MYSTERIOUSLY
MEANT

MYSTERIOUSLY MEANT ⟶ *Don Cameron Allen*

⟶ THE REDISCOVERY OF PAGAN SYMBOLISM AND ALLEGORICAL INTERPRETATION IN THE RENAISSANCE ⟵

THE JOHNS HOPKINS PRESS ⟶ BALTIMORE AND LONDON

The Johns Hopkins Press, Baltimore, Maryland 21218
The Johns Hopkins Press Ltd., London

Library of Congress Catalog Card Number 77-105363
ISBN 0-8018-1159-7

CONTENTS

≈ PREFACE ≈

IN THIS STUDY I have attempted to bring together some information about what the discovery of Greek and Latin symbolical and allegorical interpretation taught the Renaissance. It is obvious that what was learned from classical sources simply enforced what centuries of biblical exegesis had established; however, the piety of the sacred explicators prevented them from reading either the Old or the New Testament as myth. Until recent times, myth crouched at the gates of Paradise without hope of admittance.

To some extent, myth is allegory; or, perhaps, allegory is myth; but both modes of imaginative thought are little more than one or more symbols with positive or negative value attached to some natural object and provided with a predicate. A lion absolutely static stands for several nominative or adjectival virtues and vices, although in the area of physical reading a lion has no moral or theological value. When the same animal companions another beast or attends a human being, one or more of its symbolic attributes rubs off on its associate. The other creature may alter the lion's quality as easily as the lion changes that of the other creature. The meaning may be also shifted by posture, color, ornament, implement, garment, or the fashion in which garments are worn. When to this individual or group motion is applied, allegory begins; and when some other symbolic figure or figures are the object of this motion, allegory merges into myth. At this point since sustained allegory cannot be maintained for long, literalism enters and myth is created.

vii

The humanists with whom I shall deal did not talk this way, because they relied principally on what the new study of classical texts added to the medieval practices of biblical and literary allegory. When the *Republic* of Plato and the *Symposium* of Xenophon were discovered, men learned that the earliest term for "the sense beneath" was "hypo-noia." In his essay on listening to poets, Plutarch testified to the antiquity of this expression by writing, "now we say allegorical interpretations." But Plutarch, contrary to some etymological records, was not the first to use the word "allegory"; Cicero equates it with "translatio" or "the connection of many metaphors so that one thing may be said and another understood." In the *Rhetorica ad Herennium,* attributed by the sixteenth century to Cicero, allegory is "permutatio," a form of speech in which one thing is said by the words, another by the meaning. The ancient term is recalled when the rhetorician Demetrius of Phaleron defines "allegory" as something that hides (*hyponooumenon*) the real meaning. Definitions of "allegory" appear in Strabo and Longinus, but it was Quintilian who supplied the *locus classicus* for Renaissance rhetoricians of all countries.

For Quintilian, "allegory" or "inversio" is to mean something more than the words of a statement suggest or to mean something which is absolutely opposite to what the words convey. The second half of this definition also covers what Quintilian calls "ironia" or "illusio." To exemplify his definition of allegory, Quintilian uses the ship metaphor in Horace's fourteenth ode. He probably misread Horace's literal intent, but nonetheless he brought this metaphor into almost every full-scale Renaissance account of allegory and made the ship a figure that never stays long in any poetical port. Quintilian also distinguished what might now be called "historical allegory" from the other kinds. To illustrate it he points to the real persons masquerading in Virgil's tenth eclogue. Using his critical razor with reasonable care, he decides that a continued metaphor becomes an allegory, whereas a continued trope is a "figura."

As definite as Quintilian is about the meaning of "allegory," he is indefinite about "enigma" and "symbol." For him "symbol" is "nota" and "enigma" is an "obscure allegory." He warns his students, as Aristotle had warned his orators, against a too great use of metaphor; it wearies the audience and makes one's language "allegorical and enigmatic." For the Renaissance, Quintilian represented the most modern of classical opinions, although his authority was not that of Aristotle; nonetheless, if humanists looked for clearer distinctions in Quintilian's

Greek predecessors, they must have received cold comfort. When these ancients talk about something more obscure than the clear literal, or something obscure in the literal, they use "mystery," "enigma," and "hyponoia" with about the same emphasis. Heraclitus of Pontus, who allegorized and symbolized all of Homer, will after summarizing the literal append the hidden meaning with "Here Homer philosophizes." Although the Renaissance most frequently used "symbol" in the legal sense, when it employed the word otherwise, it thought of it as a motionless "sign" which the eye transfers to the brain for an agreed meaning that had been established by a long literary or theological tradition. One could not invent a symbol. Allegory which made use of symbols the way a noun uses adjectives had wider possibilities and could be invented by an artist or found by the interpreter. It was not likely to be continuous, and the interpretation having the most logical adjustments of parts to whole was the best. The custom of symbolical reading was so general that Thomas Nashe warns the readers of *Summers Last Will and Testament* not to "wrest a never meant meaning" from his book.

II

A half dozen years ago in *Image and Meaning,* and to a certain degree in the earlier *The Harmonious Vision,* I attempted to demonstrate that some understanding of what the Renaissance knew about allegory and symbol might help modern readers understand the poetry of that period. To this end I traced as well as I could the meanings of myths and signs as they moved from Greek poetry into the literatures of western Europe. I felt definitely that there were many occasions when myths and signs were not mere decorations but emphasized, or even revealed, the poet's intent. I also felt that modern man, who has abandoned allegory and invented his own private symbols, might not easily understand an imaginative mind of three centuries ago unless he knew its traditional symbolism. I hoped to establish a balance between the modern readers of this literature who insist that its meaning is superficial and nothing more and those free-wheeling interpreters ignorant of tradition who concoct inadequate and absurd readings of their own. These earlier books are my examples; this book is my reason. I have put the cart before the horse.

Twenty years ago I had intimations of what was happening but I saw through the glass darkly. In the following ten chapters I shall try to clear the glass, but I am afraid it is still fairly cloudy. During this period, historians of biblical interpretation—Wolfson, Daniélou, and Lubac—have made the Christian process apparent. There is no need to prove that it was working hand in glove with secular interpretation. Two decades ago, with the exception of a few special monographs and papers, the knowledge of Greek allegorists had not gone much beyond Decharme's study; but in recent years the fine investigations of Pépin and Buffière provided me with a running start.

In the course of the following chapters I have attempted to explain how the arguments of the apologists of the first four centuries were revived by men of the Renaissance, eager to find Christian theology and sacred history in pagan documents. With the discovery of the allegorical and symbolic readings of Homer written by his Greek apologists, men of the sixteenth century were given new reason to take up the deeper reading of Virgil, Ovid, and the mythology which had been passed on to them by medieval men. The discovery of the Egyptian remains only added to the general conviction that something essentially mysterious— philosophy, history, theology, and scientific lore—was just beneath the surface of the remnants of the past. The antiquities from the Nile were not on parchment, and the teasing nature of what they seemed to be saying turned the eyes of men toward the equally dumb remains of Greece and Rome. This passion for deciphering mystery had much to do with the efforts of painters to create mystery, and it seems only natural that men of letters should follow in their steps. It is my impression that they did, but that in this as in everything else there was a slow evolution so that the eventual alteration of attitude toward both myth and allegory had a definite effect on literature.

I am aware that I have skated over the surface and made no arabesques. I have ended up with an annotated bibliography or a thinly masked *Grundriss*. I have presented the facts as I got them—the hard way. I have no theories to offer although I have read many of the moderns who have speculated about myth and symbol. Since I am without thought I do not need interpretation. Endurance is all that is required.

At this point I want to thank the American Philosophical Society for a summer grant in 1965 and the Huntington Library for a gift of several weeks in that remarkable collection. Most of this book was written during 1967–68 when I was a fellow of the National Endowment for the Humanities.

D. C. A.

MYSTERIOUSLY
MEANT

I

❧ PAGAN MYTH AND CHRISTIAN APOLOGETICS ❧

THE WITHERING AWAY of the great Olympians can be sensed in the epics of Homer and is made plain when his champions defended his apparent irreligion with allegorical explanations. The unacceptability of the pantheon to philosophers is clear in Cicero's philosophical treatises, in the poem of Lucretius, and even in the late theologies of Plutarch and Marcus Aurelius. When the last aristocratic defender of orthodoxy, Symmachus, informed the Senate that the search for religious truth is a private matter—"we do not come to so great a mystery by one road"[1]—he may have been pleading for tolerance but he sounds very much like an indifferentist. Nonetheless, the generous views expressed in "The Oration on the Altar of Victory" are probably to be preferred to the eclectic superstitions buzzing in the skull of Constantine, Christ's Warwick, or the esoteric doctrines embraced by Julian, pagan precursor of St. John of the Cross. Pagans and semi-pagans show a nervous liberalism toward the new doctrine and an undiscriminating eagerness to tinker with their own convictions that suggest the erosion of a theology. Actually, the gods were turning into metaphors. By the fifth century, Sidonius, Count of Lyons and Bishop to the Averni, can, as a Christian, reject them all

NOTE: Unless otherwise indicated, all references to patristic writers are to Migne, *Series graeca* (Paris, 1857–1903), cited as *PG,* or *Series latina* (Paris, 1844–1903), cited as *PL.* To avoid typographical problems, Greek titles are given in Latin translation or transliteration. Volume and column numbers only are cited when the title is mentioned in the text.

[1] Symmachus, *Opera,* ed. O. Seeck (Berlin, 1883), p. 282.

in a few verses of one poem but call them back as theological tinsel in some marriage hymns written for Christian communicants.

The contest between the new and old faith began conventionally.[2] First, the Jews, spoiled of their religion and scandalized by its perversion, attacked and were counterattacked; then the idolators joined the assault. Early Gentile opinion, as it echoes in the asides of Valerius Maximus, Horace, the younger Pliny, Tacitus, and Suetonius, is contemptuous of Christian doctrine and disgusted with the vulgarity of Christianity. As the Church prospered and became politically and materially threatening, pagan responses became either occultly hilarious or learnedly serious. The first tone is heard in Lucian or Philostratus; the second probably dominated the lost book of Fronto (so charmingly confuted by Minucius Felix), Celsus' *Book of Truth* (partially preserved by Origen's rejoinder), and the vanished *Against the Christians* of the quasi-Christian Porphyry. Most of these anti-Christian complaints were written early; nevertheless, Christian apologists continued to advance their case until the time of Augustine. Paganism was obviously a tough snake that required a great deal of killing.

The records of Eusebius and the allusions of the controversialists inform us that there were other second-century apologists besides Justin, Tatian, Athenagoras, and Tertullian, whose polemics against pagans we possess. But what these four men wrote plainly provided the model schema for an apology. Some men before Christ, a synopsis might begin, had glimmerings of Christian truth, but it was so altered by devils disguised as gods it was more like a corrupted biblical imitation or a very primitive form of Christian dogma. Because Christian truth was debauched, wiser pagans assumed that the gods were either deified heroes or allegorized natural processes. Once this truth, dark in the revelation to Moses and the Prophets, was lighted by the New Dispensation, nothing could stand before it. This brief for Christianity carried the court with it after numerous public trials, but the Church's eventual victory provided questions for many centuries: Is the Bible the oldest book? Will pious pre-Christians be granted salvation? Is all non-Christian myth or legend basically historical, philosophical, physical?

---

[2] The disintegration of paganism and the Christian triumph has been handsomely described. The first serious modern study is Christian Kortholt, *De calumniis paganorum in veteres Christianos sparsa* (Rostock, 1663). The studies of C. T. Keim, G. Boissier, G. E. A. Grindle, Sir Samuel Dill, A. Harnack, and P. de Labriolle were written in the nineteenth century; more recent studies with bibliographies are W. W. Hyde, *Paganism to Christianity in the Roman Empire* (Philadelphia, 1946); A. Momogliano and others, *Paganism and Christianity in the Fourth Century* (London, 1963); and H. Chadwick, *Early Christian Thought and the Classical Tradition* (Oxford, 1966).

II

The double assault of the Christian apologist on both Jewish and Gentile criticism can be surveyed in Justin's two polemics, the *Apologia pro Christianis* and the *Dialogus cum Tryphone Judaeo*.[3] In the debate with Trypho, Justin practically invents typology[4] to convince his Hebrew opponents of their erroneous blindness, but he also indicates what must have been the common tenor of pagan jeering. Trypho had charged Christians with basing the Christ story on the legend of Perseus, and Justin responds to this accusation by attacking its lack of originality.[5] The Gentiles had long been complaining that the life and nature of Christ was stolen from the myths of Hercules, Bacchus, and Aesculapius. Justin responded by parading a series of ur-Christs so that he could ask their pagan adherents why it was possible to believe in Hercules or Bacchus and not in Jesus.[6] This was, of course, simply a means of turning the pagans' knives against them and in no sense can be considered blasphemy on the part of the defending saint, who presumed that all mythology had been invented by demons who eavesdropped on the Prophets' ecstasies and, foretasting the future, attempted to put obstacles in the way of Christianity. Learning that Christ would "tie his foal to a vine and wash his robes in the blood of the grape," the besotted devils created the myths of Bacchus and Bellerophon. In similar wise they tried to forestall and hence weaken belief in the Virgin Birth with the story of Perseus' immaculate origin. When they read that the promised Messiah would have "the strength of a giant to run his course," they concocted the myth of the demigod Hercules.[7]

The fiends spying on the manuscripts of Isaiah and Jeremiah might be the inventors of the Graeco-Roman mythology. According to Justin, however, Moses, who was more ancient than any Attic literate, is the source of all Greek philosophy. Plato's theory of creation, as expressed in the *Timaeus*, is only one indication of the enormous pagan debt to Genesis,[8] but there are numerous other obligations. Whenever the reader finds a curiously Christian idea among the litter and trash of Greek

---

[3] It is known that Justin wrote an *Oratio ad Graecos* and a *Cohortatio ad Graecos*, but the texts printed by Migne are spurious.

[4] Justin, *Dialogus, PG* VI, 562–66, 690–94, 703–6, 715–19, 723–26, 735–38, 786–87.

[5] *Ibid.*, col. 630.

[6] Justin, *Apologia, PG* VI, 358–82.

[7] *Ibid.*, cols. 410–11, 426. Certain Christian rites, such as baptism and communion, were incorporated in pagan ritual (cols. 422, 427).

[8] *Ibid.*, cols. 415–18.

philosophy, he knows its divine source. "So the seeds of truth seem to be among all men, but their [Greek philosophers] contradictions indicate the failure of men to grasp the exact meaning."[9] Justin is just new enough in controversy to be decent; hence, he is ready to grant that the Logos was always available to men, even those "considered atheists," who lived by right reason. "They who lived before Christ reasonably, and still do, are Christians."[10] As a consequence of this Christian but highly doubtful conjecture, Socrates can be held a forerunner of Christ, and there is for Justin sufficient evidence for this supposition. The Greek philosopher urged men to reject the testimony of demons and to search for the "unknown God," warning his disciples "that it is neither easy to find the Father and Maker of all, nor having found him is it safe to declare him to all." The Christian truth underlying the second half of this statement became manifest when the devils, distressed by Socrates' "vague knowledge," saw to it that he was put to death.[11]

Three other Greek contemporaries of Justin, Athenagoras, Theophilus, and Tatian, commend the half-light of the philosophers, who glimpsed, according to Theophilus, the basic truths present in divine inspiration given all wise men.[12] All of them mention the names of eminent Greek thinkers (even the Aristotle of the First Mover) who were aware of one, increate God.[13] Theophilus adds to the list the Sibyl, whom he quotes relentlessly; she is comparable in authority to the Prophets,[14] but unfortunately her pronouncements on monotheism and theodicy, like those of Homer, Hesiod, Pindar, Archilochus, Simonides, Sophocles, and Euripides are probably the fruit of human excogitation rather than divinely revealed.[15] These other apologists further agree that the pagan pantheon, if not a poetic invention, is nothing more than a roster of deified human heroes or a Mosaic revelation, once perused and badly remembered.[16]

Theophilus reminds the Greeks that all they have in the way of ancient history—the early floods of Deucalion and Clymenus—is merely

[9] *Ibid.*, cols. 338, 395, 466–67.

[10] *Ibid.*, col. 398.

[11] *Ibid.*, cols. 458–62, 335. The hallowing of St. Socrates apparently begins with Justin according to J. Geffcken, *Sokrates und das alte Christentum* (Heidelberg, 1908).

[12] Theophilus, *Ad Autolycum, PG* VI, 1143–44.

[13] *Ibid.*, cols. 1051–55; Athenagoras, *Legatio pro Christianis, PG* VI, 899–903; Tatian, *Oratio adversus Graecos, PG* VI, 810. Tatian had a squint eye for Diogenes, Plato, Aristotle, Heraclitus, and Zeno, but thinks well of Socrates.

[14] Theophilus, *op. cit.*, cols. 1063, 1110–15.

[15] *Ibid.*, cols. 1059, 1115–19.

[16] Athenagoras, *PG* VI, 888–89, 922–26, 950–51, 954, 958–62; Theophilus, *PG* VI, 1038–39, 1050, 1069, 1106, 1156, 1164–65.

a garbled version of the correct Mosaic account.[17] In a sense, the errors of the pagan theologians are somewhat innocent. At the time Moses set down the revealed truth, the remainder of mankind was totally illiterate. In due course Homer and Hesiod either badly remembered the revelation of Moses or purposely perverted the "glory of the unique God." The whole process of textual corruption, Theophilus writes, had been carefully recorded by Euhemerus, "a man of extraordinary impiety . . . who, after he had discussed the gods, concluded that they did not exist and that the universe was self-governing."[18] Aware of the nature of Greek interpretation, Theophilus offers his unbelieving opponents a fine Christian interpretation of the mysteries hidden in Moses' description of the first days of Creation.[19]

Tatian devotes a book of the *Oratio adversus Graecos* to proving that Moses lived long before the Trojan War and was the leader of the most ancient of nations.[20] He also was perfectly aware that some Greeks saw only moral or physical allegory in their traditional legends,[21] but he was also not ignorant of the double readings found in biblical texts by Clement of Rome, Barnabas, and Justin. The modes of interpretation were in his opinion utterly different, and he does not hesitate to inform the Greeks that what can be found beneath the letter of the inspired Scripture is quite opposite from what can be read into a mythology invented by lying demons.

> Believe me then, O Greeks, and do not see allegories in your gods. If you do this, the divine as you conceive it disappears for you and for us. For these demons, naturally evil, are restored by physical reading. I cannot bring myself to adore material elements or persuade others so to do. Metrodorus of Lampsacus is childish in his book on Homer when he turns it all into allegory and says that Hera, Athena, and Zeus are not what those who worship them believe but are either natural things or forces. You say the same of Hector, Achilles, Agamemnon, all the Greeks and Trojans, and of Helen and Paris. They are poetic inventions and never lived.[22]

With this opinion, Athenagoras, writing a few years later to Marcus Aurelius, agreed; he stringently criticizes the Greek allegorists, whose wealth of allegorical lore he displays and casts out as useless to believers in the true God.[23]

[17] Theophilus, *PG* VI, 1146–47.
[18] *Ibid.*, col. 1130.
[19] *Ibid.*, cols. 1075–79.
[20] Tatian, *PG* VI, 869, 879–87.
[21] *Ibid.*
[22] *Ibid.*, col. 854.
[23] Athenagoras, *PG* VI, 935–39.

When Christian apologetics moved to the West, rather than Minucius Felix,[24] it was Tertullian who was the legitimate heir of the Greeks, and it was this erudite Carthaginian who kindled the passion for discovering and separating the literal reading from the figurative understanding.[25] Like Tatian, Tertullian maintained that second or nonliteral readings were the exclusive property and privilege of the Church, because all sectarians, the Gnostics for instance, use symbols and enigmas incorrectly.[26] Pagans, whose theologians he read expertly,[27] are naturally inferior to Christian heretics in the method of under-reading; and, hence, he laughs at their continual search for significant etymological exposition and hidden physical theory.[28] The *Ad nationes* contains his principal arguments against the non-Christians, but his objections to pagan allegorical commitment come forward firmly in his *Contra Marcion.*

The superstition of the masses inspired by common idol worship and ashamed of the names and fables of their ancient dead now borne by idols turns to an interpretation of natural objects and so with cleverness covers its own disgrace by figuratively making Jupiter a heated substance and Juno one of air . . . Vesta is made fire; the Muses, water; and the Great Mother, earth. . . . Thus Osiris is buried and expected to come to life as a symbol of the regularity of the return of fruits and the restoration of life as the year turns. The lions of Mithra are emblems of arid and dry Nature.[29]

On a level with his scorn of pagan allegory, Tertullian condemns stellar theology,[30] but for him, as for Tatian, Euhemerus is a pagan of a more sympathetic complexion because he was a comfort to Christians in his sacrilegious fashion.

In the *Apologeticus* Tertullian details the human weaknesses, the occupations, and the avocations of the unholy pagan pantheon.[31] The heroes—Romulus, fratricide, rapist, and manurer of fields, and Aeneas, bastard, traitor, and fornicator—fare no better. He finds their ultimate

---

[24] In a sense, Minucius Felix's *Octavius,* probably written as a reply to Fronto (IX, 6; XXXI, 2), is the obvious ancestor of the morality play. Octavius, commenting on the belief of some philosophers in the One, says, "either Christians are philosophers, or the philosophers of old were already Christians" (XIX–XX).

[25] Tertullian, *De resurrectione carnis, PL* II, 821–22, 811; *Contra Marcion, PL* II, 316, 345–47, 356, 387, 469–70, 478, 485, 499–500.

[26] *De resurrectione,* cols. 820–21.

[27] *Ad nationes, PL* I, 587–89, 597–98. Tertullian has read Varro most carefully and mastered his categories of identity and interpretation.

[28] *Ibid.,* cols. 589–90.

[29] *Contra Marcion, PL* II, 260–61.

[30] *Ad nationes, PL* I, 606.

[31] *Apologeticus, PL* I, 329–31, 350–55.

deification beyond human mirth.[32] He knows, of course, the euhemerists' theory that the gods were formerly benefactors of mankind; and he inquires why this honor is no longer accorded men who have more recently made great contributions to society. He points out that even in the past, star-performers, Socrates, Demosthenes, Cato, Cicero, among others, were not elevated to Olympus, but coldly left "among the dead."[33] The Egyptians had far more wisdom than most heathens when they converted Joseph, "one of our saints," into their god Serapis, and Tertullian knows exactly how it came about.

> The Egyptians called him Serapis from his turban . . . of pointed shape memorializing his providing of corn and giving evidence, through the ears of corn ornamenting its edges, that the care of provisions was on his head. For the same reason that the care of the Egyptians was under his hand, they made a sacred figure of the dog at his right, and put it under his hand.[34]

Tertullian's conviction that everything holy the pagans know they learned from the Jews governs to a degree his evaluation of Greek culture. The classical poets are liars or immoral,[35] and the literature found in the Scriptures is library enough for Christians;[36] nonetheless, the Christian study of Graeco-Roman texts "partly cannot be allowed, partly cannot be avoided."[37] He also inquires, "What does Athens have to do with Jerusalem?" and almost shouts, "Away with all attempts to make a speckled Christianity of Stoic, Platonic, and dialectic composition!" But he knows many of the great philosophers well. Seneca gets a short ovation.[38] In general, however, Tertullian regards the heathen poets and philosophers as so wrong, so unoriginal that he can hardly tolerate his patristic predecessors, who quoted them because of their seemingly brief glimpses of Christian truths.[39]

Now Tertullian does not doubt that monotheism is an innate idea which is demonstrated by the fact that in moments of stress men everywhere exclaim, "Great God! Good God!" the testimony of a soul "naturally Christian."[40] But the cry also shows that Christian doctrine is

---

[32] *Ad nationes, PL* I, 598–99.

[33] *Ibid.*, col. 606; *Apologeticus, PL* I, 336–37.

[34] *Ad nationes, PL* I, 596–97.

[35] *Ibid.*, cols. 575, 587, 595.

[36] *De spectaculis, PL* I, 660.

[37] *De idolatria, PL* I, 675.

[38] *De praescriptione haereticorum, PL* II, 20; *Apologeticus, PL* I, 342–43.

[39] *De testimonio animae, PL* I, 609.

[40] *Apologeticus, PL* I, 377. Minucius Felix makes the same point (XVIII. 11) and this with other similarities suggests that he and Tertullian had some sort of relationship or used the same predecessor. See H. J. Baylis, *Minucius Felix* (London, 1928), pp. 274–359.

primal doctrine; light has come from the pagans, to be sure, "but it has flowed from the first fountainhead, and we claim as ours all you have taken from us and handed down."[41] To support this conviction, Tertullian states that Moses, a contemporary of Inachus and prior to Saturn, lived four hundred years before the founding of Troy and, consequently, fifteen hundred years before Homer, the earliest Greek writer. At this earlier date the Hebrews promulgated their concept of God, but the philosophers found it too simple.

They would not talk of Him as they found Him; they had to discuss His quality, nature, and abode. Some think Him incorporeal; others corporeal (the Platonists and Stoics). Others say He is atoms or numbers (the Epicureans and Pythagoreans). Heraclitus says fire. The Platonists represent Him as taking care of the world; the Epicureans think Him idle without human interest. The Stoics put Him outside the world. . . ; the Platonists put Him inside.[42]

Because the philosophers had this original access to truth and twisted it satanically, Tertullian, contrary to Justin, gives them no hope of grace. Pythagoras, Plato, Aristotle, and especially Socrates (who was inspired by a demon, and was both idolator and pederast), are surely damned.[43] God has hardened His heart against these men, not because they were ignorant of Christian teachings but rather because "they did not perceive God in His works and followed idolatry instead."[44]

III

Although Tertullian, father of Latin apologetics, was a man of immense learning, he is hardly in the same class either as scholar or as thinker with his two great Greek contemporaries, Clement and Origen, both Alexandrians. The former instructed the latter and probably regarded Christianity as a superlative philosophy; the latter was certainly the greatest theologian before Augustine and is the founder of Christian dogmatics and biblical criticism. Christianity, which denied both of them beatitude, is probably more indebted to them in the long run than to the blood of the martyrs; on the other hand, they are both in debt to the philosophizing Jew, Philo, and brought his Rab-

[41] Tertullian, *De testimonio animae, PL* I, 615-17; *De anima, PL* II, 648-51; *Apologeticus, PL* I, 383-88, 515-16, 519-20; *Ad nationes, PL* I, 588.
[42] *Apologeticus, PL* I, 515-20.
[43] *Ibid.*, col. 405; *De anima, PL* II, 647-48.
[44] *Apologeticus*, col. 376; *De anima, PL* II, 720; *Contra Marcion, PL* II, 511.

binical version of Greek interpretation safely into the Christian circuit.[45]

For Clement, as for his predecessors, the Graeco-Roman theology was the ultimate in superstitions,[46] but pagan philosophy, especially that of Plato, had a tincture of divine inspiration.

Before the coming of Christ, philosophy was necessary to the Greeks for righteousness . . . God is the cause of all good things, but of some before others; hence, first the two Testaments and second, philosophy. Now philosophy was given first to the Greeks until they could be called by God, because philosophy brought the Greeks to Christ as the Law did the Jews. Philosophy, therefore, prepares the way for him who would be perfected in Christ.[47]

The Greeks, Clement supposed, had their philosophy through the ministrations of inferior angels[48] and also from Moses and the Prophets.[49] The latter two sources were despoiled of "fragments of truth," which the philosophers went on to claim as their own, "masking some points, using their ingenuity to sophisticate others, and, since they were probably possessed by the spirit of perception, discovering certain tenets on their own."[50] But what they copied from the essential Christian doctrines of faith, hope, love, temperance, repentance, and fear of God, they invariably falsified;[51] nevertheless, a few sober-living men, styled "atheists" by their contemporaries, men like Euhemerus, Diagoras, Hippo, and Theodorus, "though they did not reach truth, suspected error . . . and this suspicion is a seed which can grow into the plant of wisdom."[52]

Other ancients, Socrates, who drew his ideas from Moses,[53] Orpheus, Linus, Musaeus, and Homer, who were instructed by the Prophets, philosophized "by way of a hidden sense . . . poetry is for them a veil against the many."[54] Plato, however, is Clement's great Christian before the Advent; he not only "heard right well the all-wise

[45] H. A. Wolfson, *The Philosophy of the Church Fathers* (Cambridge, Mass., 1956), I, 46–63; H. de Lubac, *Exégèse médiévale* (Paris, 1959), I, 171–77.
[46] Clement of Alexandria, *Opera,* ed. W. Dindorf (Oxford, 1869), *Cohortatio ad gentes* III. 44; II. 25–27; 29–31, 37; X. 102.
[47] Clement, *Stromateis,* I. 5. 28.
[48] *Ibid.,* VII. 2. 6.
[49] *Ibid.,* V. 14. 89–141.
[50] *Ibid.,* I. 17. 87.
[51] *Ibid.,* II. 1. 1.
[52] Clement, *Cohortatio,* II. 24.
[53] Clement, *Stromateis,* V. 11. 67.
[54] *Ibid.,* V. 4. 24. Clement states that Numa, influenced by the precepts of Moses, saw to it that no graven images were adored and taught his subjects that the mind alone apprehends the "Best of Beings" (*ibid.,* I. 15. 71).

Moses"[55] but can also be called "Moses Atticans."[56] Clement spends a large portion of the fifth book of the *Stromateis* explicating the doctrines of "Hebraizing Plato,"[57] who may have gone to the Egyptians, Babylonians, and Assyrians for some of his other knowledge but learned his religion from the Jews.[58] The Greeks, failing to find God in Nature, should more wisely have followed the almost Christian doctrine of their greatest philosopher.[59] But unlike Justin or his coeval, Irenaeus,[60] Clement, though he follows his predecessors thus far, seems unready to acquit Socrates and Plato before the presiding magistrate in the tribunal of Jehovah.

Given their acknowledged provenience, pagan writings properly understood could yield Christian messages. Clement divides all nonliteral meaning, which he calls by a variety of nondiscriminated terms, into ethical, theological, and physical comprehension, and there is no indication that he limited this sort of arcane interpretation to Christian texts alone. He is precise in his knowledge of Egyptian symbolism,[61] but he knows, too, that the Greeks "have veiled the first principles of things, delivering the truth in enigmas, symbols, allegories, metaphors, and such kinds of tropes."[62] He states that he cannot live long enough to set down the names of those "who have philosophized in a symbolical manner." The method they employed has many advantages. Truth shines more brightly in the dark, thereby revealing its edges more sharply. Nonetheless, truth should not be commonly bestowed on all or communicated "to those . . . who are not purified in soul," nor are "the mysteries of the Word to be explained to the profane."[63]

This closing decision of Clement is not unlike those proposed by the Neo-Platonic allegorizers of Homer, but his associate Origen is even more obsessed than he with grasping the spirit lurking behind the letter. His impulsion toward the occult comes not only from the practiced

[55] *Ibid.,* V. 12. 78. (It should be observed that Eusebius devotes the tenth book of his *Praeparatio evangelica* to Greek borrowings from the Bible.)

[56] *Ibid.,* I. 22. 150.

[57] *Ibid.,* I. 1. 10.

[58] Clement, *Cohortatio,* VI. 70.

[59] Clement, *Stromateis,* II. 14. 1.

[60] In his *Adversus haereses* (*PG* VII, 1047) Irenaeus states that Christ did not come just for Romans living in the age of Tiberius Caesar, "but for all men without exception, who from the beginning by His aid . . . feared and loved God, practised justice and goodness towards neighbors, desired to see Christ and hear His voice."

[61] Clement, *Stromateis,* V. 4. 19–21; 7. 41–42.

[62] *Ibid.,* V. 8. 44–55.

[63] *Ibid.,* V. 9. 56–59.

customs of his predecessors[64] and from the injunctions of St. Paul but also from his own conviction that some stories in the Old Testament are likely to turn the stomach of a decent man unless they can be explained as mythical covers of an inner mystery.[65] However, a better notion of his temper in regard to the origin of legends and their pious explication can be had from his distinguished controversy with the brilliant Celsus, long safely dead.

In his *Book of Truth* Celsus had asserted that almost all Christian doctrines were warped versions of Platonic idealism, but in addition Christians had certain other dogmas and rites eclectically put together of borrowings from the philosophy of the Stoics, the Jewish tradition, the mysteries of Mithra, the myths of Typhon, Osiris, and the Cabiri.[66] The story of Christ is no more than a concatenation of various old myths plus the remembrances of various wandering Greek and barbarian wonder-workers who had plagued antiquity.[67] Celsus was also a bit of a Janus. He explained the impious or salacious pagan stories as allegories,[68] but he refused this right to Christians. At least he did not follow his principles when he read sportive biblical events.[69] Origen thinks that all legends should be searched for their good or bad import. If this were done, it would then be discovered that demons wrote the narratives of the gods, whereas God saw to it that for moral or spiritual reasons, not for sheer Rabelesian ribaldry, the account of Noah's inebriation, Jacob's polygamy, and Lot's incest were recorded.

To turn the tables, Origen recalls Celsus' mirth over the silliness of the story of Adam and Eve and his comment that "more rational Jews and Christians were ashamed of these things and try to allegorize them." This is, indeed, an uncritical statement from a man whose compatriots allegorize the obviously analogous and purloined Pandora myth and fail to perceive in Plato's private myth of Penia and Porus the Edenic foundation, "hit on by accident" or learned from "those who interpret the Jew's traditions philosophically."[70] The special understand-

[64] Origen, *Contra Celsum*, PG XI, 1450. On Origen as a Christian apologist see Jean Daniélou, *Origen*, trans. W. Mitchell (New York, 1955), pp. 99–127.

[65] Origen, *De principatibus*, PG XI, 360–1. Actually, almost everything he read in the Bible had for him allegorical meaning. Wolfson (*op. cit.* I, 58–59) brings this out, but one should also see Origen's various homilies (*PG*, XII, 185, 198–201, 218–20, 454–56, 699, 774–75).

[66] Origen, *Contra Celsum*, PG XI, 1287–1503.

[67] *Ibid.*, cols. 951–54.

[68] *Ibid.*, col. 742.

[69] *Ibid.*, cols. 691–95, 714, 1106–14.

[70] *Ibid.*, cols. 1586, 1086–91.

ing concealed in these legends can be disclosed in other Bible tales, which Celsus assumed were all imitations of Greek myths.[71] A general rule of thumb for both pagans and Christians disturbed by a venerable but possibly dubious tale might, Origen thinks, be as follows:

> Anyone who reads the stories with a free mind, who wants to keep himself from being deceived by them, will decide what he will accept [literally] and what he will interpret allegorically, searching out the meaning of the authors who wrote such fictions.[72]

It can be assumed that this formula of personal interrogation and individual interpretation which Origen recommends for Bible students and mythographers is also useful to readers of the biography of Christ, which, in the opinion of Celsus, was conflated out of the myths of Hercules, Bacchus, and Orpheus.[73] History knew, Celsus said, a considerable number of females who were pregnant by supernatural penetration; for example, the mother of Plato had born a child to Apollo.[74] But Celsus was gravelled by various other episodes in the life of Christ. How could one prove that the dove which descended on him was the Holy Ghost? How can one prove, Origen responds, that Oedipus ever lived or that a war was fought against Troy?[75] The magic test of ends again, as always, provides Christians with assurance. The gentle religion of Christ, free of blood sacrifice and burnt offerings, and His own exemplary career are proof enough of His divinity.[76] But there is proof beyond this. Can any of the other so-called saviours of mankind show that "there are people who have reformed in morals and become better men as a consequence of their lives and teachings"?[77]

IV

After the brilliant efforts of Clement and Origen, the responsibility for Christian apologetics passed to the Latins, and during the next two centuries engaged the defending minds of Cyprian, Arnobius the Elder, Lactantius, and Augustine. The Greek exponents of the Christian his-

[71] *Ibid.*, cols. 1098–1106.
[72] *Ibid.*, col. 738.
[73] *Ibid.*, cols. 1047, 1498.
[74] *Ibid.*, col. 731.
[75] *Ibid.*, col. 738.
[76] *Ibid.*, col. 967.
[77] *Ibid.*, col. 974.

tory and theology had put together such a fine case for their superiority
that there was practically nothing new to say. Occasionally, however,
some badly informed apologist like Arnobius made the mistake of unconsciously letting his own heresies drop into the open while attacking the
position of the unconvinced pagans.

In the *Adversus gentes,* a treatise in seven parts, Arnobius opens
his denunciation by repeating most of Cyprian's *Ad Demetrianum:*
Christianity was not responsible for the troubles of the Roman Empire.
In the last two books he flagellates the modes of worship in pagan cults.
The middle sections reject the proposal of the syncretists that all religions be brought into union,[78] supports and praises Cicero's low evaluation of the Roman pantheon,[79] and expends an enormous number of
pages in reporting, mocking, and rejecting the various Greek and Latin
moral and physical allegorizers of the poets and the mythologies.[80] One
of Arnobius' central theses is the basically human origin of all of pagan
religion;[81] hence, he is not one to blame the famous Greek and Roman
atheists "for refusing to credit what is obscure." The euhemerists, he is
certain, should be praised because they have truly heaped historical
honors on a whole roster of dead heroes by supposing their deification.[82]
These views firmly enabled him to introduce the *Adversus gentes* with an
invitation to the pagan world, long given to worshipping its human
benefactors, to see at last the superlative benefactions of Christ.

Though far more readable than Arnobius, Lactantius has likewise
nothing very novel to say to the pagans in his *Divinae institutiones,*
which was written in a symbolical seven books, three of which attack the
pagans whereas four celebrate Christianity as the true religion, teaching
all men justice and proper worship and providing for its adherents a
happy life. In the adversative first books Lactantius spreads out the
pronouncements of poets and philosophers, of the Sibyl, and even of the
Delphic Apollo in behalf of monotheism.[83] These testifiers did not really
ascertain the truth, "because one cannot be so blind as fail to see it."
Actually, both the Sibyl and Hermes Trismegistus knew the Logos, and
hence were able to foresee the Advent and the Mission of Christ.[84] With

[78] Arnobius, *PL* V, 939.
[79] *Ibid.,* cols. 944–46.
[80] *Ibid.,* cols. 976–99, 1147–60.
[81] *Ibid.,* cols. 1037–38.
[82] *Ibid.,* cols. 1145–46, 1172.
[83] Lactantius, *PL* VI, 129–49.
[84] *Ibid.,* cols. 461–63, 469, 490–516.

these convincing testimonies before them, it is amazing that men still
subscribed to the shocking legends of polytheism, worshipping gods who
are born, die, and are buried in known tombs.[85] The truth is that hea-
thenism itself is subsequent to "a knowledge of the true God";[86] and,
having wandered from the original and right course, a philosopher's discussion of some apparent Christian doctrine is invariably erroneous.[87]
Although he rejects Cicero's distinction between superstition and religion,[88] Lactantius partially approves his criticism of paganism, yet blames
him for standing back and allowing "the general public to stray in idolatry." Both Cicero and Lucretius "were wiser than their fellows in their
understanding of the error of false religion, but also so much more
foolish because they did not think there was a true one."[89]

The Christian apologists culminate in Augustine, whose famous
brief against the pagans is really no fresher than those of Arnobius and
Lactantius, although his range of information is greater and his prose
more splendid than theirs. By the fifth century, deep-dyed pagans were
of the order of straw men, and, as Augustine makes so clear to Diosco-
rus, the various Greek philosophies are now unimportant compared to
the dangers inherent in the heretical opinions of the Manichaeans, Don-
atists, Arians, Eunomians, and Cataphrygians.[90] Be this as the great
bishop says; nonetheless, before the completion of the *De civitate Dei*,
he took a number of practice shots at both the flamens and the
philosophers.[91] He knew these orders well and was completely at home in
pagan practice and theory. The corridor to the *De civitate* runs through

---

[85] *Ibid.*, cols. 156–211.
[86] *Ibid.*, cols. 328–29.
[87] *Ibid.*, cols. 15–16, 390–97, 405–7, 444–46, 451–52.
[88] *Ibid.*, cols. 535–38.
[89] *Ibid.*, cols. 263–68; see René Pichon, *Lactance* (Paris, 1901), pp. 33–110, 246–62.
[90] Augustine, *Epistolae*, PL XXXIII, 437–38.
[91] In "Sex quaestiones contra paganos" (PL XXXIII, 370–86), Augustine, writing to
Deogratias, defends major aspects of Christian rite and belief against the mocking slurs of
Porphyry. In *Contra Faustus Manichaeum* (PL XLII) he is amazed that the pagans continue
to worship their gods long after they have seen them as allegories (col. 374). He tells them
that since the meanings of their fables are not very clear, "what they laugh at in the theater,
they worship in the temple" (col. 275). In the *De consensu evangelistarum* (PL XXXIV) he
points out that all pagan myths are laughable unless they can be philosophically interpreted
(cols. 1056–58), and goes on to give examples of euhemerism in the past and present and to
reveal his knowledge of etymological interpretation. The *Liber de divinatione daemonum*
(PL XL, 582–91) is, as the title suggests, an attack on oracles. For additional information see
H. I. Marrou, *Saint Augustin et la fin de la culture antique* (Paris, 1938), pp. 387–503; Sr.
Mary D. Madden, *The Pagan Divinities and their Worship as Depicted in the Works of
Saint Augustine exclusive of The City of God*, C.U.A. Patristic Studies, XXIV (Washington,
D. C., 1930).

the usual confessional in which the almost puritan memories of Augustine are purged.

> When I was a young man, I sometimes went to these sacrilegious spectacles. I heard the choristers and watched the priests raging in religious ecstasy. I was pleased with the shameless games in honor of gods and goddesses, of the Virgo Cælestis and Berecynthia, mother of all, before whose couch on the solemn day of her lustration obscene acts were sung in public which would be indecent to be heard, I shall not say by the mother of the gods or by the mother of someone among the senators or among honest men, but by one of the actors' mothers.[92]

Of these productions the mature man could say, as he does of the emasculated effeminates consecrated to the Great Mother, "interpretation failed, reason blushed, speech ceased."[93]

Augustine has objections of his own to the pantheon: its variety, licentiousness,[94] and obvious demonic possession.[95] He cites Cicero's testimony against the gods,[96] quotes from Seneca's lost book on superstition,[97] and leans so heavily on Varro's *Antiquitates* that his numerous quotations almost supply us with the vanished manuscript. As did his predecessors, Augustine votes strongly for the historical theories of "the historian Euhemerus translated into Latin by Ennius,"[98] but it is against the physical or natural interpretation of the fables of the poets and the myths of the priests that he strikes with hard hands. As one of the many examples of this form of nonsense, he cites the physical allegorization of the Attis story by Porphyry.

> The celebrated philosopher Porphyry has said that Attis signifies the flowers which adorn the spring, most beautiful of seasons, because he was cut off as the flowers fall before fruition. Therefore, they have not compared the man or the quasi-man they call Attis to flowers, but rather his genitals which fell while he was living. Moreover they did not fall . . . but were torn away. Nor when the flower was lost not fruit but sterility followed. . . . What interpretation proceeds from this?[99]

---

[92] Augustine, *De civitate* II. 4. All references to *De civitate* are to the edition of J. E. C. Welldon, London, 1924.

[93] *Ibid.,* VII. 26.

[94] *Ibid.,* IV. 10–11.

[95] *Ibid.,* II. 29; III. 5; IX. 9.

[96] *Ibid.,* IV. 30.

[97] *Ibid.,* VI. 10.

[98] *Ibid.,* VII. 16, 18–19, 27; VIII. 26.

[99] *Ibid.,* VII. 25. Augustine's citations of Varro's *Antiquitates* are numerous, but some are more significant than others. Varro apparently points out that poets rather than philosophers are responsible for the generation of gods (IV. 32) and confesses that many myths are false (III. 4). Augustine knows Varro's ways of classifying the gods and goddesses and the

Varro, Augustine continues, is silent about this sensational undermeaning, although it must not have been unknown "to this very learned man."

At first glance Augustine's continuous complaint about pagan allegory seems a trifle nearsighted in a man who is not hostile to the principal fosterers of Christian allegory and who devotes most of the second book of his *De doctrina* to the meaning of signs. There is, besides, a letter to Januarius stating that "anything made known by means of allegorical signification is more moving, delightful, and respected than if it were stated openly in words."[100] But Augustine, though he does not oppose allegory like Jovinian and, probably, Jerome, is very temperate in his attitude toward it. When he talks of a triple allegory in *De vera religione*[101] or a fourfold allegory in the later *De utilitate credendi*,[102] he is clearly discoursing on distinctions in the literal or historical reading. Probably the most open statement of his position appears in the *De civitate,* where, after summarizing some traditional allegorical interpretations of the Garden of Eden, he states that "a spiritual understanding" is permitted provided "it is also believed that the history of Paradise and the things done there are faithfully recorded."[103] In other words, once the reader is absolutely convinced of the veracity of the literal, he may then hunt for second readings. The Augustinian implication, however, is that this search is more properly in the realm of rhetoric than in that of hermeneutics. The firm rule is that one cannot believe in the literal truth of pagan myths, and, hence, there is no sense in searching out a second meaning of any sort. But when one examines the second meanings found by the Graeco-Roman allegorists, one learns they have nothing to do with divinity or deity but with natural process and physical manifestations.[104] So what is the good of it?

There are, however, orthodox readings for Christians in the better pagan literal. Much of it is nonsense, "false and superstitious fancies," but there is also instruction adaptable to the uses of truth, "and some truths in regard even to the worship of the one God are found among them." These truths are not the product of their dialectic, but "were dug out of the mines of God's Providence and everywhere scattered

---

diverse theologies (VII. 2; VI. 5–6); he quotes Varro, Cicero, and Seneca on superstition (IV. 31; VI. 9), but also notices the contradictions and absurdities in his admittedly confused efforts to expound the natural functions of the pantheon (VII. 5, 17, 28).

[100] *Epistolae, PL* XXXIII, 214.

[101] *PL* XXXIV, 165–66.

[102] *PL* XLII, 68.

[103] *De civitate* XIII. 21.

[104] *Ibid.,* VI. 8.

abroad."[105] This "Egyptian gold and silver" should be stolen by Christians who must, however, remember that useful knowledge gathered from heathen sources is poor, indeed, when compared with the solid knowledge of the Holy Scripture.[106] This opinion of Augustine may be practically illustrated by his expressed estimate of Plato and the Platonists.

Although Augustine seems to have known Plato's writings only in a limited fashion through the translations and commentaries of Cicero, Chalcidius, and Apuleius,[107] his *Contra Academicos* makes clear his rather comprehensive understanding of the major Platonic doctrines; in fact, he remarks in this work that he was confident he would find among the Platonists "what is not in opposition to our faith,"[108] and delivers a eulogy of Plato which would have charmed the Athenian's dearest disciple.[109] The praise of Plato does not end here but occurs again and again in Augustine's subsequent writings. In the *De civitate,* he rebukes the pagans for erecting temples to an inordinate number of gods and demigods but failing to dedicate even a "little shrine" to Plato.[110] "Were it not," he asks, "more in agreement with virtue to read Plato's writings in a Temple of Plato, than . . . to witness the priests of Cybele mutilating themselves?"[111] Later on, he explains why the Platonic philosophy is for a Christian better than any other rational system[112] and develops an explanation of the similarities between the two philosophies which is not exactly new. Plato could not have heard Jeremiah, as some thought, or read Hebrew Scripture, but he might have acquired his semi-Christian information through the offices of a translator.[113] Hermes Trismegistus and the Sibyl also glided near the truth. Augustine further observes that had Plato and Porphyry come to a reasonable compromise of their positions on the relation of soul and body, they would have reached the correct Christian doctrine.[114]

Augustine's cordiality to the thought and character of Plato—naturally he rejects certain of his theories—might suggest that, like a few of his predecessors, he would be inclined to accord salvation to this almost

[105] *De doctrina, PL* XXIV, 63.

[106] *Ibid.,* col. 65.

[107] Marrou, *op. cit.,* p. 34; see C. Boyer, *Christianisme et Néo-Platonisme dans la formation de S. Augustin,* Paris, 1920.

[108] *Contra Academicos, PL* XXXII, 957.

[109] *Ibid.,* col. 955.

[110] *De civitate* II. 15.

[111] *Ibid.,* II. 7.

[112] *Ibid.,* VIII. 5.

[113] *Ibid.,* VIII. 11–12.

[114] *Ibid.,* XXII. 27.

Christian theologian. There are, however, two letters, one written in about 409 and the other in about 411, which seem to make plain Augustine's position on the troubling question of the parsimony of Christian salvation. In the letter to Deogratias, he fondles Porphyry's question about the eternal fate of good men who lived before the birth of Christ and admits his own sentimental affirmative reaction in another letter directed to Bishop Evodius. There are (he writes his episcopal colleague), poets, orators, and philosophers who confessed to the existence of one, only one, God, led praiseworthy lives, and, in spite of their superstitious notions or vain forms of worship, are sometimes held up as models to be imitated.

Yet, when all these good deeds are not consecrated toward the righteous and true worship of God but to hollow pride, to human praise and glory, they fade and are devoid of profit. Nonetheless, some of these writers awake such a response in us we could wish them freed from Hell pangs . . . but human sentiments are not the same as divine justice.[115]

When interrogated about how some pagans managed almost to enunciate Christian doctrine, Augustine responded, as he did to Deogratias, in a manner similar to that of some earlier fathers but in different words.

From the beginning of mankind, at times covertly and at times openly . . . He continued to prophesy, and before He became incarnate, there were men who believed in Him . . . among the people of Israel . . . and among other peoples.[116]

These "other peoples," Augustine admits, are not mentioned in the Bible, but they must have existed. If he is right in this conviction, some of them were probably redeemed when Hell was harrowed. "All those who believed in Him," he writes Deogratias, "and lived good and devout lives according to His commandments, whenever and wherever they lived, were undoubtedly saved." The commentary on this interesting conclusion comes in the letter to Evodius, "I am still uncertain whether He saved all those He found there or certain ones He thought worthy." Who were these worthy ones? They were those who His foreknowledge revealed would have been Christians had they lived in the generation of Christ.

---

[115] *Epistolae, PL* XXXIII, 709–18. There is no tolerance in Augustine's response (col. 82) to Maximus of Madura's definition of a unique God "whose virtues diffused through the universe we adore under many names since we do not know His name. God belongs to all religions; hence, while we address separate parts of Him in our several supplications, we are really worshiping the whole God under a thousand names in a harmonious discord."

[116] *Ibid.,* col. 374.

V

These judgments of the Christian apologists about pagan theologians and philosophers returned hauntingly when men began to search the texts of non-Christians for secret wisdom or lost history. The revitalization in the Renaissance of allegory (made tired and tiresome by fifteen centuries of monkish endeavor), through the rediscovery of the Greek and Latin interpreters, the publication of the mysterious documents from Egypt, and the efforts of antiquarians to understand and explain monuments produced suspicions about the evolution and interrelations of creeds that were the beginnings of the study of comparative religion. None of this later activity could have occurred if the Christian authorities had treated the literary and philosophical texts of Greece and Rome as rigorously as they handled the parchments of their pagan opponents. Of course the world was Roman; and though the Roman gods lacked the poetic charm and beauty of the original Olympians, yet they were a great deal more moral and had, in fact, taken in Christian deities like Virtue and Piety. Be this as it may, it is also clear, no matter how loud the protest to the contrary, that the Bible was an insufficient religious library. Classical books were required for many Christian purposes, but they were gingerly opened and scanned with a *hoc caute legendum*. Since the same problem vexed some of the devout during the sixteenth and seventeenth centuries, the original reasons for having pagan shelves in the Christian library should be stated once more.

With few exceptions most of the apologists agreed that pre-Christian poets and philosophers possessed proximate truth. Some—Plato, Hermes Trismegistus, Plotinus, Cicero, Seneca—had more than others, but almost no ancient was without a grain of wisdom. Everyone knew (in fact, Justin mentioned it) that St. Paul was not loath to borrow a phrase or two from the Greek poets; hence, it was sensible for properly controlled Christians to find a use for "the gold and silver of the Egyptians." The earliest apologists knew that one had to read the pagans to refute them, but by the time of Tertullian, and especially by that of Augustine, it was becoming obvious that secular erudition was necessary for the correct study of the Bible. There was also the still more necessary fact that if the Christians were to have a learned priesthood, they would have to go to the pagans for formal training until they could establish schools of their own. But there was another side to the question.

Clement might see philosophy as the preparation for the understanding of the Christian message, but too many early fathers were sure that all pagan wisdom was either invented by demons or perverted by them from the texts of Moses and the prophets. There is an aloofness about many of these men characteristic of anyone who is convinced that he has a unique truth. With truth in their possession there was no need to know untruths or, at best, partial truths. The myths of the poets and the theories of the philosophers had seduced some Christian converts back to the old church. It was certainly reasonable to see that the enticement of the mythology might lead to fleshly immorality, whereas philosophical speculation might be a sure inductor into the society of heretics. Opinions of this nature led some members of the Church to prize the illiterate Christian, who was later to cause Christian humanists like Erasmus so much pain. But whereas Augustine and Jerome preferred an illiterate Christian to a learned renegade or heretic, they agreed that even though the study of pagan books was time-consuming and not soul-feeding, a learned Christian was a sturdy pillar of the Church militant.[117]

[117] Gerard L. Ellspermann, *The Attitude of the Early Christian Latin Writers toward Pagan Literature and Learning,* C.U.A. Patristic Studies, LXXXII (Washington, D. C., 1949).

II

✣ THE RENAISSANCE SEARCH FOR CHRISTIAN ORIGINS: THE PHILOSOPHERS ✣

IN A LETTER written to Magnus, Jerome reports his discovery of lines borrowed from Epimenides, Menander, and Aratus in the epistles of St. Paul. He approves of the apostle's allusions because, "like a true David, he used the sword of the enemy to cut off his head."[1] But it was one thing to use a few lines of verse to blunt the dagger of the pagans and another to use their ideas because they seemed filled with Christian intents. "If anyone assures you Christ dwells in the desert of the Gentiles and in the instruction of their philosophers . . . do not believe."[2] When Jerome wrote these words he was not ignorant that Justin,[3] Tatian,[4] Theophilus,[5] and Clement[6] were of the opinion that both Plato and Pythagoras had gone into Egypt to read the books of Moses. He also knew that the hated opposition, philosopher Celsus for example, claimed and proclaimed a Platonic origin of all respectable Christian principles.[7] Origen had refuted this misconception but his confutation was not widely known even by the end of Augustine's career.[8]

Confronted with the similarities between Platonism and Christian

[1] Jerome, *Epistolae, PL* XXII, 665.
[2] Jerome, *Commentarius in evangelium Matthaei, PL* XXVI, 186; *Epistolae, PL* XXII, 1148–49.
[3] Justin, *Apologia, PG* VI, 396.
[4] Tatian, *Adversus Graecos, PG* VI, 844.
[5] Theophilus, *Ad Autolycum, PG* VI, 1069.
[6] Clement, *Stromateis,* V. 14.
[7] Origen, *Contra Celsum, PG* XI, 1288, 1460, 1480, 1504.
[8] Augustine, *De doctrina Christiana, PL* XXXIV, 56; *Epistolae, PL* XXXIII, 125.

theology, early apologists were not sure exactly what to say. Sometimes they congratulated Plato and his disciples for coming close to the real truth in their conjectures on monotheism, the Logos, Creation, and the soul's immortality. Justin[9] and Clement[10] both agreed that Plato was convinced of the existence of a triune God. By the fifth century this suspicion had almost the hardened force of doctrine; Cyrillus, writing happily against the dead apostate Julian and certain of Plato's meditations on the Pentateuch of Moses, implied that the Greek had obviously envisioned a divine triumvirate in which one member was the Son of God.[11] But this conviction went beyond the limits of the Academy, for "we find among the wise men of Greece knowledge of the Holy Trinity."[12]

The ambivalent attitude toward Plato which is found in patristic writings carried Socrates' great disciple through the Middle Ages and even provided him with a school of Christian theologians in the twelfth century.[13] The logical and analytical methods of his best pupil, Aristotle, might dominate the schoolmen and provide St. Thomas, who was far from ignorant of him, with his best weapon against the Gentiles; by the beginning of the fifteenth century, however, Platonism was once again reviving and coming now to the rescue of an overintellectualized Christianity. The increasing popularity of the Averroistic doctrine of the double truth as the way out of the dilemma of faith was, of course, best subdued by Platonism; hence, when Pletho put the two great Greek philosophers side by side, he could see that Plato was far more Christian than Aristotle because he preferred the one to the many, stasis to kinema, creation in time to infinite existence. There were, naturally, many other flaws in Aristotle. He made no statement about the immortality of the soul; he defined virtue as the mean between extremes; he

---

[9] Justin, *Apologia*, PG VI, 420.

[10] Clement, *Stromateis*, V. 14. 89–100.

[11] Cyrillus, *Contra Julianum*, PG LXXVI, 551–54.

[12] *Ibid.*, col. 919. He supposes (col. 546) that both Plato and Pythagoras visited Egypt in order to study Moses' writings and, consequently, knew more about God than other Gentiles (cols. 574, 907). One of the fullest accounts of the notion is to be found in R. Arnou, "Platonisme des pères," *Dictionnaire de théologie catholique* (Paris, 1935), XII, 2258–393.

[13] Since there is an enormous literature on this matter, only a few important monographs can be mentioned: R. von Stein, *Verhältniss des Platonismus zur Philosophie der christlichen Zeit* (Göttingen, 1875), III, 67–184; R. Klibansky, *The Continuity of the Platonic Tradition during the Middle Ages* (London, 1939); E. Garin, *Studi sul Platonismo médiévale* (Florence, 1958); E. Bréhier, *La philosophie du moyen âge* (Paris, 1949), pp. 134–45, 150–58; M. D. Chenu, *La théologie au douzième siècle* (Paris, 1957), pp. 108–41. There are many individual Fathers and Doctors who looked toward Plato; see R. J. Henle, *St. Thomas and Platonism* (Hague, 1956); and P. L. Gaul, *Albert des Grossen Verhältnis zu Plato* (Munich, 1913).

thought man's chief end was temporal beatitude.[14] Reading this analysis, Gennadius went to Aristotle's defence and sent the usual pious controversy roaring down the ways; then Cardinal Bessarion stood up for Plato, remembered how the Fathers used him for the confirmation of Christian doctrine, and how in most questions he was seated far closer to Christian idealism than any other non-Christian philosopher. It was greatly to Plato's credit, too, he thought, that Dionysius, St. Paul's eminent and witty convert, had read him so carefully; and though the Athenian's theories of pre-existence and of the *Anima Mundi* were a bit bizarre, these errors avoided, his concepts of the Divine Attributes, the Trinity, Creation, and human immortality are much more orthodox than cherished Aristotle's anticreationism and his concept of a restricted providence.

The ensuing debate about the Christian coloration of Plato and Aristotle which involved Theodore of Gaza, Michael Apostolius, Georgius and Andreas Trapezuntius, Johannes Argyropoulos, and Niccolo Perotti eventuates in the Florentine school of Platonists directed by Marsiglio Ficino, which made Plato and the Platonists the heroes of the philosophical Renaissance. For these idealists the Athenians and the Alexandrians said many things that translated like Mosaic or Pauline utterances and were too close to the text of Scripture to be merely coincidences. The close scrutiny of Platonic texts by these devotees produced in them a conviction that all systems of thought were capable of being brought into a harmony resembling the primitive philosophy which had been fragmented and diminished by the rusting passage of time. Ficino's *Theologia Platonica de immortalitate animorum* broods on the hypothesis that a pagan theology descending from Zoroaster through Hermes Trismegistus to Orpheus, Pythagoras, and Plato is concurrent with the divine transmission of Christian theology and is useful in expounding it. Ficino's book on the soul's immortality is, therefore, the Renaissance's first in a series of obsessive attempts to gather into one grave plaque the parts of the primal theology,[15] known from

---

[14] Pletho, *De Platonicae et Aristotelicae philosophiae differentia*, PG CLX, 890–932; see J. W. Taylor, *Georgius Gemistus Pletho's Criticism of Plato and Aristotle* (Chicago, 1921), and François Masai, *Pléthon et le Platonisme de Mistra* (Paris, 1956). For Bessarion's views see his *In calumniatorem Platonis libri quatuor, Opera* (Venice, 1516), pp. 1–88, and J. W. Taylor, "Bessarion the Mediator," *APA Transactions*, LV (1924), 120–28. One of the best accounts of the Renaissance rediscovery of Plato, though subject to correction, is still J. J. Brucker, *Historia critica philosophiae* (Leipzig, 1766), IV, 1, 41–61.

[15] Of the large literature on Ficino and the Florentine Academy, which really begins with A. delle Torre, *Storia dell'Accademia Platonica di Firenze* (Florence, 1902), the following studies of the *Theologia* are valuable: P. O. Kristeller, *The Philosophy of Marsilio Ficino*

dialogues of the Divine with the first of mankind. Not all editors and translators of Plato agreed with the Florentine notion of a double line of theological descent; Giovanni Serrano, for instance, clung to the other opinion of the apologists that "Plato drew these symbols from Jewish doctrine."[16] But Ficino had been moved in his choice of dual ways by several experiences. He had read Proclus' *Theologia Platonica;* he had been unable to controvert the Epicurean ideas of Lucretius;[17] he believed that the soul was man's proper study;[18] and he saw all philosophies as an ascent from darkness to light, from flux to permanence.[19] In the writings of Plato he found all departments of human thought reduced to "the worship of the known God and the immortality of the soul, truths incorporating all knowledge, all rules of life, and happiness itself."[20]

II

What Ficino and his young associate Pico della Mirandola detected in the Platonists became a passion which drove other thinkers to look for God's whole in an infinitesimal number of parts, some of which were hardly godly. The search for a primitive but divinely communicated philosophy occupied men for two centuries and in due course fathered a shadowy form of cultural anthropology. Originally the process was essentially interpretive. More than fifteen hundred years had gone into seeking the New Testament in the Old Testament and moral and spiritual allegories of several kinds in both books. The custom pursued to a sacred nausea had become tritely sterile. It was so comically boring that Protestants were vigorously opposed to it, except when it helped them over a bad or adversative place in the divine oracles. It was, consequently, refreshing to discover that pagan scripture, once the verdigris of time was scoured away, had an almost smiling Christian message. Probably the first philosopher after the Florentines to see the virtue of

---

(New York, 1943); G. Saitta, *Marsilio Ficino* (Bologna, 1954), pp. 29–129; M. Schiavone, *Problemi filosofici in Marsilio Ficino* (Milan, 1957), pp. 17–189; R. Marcel, *Marsile Ficin* (Paris, 1958), pp. 647–78.

[16] Plato, *Opera,* ed. Giovanni Serrano (Paris, 1578), sig. ***1.

[17] Ficino, *Opera omnia* (Basel, 1576), p. 660. Two of his letters, "Concordia Mosis et Platonis" (pp. 866–68), and "Confirmatio Christianorum per Socratica" (p. 868) are **very** important.

[18] *Ibid.,* p. 657.

[19] *Ibid.,* pp. 670, 761.

[20] *Ibid.,* p. 78. Bessarion, *Opera* (p. 44) spread the net more widely: "The theology of Plato was so dear to the holy Doctors of our faith that each time they wrote something on God, they have not only wished to be inspired by his opinions but have actually used his **very** words."

harmonizing pagan philosophers and poets with the publications of the Holy Spirit was Agostino Steuco of Gubbio, Bishop of Kisamos.[21]

A master of languages and hence polymath, Steuco published in 1535 his *Cosmopoeia vel de mundano opificio,* which not only brought all of human knowledge to the aid and comfort of Moses' creation chapters but was also the steam-heated seminary for the *De perenni philosophia libri X* published in 1540 and several times reprinted. Steuco's hardly complicated or unexpected hypothesis is that sinless Adam conversed with God and angels, learning the "perfect theology" which he dispensed to his descendants during the following nine centuries of his life. In the six hundred years between Adam's death and the Flood, the celestially rendered doctrine deteriorated, but after that catastrophe, chaos and barbarism naturally ensuing, the Edenic theology completely disintegrated. Some of the Noachides, the Chaldeans, among whom lived Abraham and Noah's daughter-in-law, the Cumean Sibyl, preserved the *De doctrina Christiana* of Adam better than others. At that time all wisdom probably depended on oral transmission (Steuco is not certain when writing was invented), and the primitive theology became confused and corrupted as it was handed down orally.

The Hebrews were the best custodians of the Adamic bequest, and, consequently, those nations whose languages are derived from Hebrew —Chaldea, Babylon, Assyria, Egypt, and Phoenicia—preserved fragments of this philosophy (sometimes almost perfectly, but at other times debased by ugly fictions), better than non-Semitic races. From these more ancient and more civilized countries, regarded by them as barbaric, the Greeks, an astonishingly recent people, obtained their myths, theologies, and philosophies. Curiously acritical of their own origins, the Greeks prided themselves on their antiquity, but they had no documentary or monumental means of proving this illusion. Before Homer and Hesiod, the poetical codifiers of their philosophy and their first theologians, they could only name Orpheus, Linus, and Musaeus, poet-theologians whose writings are spurious and sparse. It is quite probable, of course, that many men wrote books before Homer and Hesiod's generation; in fact, these two poets must have had teachers whose books have vanished. It is known, writes Steuco, that Hermes Trismegistus wrote more than one hundred thousand books of which hardly a handful remains. If these lost volumes could be found, we should come a little closer to the verities contained in the pure text of the primitive theology.

[21] T. Freundenberger's *Augustinus Steuchus* (Münster, 1935), is apparently the only monograph on this philosopher.

Fortunately this text, vastly corrupted after the Flood, has been revised by Moses and restored by the new Christian revelation. In spite of these happy editorial events, Steuco thinks it worthwhile to search for vestiges of the "perfect theology" in the whole world's library because he is convinced that much of what he will discover here will help to establish the unique truth of Christianity.

Through hundreds of large pages, Steuco proves this idea again and again. Like so many Renaissance men, he never seems tired of repeating himself. He finds in Plato, Aristotle, Trismegistus, Proclus, Porphyry, Plotinus, the Magi, and the Sibyls (to mention a few of his informers), the concept of a Divine Mind reproducing itself hypostatically. The Arabs as well as the Delphic Apollo admit to this belief;[22] the natural theologians, Empedocles, Parmenides, Zeno, and Melissus speak of a creating God who animates His works.[23] Aristotle's *History of Animals* closely concurs with Genesis in a doctrine of creation, a principle that Aristotle, like Plato, got straight from Hermes Trismegistus.[24] In the second half of his fat treatise, Steuco searches the pockets of all pagan philosophers for the honest possession of basic Christian dogmas. The nauseating Aristotelian theory that the world is eternal can be shown to be nothing more than a mistranslation; Aristotle, like numerous Church Fathers, is not talking about the created universe but the Hebraic *tohu bohu*.[25] Although most of this theological knowledge came down the protoplasmic line from Adam, much of it is also from Moses, "most ancient of authors," the instructor of both Zoroaster and Hermes Trismegistus.[26] Steuco courses along and with very little difficulty finds that Christian opinions about angels and demons, immortality, ethics, postmortem rewards and inflictions, the destruction and re-creation of the earth are abundantly present as mementos of the Adamic heritage in most pagan philosophers.

Although Steuco was probably first in the procession from Ficino,[27] he was closely followed by Stefano Convenzio, whose *De ascensu mentis*

---

[22] Steuco, *Opera omnia* (Venice, 1591), III, 41–43.

[23] *Ibid.,* pp. 48–9.

[24] *Ibid.,* pp. 72v–73v.

[25] *Ibid.,* p. 102v. Steuco's position is opposite to that of Giovanni Francesco Pico della Mirandola, whose *Examen vanitatis gentium et veritatis Christianae disciplina* (Mirandola, 1520), is an attempt to weigh pagan theologies against Christian doctrine to show how lightweight the former are. The book is principally an attack on Aristotle, but other philosophers are knocked down in the course of it.

[26] *Ibid.,* p. 113v.

[27] G. Saitta, *Il pensiero Italiano nell' umanesimo e nel rinascimento* (Bologna, 1950), II, 71–156.

in Deum ex Platonica et Peripatetica doctrina was issued at Venice in
1563. With the help of Plato, the Neo-Platonists, and Aristotle, this
mystical philosopher describes the descent of the pre-existent soul to the
body's cave, where, as "God's ornament," it imitates superiors and dominates inferiors.[28] Aristotle is called on to describe the soul's union with
the body and the nature of the soul's self-knowledge;[29] then one is instructed in the various ladders of erotic ascent as constructed by Plato,
Aristotle, and Plotinus. Although he always talks with a Christian
mouth, Convenzio never openly embraces Steuco's theory of the original
"perfect theology." In his preface, however, he praises Plato for his
constant assistance to Christians and the Platonists for their Christian
doctrines of the soul.

In 1577, Francesco de Vieri, professor of philosophy at Florence,
recorded in his *Compendio della dottrina di Platone in quello che ella è
conforme con la fede nostra* a series of almost unbelievable similarities
between Christian doctrine and the philosophical tenets of Hermes Trismegistus, Pythagoras, Aristotle, and particularly Plato and Socrates.
The writings of St. Paul, Vieri sagely observes, are filled with Platonic
notions, and even St. Thomas seems to have found his proofs of God's
existence in the tenth book of Plato's *Laws*.[30] The right comprehension
of the true God as known to Moses, Solomon, and St. Paul can also be
discovered in the *Republic, Symposium,* and *Phaedo;* in fact, to Vieri,
the first chapter of Romans sounds very much like Diotima speaking.[31]
Man, this Florentine contends, has two forms of divine wisdom available to him; some of it is obscure, as in the Old Testament or the poetic
myths; some is clear, as in the New Testament, Plato, and Aristotle.[32]
The clearest of pagan philosophers speak of a triune God, creating
instantly for His own glory, and, as the *Timaeus* states, to communicate
His goodness.[33] Without too much striving Vieri uncovers a reasonable
amount of Christianity in Plato. Faith, hope, and love are Platonic
principles. Hell, Purgatory, and Heaven are to be found in the *Phaedo*.
Angels and devils are mentioned and described in the *Symposium* and
Republic. The beatific vision may be seen in the *Philebus* and *Timaeus*.[34]

Neither of these successors of Steuco looks askance at Aristotle,

---

[28] Convenzio, *op. cit.* (Venice, 1563), pp. 11–18.
[29] *Ibid.,* pp. 31–47.
[30] De Vieri, *op. cit.* (Florence, 1577), pp. 40–46.
[31] *Ibid.,* pp. 5–19.
[32] *Ibid.,* pp. 20–23.
[33] *Ibid.,* pp. 85–102.
[34] *Ibid.,* pp. 157–97.

although Plato and his school yield the best support to their syncretic hopes and convictions. The Professor of Platonism at Padua, Francesco Patrizzi, is neither so generous nor so neutral as they. His *Discussio peripateticarum* (Basel, 1581) and his *Nova de universis philosophia* (Ferrara, 1591) are both devoted to a fanatical exposition of Platonic Christianity and a vigorous, almost muscular, assault on virtually anything Aristotle ventured to say that touches in any fashion the dogmas of the church. In the first part of the *Discussio* the reader is offered as large an anthology of every hostile comment on Aristotle's ideas, morals, and manners as Partizzi could discover in Greek and Latin sources, because he is bent on exhibiting Aristotle as an ungrateful pupil, perverting or attempting to discredit everything proposed by his teacher Plato, whom he envied so much. In the preface to the *Nova philosophia* Patrizzi complains to Pope Gregory that the writings of Aristotle, who granted neither omnipotence nor providence to God, are the textbooks of European scholars and monastics; in contrast, the Christian dialogues of Plato, the theologies of Plotinus and Proclus, the "little book of Hermes Trismegistus containing more piety than all of Aristotle," are almost unknown and unread. These philosophers neglected in schools and monasteries could be favorably compared, he thinks, to Moses; most early Fathers, he continues, from Justin to Augustine, though they have nothing but ill to say about Aristotle, thought of Plato and the Platonists as "easily Christian." The formal development of this persuasion of the redemption of the philosophical idealists had already occupied the latter half of the *Discussio,* where the warped Platonic plagiarisms of Aristotle and the semi-Christian convictions of the Platonists are fully delineated. Patrizzi even found in Plato a prediction of the birth of Christ which antedates Virgil's annunciation by four hundred years.

Ficino was satisfied to summon the classical philosophers to the support of Christian notions of immortality; Patrizzi organizes both a metaphysic and physic on the ground of a Christian Platonism in the *Nova philosophia.* The organizing principle is the elimination of Aristotelian dualism so that the omnipotent and omniscient Jehovah, cheered on by Plato and his school, can triumph over omnipresent matter. The argument based on the presentation of innumerable quotations from the esoteric Platonists is parcelled out into four large areas on the slopes of comprehension which are named *Panaugia, Panarchia, Pansychia,* and *Pancomia.* The reader follows the primal light as it descends from the Absolute and helps to irradiate theology, pneumatology, psychology, and the commonest of elemental phenomena. The thinking is highly original in this large volume and prepares the reader, if he lives long enough, for the seventeenth-century theosophic vagaries of Henry More. In a series of appendices to appendices, Patrizzi provides the full Greek and Latin texts of Zoroaster, Hermes Trismegistus, and Aesculapius, the Platonic authorities from whom he had drawn his basic doctrines and whom he had already quoted *ad libitum*. In addition to this double supply of philosophical richness there is also an adjunct essay demonstrating the Chaldean and Egyptian origins of many of Plato's ideas. This essay is accompanied by an "Aristoteles exotericus," systematically demonstrating the correctness of Plato and the impious blunders of Aristotle on essential Christian principles.[35]

The crescendo of praise for Plato was muted to a universal shout in 1594 when Giovanni Crispo, poet friend of Tasso and Caro, finished the first volume of a projected five-volume work, *De ethnicis philosophis caute legendis disputationum,* and printed it at Rome. The subject of this volume (two additional ones are said to have been written but never printed) is the soul and its immortality, a doctrine which alone made Christianity possible and acceptable. The proud Crispo is determined to show that the Roman Church alone is right and that readers who follow the pagan philosophers, especially Plato and the Platonists, are likely to be led into heresies. Although he knows Ficino's translation of Plato, it is probably by no whim that he recommends and uses the two-language edition by Serrano, because the Latin translation is more accurate and closer to the Greek. Throughout his book, Crispo repeatedly refers to "our Platonizing theologians," but it is only Steuco and Ficino, Ficino particularly, who are called by name and personally corrected. Ficino is castigated for his heretical theories about the soul and about angels,[36] for his Christianization of the myth of Prometheus,[37] for his teachings on pre-existence and metempsychosis.[38] According to Crispo, Ficino's obsession is "that he wants Plato to be the basis of everything; hence, first he deceives himself, then others." In this idealistic monomania, Crispo thinks, Ficino may be imitating St. Thomas, who tried to bring the Church into agreement with Aristotle. "I have no other desire," Crispo states, "beyond keeping Christian truth separate from pagan impurities."[39] This decision follows his remarks in his preface, where he

[35] Saitta, *Il pensiero,* II, 521–67.
[36] Crispo, *op. cit.* (Rome, 1594), pp. 105–6.
[37] *Ibid.,* p. 236.
[38] *Ibid.,* pp. 443–46.
[39] *Ibid.,* p. 307.

complains of those who by means of the "machines of allegory" adjust the pagan philosophers to the pattern of the evangelists and venerate Plato as a "Moses Atticans." The book, which arose from this antithetical point of view and was as logically arranged as a scholastic could wish, should certainly have overwhelmed the Platolatry Crispo so abhorred.

The *De ethnicis philosophis caute legendis disputationum* is partitioned into twenty-four major divisions. In each division Crispo anatomizes some cherished pronouncement of Plato or the Platonists about the nature of the human soul. Among the important hypotheses which fall under Crispo's stern scrutiny are those postulating that the individual soul is part of the *Anima Mundi,* that all souls were created at the beginning of time and descend in the sequence of generation, that the number of souls is equal to that of the stars, that souls are corporeal and permanently joined to body, that not every soul is immortal, that the soul remembers its former state, that man has three souls, and that the soul migrates. In each instance, Crispo first summarizes the opinions of the philosophers, cites the objections of the Fathers, Doctors, and Councils, as well as scriptural references to the contrary. He does not find these negative votes hard to assemble because in all these celestially worthy matters (and he discourses almost elegantly on them) not only theological errors but also more offensive and damnable heresies have arisen from the infatuation of some vagrant group of Christians with one of these tantalizing theories of the philosophers.

III

The coldly solid objections of Crispo, poet as well as philosophizer, against the Platonizers who groped for Christian sparkles in the dustbins of the heathen theologians were not a decade old when Muzio Pansa, also a Christian poet, continued the discussion of divine transmissions for the seventeenth century by endorsing the theories of Ficino, Steuco, and Patrizzi and adding several new pagan philosophers to the approved list. The *De osculo ethnicae et Christianae philosophiae* printed in 1601 at Chieti, where its compiler was the local physician, is, according to its prospectus, only a quarter of the work projected. Volumes two to four, which would have revealed the international Christian knowledge of the Trinity, angels, demons, Creation, immortality, plus some pagan glimpses of the Judaeo-Christian religious history augmented with a complete account of Christian doctrine as expressed by

Greek, Arab, and Latin philosophers and poets, were either never written or, if written, were never sent to the printer.

In his first volume, Pansa's three-hundred quarto pages do little more than expose the general human agreement about a triune God and His attributes. This knowledge came to men through the normal two sources: the *lux divina,* which shone in "the perfect theology" taught to Adam and the book of the world, the *liber mundi,* fervently read by piously inclined philosophers. The Chaldeans were first to suspect the existence of a triune God, but this knowledge transmitted to the Hebrews was passed on by them to the Egyptians, Phoenicians, Greeks, and Romans.[40] Long before Plato told them, men knew that God was wisdom and that unless they were aided by God they could never know Him. To obtain a total comprehension of God, one must first purge one's soul of its unspiritual excrescences according to the methods taught by Zoroaster, Trismegistus, Pythagoras, Plotinus, Orpheus, and the mages of Persia and India.[41] The wiser ancients, Pansa supposes, scorned polytheism[42] because they were conscious of their own innate comprehension of the divine. All of these inspired ones—Euripides, Xenophanes, Socrates, Plato, Orpheus, Homer, Hesiod, Empedocles, Sophocles, Pindar, to mention only a few—believed in a divine unity and were certain in an approximate Christian manner of the causes and origin of evil.[43] It is true that some of Pansa's osculators compared God —and so do Christians—to fire or air, but then Orphic metaphors of this nature may be found here and there in the New Testament.[44] Parmenides, for example, anticipated Christian doctrine by describing God as infinite, immaterial, indivisible, perfect, eternal, and circular.[45] Of course (Pansa admits) it sometimes requires explicatory effort to uncover Christian thought in pagan poets and philosophers, but there is excellent reason for this. Those of the ancients who were sure in their conviction of only one God were not going to risk a death like that of Socrates by confessing their beliefs to illiterate plebeians; hence, they veiled their wisdom in enigmas and phrased what they wrote in metaphors so that they would not only be protected, but so that their sound theology would also be preserved from the corrupting distortions of vulgar minds.[46]

[40] Pansa, *op. cit.,* p. 2.
[41] *Ibid.,* pp. 7–26.
[42] *Ibid.,* pp. 35–38.
[43] *Ibid.,* pp. 40–59.
[44] *Ibid.,* pp. 71–74.
[45] *Ibid.,* pp. 103–10.
[46] *Ibid.,* pp. 182–83.

Pansa delights his readers with an extensive account of the Christian thinking of Plato, Aristotle (he prints his "Hymn to Virtue"),[47] and all their disciples and agreeable successors. He quotes philosophers and poets who, impregnated by "the perfect theology" transmitted through Moses, describe God as infinite in beauty, power, duration, place, action, vision, and understanding. This string of divine attributes brings Pansa to a final account of God's providence and love for the creatures. Beginning with Orpheus a large assembly of early poets and wise men believed in the Christian doctrine of Providence as expounded by the Roman Church; in fact, Homer's description of the golden chain of Zeus and Plato's spindle of necessity are allegorical representations of the doctrine of Providence.[48] Pansa finds that if one sweeps the theories of Epicurus out of the way, all other ancients agree in the belief that Providence does not interfere with the functions of free-will.[49] He discovers in Greek sources the "Word of God lovingly creating all from Chaos and Night," for what is the Celestial Venus, so celebrated in antique song, but an alternate redaction of the Mosaic creation? The final chapters of the *De osculo* recount on the authority of Aristobulus, Philo, Josephus, and a concourse of early Fathers, the migration into Egypt of almost all early Greek poets and philosophers to gain instruction in the true theology.

Pansa's irenics was succeeded by other attempts to find Christian light in pagan gloom. George Pacard, a conventional rational theologian, devotes almost six hundred pages of his *Théologie naturelle* (Paris, 1606) to the Gentiles' knowledge of one God, Providence, and comparable items of faith. He finds Aristotle's realistic materialism alone inexcusable because he might have consulted Numenius, who states that Musaeus was Moses, or Diodorus Siculus, who recounts the Mosaic instruction of the Egyptian divines.[50] Pacard writes as if he were almost without predecessors, but Raimondo Breganio, a Dominican, assembled in Venice in 1621 a portable version of Steuco in his *Theologiae gentium de cognitione divina enarrationes*, which was greatly dependent on earlier expositors. After commending both Hermes and Socrates for regarding their comprehension of God as a gift of grace,[51] Breganio lists the non-Christians to whom God condescended to make revelations, and traces the dissemination of the "perfect theology" as it flowed from

---

[47] *Ibid.*, p. 199.
[48] *Ibid.*, pp. 297–98.
[49] *Ibid.*, pp. 303–11, 325–26.
[50] Pacard, *op. cit.*, 435–37.
[51] Breganio, *op. cit.*, pp. 16–17.

Adam to Moses to the Greeks.[52] Plato, who lived after the time of David and learned from both Moses and the Prophets, quotes the Old Testament (Breganio got this from Eusebius) fourteen times;[53] nevertheless, one should not swallow all that the heathen philosophers said but keep Jerome's remark in mind and read the pagans only for what they have retained of the truth.[54]

Shortly after the publication of Breganio's defence of divine condescension, books supporting Patrizzi's case for the Christian recognition of Plato and the Platonists by Livio Galanti and Pierre Halloix appeared. Galanti excuses the patristic detractors of Plato for their failure to discover in the highly poetical language and subjectively allegorical structure of the dialogues the essential Platonic parallels with Christianity.[55] Although he urges his readers to use Plato's texts with caution, he himself finds both the Garden of Eden and the beguiling Satanic serpent in the *Phaedo*.[56] Halloix, a Jesuit, subscribes to the time-honored notion that Moses taught Plato[57] and finds a premonition of the Advent in the closing remarks of Socrates.[58] This inclines him, as it had inclined others, to assume the salvation of Socrates, Erasmus' "Sanctus Socrates,"[59] because he believed in Providence, was led by tutelary angels, respected one God who rewards and punishes in the hereafter, loved justice, urged men to pursue virtue, and foreshadowed with his own death the crucifixion of Christ.[60]

Book upon book in which the relation between the theology of the Church and that of the pagan philosophers was traced, even to the extent of annotating the Holy Bible with comments derived from heathen letters,[61] came in profusion to grace the bookstalls of the seven-

[52] *Ibid.,* pp. 33–35, 51–57.

[53] *Ibid.,* pp. 147–56.

[54] *Ibid.,* pp. 166–70.

[55] Galanti, *Christianae theologiae cum Platonica comparatio quin imo cum tota veteri sapientia ethnicorum, Chaldaeorum nempe, Aegyptiorum et Graecorum* (Bologna, 1627), pp. 16–25.

[56] *Ibid.,* pp. 137–41, 200–1.

[57] Halloix, *Illustrium ecclesiae orientalis scriptorum qui sanctitate iuxta et eruditione . . . vitae et documenta* (Douai, 1633), I, 236.

[58] *Ibid.,* I, 10, 232–3.

[59] Erasmus, *The Colloquies,* trans. Craig Thompson (Chicago, 1965), pp. 67–68.

[60] Halloix, *op. cit.,* II, 333–51.

[61] The custom of collecting parallels between pagan literature and the Bible may begin for modern times with Georg Wicel, *Parallela affinia sive correspondentia ex nostris hoc est sacris et gentilium libris* (Mayence, 1544). In his 1633 oration "Farrago rituum sacrorum et secularium," Johannes Dilherr finds Acts 5:29 in the *Apology;* Acts 17:28 in Aristotle's *Parts of Animals;* Colossians 3:17 in the eighth Platonic letter; and Wisdom 15:12 in Epictetus, Terence, Cicero, Plutarch, and other ethnics. The oration appeared in two parts in *Opuscula quae ad historiam ac philologiam sacram spectant* (Rotterdam, 1693), VIII, 10–16, 287–91. A

teenth century. The suppositions proposed by most of them differed very little from those laid down by the earliest apologists. Originality is not an attribute of theological contention in any era, and the seventeenth century was no exception to common experience. The patent similarities between the pagan and Christian systems were explained as a consequence of the revelation to Adam, duly perverted until Moses renewed its original luster and instructed not only the Jews but also visiting delegations of pagans. This was one explanation. A second theory was that fallen angels, overhearing (with sin-obstructed ears) the lucid predictions of the prophets, attempted to befuddle potential Christian believers by inventing similar but somewhat erroneous myth-fulfillments gladly adopted by the pagan world. Finally it was imagined that God had made a universal revelation of Himself to all men via the operations of the Natural Light, but that some men, Hebrews for instance, were less myopic or light-dazzled than others. All of these propositions were backed by infinite quotation and analytical adjustment of suitable non-Christian legend and speculation. Most of the adherents of these positions were foster children of Platonism, the stepmother of the Christian Church. But if these theories were sometimes tentatively put forth on the Continent, it was in England, home of aberrant doctrine, that they merged to make a school.[62]

IV

One should not be so irreverent as to observe that Henry More and his Cambridge colleagues did not always draw precise borders between Platonism and Neo-Platonism. More's poetic "Psychathanasia" is manifestly the work of a philosopher who was more of a Plotinist than a Platonist. The God so carefully delineated by More is like Plotinus' god superior in his eminence to the Platonic Idea.[63] He is, besides, the station toward which the mortal mind, which knows Him innately, returns via the route of contemplation. "It remains, therefore, undeniable that there is an inseparable Idea of a Being absolutely Perfect, ever

book on the same matter is Filippo Picinelli's *Lumi riflessi ò dir vogliamo concetti della sacra Bibbia osservati ne i volumi non sacri* (Milan, 1667). The most impressive of these efforts to annotate the Bible with pagan references is Johannes Bompart's *Parallela sacra et profana sive notae in Genesim* (Amsterdam, 1689). Here one learns that Genesis I:1 is *Metamorphoses*, I, 5–7, 15–20; that Sara's words in Genesis 21:10 are those of Achilles to Briseis in *Heroides*, 76–77; and that when Hagar complains under the fig tree in Genesis 21:15, her words are repeated by Statius in *Thebiad*, IV, 780–81.

[62] The best account of the movement is still Ernst Cassirer, *Die Platonische Renaissance in England und die Schule von Cambridge* (Leipzig-Berlin, 1932).

[63] More, *A Collection of Several Philosophical Writings* (London, 1662), pp. 48, 85.

residing, though not always acting, in the Soul of Man."[64] The perversion of the true spiritual religion by fallen angels, who reduced all to an "animal state," which is that of the polytheistic faiths, is the theme of a large section of More's *An Explanation of the Grand Mystery of Godliness.*[65] This work, if supplemented by *The Mystery of Iniquity* and the *Antidote against Idolatry,* could be considered almost the last Christian *apologia* against paganism. Pythagoras, Plato, and his disciples are generally exonerated of heathen blame because they had their philosophy from the books of Moses; in fact, they are "the best Cabbala that I know of *Moses* his text."[66] But in addition to reading the Pentateuch, Plato was likewise a Greek minor prophet who "seems to have had some knowledge and presage of the coming of Christ: in that being asked how long men should attend to his writings, he answered, till some more holy and divine Person appear in the world, whom all should follow."[67]

More's learned colleague Ralph Cudworth, who put down all his reading notes in a fantastic number of printed and unprinted quires to be fluttered against the atomic atheists, repeatedly notices that polytheists thought all their lesser gods derived from "one increate being" or, at their ridiculous worst, were theological "monarchists."[68] Cudworth has no difficulty determining the monotheism of the Sibyls or of Zoroaster;[69] he even discloses the Trinity in Orpheus,[70] who was, in his estimation, a historical personage even though he may not, as some said, have written the Orphic verses. The traditional transmission story, which appears almost midway in his treatise,[71] is that the Greeks, contrary to the opinion of Philo, learned from the Egyptians, who naturally learned from Moses. After this gambit he can follow the usual divine course through Egyptian theology and the theologian Hermes Trismegistus to Homer, Hesiod, Sophocles, Euripides, Pythagoras, and the pre-Socratics. Unlike many of his predecessors, Cudworth congratulates neither Socrates nor Plato on their rational views of the true Jehovah. The golden legend cherished by some Christians that Socrates died because he rejected the Greek pantheon for his personal monotheism is branded by Cudworth as "a vulgar error." Socrates and Plato were both polythe-

---

[64] *Ibid.,* p. 13.
[65] More, *The Theological Works* (London, 1708), pp. 39–67.
[66] More, *Conjectura Cabbalistica* (London, 1662), pp. 43–5, 84, 87, 100.
[67] *Ibid.,* p. 95.
[68] Cudworth, *The True Intellectual System of the Universe* (London, 1743), pp. 230–31. Cudworth observes that even the shrewdest opponents of Christianity—Celsus, Porphyry, and Julian—were all monotheists (pp. 270–74).
[69] *Ibid.,* pp. 283–87.
[70] *Ibid.,* pp. 304–5.
[71] *Ibid.,* pp. 310–12.

ists,[72] but Plato did believe in one supreme creating god. Although his trinitarian theory is far better than that of the "pseudo-Platonists" and has "an admirable correspondency" with Christianity,[73] it is by no means so reasonable as the Christian three-in-one hypothesis. Cudworth calls the roll of all those venerable pagans—Cicero, Varro, Seneca—who rejected polytheism and voted for one god only or for a head god who had powers and attributes not unlike those of the true God. He is not amazed at the number of ancient monotheists, because an atheist in the exact import of the word is a rational impossibility.

Sometime between the publication of More's philosophical volumes and Cudworth's voluminous attack on atheism, the study of comparative religions began with the printing of John Spencer's *Dissertatio de Urim et Thummin* (1669/1670) which was eventually incorporated in the *De legibus Hebraeorum ritualibus* of 1685. In the short book of 1669, Spencer proposed that although the Jewish custom of lot-casting is obscure in origin and may have been known as far back as the time of the sons of Noah, the Jews probably learned it from Egyptians during the Captivity.[74] In the succeeding larger work he states that the enigmatic rites of Hebrews and Egyptians were strangely similar. But no one with any historical caution would assume that the Hebrews taught the Egyptians, because the hieroglyphic literature of Egypt was definitely older than the age of Moses "and the Egyptians long before his time were accustomed to hide their holy dogmas under mystical symbols and figures." It is Spencer's contention, too, that the Chaldean mages and Persian wisemen were all before the age of Moses.[75] The Jews, when not prohibited by their laws, were inclined to adopt many Gentile customs.[76] Circumcision, for example, was borrowed from the Egyptians.[77] The

---

[72] *Ibid.*, pp. 400–401.

[73] *Ibid.*, pp. 405–6, 552–61, 576–601.

[74] Spencer, *op. cit.* (Cambridge, 1727), pp. 920–1038. An effort in the same direction is found in Christian Kortholt's *Tractatus de origine, progressu, et antiquitate philosophiae barbaricae* (Jena, 1660), where it is held that Moses and the Greeks—Thales, Pythagoras, Democritus, and Plato—were instructed by the Chaldeans and Egyptians in astronomy and mathematics. The Persian magi, the Indian Gymnosophists, and the Druids were also taught by these masters long before the time of the Greeks. Kortholt concludes his thesis with "I intended now to go on with the Greeks, but necessity intervenes and I shall save it for a better time."

[75] *Ibid.*, p. 212. Somewhat earlier (p. 210) he had conjectured that Moses could read hieroglyphics.

[76] *Ibid.*, pp. 639–63, 730–38. The clamor against this wicked theory was over-loud. In 1656, for example, Philippe de Ribondeault of Geneva argued in his *Sacrum Dei oraculum Urim et Thummin* that Homer, Pythagoras, Herodotus, Thucydides, Xenophon, Plato, and the rest read the Septuagint and hence knew the Hebrew mysteries. His book is reprinted in Blasius Ugolinus, *Thesaurus antiquitatum sacrum* (Venice, 1751), XII.

[77] *Ibid.*, p. 55.

Christians did not lag behind the Jews in this respect. The pagan custom of lustration and divine feasts were naturalized by Christians as baptism and the eucharist;[78] in fact, it was not uncommon for "purified and emended" ethnic ceremony to be converted into Christian rite. Christian burial ceremonies—singing and flute-playing at funerals, the ritual washing of the corpse, public mourning, the ritual at the tomb, the erection of a memorial, and the funeral feast—were all of pagan origin.[79] God, Spencer thought, prevented the triumph of superstition by absorbing pagan customs which were innocent or prefigured His mysteries into His church. Tertullian's well-known account of the conversion of Joseph into the god Serapis is a good example of the sensible divine process. When Joseph died, Spencer imagines, the Egyptians (perhaps it was the Israelites) accorded him divine honors and made his coffin and the ox his ceremonial symbols. God altered these superstitious pagan symbols into the Ark of the Covenant and the cherubim. Spencer can, of course, find other parallels like this euhemeristic example of Tertullian's to support his doctrine of divine condescension.[80]

The incredible surmise that Moses was not the oldest of the world's writers and that both Jews and Christians might have imitated prior pagan theologies and ceremonies did not go down very easily in seventeenth-century Europe. A score or more of distinguished theologians came to the defence of Hebrew priorities. Spencer made a few converts, but not many of the sort who came immediately to his aid. His views were eventually supported by Juricu and Warburton, but only John Marsham sprang up immediately to back this heretical suggestion. Marsham had, he informs us, always wondered why the Jews, a people famous for their aloofness and proud of their place as the chosen of Jehovah, would have leaked the theological secrets of the Promise to Gentiles. However, he presumes they lived so long as slaves among the Egyptians that they must have taken over a great amount of primitive Egyptian doctrine. Everyone stood ready to assume that the Greeks, who had to travel down to the Nile, were taught by Egyptians, Marsham declares, so why should the Jews who lived in Egypt not pick up

[78] *Ibid.,* p. 688. An enormously learned study of the question of the origins of Christian rituals appeared at Lyon in 1635 by Luigi Novarini as the *Schedismata sacro-prophana, hoc est observationem antiquis Christianorum, Hebraeorum, aliarumque gentium ritibus in lucem eruendis,* which is an encyclopaedia of the universal religious practices of ablution, baptism, blessing, crowns, charity, fasts, founts, holy oil, etc. After indicating how widely these rites are employed, the author reminds his readers that they are all derived from Christian sources.

[79] *Ibid.,* pp. 1135–60.

[80] *Ibid.,* pp. 879–81.

Egyptian customs? "Many of Moses' laws are based on ancient custom." When he said this, Marsham was sure that Moses forbade rites or dogmas offensive to Jehovah, but, as he adds, Moses revised and adopted other Egyptian ceremonies for Hebrew use. By scrutinizing the Decalogue Marsham found examples to support his views. Many ancient Egyptian principles, like respect for parents, are recommended by Moses to the Jews.[81] Marsham was no more successful than Spencer in avoiding the censure of the Christian orthodox, but by coming to the aid of Spencer, he may have helped advance the study of the historical evolution of Christianity.[82]

Although both Spencer and Marsham planted the seed of a rational consideration of the development and refinement of religion, the old theory that all men shared commonly in the Divine Light continued to be discussed. In 1679 the keeper of the archives at Gotha, Tobias Pfanner, printed a *Systema theologiae gentilis purioris* at Basel, where, after pondering the various ways—natural reason, knowledge of Scripture, philosophical excogitation—in which the pagans came close to Christian beliefs and had ceremonies in common, Pfanner attempts to make fine discriminations between pagan and Christian doctrines about God, the Trinity, Christ, Creation, angels and demons, Providence, and Free

[81] Marsham, *Chronicus canon Aegypticus, Ebraicus, et disquisitiones* (London, 1676), pp. 146–50. This book is one in the great chronological debate in which J. J. Scaliger, J. Gualter, I. Voss, T. Lydiat, D. Petau, and others took part. The problem of which people was most ancient, which produced the heresy of Isaac de la Peyrere, had to await the publication of William Jameson's *Spicelegia antiquitatum Aegypti* and Jacob Voorbroek's *Origines Babylonicae et Aegyptiacae* for reasonable clarification. The famous theologian, Herman Wits, who attacked both Spencer and Marsham in *Aegyptiaca et Dekaphulon sive de Aegyptiacorum sacrorum cum Hebraicis collatione libri tres* (Amsterdam, 1696), nevertheless agrees with both men that the Jews and Egyptians seem to have many religious ideas and rites in common, but he insists that the Egyptians got them all from the Jews, or that the apparently borrowed notions and customs were common to many races, or that the Egyptian forms were inferior to those of the Jews. He notices that some Egyptian customs, such as incestuous marriage, would have been obnoxious to Jews. He can find no historical evidence that the Egyptians were the most ancient people; in fact, it is clear to him they were posterior in time to the Hebrews.

[82] A great many books gravid with learning and supporting one or other of the conflicting views on the antiquity of peoples appeared prior to Spencer's and Marsham's publications. Gerard Vos printed the first two books of his heavy handed *De theologia gentili et physiologia Christiana sive de origine ac progressu idolatriae* at Amsterdam in 1642. The interest in ancient astronomical theology is responsible for Guy Scheffer's *Coelum poeticum seu sphaera astronomica* (Prague, 1686) and Philip von Zesen's *Coelum astronomico-poeticum, sive mythologia stellarum fixarum* (Amsterdam, 1682). A similar, but much slighter book, is the *Theologia gentilis* of Daniel Clasen, which was printed at Frankfort in 1684 with the purpose of demonstrating again the Biblical provenience of all pagan ceremonies dealing with the underworld. Clasen thinks that Moses and Aaron were transmogrified into Minos and Rhadamanthus. The *De religione gentilium* of Edward Herbert should be mentioned here as supporting the claims of Natural Light in religious development, but its aims were hardly those of Vos and Clasen.

Will. He eliminates a number of pious pagans whose admirable Christian beliefs he found wide of the mark, but he has high respect for Plato, "of all Gentiles the most skilled and fortunate seeker after truth, who rarely errs." Next in merit to Plato is Plotinus, who "just missed being Christian." Pfanner's Protestant views on these important details were shared by Louis Thomassin, a priest of the Oratoire, who devoted six fantastic volumes to the discovery of Christian doctrines in all Greek and Roman writers.

Thomassin's *La méthode d'étudier et d'enseigner Chrétiennement et solidement les lettres humaines par rapport aux lettres divines et aux écritures* came out between 1681 and 1695 at Paris and is far more difficult to read than it was to write. He bases his enormous effort (and this was by no means his only learned labor) on the devotion of the Fathers to pagan literature. Ambrose, for example, urges Christians "to seek in the fables the shadows and counterfeits of Jesus." Moses quoted some heathen Canaanite poetry in Numbers. Christian poets have often availed themselves of pagan rhetorical ornaments. After Moses, who was the first theologian, the pagan poets, instructed by Natural Light, tarnished patriarchal tradition, or Hebrew teachers, were the next religious philosophers. Thomassin finds Moses speaking in Homer and stresses the value to Christians of the truth lurking in the texts of pagans.

Young Christians, he states, should read pagan literature with care, but they should also understand that the apparent impieties they find in it are divinely placed there for moral instructions. They must also realize the allegorical nature of non-Christian letters. Physical and astronomical lore often hides in myth, and often, too, it is a cover for human history. Thomassin illustrates this pedagogical admonition with lengthy summaries of the epics of Homer and Virgil which enable him to show a dozen or more basic Christian dogmas in each poet.[83] After this particularized study of the greatest Greek and Latin poets, he traces the major moments in Christian history—Creation, Antediluvian Giants, the Deluge, the Four Ages, and so on—through the pages of pagan literature. His two early volumes on Graeco-Roman literature are followed by two more on pagan historians, all of whom testified to certain Christian convictions. In 1695 came the volumes on the philosophers.

If there is Christian inspiration in pagan fine letters, there is for Thomassin even more pious doctrine in the philosophers. Moses in-

[83] Thomassin, *op. cit.*, I, 328–434.

structed the primitive Greek poets and they, in turn, taught their wisdom to Socrates and Plato. Thomassin proves that Plato lived too late to converse personally with any of the Hebrew prophets, but this does not make impossible an acquaintanceship with some of the translators of the Septuagint. Plato's clear understanding of the Creation, angels, an infinite God, and the uncertainty of discursive knowledge suggests that he either read Moses or had a private revelation from the Natural Light.[84] On page after page, Thomassin follows the development of Christian ideas as they are expressed by Plato, reexpressed by the Platonists, and then appear in the writings of Cicero or Seneca. Thomassin's attempt to trace the remnants of Christian ideals in pagan texts was the most elaborate of all such seventeenth-century efforts and was almost the last. The comparative study of religions had begun, although it was not yet freed from the pious inattention of the Christian theologians. Wiser heads no longer saw in an Ethiopian or Central American account of a flood proof of biblical accuracy because analogues of this nature were perceived to demonstrate the primitive convictions of human fearfulness. The passion for allegory ceased to possess men like a taste for strong drink; myths became myths whether they were Hebrew, Persian, or Greek. The search for an elaborate pattern of a universal theology divinely revealed was ended now that men like Bayle, Fontenelle, and the French rationalists were making themselves heard.[85] The supernatural had begun to lose its prefix.

V

Although Augustine was disinclined to assign these pagan pre-Christians even a degree of salvation, other Fathers were not so sure of the eternal fate of pious philosophers who seemed to have thoughts suitable for companions of the Holy Ghost or at least for constant readers in the Mosaic library.[86] Were these men condemned, one inquired, to the eternal bonfire because they had the misfortune to live

[84] *Ibid.,* IV, 321–28.

[85] In 1693 Albrecht Rotth's *Trinitas Platonica* discussed the pros and cons of this very tedious subject to conclude that the Trinity of Plato was not that of Christians. The *Le Platonisme dévoilé* of the Arminian divine Matthieu Souverain, published at Cologne in 1700, treated Plato as a kind of primitive man and underscored with horror his superstitious opinions accepted by Christians (pp. 51–68). A series of discourses by J. J. Zimmerman casting doubts on Plato's so-called Christianity were printed posthumously in J. G. Schelhorn, *Amoenitates literariae* (Frankfort and Leipzig, 1728–30), IX, 827–985; XI, 93–212; XII, 369–510.

[86] Louis Capéran, *Le problème du salut des infidèles* (Paris, 1912), pp. 110–32.

prior to the Advent or were they, like the patriarchs, susceptible to salvation when Christ harrowed Hell on Holy Saturday? Dante installs a group of these virtuous heathen in Limbo and permits one of them to take him to the edge of Purgatory and another to go a bit farther. In the nineteenth canto of the *Paradiso,* he puts the matter up to the divine Eagle, but that symbolical and clear-sighted bird backs off from the problem and provides an ambiguous solution. At Judgment Day, many will cry "Christ! Christ!" who are not so close to Him as some who never knew Him. Abelard writes that divinely inspired philosophers like Plato were similar to the Hebrew prophets, were by no means true idolators, knew mysteries like the nature of the Trinity, and, hence, understood the possibility of eternal salvation.[87] Although St. Thomas agrees that these early good men lacked a saving faith in the incarnate Christ, he assumes that they might be saved during the Descent into Hell because they all plainly believed in and trusted Providence.[88] The rough problem of the salvation of Socrates, Plato, Cicero, and Seneca was still a relatively unsolved matter when the Renaissance began.

In his preface to Cicero's *Tusculan Disputations,* Erasmus inspects the possiblity of Cicero's salvation. The Roman believed in the existence of a supreme God and the immortality of the soul. He lived as pure a life as Job. He did not oppose idol-worship, but neither did the Apostles before the coming of the Holy Spirit. "To the Jews before the publication of the gospels a certain rough and half-light faith was enough. What about those who have not known Moses' laws? What hinders it that even a little knowledge will make for salvation, especially when he leads not only an innocent but a holy life?" In the well-known passage of the "Convivium religiosum," Erasmus states through several of the speakers his conviction that Cicero, Plutarch, and Socrates are saved. When he reads Cicero, he kisses the book, and as for Socrates, "I can only cry out, 'Sancte Socrates ora pro nobis.'"

Luther took violent issue with Erasmus' Christian generosity although he stood ready to admit certain heathen like Melchizedek, Job, and Naaman the Syrian to the sweet society of the blessed. In his *De servo arbitrio* (1525) he attacks the assumed merit of certain pagan heroes and asks Erasmus how these men could have taught morality without knowing what it was? He calls out Regulus and Scaevola as men favored by his Catholic opponent and inquires if Erasmus was sure he

[87] Abelard, *Introductio ad theologiam,* PL CLXXVIII, 1012, 1034, 1056; *Theologia Christiana,* PL CLXXVIII, 1179.
[88] St. Thomas, *Summa theologia,* II. 2. Quaest. 2. art. 7.

knew their hearts. "Did they not pursue their personal glory and so detract from God's glory, attributing merit to themselves and to no one else?"[89] Melanchthon, who thought the Gospel was proclaimed in the time of Homer and Thales,[90] excused no pagans; the Law was available to all and they had salvation in it.[91] The French Protestants assumed a similar unrelenting point of view, which arises from the supposition found in the first pages of Calvin's *Institutes* that God had imprinted a sense of Himself in all men. The Genevan presented the centurion Cornelius and Naaman the Syrian as witnesses to this premise. They were changed by God's innate impression, but other pagans were not spiritually altered by this internal experience. Hence, the other pagans face eventual damnation without excuse.[92] As a matter of fact, Calvin concludes that they may have been given this knowledge in order to increase their damnation.[93] The nasty Jehovah of Calvin was happily not the God of Zwingli, who in his *Exposition of the Christian Faith* opened the doors of salvation to many men, and, in the opinion of Luther, almost closed them to himself by this too generous gesture. In his dedication to Francis I, Zwingli gives the king a promising glimpse of the City of God.

> You will see Hercules, Theseus, Socrates, Aristides, Antigone, Numa, Camilla, the Catos, the Scipios; you will see Louis the Pious, your predecessors the Louises, the Philips, the Pepins, and all your ancestors who are dead in the faith. In sum, there has not been a good man, not been a holy mind, not a faithful heart from the beginning of the world to its burning whom you will not see with God.[94]

The kindly and relaxed decision of Zwingli was adopted by the Arminians, who were battered by Calvinistic polemic for accepting it. In the famous Thirty-one Articles, Arminius set down three items pertinent to this question. "If the pagan," he stated in one, "and those who have

---

[89] Capéran, *op. cit.*, pp. 242-6.

[90] Melanchthon, *Opera*, ed. G. Bretschneider and H. E. Bindseil (Halle, 1834-60), XXIV, 230.

[91] *Ibid.*, p. 925. On this matter see P. Drews, "Die Anschauungen reformatorischer Theologen über die Heidenmisson," *Zeitschrift für praktische Theologie*, XIX (1897), 202-3. About this time Conrad Mudt (Mutianus) wrote Spalatin, "the Christian religion did not commence with the Incarnation, for it was before time as the birth of the Word. What is Christ after all if not, as Paul says, the Wisdom of the Father? Now this Wisdom has not been divulged exclusively to the Jews; it has shone among the Greeks, Italians, and Germans although their religious customs were different from those of the Jews." The letter is reprinted in J. Janssen, *Geschichte des deutschen Volkes* (Freiburg, 1891), II, 30-31.

[92] Calvin, *Opera*, ed. W. Baum, E. Cunlitz, E. Reuss (Brunswick, 1863-82), XLVIII, 227; II, 425.

[93] *Ibid.*, XXVIII, 488-89, 644.

[94] Zwingli, *Werke*, ed. M. Schuler and J. Schulthess (Zurich, 1828-42), IV, 65.

no knowledge of God do what they can by nature, God will not condemn them but recompense their works by a greater knowledge which will bring them to salvation." This flat but firm definition of universal grace was supported by Arminius' thesis that divine mercy was extended to anyone who did as well as he could and by his conviction that men who never read the Gospel were, nonetheless, inwardly informed about Christ by the Holy Spirit or by angelic tutors.[95] The essential Roman position was, for a change, as rigid as that of Wittenberg and Geneva.

The pattern for the Roman attitude had been set by Augustine in his letter to Evodius.[96] In this epistle, he spoke well of right-living pagans who anticipated the Christian notions of God, Creation, and human conduct. With spiritual tears in his eyes, Augustine regretfully denies these men any prospect of redemption. Although there were noteworthy exceptions to his attitude, the Church itself clung to his conclusions. In the fifteenth century, Tostado, Bishop of Avila, argued that Socrates, Plato, and others may have found their way into a Dantean limbo from which they were released during the infernal visitation of Christ because of their belief in "an unknown God."[97] A century afterwards, both Vega and Soto held that "a kind of natural faith" was an assurance of salvation, a false doctrine readily refuted by Medina, Cano, and Suarez.[98] The same negative attitude was supported at the sixth session of the Tridentine Council on January 13, 1547/48, a clear indication of how widely the generous infection had spread. In 1565, Michel de Bay argued for the salvation of pious pagans in the first part of his De meritis only to have his opinions declared Neo-Pelagian in a Bull of Gregory XIII. Leonardus Lessius, a Jesuit well-known in England, was subsequently disciplined for advancing arguments in favor of universal grace, a popular hypothesis discussed at some length by Franciscus Collius and François de la Mothe le Vayer in the seventeenth century.

The De animabus paganorum libri quinque, published in Milan in 1622 by the Ambrosian Collius, opens with theoretical theology and an analysis of the assumptions of some great predecessors like Claude

---

[95] Arminius, *Opera* (Leyden, 1629) pp. 156, 158–59. Arminius attacked the opinions of Perkins' *Armilla aurea* of 1590 in his 1612 *Examen modestum libelli* and his conclusions were attacked almost at once by Tilenus in his *Consideratio sententiae J. Arminii de praedestionatione, gratia Dei, et libero arbitrio hominis* (Frankfort, 1612).

[96] Augustine, *Epistolae, PL* XXXIII, 710.

[97] Capéran, *op. cit.*, pp. 213–15. S. Harent's essay on "Infidèles" in the *Dictionnaire Théologie Catholique*, VII, 2, 1726–1930 adds a great amount of supplementary material.

[98] *Ibid.*, pp. 253–58, 272–81.

Seyssel, who assigned the better pagans in his *De divina providentia* the same future as that of unbaptized infants.[99] Collius maintains that pre-Christians were capable of good and were aided by Grace in virtuous practices but were too insufficient in themselves to follow the dictates of Natural Law for long.[100] On rare occasions an infidel might achieve a perfect love of God, but a natural love of God was no better an assurance than natural virtue in the quest for salvation. Hence, if these candidates for redemption were granted a Christian hereafter, it was nothing more than a gift of divine mercy.[101] God, he adds, does not ask man for the impossible or demand of him an unobtainable end.[102] To aid man God made use of the non-Christian senses. He gave apparitions to the eyes, supernal voices muttered in the ears, angelic illuminations shown in the hearts. Through these experiences many of the descendants of Seth, Japheth, and Shem are dead in the faith.[103] The greater portion of Collius' treatise is given over to the careful, almost fanciful, examination of the eternal chances of individual pious infidels; he decides to save Melchizedek, Job together with his comforters, the three Magi, and the Sibyls. The prospects of the Queen of Sheba, of Anaxagoras, and of Epictetus are in doubt. Balaam is surely damned and has in Hell the company of Orpheus, Homer, Pythagoras, Heraclitus, Plato, Socrates, Aristotle, Diogenes, and Plotinus. Collius rejects as an ordinary legend the so-called successful intercession of Gregory the Great for the salvation of Trajan, and concludes his series of vindications and convictions by reopening the cases of Origen and Tertullian and damning them both.

The *De la vertu des payens* (1642) of François de la Mothe le Vayer was certainly inspired by the *De animabus paganorum*. The views that La Mothe le Vayer expressed in the theoretical and practical sections of his book are supported by thirty learned folios of "Preuves des citations" with which the volume concludes. It is assumed that the Light of Nature was never so diminished that men could not see the truth; hence, just as the faithful are sometimes vicious, so the infidel was sometimes virtuous, "although they are never worthy of the merit given by faith."[104] The discourse breaks into three argumentative theoretical sections: the age of the Law of Nature (the time from Adam to the circumcision of Abraham), the age of the Mosaic Laws, the age of

[99] Collius, *op. cit.*, pp. 20–50.
[100] *Ibid.*, pp. 20–36, 41–2.
[101] *Ibid.*, pp. 54–71.
[102] *Ibid.*, pp. 83–90.
[103] *Ibid.*, pp. 90–152.
[104] La Mothe le Vayer, *Oeuvres* (Paris, 1662), I, 560.

Grace (the Nativity to Doomsday). Substance is granted La Mothe le Vayer's theory by the Old Testament's account of Abel, Seth, Enoch, and Noah, "men beloved of God," and by the fact that Melchizedek and Abraham were both originally Gentiles. However, if pious pagans before Moses are salvaged for salvation, the eternal futures of those born after the divinely given Mosaic laws, which are in themselves a Church, are more difficult to assess. Trent had supported the view that only faith saved, which the theologians expounded as a faith in Christ or, in the case of Jews, a belief in and an expectation of the coming of a Messiah. This fine discrimination left many of the pious pagans admired by Justin or Jerome quite out of the heavenly choir. The Doctors of the Church, La Mothe le Vayer observes, get around the Tridentine position by arguing that not all infidels were idolators and hence had "explicit faith." He can quote Sepulveda and Seyssel on this point, for the supposition is that unless pious philosophers are saved, the Hebrew people must be deprived of beatitude. The opinions of Dionysius, Justin, Chrysostom, Anselm, Clement, Thomas, Tostado, Soto, Erasmus, Sepulveda, Gretzer, and Trigault—all in agreement—are brought to the comfort of Plato and the rest. The salvation of these pagans is offered as a normal result of God's goodness and sense of human worthiness helped by the pagans' own love of a unique God and their surrounding neighbors. There is, however, a group of metaphysical experts who were convinced that since the Incarnation and the Apostolic mission no one in the whole world could be saved without a belief in Jesus Christ. "But did everyone in the world know about Him?" La Mothe le Vayer inquires. Not all men knew of Alexander the Great at the very moment of his conquests, and there is increasing evidence from voyagers' accounts that many peoples have never heard of Christ. The pious and ignorant are thus given a chance by La Mothe le Vayer for salvation even at this eleventh hour.[105]

La Mothe le Vayer discourses at length on the piety and salvation of Socrates, Plato, Pythagoras, Epicurus, and Confucius, though he is not necessarily convinced of the virtues of all the followers of these righteous infidels. In his opinion, the fate of Aristotle is dubious but hopeful, and he obviously would like to save Julian the Apostate, whose manifest virtues must be commended even though his attitude toward Christianity is deplorable. During the remainder of the seventeenth

---

[105] *Ibid.*, pp. 565–81. Pfanner, who devotes the concluding section of his book to the salvation of pagans (*op. cit.*, pp. 490–518), mentions this as a possible kindness, but agrees with Luther that only those who believe in Christ and are baptized can be redeemed.

century, the question of the redemption of the pious pagans twisted back and forth between optimistic and pessimistic convictions so that a dead philosopher saved by one human redeemer might be sent to the Pit by another.[106] The whole procedure was an interesting theological game at which both Catholics and Protestants amused themselves. It can be seen in a well-lighted way by surveying the undulations of the postmortem situation of Seneca.

VI

The eagerness with which some seventeenth-century theologians hunted out evidences of Christian doctrine in pre-Christian philosophers or even in post-Resurrection unbelievers like Plutarch and Seneca resulted in controversies that now seem pathetically amusing. Having mistranslated a section of Josephus' *Contra Apion,* Ficino stated as a result that Aristotle was a Jew.[107] This announcement abetted by Christian interpretations of the opening phrases of Aristotle's *De mundo* got the story into the public mind via such popular universal histories as Gilbert Génébrard's *Chronographia.*[108] The assumed Jewishness of Aristotle, which was not questioned too loudly until 1702,[109] stands behind Johannes Faust's *Examen theologiae gentilis quam docuit Aristotle,* which appeared at Strassburg in 1667. The pious predications of other

[106] The Protestant attitudes on the problem varied according to the inner nature of the theologian. Moise Amyraut stated in his *Brief traité de prédestination* (Samur, 1634) that God was too merciful to condemn men who harkened to Providence and lived righteously even though they had never heard of Christ (pp. 80–83). His position was denounced at the Synod of Alençon in 1637 and condemned as Arminian at Charenton in 1645. Ezekiel Spanheim, the great Protestant scholar, attacked it, and Justus Sieber, in his thirty-four highly supported theses, the *De Salute Christiana et philosophica, id est, de Christianorum vera et philosophorum gentilium et Hermetis Tresmegisti, Platonis, Aristotelis, Ciceronis et Senecae praeprimis falsa beatitudines considerationes* (Dresden, 1657), lumps him with Zwingli. Sieber supported the view of Calvin that the pious pagans knew and ignored the true God and that their quasi-Christian ideas are filled with fallacies. Daniel Colberg, writing at Rostock in 1680, is more liberal in his *Unicum, proprium, adaequatum remedium therapeuticum atheologiae* in that he posits the instructive forces of Natural Light although he realizes that it revealed proper worship only in a negative way. The pagan mystery religions, which seem close to Christianity, are not positively Christian. In the early eighteenth century, David Martin devoted a section (pp. 458–64) of his *Traité de la religion naturelle* (Amsterdam, 1713), to the subject and agrees with Augustine's theory of "peccata splendida" and points to the absence of any positive biblical reference to the salvation of pious unbelievers. If salvation came through Natural Light, he wisely observes, there would be no point to either the Incarnation or Redemption.

[107] Ficino, *De Christiana religione, Opera omnia* (Basel, 1576), p. 30; see Josephus, *Contra Apion,* ed. T. Reinach, trans. L. Blum (Paris, 1930), pp. 175–82.

[108] Génébrard, *op. cit.* (Paris, 1567), p. 80.

[109] Thomas Crenius, *Animadversionum philologicarum et historicarum liber* (Leyden, 1702), pp. 107–10.

heathen like Plotinus found explanation in books like P. H. Pladek's *De tribus hypostasibus Plotini* (1694), and there was a whole series of altruistic attempts to find the proper message in Hippocrates. To this end C. Drelincourt wrote his *De divinis apud Hippocratem dogmatis sermo,* which was published in 1689; Johannes Stephanus wrote a *Theologia Hippocratis in qua Platonis, Aristotlis, et Galeni placita Christianiae religioni consentanea exponuntur* in 1700; and a certain D. W. J. D. defended the wise physician in *Hippocrates atheismi falso accusatus* in 1718. The latter of these books was for the confounding of the sceptical N. H. Gundling, author of the *Historia philosophiae moralis,* whose doubts about pagan Christianity brought one of the last Christian champions of non-Christendom, Jacob Zimmerman, to the fore. In 1728 Zimmerman wrote an *Exercitatio de atheismo Platonis,* and in the following year, when Gundling had spoken adversely, he not only printed a *Vindiciae dissertationes de atheismo Platonis* but augmented his arguments with a second memoir, the *De praestantia religionis Christianae collata cum philosophia Socratis.*[110] But the controversy over the Christianity of Seneca is far more exciting, if that is the proper word.

The possibility that Seneca was a Christian convert, a conviction congenial to men of the Middle Ages, depends on a few confused allusions in early Fathers of the Church and on fourteen letters (known to medieval men in more than three hundred manuscripts) assumed to be his correspondence with St. Paul. The allusions begin with Tertullian's "Seneca saepe noster,"[111] a phrase repeated by Jerome.[112] Lactantius never suggests that Seneca was a Christian convert, although he respects his metaphysical opinions.[113] How far any of these testimonials would have misled the Church without the paragraph in Jerome's *Liber de viris illustribus,* one does not know, but it was evidence enough for most men.

Lucius Annaeus Seneca of Cordova, disciple of the stoic Sotion, and paternal uncle of the poet Lucan was most continent of life. I would not place him in the catalogue of saints if I were not encouraged by letters read by many between Paul and Seneca and Seneca and Paul. Although he was Nero's teacher and most powerful in his time, he says in them he would like to be regarded by his fellow citizens as Paul was by the Christians. He was put to death by Nero two years before Peter and Paul won martyrs' crowns.[114]

---

[110] J. G. Schelhorn, *Amoentates literariae,* IX, 827–968; XI, 93–212, 369–510.
[111] Tertullian, *De anima, PL* II, 682.
[112] Jerome, *Adversus Jovinianum, PL* XXIII, 222–352.
[113] Lactantius, *Divinae institutiones, PL* VI, 136–37, 299, 579, 724.
[114] Jerome, *De viris illustribus, PL* XXIII, 662.

The actuality of an epistolatory exchange between the Stoic and the Christian Apostle was further substantiated for many men by St. Augustine's remark about "Seneca who lived at the same time as the Apostles and from whom there are a number of letters to the Apostle Paul."[115] Augustine writes an ambiguous annex to this remark when in the *De civitate* he describes Seneca's antisemitism. "The Christians . . . he [Seneca] did not dare to mention either for praise or blame, fearing that if he praised them, he would do so against the traditions of his nation, or if, perhaps, he blamed them, he would do so against his own will."[116] But Augustine, it is clear, does not plainly write "Seneca" in his catalogue of saints.

Although Jerome quotes a phrase in the *Vita* from the twelfth letter of the so-called correspondence, there is no indication, on the other hand, that Augustine had seen these letters. It is also possible, though some modern scholars doubt it, that the forger of the file cleverly inserted Jerome's quotation in what could be the proper epistle. The authenticity of the correspondence was generally acknowledged in the Middle Ages, and both Peter Abelard and Peter of Cluny quote from the letters.[117] No one at this time seemed to notice that Jerome had also bestowed quasi-saintliness on Philo Judaeus and Flavius Josephus as well as on Seneca. So until men of the Renaissance with a better sense of classical style and ancient history peered at the letters and the legend, the friendship of the Apostle and the philosopher, supported also by the spurious testimony of the spurious Pope Linus, was mentioned with awe and their letters written in a foul Latin were read with pious breathlessness.[118]

Of the fourteen letters, all of them brief, six are signed by Paul and the remainder by Seneca. St. Paul's letters are not only uncharacteristically terse but also very nondescript. For a man of God he seems too pleased to be known to the famous Seneca and sympathetically under-

---

[115] Augustine, *Epistolae, PL* XXXIII, 659.

[116] Augustine, *De civitate* VI. 10–11.

[117] Abelard, *Sermones, PL* CLXXVIII, 535–36; *Introductio ad theologiam, PL* CLXXVIII, 1083–84; *Theologia et philosophica, PL* CLXXVIII, 1164. Peter of Cluny, *Tractatus contra Petro Brusiango, PL* CLXXXIX, 737.

[118] Amedée Fleury's *Saint Paul et Sénèque* (Paris, 1853) is an anthology of allusions to the relationship between the two men (pp. 269–399) in order to establish their friendship. The discussion is not dead, but modern scholars seldom take the letters seriously; see P. Benoit, "Sénèque et St. Paul," *Revue biblique,* LIII (1946), 7–33; A. Momigliano, "La leggenda del Cristianesimo di Seneca," *Rivista storica italiana,* LXII (1950), 325–44; A. Kurfess, "Zum dem Apokryphen Briefwechsel zwischen dem Philosophen Seneca und dem Apostel Paul," *Aevum,* XXVI (1952), 42–48; J. N. Sevenster, *Paul and Seneca* (Leyden, 1961).

stood by him. He is not unhappy to learn that Seneca has talked about him to the Emperor and Empress and hopes no ill will come of this. In his final letter, he talks as in a dramatic climax to a half-convert. "You must make yourself one who proposes Jesus Christ by showing, with a celebrating rhetoric, the unblameable wisdom, in which you are almost adept, to the temporal king, to his household, and to his trusted friends, whom you will find it difficult or nearly impossible to persuade, since most of them will not at all incline themselves to your suggestions." Seneca, in his turn, hopes Paul will oversee a book he has written and intends to read to Nero; he hints at some Pauline offense to the Empress; he admits to reading Paul's letters to the Galatians, Corinthians, and Achaeans and to writing an essay on Paul's ideas for an astonished yet admiring Emperor. He also proposes that Paul improve his prose style—he is too enigmatic—and sends him a rhetorical handbook to this end. As an almost Christian believer, he exhorts the Christians patiently to endure their persecutions as the pagans had endured the oppressive excesses of various tyrants.[119]

Some of the earliest humanists grasped at this fine Christian tradition that made Seneca "one of ours." The letters were known, for instance, to Petrarch, who reminds the great Seneca of his Christian knowledge and friendships when he wrote familiarly to him from Parma on August 1, 1350.[120] Lefèvre d'Etaples, editing the letters of Paul in 1517, reported, as Petrarch and others had done, that Seneca had dedicated a treatise on the virtues to St. Paul. This was probably the book Seneca asked Paul to criticize, but if "this book today no longer has the same title, it is because of anti-Christian malice."[121] In spite of all this, Lefèvre doubts that Seneca was regenerated as a Christian; although he knows that Seneca spoke admiringly of Christ, he failed by his suicide to imitate the martyrs and clearly preferred to follow the pagan way of Cato and Lucretia.[122] Erasmus, who edited Seneca in 1515, hardly tolerates the received opinion when he composed the preface to these letters in the revised edition of 1529 and attacked their authenticity on both stylistic and historical grounds. Joost Lipse, greatest of

[119] *Epistolae Senecae ad Paulum et Pauli ad Senecam,* ed. C. W. Barlow, Papers and Monographs of the American Academy in Rome, X (1938).
[120] *Lettere delle cose familiari,* ed. G. Fracassetti (Florence, 1892), V, 146–52.
[121] *Epistolae divi Pauli apostoli . . . epistolae ad Senecam sex* (Paris, 1517), p. 176. Two spurious Senecan treatises, the *De quatuor virtutibus* and the *De remediis fortuitorum* were both edited and translated several times during the sixteenth century. The latter work is a moral dialogue between Sense and Reason. Sense will describe an affliction, "I have lost all my children"; then Reason comforts her with, "This is a common complaint."
[122] *Ibid.,* p. 179.

sixteenth-century Stoic-Christians, also rejects the letters as spurious, though he admits that he hesitates to oppose the testimony of the Fathers and other venerable men.[123] He exalts the natural but nonetheless Christian inclinations of Seneca, who proved for him the actuality of a Providence by coming from God "to teach us austerity." Seneca was a man "on a par with the holy Doctors."[124]

The quarrel about the authenticity of the letters and the Christianity of Seneca swirled through the seventeenth century; but as the century aged, the case against Seneca's Christianity and salvation became stronger, though men came to this conclusion with the greatest of regrets. Collius approves of many of Seneca's notions of the divine, but he cannot read the letters as genuine, sees numerous non-Christian ideas in the corpus of the philosopher, and sadly places him in Hell.[125] La Mothe le Vayer does not agree with Erasmus' theory that Jerome knew the letters were fake, but, believing Seneca was a Christian, spoke well of them so that Christians would read Seneca's other writings. He associates the correspondence with other Christian forgeries and thinks both Jerome and Augustine, had they taken more time, would have rejected the Seneca–St. Paul letters as spurious. He is forced to assume, "because there is not even a suspicion he was a Christian," that Seneca is damned; but "no one knows the ways of God" and mercy can bring good out of evil.[126]

The final thrust against Seneca's Christian prospects came in 1668 with Gotofrid Kaewitz's *De Christianismo Senecae.* In this work, the Wittenberg theologian generously brings forward the evidence in behalf of the philosopher. Callisthenes mentions a Seneca who was tenth bishop of Jerusalem and some think he is L. A. Seneca. Others assume he is alluded to in Philippians 1:12–13, and in St. Linus' *On the Passion of St. Paul,* where the expression "institutor Imperatoris" occurs. There are also the fourteen letters. This is for Kaewitz the optimistic evidence, but there is material to the contrary. No Father states that Seneca was converted; Augustine describes him as a scorner of Jewish customs and ceremonies; his writings make clear that Nature was his god; he did not believe in immortality; according to Tacitus he prayed to Jupiter; he

[123] Lipse, *Opera omnia* (Antwerp, 1637), I, 328, 389.
[124] *Ibid.,* IV, 456.
[125] Collius, *op. cit.,* II, 20–41.
[126] La Mothe le Vayer, *op. cit.,* I, 672–83. In his *praeloquium* to his translation of the holy Marcus Aurelius, Thomas Gataker decides that Seneca is inferior to his hero and to Epictetus, both of whose views are similar to those of Christ; see *Opera critica* (Strassburg, 1698), p. D2.

committed suicide. After books of this demolishing nature, men contented themselves (as they did with Plato, Plutarch, and other former
possible converts to Christ) with dispassionate descriptions of their
favorite's general philosophical views. As a consequence, the whole
direction changes and one could read toward the end of the seventeenth
century reasonably modern analyses like Nicolas Hardschmidt's *De Seneca notitia Dei naturali* (Jena, 1668) ; Joost Sieber's *De Seneca divinis
oraculis quodammodo consonans* (Dresden, 1675) ; J. A. Schmidt's *De
Seneca ejusque theologia* (Jena, 1686) ; or J. P. Apin, *De religione
Senecae* (Wittenberg, 1692). Men were becoming increasingly aware
that a heathen could have Christian ideas without having any contact
with Christianity. Even the Natural Light was beginning to take form as
the collective imagination of mankind.

III

❧ THE RENAISSANCE SEARCH FOR CHRISTIAN ORIGINS: THE SACRED HISTORY ❧

IN DEFENDING THE DOCTRINES and ritual of the Christian Church, the earliest apologists accused Greek philosophers of pilfering their more satisfactory metaphysical and ethical conclusions from the divine instructions to Moses, which had been conveyed by him and his Hebrew adherents to the other Semitic peoples. This hypothesis, rigorously pushed, was presumed to still the complaints of Celsus and others about the servile imitativeness of Christian idealism. The same method of theoretical undercutting was used against the sacred histories of the Greeks and the Latins; in fact, these modes of rational rebuke had been invented by doubters among the Greeks before they were taken up by the Christian opposition. Charged by pagan controversialists with deriving the heroes of both Testaments from other pantheons, the apologists first described the rather scurvy moral lives and ignoble manners of Greek divinities. With the reports of scandals in ethereal places went the assumption that men and women were alone capable of such fleshly misdoing. When the Olympian ventured on something more Christian than murder or rape, it could be pointed out that he was unoriginal, a poor réchauffé of one or more Hebrew patriarchs, prophets, or heroes.

Although he is not called on by the earliest apologists, Euhemerus of Messina, born almost four centuries before Christ to plague heathen theologians, and author of the wryly named *Sacred History,* which Ennius turned into Latin and verse, was a useful ally for the second generation of defenders of the Faith. To Theophilus, this father of

53

anthropology was an impious critic of the gods as well as a materialist who assumed the universe to be self-sustaining and self-governing.[1] Tertullian read Euhemerus more carefully and knew Augustine's favorite mythographer, Varro, as well; hence, as he turns over the myths of Coelus, Terra, Saturn, Ocean, or Cronus, he reveals the ordinary human actions and responses of these allegedly divine beings. He has Christian amusement over Saturn, who first enjoyed the hospitality of Athens and then migrated to Latium to found the city of Saturnia. "His actions openly inform us he was human and as such came of human parents; therefore, he was a man and not born of Coelus and Terra."[2] Even Euhemerus' theory that gods were once men who discovered or invented something beneficial to mankind came under Tertullian's jaundiced eye. Discovered benefits like the grape or human inventions like wine were first supplied and revealed by God.[3] Tertullian's contemporary Minucius Felix also read Euhemerus' roster of men deified "because of their worth as courageous leaders or benefactors" and recollects that in each case the man of Messina recorded the vital statistics about each divinity. The Christian who desires further information about these quondam men who now inhabit Olympus can read Prodicus, Persaeus, Alexander's letter on the Egyptian gods, Nepos, Cassius, Thallus, and Diodorus Siculus.[4] Euhemerus' *Sacred History* was clearly provided with footnotes.

In his *Protrepticon*,[5] Clement of Alexandria is fairly pleasant about Euhemerus, associating him with Nicanor, Diagoras, Hippo, and Theodorus, celebrated pagan atheists, who lived soberly and had clearer insight than their fellows into the origins of the gods. This congregation of heathen muckrakers, beloved by the early Church, was also assembled by Arnobius, who terminates his preface to the Gentiles on their superstitious foolishness with some suggestions for further private study.

Of course we can demonstrate that all those whom you call gods were men according to Euhemerus of Acragas, whose works Ennius translated into the Latin language so all might understand, or by Nicagoras of Cyprus, Leon of Pella,

---

[1] Theophilus, *Ad Autolycum*, PG VI, 1130; see Cicero, *De natura deorum* I. 42. 119; Sextus Empericus, *Adversus Physicos*, I. 17. 51. Athenagoras, who states that the gods were once men, bases his conclusion on Herodotus and on Alexander's famous letter to Olympias which retails the human origins of the Egyptian Pantheon; see *op. cit.*, PG VI, 929–36, 1049, 1133.

[2] Tertullian, *Ad nationes*, PL I, 601–3 and *Apologeticus*, PL I, 329–31, 350–55.

[3] *Ibid.*, col. 334; *Ad nationes*, PL I, 608.

[4] Minucius Felix, *op. cit.*, XXI, 1–9.

[5] Clement of Alexandria, *op. cit.*, II. 24. "Those to whom you bow were once like you" (IV. 55).

Theodorus of Cyrene, or Hippo and Diagoras, both of Melos, or a thousand other authors, who with great care and labor have brought to light with great lucidity matters which were hidden.[6]

The reading assigned by Arnobius may have been done by numerous Christians; it was clearly known to Lactantius, whose essay on the mortal beginnings of the Graeco-Roman gods constitutes the first book of the *Divine Institutes*.

There are some historians, Lactantius states, who hold that the gods were originally valorous men like Hercules, inventors of bread or wine like Ceres and Liber, or discoverers of human arts like Minerva and Aesculapius. Close investigation, however, reveals Hercules to be little more than a muscle-man, who killed himself when his strength began to fail. In the cases of the inventors and discoverers, it was invariably the God of Lactantius, like that of Tertullian, who furnished the grain and the grape as well as the knack for turning them into bread and wine.[7] This happy conclusion logically followed Lactantius' biographies of Saturn, Jupiter, and other Olympians, biographies based on documents furnished by Ennius' Euhemerus, by Thallus, Nepos, Cassius, Diodorus Siculus, and Varro, which enabled Lactantius to apply Christian common sense to freakish pagan myth. Ganymede is said by mythographers to have been snatched up by Zeus, who disguised himself as an eagle. Clearly this story is nonsense. A body of soldiers preceded by an eagle standard or a ship with an eagle figurehead on the prow was obviously employed to kidnap the handsome youth. With this wisdom before him the Christian also knows more about the salacious bull that galloped off with the weeping Europa. Like Tertullian and Arnobius, Lactantius uses the history of Euhemerus to retell the ordinary human events in the sorry life of Saturn and other heathen gods. When deification of great men is practiced in one's own day, he writes, the origin of the old-fashioned gods is not difficult to detect.[8] What was occurring in Lactantius' generation was to his mind illustrative of Euhemerus' account of King Jupiter's wandering and institution of his own worship in various places of the visited world.[9] Euhemerus, "no fabulist but an historian who gravely investigated matters," was well known to Augus-

---

[6] Arnobius, *Adversus gentes*, PL V, 1022–23. In his poem *Adversus gentium deos* (PL V, 202–11), Commodianus speaks of the humanity of Saturn, Jupiter, Neptune, Apollo, and other deities.

[7] Lactantius, *Divinae institutiones*, PL VI, 209–11.

[8] *Ibid.*, cols. 165–201.

[9] *Ibid.*, cols. 242–54.

tine,[10] who placed full reliance on his imitator Varro's *Antiquities Human and Divine* when he girded himself to demolish the gods of the recalcitrant Romans.

II

Euhemerus, whose laureate Ennius was edited or reprinted at least eight times between 1564 and 1627, together with some of his myth-disintegrating predecessors, Hecataeus of Miletus,[11] Ephorus,[12] and Leon of Pella,[13] was well known to Renaissance men. With the publication in 1624 of the *De historicis Graecis* of Gerard Vos,[14] one of the editors of Ennius, Euhemerus' literary remains were practically complete. If a seventeenth-century scholar consulted the authorities summarized or cited by Vos, he would learn that Aelian[15] placed Euhemerus on a list of proscribed atheists and that Plutarch not only repeated Callimachus' epigram about "the proud old man vomiting impious books"[16] but also, lamenting in *Isis and Osiris* "the war of antiquity" which he perceived to be destroying religious faith, added a warning for his own disenchanted generation about the falsehoods of Euhemerus.

This opens a wide gate to the atheists and to him who makes the gods men and gives wide scope to the lies of Euhemerus the Messinian, who composed books on his

---

[10] Augustine, *De civitate,* VI. 7. Augustine uses Varro's account of Janus, Jupiter, Saturn, Mercury, Apollo, Mars, Vulcan, Neptune, Sol, Orcus, Liber, Tellus, Ceres, Juno, Luna, Diana, Minerva, Venus, and Vesta. The relationship between Varro and Augustine has been studied in E. Scharz, "De Varronis apud sanctos patres vestigiis," *Jahrbücher für classische Philologie, Supplementband,* XVI (1888), 407–99, and by R. Agahd, *M. Terenti Varronis, Antiquitates rerum divinarum, ibid.,* XXIV (1898), 5–220. Just as Lactantius supplies many fragments of Euhemerus, so Augustine is largely responsible for most of what is known of the lost book of Varro.

[11] Hecataeus identified Geryon with a King of Epirus whose herds were stolen by Hercules; he also said that Cerberus was only a large serpent; see *Fragmenta historicorum Graecorum,* ed. C. and T. Muller (Paris, 1841), I, 27.

[12] Our information about Ephorus comes from Strabo, *Geography,* IX, 12, who also held (*Fragmenta,* I, 255) that Zeus was no more than a Greek citizen.

[13] Leon of Pella, or Leon the Egyptian, probably the author of a *History of the Gods of Egypt,* is mentioned with great favor by Tertullian (*De coronis, PL* II, 86) and Tatian (*Oratio, PG* VI, 865). It is however, Hyginus, a communicant of the heathen church, who supplies the fullest detail, reporting that "Leon who wrote about Egyptian matters" said that when Bacchus was ruling Egypt and subjecting Egyptians to civilized benefits, a certain Ammon came from lower Africa bringing herds of domesticated animals. As a reward for discovering the domestication of animals, Ammon was given land near Thebes and was represented in statuary and painting with symbolical horns; see *Astronomica,* ed. E. Chatelain and P. Legendre (Paris, 1909), p. 28.

[14] Vos, *Opera omnia* (Amsterdam, 1686), IV, 96–97.

[15] Aelianus, *Varia historia* II. 31.

[16] Pultarch, *op. cit., De placitis philosophorum* I. 7.

false and unfounded mythology and disseminated atheism all over the world, reducing all deities to generals, admirals, and kings who may have existed in the past, copying it all from letters of gold in the Isle of Panchaea. Now no barbarian or Greek except Euhemerus alone has ever met these Panchaeans and Triphylians, who do not exist nor have ever existed in any part of the world.[17]

In order to read these letters of gold, a man of the Renaissance was forced to ship with Euhemerus on one of the oldest of imaginary voyages.

The Land of Panchaea visited by Euhemerus in fancy was known to the geographer Strabo.[18] But for a proper description one must go to Diodorus Siculus who used the text of Euhemerus to describe the land first surveyed by Uranus, which, when Zeus was later king of the earth, became the place to which gods born in Crete migrated. Here was to be found a stele of gold, memorializing the deeds of early gods and copied by Euhemerus[19] in the first *corpus inscriptionum*. Diodorus does not quote, but Eusebius summarizes the inscription. It read somewhat like this: "Certain of the elder gods, the sun, moon, and stars, are eternal; but gods like Hercules and Dionysus are simply mortals raised to divinity." Euhemerus wrote his special book about the gods, Eusebius announces, so men did not have to depend on the "monstrous stories" invented by Homer, Hesiod, and Orpheus;[20] and though the mythography of Euhemerus was as familiar to pagans[21] as the Land of Panchaea,[22] it is again Lactantius who preserves enough of the text to supplement the Eusebian epitome. Depending on the poetic version of Ennius, Lactantius talks about Saturn, son of the man Uranus, who was warned by an oracle not to let his sons reach maturity. "He killed them,

---

[17] Plutarch, *op. cit., Isis et Osiris* 475–76.

[18] Strabo, *op. cit.*, II. 3. 6; II. 4. 2; VII. 3; for the fragments of Euhemerus see *Reliquiae,* ed. G. Némethy (Budapest, 1889).

[19] *Ibid.*, V. 42–7.

[20] Eusebius, *Praeparatio evangelica* II. 2. 59–61. Here it is stated that Uranus was the first king to sacrifice to the gods, and his descendants are traced to the age of Zeus, who got the Curetes on Hera, Proserpine on Demeter, and Athena on Themis. Entertained in Babylon by King Belus, Zeus then went to Panchaea where he set up the altar to Jove.

[21] Athenaeus (*Deipnosophistae* XIV. 658) reports that, according to Euhemerus, Cadmus was a cook, who eloped with the king's flute-player Harmonia. In Cicero's *De natura deorum*, Cotta calls the euhemeristic theory that gods were invented to curb the viciousness of the duller citizens "absolutely and entirely destructive of religion" (I. 42). Here (III. 53, 57) and in the *Tusculanae disputationes* (I. 29), Cicero mentions the various burial places of Zeus, Aesculapius, and Dionysus. Columella provides Euhemerus' account of the origin of bees, which is contrary to myth (IX. 2. 2–3). For Euhemerus' statement about the human kingship of Zeus see Némethy (*op. cit.*, p. 58), but L. Müller, *Q. Enni Carminum reliquiae* (St. Petersburg, 1884) does not accept the paraphrase as a true fragment.

[22] Virgil, *Georgics* II. 139; Tibullus, III. 2, 23; Ovid, *Metamorphoses* X. 309; Claudian, *De raptu Proserpinae* II. 81.

but did not eat them!" When Saturn's wife Ops gave birth to Zeus, she sent him to Crete to be safely and secretly brought up. Here as a youth, under the tutelage of Pan, he erected a mountain altar to Coelus, "who had died in Oceania and was buried in Aulatia." Later Zeus made five tours of the world, bestowing crowns on friends and relatives and innumerable benefits on men until he died and was buried in Cnossus, where his tomb inscribed "Zan Kronou" could be seen for a long time.[23]

Whereas Euhemerus delighted the Christians by reducing the tall Olympians to human dimensions, his imitator Palaephatus, whose *The Incredibles* was frequently printed in the sixteenth and seventeenth centuries, engaged himself to explain Greek myths which were beyond ordinary belief. In the preface of his book, which is more agnostically ingenious than religiously wise, he states that ignorant men believe everything they hear, but wise men, who look carefully into things, believe nothing whatsoever. He intends, he warns the reader, to steer between total belief and absolute disbelief, for he is convinced that no legend is ever preserved which does not have some tincture of truth. Nothing, he says, has ever happened that does not recur again and again. "But certain poets and mythographers have deliberately made these old tales incredible and astonishing in order to dazzle the minds of men." To be certain of his facts, Palaephatus claims to have visited the scene of each interpreted myth and talked to the old men of the area; consequently, each of his fifty-one chapters opens with the constructions, "they tell" or "they say."[24]

In the course of his junkets, Palaephatus discovered that Actaeon

---

[23] Lactantius, *op. cit., PL* VI, 165–201, 209–11. Firmicus Maternus (*op. cit.,* VII) depends on the evidence of Euhemerus to rationalize the legend of Proserpine, writing that she was the mortal child of the Sicilian Princess Demeter and was courted by so many suitors that her mother could not decide among them. Pluto, a rich countryman, was so tormented by his passion for her that he carried her off by force in a swift chariot. Princess Demeter summoned her cavalry and pursued him closely until he drove into Lake Pecos, where both he and Proserpine perished. The citizens of Enna consoled the stricken Princess Demeter by making up a legend about the kingdom of Hell, but Demeter firmly believed Proserpine had been carried by ship to Syracuse. Unable to find her daughter here she wandered the earth in search of her. Generously welcomed in Athens she bestowed a gift of wheat, until then an unknown cereal, on the Athenians. In return for this boon they raised her and Proserpine to the rank of goddesses.

[24] Palaephatus, *De incredibilibus,* ed. N. Festa (Leipzig, 1901); the work is so slight I shall not give page references. In his *Quaestiones Palaephatae* (Bonn, 1892), pp. 10–20, F. Wipprecht describes the use made of this book by Jerome, Orosius, and Eustathius. Orosius places special emphasis on the story of Cadmus (*Historia, PL* XXXI, 722), who was, according to Palaephatus, merely a wealthy Phoenician who destroyed the armies of Draco before Thebes. The *De incredibilibus* was popular reading in the Renaissance; there were more than twenty editions in Latin, with or without a parallel Greek text, before 1788; an Italian version appeared as early as 1545 and a French version in 1558.

was not literally devoured by his hounds but was eaten up by the cost of his extravagant hunting, that the Centaurs were skilled horsemen of Thessaly, famous as pursuers and stabbers (Kentores) of wild bulls, that Medea did nothing worse than invent hair-dye, and that Daedalus escaped from Crete in a fast boat, whereas Icarus fell overboard in a storm. The touching story of Admetus and Alcestis is turned into a purely military affair in which Hercules by defeating Acastus restored his sister-hostage Alcestis to her husband. The Hydra was no monster but a citadel belonging to King Lernus; Niobe was really pictured in stone by a sculptor to mark her children's tomb; and the trees that danced to Orpheus' music were only bacchantes waving leafy boughs. By revealing the true history behind these myths, Palaephatus hoped to purge them of their dubiety. Unlike Euhemerus, he never questioned the existence of the pantheon; the twelve major gods and goddesses are never stripped of their divinity by his skeptical pen.

A second son of Euhemerus is Diodorus Siculus, author of a *Universal History,* which begins in 1184 B.C. with the destruction of Troy and concludes with the Gallic Wars. The *Universal History* is, of course, an international muddle of historical and mythological material drawn from lost historians of greater merit than Diodorus. It was, however, well received by the Church because Justin, either using a poor manuscript or badly quoting from memory, found in Diodorus pagan witness to the divine inspiration of the Mosaic laws.[25] The evidence adduced by this earliest of apologists was solemnly repeated by others and secured for Diodorus a reasonable amount of Christian respect and acclaim. The Renaissance honored the *Universal History* with frequent editions and translations. Henry Cogan, who made the work English in 1653, describes in his preface Diodorus' high standing with Church Fathers; George Booth, an early eighteenth-century translator, praises the Sicilian for "his respect to the Providence of God." Unlike Euhemerus, Diodorus is carefully agnostic and never announces his disbelief in the divine, although he talks long and confusedly about the deities and their careers in this world before they put off mortality for immortality. He avoids, as he says, mentioning the "several notions of the gods

---

[25] Justin (*Cohortatio, PG* VI, 256–60) writes something which translates: "It is a tradition among Jews that Moses attributed his laws to the God called 'Jahve' either because these laws were considered the result of a wonderfully divine plan or because it was thought the people would be more ready to obey them when they knew the power and dignity of the lawmakers." What Diodorus actually writes (I. 94) is that a whole group of legislators, Mneves, Minos, Lycurgus, Zathraustes, Zalmoxis, Moyses, claimed divine sources for their decrees in order to get them properly observed.

formed by the first introducers of divine worship";[26] but he does not discard, as "Ephorus, Callisthenes, and Theopompus had done," all mythology.[27] It is Diodorus' conviction that one should not inspect a myth too closely, because "we do not believe that Centaurs composed of two different bodies ever existed, but in the theater we applaud such versions of myths and honor the gods."[28]

Diodorus is inclined to linger over the stories of national heroes whose efforts for mankind have been symbolized by sacrifices, and it is evident that at times he thought of the pantheon as composed of famous men and women retired into divinity. He would, however, never make this statement on his own if he did not have the authority of someone else. He consults among many peoples the Atlantians, who said that gods had been born among them and reckoned Uranus as their first king. In addition to his regal virtues, Uranus was an inspired benefactor in the sciences of agriculture and astronomy; hence, it was assumed that after "he had passed from among men," he became a god.[29] With similar pedantic care Diodorus traces the history of the children of Uranus and of the "second Zeus," who was given the name "Zen" after he had left the world because he was not only a teacher of the living but also the cause of life itself.[30] Repeating the divine myths as if he were simply writing chapters in the history of the world, Diodorus describes one god overcoming another, committing murder, adultery, or incest as if he were simply an earthly monarch, a tyrant of Megara or Argos.

When he attempts a rational explanation of an incredible mythic event, Diodorus usually succeeds in making the episode even more unbelievable.[31] He does not avoid allegorical devices for eluding factual difficulties and gets round Dionysus' five sets of parents in this fashion,[32] but allegory is not his forte. He always sees himself as a calm and judicious historian, sifting the documents in order to write eagerly about the human exploits of gods and goddesses while they still decorate the lower world. In a sense, he anticipates the medieval attitude toward gods

[26] Diodorus, I. 6.

[27] *Ibid.,* IV. 1.

[28] *Ibid.,* IV. 8.

[29] *Ibid.,* III. 56–61.

[30] *Ibid.,* VII. 61; V. 71.

[31] An example is found in *ibid.,* I. 19 when Diodorus explains Hercules' rescue of Prometheus, "governor of Egypt," made distraught to the point of suicide by the ravages of the Nile. The Nile was at this time called "The Eagle." Hercules forced the Nile or Aëtus to return to its channel, and certain Greek poets subsequently reported that "Hercules had killed the eagle that was devouring the liver of Prometheus."

[32] *Ibid.,* III. 62.

perfectly at home among men. Sir Orpheus, Duke Apollo, Lady Venus would have assumed their normal roles in the *Universal History* had Diodorus lived some centuries later. If he had also permitted his gods and heroes wider travels he might have been the first to track them into the far reaches of Europe where they founded nations, named cities after themselves, and established aristocratic orders like that of the Golden Fleece.[33]

III

The wanderings of men elevated to godhood or the migrations of heroes from the narrow world of Asia Minor into the enormous fields of Europe not only furnished the major nations of the West with Trojan ancestors but also put a stout mallet into the willing hands of Christian euhemerists. By the opening years of the sixteenth century the authentic opinions of patristic apologists and pagan pupils of the Messinian were being propagated by the printers; but the discovery and publication by Giovanni Nannio of Viterbo of the texts of very ancient and very lost historians was far more exciting and useful to those who wanted to demonstrate that all of pagan mythology was distorted history purloined from Moses. Among the dozen historical sources preserved in the counterfeits of Nannio was the *History of the Chaldeans* written by Berosus of Babylon, who had been read and respectfully cited, though not in this 1497 edition, by Justin, Clement of Alexandria, Tatian, Eusebius, and Theophilus. Although there were early doubters, his forged credentials and text were widely accepted until the eighteenth century.

In its Nannian manifestation, the *History* of Berosus begins with the Flood and the salvation of Noah (Janus, Coelum), his wife (Titea, Terra, Vesta), and their three sons and daughters-in-law. The reader follows these founders of human society as they move eastward, westward, and southward surrounded by their numerous offspring and the copious annotations of Nannio of Viterbo. The fictions of "Ananias" Nannio found better literary form and wider reputation when Jean Lemaire de Belges used the "Deflorations de Berose," as he called them, and several shelves of real and similarly fabricated authorities to write

<hr>

[33] J. D. Cooke, "Euhemerism: A Mediaeval Interpretation of Classical Paganism," *Speculum*, II (1927), 396–410; P. Alphandery, "L'Euhémérisme et les débuts de l'histoire des religions au moyen âge," *Revue de l'histoire des religions*, CIX (1934), 5–27; J. Seznec, *The Survival of the Pagan Gods,* trans. B. F. Sessions (New York, 1953), pp. 11–26.

his *Illustrations de Gaule et Singularitez de Troye,* which appeared in the first decade of the sixteenth century and, like the text of the pseudo-Berosus, was regularly reprinted. In due course, the falsifications of Nannio of Viterbo were translated into Italian and French. Though there was no exact English version, there was the fascinating *An Historical Treatise of the Travels of Noah into Europe,* written by Richard Lynche and published in 1601.

Lynche is committed, of course, to the British fiction of a Trojan past; hence, in order to get to founding-father Dardanus, he begins with Noah, surnamed Gallus, and follows the chronicle of that "authenticke writer, Berosus . . . who of all others most accordeth with the writings and holy workes of Moyses." Noah lives with Titea and their three sons in the town of Enos, established by Cain, with all his fellow giants, most of whom are libidinous, or vicious, or both. The giant soothsayers and astronomers predict a great deluge, so Noah, his wife, his sons, and his daughters-in-law, Pandora, Noela, and Noegla, enter an ark and are preserved. After the Flood, Noah begets thirty children (among whom are Prometheus, the sixteen Titans, Oceanus, and Thetis) and wanders about the world, all of which is now completely in his gift. The Scythians, consequently, remember him as Ogyges, Olybama, Arsa, and also as Janus, discoverer of vintage. After numerous years Noah leaves Armenia, his capital, to rule his kingdom of Italy; but while he is gone his viceroy and nephew Sabatius Sage, or Saturn, discovers that Jupiter Belus is plotting against him and flees for safety to his grandfather in Italy. Settled in Italy, Saturn and his son Sabus, father of the Sabines, instruct the natives in agriculture and religion. Then, 440 years before the founding of Troy and 1,960 years before the birth of Christ, Noah, ripe in years, dies.

The death of this good King and Patriarke possessed almost all the people in the world with great sorrow and lamentation, and especially the Armenians and Italians, who in most honorable manner celebrated his obsequies with such their then used rites and ceremonies, and afterward dedicated and attributed unto him divine honors and godlike adoration . . . their children and successours called him Ianus, Geminus, Quadrifons, Enotrius, Ogyges, Vertumnus, Prometheus, Multisors, Diespiter, and Jupiter.[34]

[34] Lynche, *op. cit.,* sig. C₃ v. As early as 1580, de Mornay discussed the theory in his *De la verité de la religion Chrestienne* (Paris, 1585), pp. 430–58. Within these pages, de Mornay reminds his readers that they can no more expect to find Jewish history in pagan literature than they could hope to read French history in the annals of Peru. The Scriptures were written at the time uncivilized Greeks and Romans were still eating acorns. In due course the Greeks went to school in Egypt and there learned Jewish theology; later

The chronology and history of the pseudo-Berosus, adopted by Lemaire de Belges and Richard Lynche, was even used by local historians like Johann Bertels in his *Historia Luxemburgensis*[35] and almost always by national historians who wanted to supply their fellow citizens with praiseworthy ancestors; but not all men agreed with the chronology, and the problem of the true age of the earth grew to be more than a mote to trouble the eye of the national historian. The earliest of Christian apologists could deflect pagan taunts on the antiquity of the Jews by raising their voices; but by the time of St. Augustine Christians began to be distressed by the possibility that the world could be older than the creation date of 5,199 B.C. set by the Septuagint.[36] A controversial storm over the discrepancies in the universal calendar was roaring by the end of the sixteenth century;[37] during the next hundred years the attempts at a chronology by Scaliger, Vos, Marsham, Petau, Usher, Voorbroek, not to forget the wild guesses of Newton, made a grand chaos of comparative world history. Disturbing theories like the Preadamite notions of Isaac de la Peyrere created momentary spiritual crises,[38] but orthodox Christians were not shaken in their belief that Moses' writings were the oldest of all books and the source of all other ancient histories. The historical philosophy of Walter Raleigh, which governed his examina-

---

Hecataeus wrote a history of the Jews, and the Bible was translated into Greek. Pagans have objected to some Old Testament stories as fabulous, but where is fable wanting? One does not believe much of what Homer writes, but one never doubts there was a Trojan War. Many peoples have some account of a Creation. According to Berosus, many men of ancient times lived for hundreds of years. The Flood story is known even in Brazil and New Spain. Ham is Zoroaster to the Chaldeans; Jupiter Ammon is his name among the Greeks. The story of Nimrod is translated as that of Jupiter Belus. The pagans may say the burning of Sodom is a Jewish version of the fall of Phaeton, but the ruins of the city can still be seen. The historian Eupolemus knows Abraham as a great astronomer, who went to teach his science in Phoenicia. De Mornay suggests that heathen writings can verify Hebrew history, but that they do not supply it with basic facts.

[35] Local histories of the Renaissance usually began with the arrival of a founder from Troy or Mt. Ararat. An example is the chapter on local religions of Luxemburg by Abbot Bertels, which was printed separately in 1606 at Cologne as *Deorum sacrificiorumque gentilium*. In this book, based on the pseudo-Berosus, one is told that Luxemburg was founded by Trebeta, idolatrous son of King Ninus, founder of idol-worship. Bertels is convinced that Saturn was driven to the West by Ninus together with Mercurius Luxembergensis and Mars Luxembergensis. For him Janus is Noah and Titea, Vesta; Saturn is a pagan prefiguration of St. Peter. Although the Abbot's theories are as unorthodoxly absurd as most, he did uncover valuable material about his little corner of primitive religion.

[36] Augustine, *De civitate* XII. 10; XVIII. 40.

[37] The best contemporary summary together with some official conclusions is found in Etienne Fourmont, *Reflexions critiques sur les histoires des anciens peuples*, Paris, 1735; recent accounts are to be found in P. H. Kocher, *Christopher Marlowe* (Chapel Hill, N.C., 1946), pp. 42–5 and Ernest Strathman, *Sir Walter Raleigh* (New York, 1951), pp. 199–218.

[38] D. C. Allen, *The Legend of Noah* (Urbana, Ill., 1949), pp. 132–37.

tion of materials and the writing of his *History of the World,* is a case in point.

Raleigh assumes that Moses not only had oral tradition behind him but also the library of manuscripts written by Enoch, which is mentioned by Tertullian, Origen, Augustine, Bede, Procopius, and others; but these once authentic texts are not now entirely to be trusted because they have deteriorated as a result of "fabulous inventions . . . breaking into parts . . . delivering it over into a mystical sense . . . wrapping it up mixed with other their own trumpery." The Greeks and other unblessed nations have sought to obscure the truth in hopes that after-times would hold it for an invention of poets and philosophers "and not as anything borrowed or stolen out of the books of God."[39] Raleigh knows, like all other historians, exactly what has happened, because he too had read the pseudo-Berosus.

The sons of Cham, he writes, inherited the vices of Cain and became the fathers of the sun-worshiping Chaldeans through whose instigations the Phoenicians and Egyptians abandoned the true God and raised altars to the notorious twelve deities who eventually dominated the Greek pantheon. In time men sank even lower spiritually, paying religious homage to beasts, plants, elements, and the passions and affections of the human mind. The heroes of the Old Testament also got themselves curious names. Adam passed into pagan legend as Saturn. Cain, who married his sister, was known as Jupiter. Jubal, Tubal, and Tubalcain were transformed into Mercury, Vulcan, and Apollo. Eve became Rhea, to be worshiped in time as Venus. The sons of Noah are the three sons of Saturn; and Eden with its apples and serpent was transferred to North Africa as the Garden of the Hesperides. The Old Testament prophecies of Christ degenerated into the myths of Hercules. In other words, the Pentateuch was corrupted by the Babylonians, Chaldeans, and Egyptians before the Greeks got their perverted versions and tricked them out with Olympian foolishness.[40] "Yet it cannot be doubted, but that Homer had read over all the books of Moses, as by places stolen thence almost word for word may appear."[41]

[39] Raleigh, *op. cit.* (Edinburgh, 1820), I, 178. He was aware of the falsifications of Friar Annius (VI, 76).

[40] *Ibid.,* I, 181–85.

[41] *Ibid.,* I, 195. In the seventh chapter, Raleigh distinguishes Noah from Ogyges, Deucalion, and other survivors of universal deluges. He sees Noah, as had Tertullian, in the pagan robes of Saturn, Uranus, and Jove; he fancies him as Janus. Thanks to the pseudo-Berosus, he notices that Noah was also known as Coelum, Sol, Vertumnus, Triton, Liber, and especially as Bacchus or Dionysus (pp. 224–27). Similar identifications were made by Edmund Dickinson in his "Diatribe de Noah in Italiam adventu" printed in 1655 at

Raleigh, like other seventeenth-century scholars, was a great stealer of footnotes; yet it is plain that he had read some of the theorists, Steuco of Gubbio, for instance, with reasonable care. He was, of course, not out of line with the normal course of English thought, as evidenced by Lynche's essay or by the *De descensu domini nostri Iesu Christi ad inferos,* which had been written by Hugh Sanford at a time somewhat earlier but was only given to the press in 1611 by Bishop Parker. Sanford assumed that the Jews had taught the Egyptians and Phoenicians, who were the teachers of the Greeks; with this lore passing orally through several languages, names naturally got very distorted. There might be, he thought, a vowel or consonant substitution, as when "Abaddon" became "Apolluon." Fine details of pronunciation might be misheard, and so "Japeth" could become "Iapetus." Initial letters were likely to get aspirated, and so "Elohim" might change to "Helios." Besides these philological shifts, there was Sanford's second epigraphic law that "things which are commemorated in Scripture as most worthy to be known to Jehovah's worshipers are confused and distorted into fables."

Following the evidences of ancient history and his three linguistic laws, Sanford discovers that Isis is the mother of Moses and that Moses was also known as Misen, Mises, and Moso. Sanford finds it more reasonable to identify Moses with Bacchus of Nysa, a place-name which is an anagram of "Syna" or Sinai. Reading Nonnos' epic about Bacchus, Sanford noticed the name Maira, the dog-star, a distorted form of the name of Moses' sister Miriam. Orus is Aaron; and Caleb, which means "dog" in Hebrew, is Bacchus' companionable pet. With similar deftness, the pagans converted Jacob into Pan, Joseph into Osiris and Apis, Balaam into Silenus, Joshua into Hercules, and the Giants into the Canaanites. In each instance Sanford can explain the process of transmogrification, but one example will suffice. When the Christian reader understands that Og of Basan is Typhon and then juggles the letters of that name into Python, he comprehends the biblical origin of Ovid's Apollo legend.[42] Behind these philological manipulations of Sanford are the attractive speculations of previous harmonizers like Ficino, Steuco, and Pansa; but the search for biblical faces in the gallery of pagan gods and heroes was one of the numerous Christian obsessions of the Renaissance, an obsession that does not fade out even when the sun of the

Oxford as an appendix to *Delphi Phoenicizantes.* I have used the reprint in *Opuscula quae ad historiam ac philologiam sacram spectant* (Rotterdam, 1693), I, 151–94.

[42] Sanford, *op. cit.,* pp. 8–37.

Enlightenment rises. Huig de Groot or La Mothe le Vayer may write only briefly about this matter, but other men devoted most of their lives to supporting the hallucination; in fact, the preparation of a specialized and affirmative study of the monomania became a legitimate requirement for a doctorate in theology.[43]

Asking themselves how man, once filled with heavenly light or knowledge, managed to sink into heathen darkness, scholars famous for their writings in classics or theology put together histories concerning the causes and growth of idolatry. The subject had been briefly discussed by some of the Church Fathers, and the Jewish view of the matter was known to the seventeenth century in Dionysius Vos' Latin rendering of Moses ben Maimon's *Yad-Hachhazakah,* but much remained to be said. Not all of these histories were written by Protestants, but those that

[43] In 1627 Huig de Groot found out many evidences of Moses' primacy in theological and historical matters as well as biographical details about him in the Orphic hymns; see *De veritate religione Christiana, Opera* (London, 1679), III, 9–26. La Mothe le Vayer (I, 602–3) records the parallels in the careers of Samson-Hercules, Joseph-Hippolytus, Nebuchadnezzar-Lycaon, Tantalus-Dives, Isaac and Jeptha-Agamemnon, Baucis and Philemon-Lot, Pandora-Eve, St. George and the Dragon-Perseus and the Orc. Besides treatises concentrating on these proofs, substantial accounts are found in many books: Johannes Micraelius, *Ethnophronii liber contra gentiles de principiis religionis Christianiae dubitationes* (Stettin, 1647), pp. 102–23; J. H. Ursinus, *Analectorum sacrorum libri sex* (Frankfort, 1658), pp. 207–9, 219–31, 237–39, annotates the Bible with myth as Johannes Bompart does for Genesis (see Chapter Two, note 61). In the same general tradition are G. Moebius, *Tractatus de oraculum ethnicorum origine, propagatione, ac duratione* (Leipzig, 1660), pp. 2–7, and Christian Worm, *De corruptis antiquitatum Hebræarum* (Copenhagen, 1693), where it is asserted that Pythagoras studied under a disciple of Moses and talked with the prophets (p. 97); hence, Worm probably felt justified in identifying Moses and Aaron, as others had done, with Minos and Rhadamanthus (p. 42), Saturn and Rhea with Moses and Era (pp. 58–59), Samson and Polyphemus (p. 89), Hercules with Joshua (pp. 217–18), and Andromeda and Perseus with Jonah and the Whale (pp. 171–72). These references are to the 1744 reprint in the second volume of Ugolini's *Thesaurus.*

Separate parallel studies of pagan and biblical figures became popular as university doctoral theses such as Georg Schubart's *De diluvio Deucalionis* (Jena, 1642); Andreas Roetel, *Deorum gentilium praecipuorum origines ex sacra scriptura derivatas* (Jena, 1674); Johannes Emmerling, *Schediasma de Schilo in Silenum atque Mose in Bacchum a profanis converso* (Jena, 1667); Christian Wolff, *Quod Hercules idem sit ac Josua* (Leipzig, 1706); Daniel Ram, *Hercules et Samson seu dissertatio mythologico-critica* (Copenhagen, 1707); Johannes Moneta, *Problema mythologicum utrum immolatio Phrixi eadem sit ac Isaaci necne* (Wittenberg, 1721); Johannes Matthaeus, *Quod bene vortat Nisum Samsonis symbolum* (Wittenberg, 1724); Melchior Mehl, *Pterelaum Samsonis symbolum* (Wittenberg, 1724); and Nicolaus Zobel, *De lapsu primorum humani generis parentum a paganis adumbratio* (Altdorf, 1730). An interesting variant of the vogue was followed by Jonas Ram in *Ulysses et Otinus unus et idem, sive disquisitio historica et geographica, qua, ex collatis inter se Odyssea Homeri, et Edda Island* (Copenhagen, 1702). Ram, who discovered evidence of Noah's visit to Norway in the founding of the town of Noatun, proposes that there is extra-Homeric evidence that Ulysses' wandering was not restricted to the Mediterranean; hence he is moved to associate him with Odin and identify Asgaard with Troy. Odin is also the same person as Priam, whose wife Phrygica is, of course, Frigga. The Cyclopes are the Irish; Aeolus is England; the Laestrygonians are either the French or the Germans; Circe's realm is Denmark, etc. Each Odyssean adventure is repeated in the Eddas.

were had the irritating custom of emphasizing the heathen superstitions and religious rites practiced by the Catholic Church.

The controversy over the pagan bases of various Catholic rites like image-worship, holy water, and incense was as hot as the argument between the two Christian divisions about the inspiration, antiquity, and genuineness of the Sibylline oracles. Although the investigation of Catholic antiquarians into religious origins, which produced books like Giovanni Casalio's *De profanis Aegyptiorum, Romanorum et sacris Christianorum ritibus libri tres* (Rome, 1681) and Noël Alexandre's *Conformité des cérémonies Chinoises avec l'idolatrie Grecque et Romaine* (Paris, 1700), are admirable building blocks in the history of the evolution of human religions, Protestants generally failed to see anything suggestive of religious evolution in their attacks on Roman Catholic paganism and compiled books like G. Meier's *De papatu per ethnicisum impraegnato* (Frankfort, 1634); J. Valkenier's *Roma paganizans* (Franecker, 1656); or S. Jones's *De origine idolatriae apud gentes et Christianos* (Lyons, 1708).[44] Actually, the first British history of idolatry was deeply steeped in anti-Roman bias.

In 1624 *The Original of Idolatries, or the Birth of Heresies*, appeared in London and was attributed by its translator Abraham Darcie to the great scholar Isaac Casaubon, who had died seven years before. Anyone who knew Casaubon's writings should have been aware before he finished the first paragraph that this book was not from the hand of James I's librarian and captive scholar. After listing the rites ordained by God and debased by Adam's successors, the book complains

---

[44] A later example of this sort of polemic is Paul Stockmann's *Elucidarius deorum dearumque gentilium, variaeque idolatatriae in usum antiquitatis studiosorum, necnon ad loca tam Scripturae S. quam profanorum scriptorum, huius argumenti, facilius intelligenda et explicanda, e probatis autoribus congestus et in ordinem alphabeticum redactus* (Leipzig, 1697). This is a catalogue of pagan saints commencing with Abarbarea, a Homeric nymph, and concluding with Zwantewytus, who was worshiped on the Island of Rugia. Stockmann thinks Satan took advantage of the example of the Trinity to urge polytheism as the proper religion. All Gentiles, descended from Cain and dependent on Natural Light, agreed to this heresy, although from the very beginning of things, it was known that God revealed Himself through His voice and that the evidence of natural phenomena was not enough. As a result of the satanic hypothesis, pantheons developed; but it also must be understood that as a consequence of the betrayal there is some truth behind each myth. This theory is supported by the well-known fact that Janus is Noah, the Giants are the builders of Babel, and Hercules and Omphale are Samson and Delilah. Pagan worship in substance is not unlike the theology of the Roman Church, which, Stockmann thinks, is regrettable because men like Plato almost saw the truth, and even in America Indians had heard of God, the Son of God, the Flood, and the Destruction of the World. The Hurons preserve tales about Joseph; the people of Yucatan practice circumcision; Mexicans keep the Sabbath and follow Levitical custom. These similarities are, however, not the revelations of Natural Light but the obvious results of Solomon's voyages to Ophir, which spread Jewish doctrine and rites throughout the world.

like a true member of the better class that the bishops of Rome were so busy adapting pagan and Jewish ceremonies to Christian use that they made no socially important Roman converts during the first three centuries of the Church's existence. It attributes the word "mass" to the flamens' custom of concluding a sacrifice with "licet missa est," and finds the word unchristianly used by Turks in their term "messelmen." Holy water, processions, candles, the round host, and similar Roman vagaries are fully credited to the priestly methods of heathendom. The book was hardly for sale before Isaac Casaubon's son, Meric, brought out a vindication in which he denied that his father, "while not excusing the superstitions of popery," had aught to do with this text translated by "Abraham d'Acier, a Genevan," and flatly states "that this your admired Pamphlet, this your Allobrogicall Dormouse indeed, came stealing out in a corner by owle-light, (no good signe of a Sincere Booke) and was Printed in French three yeeres before M. Isaac Casaubon was borne."[45] But this was only the beginning.

A fantastically detailed and, consequently, pedantic history of the debasement of Christian worship, which would in time be equalled in scholarship only by Van Dale's *Dissertationes de origine ac progressu idolalatriae et superstitionum* was next composed by Gerard Johann Vos, a Dutch scholar who was a canon of Canterbury. Dedicated in its 1641 version to Charles I, it is the 1668 posthumous printing which dazzles the eye with the splendor of its almost two thousand quarto pages. The preface of Vos's *De theologia gentili et physiologia Christiana, sive de origine ac progressu idololatriae* informs the "benevolent reader" that the Gentile mistake of looking to Nature rather than to the God of Nature has proliferated the Joves and Junos, who are found in every sacred acre of the world. The gods, multiplied by the Syrians and Egyptians before the Greeks had their turn with them, are simply thin slicings of Adam, Noah, Joseph, Moses, Joshua, and Samson. Great patches of the first half of Vos's book are devoted to the borrowed Hebrew theologies and sacred histories of the ethnics. Neptune is one of the sons of Noah; Vulcan is Tubalcain; Nimrod is Bel or Mars; Saturn is Noah and Abraham; but Noah is, furthermore, Prometheus and Liber. Not to be outdone by his Old Testament predecessors, Moses is Liber, Osiris, Monius, Mises, Moso, and Milichus.[46] Picking up San-

---

[45] M. Casaubon, *The vindication or defense of Isaac Casaubon against those impostors that lately published an impious and unlearned pamphlet, intituled The Originall of Idolatrie, etc., under his name* (London, 1624), sigs. M1v-M2.

[46] Vos, *De theologia*, pp. 226–29.

ford's Nysa-Sinai intimation, Vos develops the Moses-Bacchus relationship still further. Both heroes spent a good deal of time in the Arabian
desert, and the Dionysian laureate Nonnos probably had the crossing
of the Red Sea in mind when he wrote of his hero that "he took to his
heels and ran in fear too fast to be pursued/ until he leaped into the gray
waters of the Erythraian Sea."[47]

There is little doubt that Vos knew more about world religions
than almost anyone else in his generation. He can run after his deities as
fast as they migrate, and even when they modify and disguise their cults
he can uncover them with learned ease. For example, the Egyptian
Thoth went to Germany, changed his name to Woth, then Wothan,
Woden, Wode, and finally altered the initial letter and became Gode;
but he was pursued and unmasked by Vos. Many of these gods put on
animal limbs or features or were accompanied by symbolical animals
that, consequently, were sympathetically worshiped. Often the god was
merely an element or a complexion or an abstraction like Peace or
Health or Safety, and so got deified. Plunging into the thickets of the
past, Vos sought all these facts out, and by reading volumes in classical,
oriental, and European languages, ran down the scale of idolatry from
the veneration of famous men to the religious cultivation of cicadas and
onions. Thoroughly skilled in all branches of science too, he writes full
zoological descriptions of the nature and habits of each creature as he
descends the ladder of idols from elephants to poisonous insects. There
is little about shellfish that he can be told by those who fear and pray to
the oyster. Between the first and final forms of his book, the theory of
Hebrew-Gentile transmissions was given a new twist when Samuel Bochart, a pupil of the British theologian John Cameron, published his
Geographia sacra seu Phaleg et Canaan at Caen in 1646.

The first four books of Bochart's impressive and magistral work go
over the old well-trodden ground of the history of Noah and his sons, or
rather Saturn and his brood, and retell how they wandered about and
colonized the postdiluvian world. Bochart composes a history of these
founders of nations (pausing to associate Chanaan with Mercury, Nimrod with Bacchus, and Magog with Prometheus) until the time they
established colonies and set up capital cities all over the earth. The
second and highly influential part of the *Geographia sacra* advances his
major hypothesis. Drawing on words and phrases found in Herodotus,
Varro, Eustathius, and other sources, but especially on the Punic speech

---

[47] Nonnos, *Dionysiaca*, XX, 352–53.

of Hanno in Plautus' *Poenulus* (V.1), which he turns into Hebrew, Bochart sees the Phoenician merchant adventurers as the people who spread Hebrew history and theology from Taprobane to Ophir.

When he discusses the transmission of Hebrew history into pagan legend, Bochart does not put the argument as hard as Vos or as Vos's Countryman Daniel Heinz, who popularized the Moses-Bacchus identification in his notes on Nonnos. When Bochart wrote his essay on Bacchus, he not only put together erudite material from ancient and contemporary sources, but also, after recapitulating Vos's proofs for the identification of Moses and Bacchus, took issue with the *vir magnus* and presented evidence to show that Bacchus is not a badly reworked Moses. It is his general thesis that episodes from all sorts of history, both true and mythical, got mingled in all ancient accounts, and that, in most cases, these apparent borrowings are really accidental parallels. The reason why some of these biographies seem to have derived from the Pentateuch histories, and especially from that of Moses, is that Cadmus, who led the Phoenicians into Greece, lived in the age of Joshua when the memory of the life and career of Moses was still fresh.[48] The theory of the Phoenician migrations and of these peoples as the medium through which the culture of the Near East was given to the West took with this book a firm grasp on men's minds which it did not relinquish for a long time.[49]

[48] Bochart, *op. cit.,* in *Opera omnia* (Leyden, 1712), III, 440–47.

[49] In his *Delphi Phoenicizantes,* Dr. Edmund Dickinson (note 41) identifies Phoenicians with Jews and gets a historical identification between Moses and Bacchus and Joshua and Apollo. Og of the Amorites, or Giants, is either Typho or Python destroyed by Joshua-Apollo on the way to Delphi or the Promised Land. Joshua is, likewise, Hercules, who assisted the gods or Israelites in their fight against the Giants or Canaanites. If Joshua is Apollo, Nun is Jove, who is described in this manner by the Greeks, who call him "mind" or "noun." Delphi is another name for Shiloh, whither Joshua transferred the Ark and the Tabernacle about the time Cadmus came to Greece. Dickinson identifies the Spartans as a Hebrew colony in Greece brought in by Cadmus, whose Hebrew name is Kadam ("one who goes before"); this is all consonant with Nicander's statement in the *Thebaici* that Cadmus was educated in Palestine (pp. 1–5, 7–20, 28–73, 76–96, 119–34. Zachary Bogan, who stirred through Homer for biblical material, provided this book with a concluding essay on the Typhon-Python problem.

After Bochart championed the Phoenicians, they began to be loaded with the responsibility for the spread of idolatry. Stillingfleet, Gale, and Huet are his great disciples, but there were innumerable small adherents like M. Morlot, who devoted the opening pages of his *De idolatria gentili* (Strassburg, 1688), to this matter. In 1684 the celebrated Jacob Gronov discovered Pekah, son of Remalia, in the Old Testament and argued from the Greek form of Romeliou that Romulus was of Hebrew-Phoenician origins. See his "De origine Romuli" in J. E. Kapp, *Clarissimorum virorum orationes selectae* (Leipzig, 1722), pp. 574–613.

Bochart also stood behind Armand Maichin's *La theologie payenne,* 1657). Maichin believed that all once knew God through Adam's instruction; but that when Noah attempted to restore the old faith after the Flood, he was thwarted by the heresies of his children. The temple erected to God as Hammon by Ham in Libya became a shrine of

Bochart's temper, unlike that of Vos, is strictly historical; hence, the British counterpart of the Hollander is the Puritan divine John Owen whose *Theologoumena pantodapa, sive de natura, ortu, progressu, et studio verae theologiae libri sex,* was published at Oxford in 1661. While agreeing with Clement of Alexandria that some of the original philosophy lost in the Fall has been recovered by human speculation and revelation,[50] Owen assumes that all that the Greeks and their heritors possessed in the way of history or metaphysics came to them from the Hebrew and was transmitted by other Semitic peoples like the Phoenicians. He finds Jewish dietary laws in Virgil and Ovid[51] and Ham's mockery of Noah in Saturn's emasculation of his father. He does not think, as do other naive historians, that Noah's daughter-in-law was the Cumean Sibyl, and he rejects the whole Sibylline corpus of prophecies as spurious and the work of Christian heretics.[52] He sees the first seed of all idolatry in Eve's readiness to trust the suggestions of a serpent in preference to the edicts of God. Once touched with this fatal blight, men either became Sabians, who adored heavenly bodies, or Hellenes, who worshiped important dead men and women.[53] The Bible informs Owen about the course taken by the Jews in their wanderings away from Jehovah, but he also has enough data in the way of nonbiblical records to describe British idolism beginning with the aniconic remains at Stonehenge.[54] He refuses to talk about the antiquity of the "Chinese fables"; consequently, he ascribes the origin of culture to the Jews and reproduces, as one of his proofs of their invention of writing, a very ancient, possibly Mosaic, Hebrew inscription from an altar discovered by a Franciscan at the base of Mt. Horeb.[55]

A year after Owen's book appeared, Edward Stillingfleet, who was

---

Jupiter; the Temple of Dodon built by Dodanim, son of Javan, in Epirus became a demonic church. In spite of this falling off, men managed almost to reach God by the ladder of Nature (pp. 9–22). The legend of Orpheus indicates how close the pagans came to divine wisdom, but usually they had only a natural theology based on Nature, a fabulous theology established by poets, and a political or sacerdotal theology used to hold people in check (pp. 52–54). Maichin is fully acquainted with the ancient mythographers and allegorizers (pp. 120–21) and uses their conclusions for his own physical and moral analyses of the fables (pp. 128–50). He identifies the major gods with the major Old Testament figures (pp. 151–70), whose legends were spread about by Jews leaving Palestine. At the end of his book, he demonstrates how well pagans knew Christian doctrine and ritual (pp. 157–300).

[50] Owen, *Theologoumena,* p. 63.

[51] *Ibid.,* pp. 159–60.

[52] *Ibid.,* p. 167.

[53] *Ibid.,* pp. 187–260.

[54] *Ibid.,* p. 351.

[55] *Ibid.,* pp. 292–321. Owen rejects the theory which proposed Adam wrote a library of books condensed in the early chapters of Genesis.

not yet thirty, brought out his *Origines sacrae, or a Rational Account of the Grounds of Christian Faith, as to the Truth and Divine Authority of the Scriptures.* Learned and thoughtful beyond his years, the future Bishop of Worcester proposed to investigate the irreconcilability of "the Times of the Scripture" with that of ancient nations, the inconsistency of a belief in the Bible with the principles of reason, and the "account which may be given of things from the principles of Philosophy without the Scriptures." Following out these topics suggested by Deists, the first book of the *Origines* exposes the dense obscurities and contradictions of Phoenician, Egyptian, Chaldean, and Greek history and chronology. The second book vouches for the veracity of Moses, the prophets, and the New Testament on the basis of Christian miracle[56] and fulfilled prophecy. The last book demonstrates how badly secular philosophy has criticized or offered alternate concepts to the Christian doctrines of God, the Creation of the universe and mankind, and the problem of evil.

Taking the position that the full account of "the original and general tradition" is alone preserved in the Bible, Stillingfleet follows the planters of colonies, who knew the truth but were so engaged in mundane struggles that "they soon lost record of the origins of their nations let alone of man himself." One should, he thinks, not put great stock in Sanchoniathon, "much junior to Moses," or in Hermes Trismegistus, or in Manetho and Berosus, "the true, not the counterfeit of Annius." The Greek authorities are no better. In fact, their earliest theologian, Orpheus, lived about the time of Gideon, and they have no historians before the reign of the first Cyrus. Their gods were nothing more than eminent persons, a fact that "the subtiller Greeks" would not admit, "which made them turn all into Allegories and Mystical senses to blind the Idolatry they were guilty of the better among the ignorant."[57]

The young Stillingfleet did not hesitate to take issue with some of his fantastically famous elders. The "learned Bochart," who supplied him with many of his origins is not spared if necessary; Patrizzi, whose conversion of Plato to Christianity took place seventy-five years earlier,

---

[56] The teasing problem of miracles (especially those attributed to Vespasian), which occurred among the pagans or were performed by pagan wonder-workers, comes forward time and again. J. H. Muller's *De miraculis Vespasiani* (Jena, 1707), has a bibliography on the question. In 1714 Frederick Gregorii looked through the classical records for various miracles like that of Androcles and the lion and Arion and the dolphin to conclude that God used miracles to manifest Himself to the Gentiles. In his *De miraculis Providentiae apud gentes antiquas* this Leipzig savant argued that if miracles in pagan quarters teach a Christian lesson they are divine in source; if not, they are the machinations of demons. Since Vespasian's miracles did nothing for the Church, they were satanically produced.

[57] Stillingfleet, *Origines sacrae* (London, 1662), pp. 14, 16–24, 28–32, 45–55.

is blasted for his Christian elevation of Hermes Trismegistus, whose books are "a meer Cento, a confused mixture of the Christian, Platonick, and Egyptian doctrine together."[58] By avoiding the tyranny of authorities, Stillingfleet attempts to understand the corruption of tradition and look for the plain "marks" of the original. Tradition lost authenticity with the decay of learning, the spread of idolatry, the confusion of tongues at Babel, the "fabulousness of the Poets," who "put a new face" on their borrowings and so fabricated the mythology. The men of letters who are responsible for mythological corruption were prone to attribute what was done by some ancestor of mankind to a hero of their nation. They also read a Hebrew statement literally and not as an idiom and translated some Hebrew attributive adjective or proper noun into something similar. Poseidon, for instance, comes from "Punick" Phsytz ("large and broad"), which is from Genesis 9:27, "God shall enlarge Japhet." Japheth then becomes Poseidon by omitting the sense of an oriental equivocal phrase and attributing the actions of several persons "to the one who was the first and chief of them."

With the aid of such historical principles, Stillingfleet arrives at the spot where he can discern "the footsteps of Scripture-history" in the "Heathen Mythology." The Hebrew names for God, Chaos, and Creation are preserved in the fragments of Phoenician theology translated out of Sanchoniathon by Philo Byblius. Everything that is said about Saturn, first of men, applies much better to Adam. The stories of Enoch and Methuselah were combined to make that of Inachus. Noah's memorials are conserved in the legends of Saturn, Janus, Prometheus, and Bacchus; those of his three sons are confused into the myths of Jupiter, Neptune, and Pluto. Drawing to some extent on Vos, Stillingfleet finds Abraham in the pantheon of Phoenicia and identifies Sara as Anobret, a nymph by whom Saturn had a son, Jeoud (Hebrew *Jehid,* "only son," Genesis 22:1). Jacob's trials under his uncle Laban are described as those of Apollo in Callimachus' hymn to that god, whereas his anointing of the stone at Bethel established the "custome of anointing stones among the Heathens." The traditional evolution of Joseph into the Egyptian Apis and the identification of Bacchus-Dionysus with Moses get their customary pages in Stillingfleet's religious records.[59]

[58] *Ibid.,* pp. 122–23.
[59] *Ibid.,* pp. 578–97. In 1668, Barthold Brammer brought out at Kilon a *Veritas creationis mundi prout a Mose descripta est ostensa in traditionibus gentium ac vetustissimus antiquitatis profanae monumentis ad convincendos atheos.* In the first half of this book he attacks the Creation theories of Vanini and La Peyrere, men who did not think the Hebrews the eldest race. In his opinion Moses wrote down God's direct discourse. He knows Steuco, Pansa, and

When Stillingfleet was completing his *Origines,* a very learned Englishman, somewhat his senior, was laboring at a book that would be published in three parts, each of which would be further augmented before a complete version was available for the general public. Theophilus Gale, a Nonconformist who willed his nonphilosophical books to Harvard, finished and published the separate sections of his *The Court of the Gentiles: or Discourse touching the Original of Human Literature both Philologie and Philosophie from the Scriptures and Jewish Church* at Oxford in 1669, 1671, and 1678. The "advertisement" of this ponderous treatise states that Gale had the idea of the Hebrew provenience of everything worth knowing all by himself and was pleased to learn, after reading Steuco, Vos, Sanford, Bochart, Owen, Stillingfleet, and others that his original views were endorsed by both Protestants and Papists. Stimulated by these assurances, he read sources like Plato, Sanchoniathon, and Manetho and corresponded or conversed regularly with Bochart. He asks his readers not always to expect logical or mathematical proofs of his theories, because he was forced "to make use of annals and records of antiquitie which are not so authentic as could be desired; yea, sometimes, when memoirs fail us, of conjectures, which peradventure are liable for many exceptions." Gale is particularly anxious to demonstrate that all sensible Greek metaphysical theories like Plato's are "broken traditions" from the Bible and the Jewish Church and not discursively developed by the philosophers. To assume that these rare ideas can come from Natural Light is to "prove a foundation for Atheisme," a nonphilosophy "sucked in from reading Ethnic Poets and Mythologists."

Gale, it is not surprising, takes it all back to Moses; although Plato may admit his debts to Phoenicians, Egyptians, Chaldeans, and Syrians, Gale knows he was really concealing the word "Jews" under these names. Hebrew is the matrix of all languages, and Hebrew theology is the inspiration of all impressive human thought. Everything the Gentiles know is owed to Jewish discovery. Astronomy is the invention of Abraham, arithmetic and geometry of Moses, navigation of Noah, architecture of Solomon.[60] Embracing fervently the hypotheses of Bochart, Gale sends his Phoenicians (really Canaanites "ashamed of their national founder") on colonial expeditions to Spain and Africa under the conduct

---

the other supporters of pagan Christianity; hence, he makes the common connections between the pantheons and the Old Testament. To prove his point he annotates the Creation chapters of Genesis with a superabundance of classical annotations.

[60] Gale, *The Court of the Gentiles,* I, 14–17.

of Hercules and to Greece as followers of Cadmus. Adventurous beyond imagination, they even sailed to Ireland, where the name Ibernica or "Iber + nae," Phoenician for "utmost habitation," preserves their memory. Wherever they went, the Phoenician pioneers spread Hebrew culture and civility, using the written language devised by Moses. Moses the philologian is, therefore, the same as Hermes Trismegistus who, the Egyptians say, gave them their hieroglyphics. Having pilfered a good deal of this material from his friend Bochart, Gale separates all myths into those invented by statesmen for political advantage and those based on natural phenomena and contrived by the better philosophers as counters to the polytheistic mythology.[61]

Having advanced his not very original theory, Gale discloses the Hebraic borrowings of the pagan mythographers and mythological poets. He takes over the references and illustrations of his numerous predecessors and sometimes supplies additional data. The by now rather stale identification of Moses with Bacchus-Dionysus is repeated, but it is also noticed that both heroes were handsome, both doubly mothered, both titled "legislator," and both horned.[62] Not content with letting well enough alone, Gale steps back from this exercise and agrees with Bochart that "Nimrod is the true source of the Bacchus myth." Having demonstrated that all mythologies are misrenderings of Jewish history, Gale devotes the remainder of his bulky book to proving that all ethnic poetry, theology, philosophy, and ritualistic religion were cast in Hebrew moulds but are now very much misshapen.

IV

During the latter part of the seventeenth century, learned studies of religions other than Christianity, studies which would multiply with each passing year, made it clear to those who preferred clarity that most religions had much in common and that all of them grew from certain primitive fears and hopes.[63] In 1663, shortly after Stillingfleet published

---

[61] *Ibid.,* I, 22–50.

[62] *Ibid.,* I, 1, 24–36. One of the best analyses of idolatry is Tommaseo Campanella's "Examen gentilismi" appended to his *Atheismus triumphatus seu reductio ad religionem per scientiarum veritatis* (Rome, 1631), pp. 109–20. Campanella sees five ascending stages of idolism: worship of subhuman creatures, of men, of elements, of heavenly bodies, and of incorporeal good or evil spirits.

[63] In his *Exercitationum theologicarum trias* (Wittenberg, 1667), Andreas Sennert attempts to prove the continuity of religious influence from Judaism to Ethnicism to Christianity to Mohammedanism. He holds the second and fourth stages of this evolution to be deviations of the first and third. Ten years after Sennert, Johannes Henning compiled a scholarly his-

his *Origines,* the posthumous *De religione gentilium errorumque apud eos causis* of Edward Herbert, Lord Cherbury, whose earlier announcement of the five innate religious principles had furnished the Deists and other non-Christian students of religion with working principles, was published in free-thinking Amsterdam. The manuscript of the *De religione* had reposed in Herbert's study since his death in 1648 and was found and given to the printer by Isaac Vos, son of Gerard. Seven years after its first printing there was a second Dutch edition; finally in 1705 it was translated into English by Lewis, because "it is seldom met with, and rarely known, but only by Curious Enquirers into, and Diligent Searchers after Polite Learning."[64]

Herbert admits that his survey of the Greek and Roman pantheon is one aspect of his search for evidences of a universal Providence. The Church Fathers, who are imitated by "current theologians," scorned the Gentile cults and condemned "the greater part of mankind to eternal punishment." But when Herbert read the ancients he discovered that some of their deities were not only men but bad ones, and he is sometimes stunned by the ridiculousness of their religious rites. He learned, too, that the God of the Gentiles was Nature or some imperfect power like the whole sky or a bright planet. Sometimes God was only a dead emperor or something above normal human comprehension and naught more. Nonetheless, he also found, they really knew "our God" and clearly designated him by titles like Summus, Optimus, and Maximus.

Here, as elsewhere, Herbert assigns the responsibility for human superstition to a priesthood, which is unbelievably cruel enough to condemn good men who were ignorant of Christianity to Hell. He wishes modern divines would learn tolerance; but all of them agree that after the Fall, with the exception of a few men saved by God's election or Christ's death, the majority of mankind, "even those who never knew Christ's name," are subject to eternal damnation. If a heathen lived a good life he is styled only as "moral" and sent to Hell, a decision "unworthy of God." Herbert cannot, in fact, imagine that such a God could be happy, knowing creatures whom he had made and infused with

---

tory of paganism, *De polytheismo gentilium* (Marburg, 1677), which follows the direction of Herbert but avoids his anticlericalism. Henning attributes, like Machiavelli, all perversions of true religion to ambitious princes. For the first time, antiquarian objects begin to be used as frequently as texts for studies of antiquity; and in this connection Johannes Stiegler's *De theologia gentili ex antiquis nummis eruta et antiquitate illustrata* (Wittenberg, 1659), shows how a numismatist can come to the aid of the religion's history.

[64] Herbert, *The Antient religion of the Gentiles, and the causes of their errors,* trans. W. Lewis (London, 1705), p. xiii.

souls were foreordained to be spiritually condemned. He approves of a few decent divines who thought Christ revealed himself to pious pagans at the last moment of their lives, and of the notion of "hairsplitting scholastics" that "those who did what they could had saving grace"; but none of this can be proved satisfactorily by history, tradition, or theory. He applauds Collius' conclusions that some pagans who unconsciously followed Christian ideals got grace.

According to Herbert, religion begins when men, noticing the transitoriness of things on earth, look toward the skies and see permanence in the fixed stars and mutability in the planets. They are likely, after such discoveries, to regard these bodies either as gods or as ministers of God. In time they begin to endow them, the sun and moon in particular, with human senses and deem them worthy of worship. From this worship men move naturally to that of a Supreme Being who creates and controls all. At this stage a priesthood arises with required rites, temples, and oracles. Knowing man once adored the skies, the priests teach him to worship the earth, the "antiqua mater" who married the sky. They invent names for these celestial masses: Isis and Serapis in Egypt, Daantes and Astarte in Phoenicia, Saturn and Ops elsewhere. In time the elements, identified with divine names, are brought into the pantheon as children or relatives of the original pair, and the Gentiles have a sacred history.

Depending greatly on Vos, Herbert puts together a rather confused history of worship. Primitive worship of fire became in time the cults of Vulcan and Vesta, that of water, the adoration of Osiris and Neptune.[65] Eventually the "Deus Summus"[66] was discovered by more sapient philosophers.[67] But the proper worship of the unique God was perverted by the priests, "fearing there would be no need for their services."[68] Herbert rejects previous theories by asserting that Christian rites and ethics, when seemingly followed by non-Christians, are not the consequences of imitation but of natural reasoning.[69] Left to himself, man would have come to the right church, but the priesthood not only took the administration of the world out of God's hands and gave it to a multitude of invented spirits but saw to it that scandalous fables were told about these lesser creatures. Herbert finds in these legends the further ambitious activities of greedy priests, because these lascivious and wicked tales could have been erased by public edict if the clergy had

[65] *Ibid.*, pp. 1–17.
[66] *Ibid.*, pp. 113–26.
[67] *Ibid.*, p. 227.
[68] *Ibid.*, p. 245.
[69] *Ibid.*, pp. 262–94.

not preferred to read allegory into them, "allegory that the priest could explain as if these nuts of foolishness contained kernels of truth."[70]

In a way Herbert's posthumous book marked the beginning of the end for the whole theory that etymological investigations and comparative biographies would show the Old Testament behind all other religious theory and history. The monomania that plagued so many Christian scholars was being cured, and the fact that Herbert's book could be finally published was an indication of the advancement of learning. Within two decades Anton van Dale, master of the excruciatingly minute learning so highly regarded by the seventeenth century, published a *De oraculis veterum ethnicorum dissertationes duae* (1683) in which he proved with numerous diverting anecdotes that all oracles were religious fakes. The discussion of predictive utterance which began with Plutarch's "Cessation of Oracles" ended after more than a thousand years of talk with this rational evaluation of prophecy. Contradicting the common Christian statement that pagan oracles were the work of devils and ceased at the birth of Christ, van Dale, without saying so much, implied that Christian predictions were in the same category. He had an uneasy habit of reciting, for illustrative purposes, recent events such as the story of the Ursulines and the devils of Loudon.[71]

The appearance in the same year as van Dale's book of Bayle's *Pensées Diverses sur la Comète* indicates another advance in the rational study of religion, because while ostensibly eradicating the fear of comets (a fear long before put aside by intelligent people), Bayle is really intent on revealing that the superstitious rites and beliefs of the heathen are still to be found in the practices of the Roman Church.[72] Shortly after this reasonable demonstration, van Dale's book was given general currency when Fontenelle rearranged the arguments, softened the awk-

[70] *Ibid.,* pp. 295–312. Cherbury's bones were, of course, regularly dug up and hanged in chains. In his *Examen cherburianismi sive de luminis naturae insufficientia ad salutem* (Jena, 1675), Johannes Musaeus wreaks havoc with theories about pagan virtue by asking that virtue be defined and taking as his thesis the conviction that there is no safety without Revelation and no sound Revelation without Incarnation (p. 11). G. N. Seerup's *De legis Mosaicae divina origine et auctoritate diatribe adversus Edoardum Herbertum* (Copenhagen, 1678), takes the position that naught is better than Mosaic principles based on Revelation and that Herbert's notions resulting from either reason or nature are extraordinarily dubious. In the *De tribus impostoribus* (Kilon, 1680), Christian Kortholt has it out with Herbert, Hobbes, and Spinoza. He argues (pp. 4–92) that Herbert's *De religione* estimates the Bible no higher than the Talmud or the Koran and places Christianity on the level of paganism.

[71] J. R. Carré, *La philosophie de Fontenelle* (Paris, 1932), pp. 416–58; F. Manuel, *The Eighteenth Century Confronts the Gods* (Cambridge, 1959), pp. 15–53.

[72] W. Rex, *Essays on Pierre Bayle and Religious Controversy* (Hague, 1965), pp. 30–74; A. Prat's preface to his edition of the *Pensées diverses sur la comète* (Paris, 1939), pp. v–xxx, contains the germ of Rex's analysis.

ward and heavy scholarship, added sardonic twists and turns to some of the more diverting illustrations, and turned it into the *Histoire des oracles* for the amusement and enlightenment of sophisticated France. Fontenelle's revision of van Dale was rendered into English as *The History of Oracles and the Cheats of Pagan Priests* by the formidable bluestocking, Aphra Behn, about the same time as Herbert's *De religione* was translated; the British were, thereby, given a double helping of religious reasonableness.

Shortly after Fontenelle finished his popularization of van Dale, he wrote a short essay on how fables began among those nations that were ignorant of "the traditions of the family of Seth." When such people related an experienced marvel, proposed Fontenelle, they were not different from modern men who embellish their narratives with something curious to make them more interesting and to win over their audiences. From the yarns of these contemplative but crude primitive philosophers, gods and goddesses were born. Someone had to be found who could toss lightning, make winds blow, and create storms at sea; hence, gods who were human in form but larger than humans were invented to see that these natural phenomena occurred. Actually the gods were mirrors of their creators. When mankind was brutal, gods, as in the time of Homer, were brutal; when mankind became wise and just in the age of Cicero, the gods followed their example. "The history of fables is the history of the errors of the human spirit."[73]

In spite of these solid efforts of the rationalists, the conviction that pagan theologies and histories were wastings of Adam's teachings or foolishly imitated recapitulations of Jewish encyclopaedias continued to flourish. In 1696, a decade after Fontenelle's publications, van Dale tried again with his *De origine et progressu idolalatriae et superstitionum*. The title, by now commonplace, may have been consciously sarcastic, because van Dale not only took vigorous issue with precursors like Vos but also made it very plain that primitive Judaism was just as crude and idolatrous as the ethnic cults which were thought to imitate or pervert it. The book, loaded as usual with esoteric learning, was a real body-blow to the Christian obsession, but religious convictions are as slow to cure as malignancies. Forty years later, Arthur Young, nettled by Spencer's Egyptian primacy theory, went over the whole matter again in the two volumes of his *An Historical Dissertation on Idolatrous Corruptions in Religion*; but without knowing it, Young is really at-

[73] Fontenelle, *Oeuvres* (Paris, 1767), III, 296.

tempting to galvanize a corpse. He who wishes to witness the death throes of the Jewish origins hypothesis should read the efforts of Bochart's best pupil, P. Daniel Huet, Bishop of Soissons and Avranches, a man miraculously learned, liberal, and reasonable.

In September of 1691, Huet wrote Huygens that "those who were most rational were the enlightening nations in their flourishing age and the great ancient philosophers who believed and supported dogmas similar to or only less credible than Christian doctrines."[74] By the time that Huet expressed himself so soundly he had published his *Demonstratio evangelica* (1679) and had just issued his *Alnetanae quaestiones de concordia rationis et fidei* (1690). Neither book really shows him at his best as a thinker, but his vast knowledge shines through the folds of memory in each page and gives us a man willing to compromise, perhaps, but also happily married to a comfortable hypothesis.

Homer, Huet thinks, may have been an Egyptian and not a Greek; further, he read all of Moses' writings and took over his sacred history and his theology. Hesiod, subsequently, learned all that he knew from Homer.[75] Huet hesitates to deny that Moses did not appropriate Egyptian laws, doctrines, and rites which were inoffensive to Judaism, but he rejects the theory found in Simplicius that all of Moses' theology was originally Egyptian. "To be sure this false notion sticks in many minds that Jews were, as many Gentile writers state, the pupils of Egyptians; but if they were better versed in Jewish customs and primitive history, they would perceive that Hebrew theology is worlds apart from that of Egypt because the Jews are from Chaldea."[76] Huet admits that the long escape of time has made it very difficult to find Jewish truth in ethnic fabulation; nonetheless, adopting the thesis of his master Bochart, he decides that Moses was converted by the Phoenicians into the gods Taautus and Adonis. The second metamorphosis fits very snugly, because Adonis was born in Arabia where Moses dwelt, and was, in his myth, hidden in an ark entrusted to Proserpine. When this deception was uncovered, a consultation of heavenly powers awarded his custody to Venus, Proserpine, and Zeus, each of whom was to enjoy his company for a third of the year. In similar wise, Moses was hidden for three months by his mother, found by Pharaoh's daughter, and frequently went to worship Jehovah. Adonis is, of course, the same as Bacchus, Mercury, Osiris, Apollo, and Helios; hence, since Moses is Adonis, he is

[74] C. Huygens, *Oeuvres complètes* (The Hague, 1888–1950), X, 144.
[75] Huet, *Demonstratio evangelica* (Venice, 1732), p. 53.
[76] *Ibid.*, p. 94.

also these other gods.[77] Huet finds the rites of Adonis in the history of Moses and his garden in Eden; in fact, by looking about, Huet discovers Moses in the pantheons of Persia, China, Japan, Mexico, and the primitive religions of the Germans, French, and English.[78] He is, of course, best found in Greece and Rome, and in the latter country he was worshiped as Romulus.[79] Having worked out this universal scattering of the Moses story, Huet makes a similar relation of the universal manifestations of Joshua as Hercules.[80]

At the conclusion of the *Demonstratio,* Huet criticizes the pedantic allegorizers of the Bible,[81] an unusual position for a Roman Catholic of his generation to assume. But while he demands moderation among Christian exegetes, he praises Metrodorus, Heraclitus, Porphyry, Plutarch, Eustathius, Dio Chrysostom, Cornutus, Palaephatus, Fulgentius, allegorical and euhemeristic interpreters of Homer, whose careful veiling of his doctrines would have deprived men "unless there were those who dispelled the shadows and worked to dig out what was hidden."[82] In his later *Alnetanae quaestiones,* Huet retraces in an opening dialogue with his friend Hamel the traditional problems of the conflict between belief and reason, philosophy and religion, but swiftly moves on to a comparison of the central tenets of Christianity with those of the pagan philosophers. Here he looks back to the conclusion of the *Demonstratio* by remembering that Plato, confronted with the myths of his ancestors, either rejected them absolutely or explained them in allegory. He applauds Plato's employment of the second method because he holds that all pagan ideas should be carefully contemplated—in this he is at one with his contemporary countryman, Louis Thomassin—in order that a Christian may better understand the truths of Christianity.[83]

Although there are nations, like the Tartars and the Canadians, who have no knowledge of a unique God, Huet finds it difficult to learn of other pagans who do not cherish a monotheistic belief.[84] The several attributes of God, the nature of the Trinity, the existence of good and bad spirits between God and men, a nondualistic Creator who made man in his image with an immortal soul, all or some of these essential Christian ideals are to be found in Plato, Aristotle, Pythagoras, Plo-

[77] *Ibid.,* pp. 74–90.
[78] *Ibid.,* pp. 102–11.
[79] *Ibid.,* pp. 144–52.
[80] *Ibid.,* pp. 205–10.
[81] *Ibid.,* p. 741.
[82] *Ibid.,* pp. 748–49.
[83] Huet, *Alnetanae quaestiones de concordia rationis et fidei* (Paris, 1690), pp. 94–95.
[84] *Ibid.,* pp. 97–102.

tinus, Proclus, Iamblichus, Cicero, Seneca, Prophyry, Homer, Virgil, and the religions of Persia, India, China, Japan, Peru, and Cuba.[85] Renewing the tired unification theory of Ficino and Steuco, Huet once again proceeds to compare patriarchs, gods, and heroes as he had done in his earlier book. By an allegorical scrutiny of ethnic legend, he discovers a general knowledge of the incarnation, the mission, miracles, death, resurrection, and ascension of Christ throughout the known world. Certain libertines had expressed mocking doubts about a virgin birth, but Huet, thanks to his reading in a vast library, loaded with travelers' narratives, can silence these agnostics by listing the ancient heroes and demigods born to virgins. "Avicenna states that this is not at all an uncommon phenomenon in lands below the equator."[86] Gifted with an eager heart and great erudition, Huet discovered that most Christian rites, beliefs, and moral convictions were known and practised among nations outside the pale of Christendom.

Huet was on the edge of a great anthropological discovery, but his Christian convictions blinded him. There were other hindrances that he could not avoid. The early Renaissance had recovered the lost epics of Homer and with them they had also discovered the ancient Greek allegorists who attempted to purify the *Iliad* and *Odyssey* of impieties by a correct exegesis not too different in method from that applied to the Scriptures. Homer was not, of course, as venerable as Moses, but the pagans had no other writer before him, and his Christian testimony, like that of Plato, carried enormous weight for Renaissance men.

[85] *Ibid.,* pp. 117–72.
[86] *Ibid.,* pp. 233–64.

IV

◄ UNDERMEANINGS IN HOMER'S *ILIAD* AND *ODYSSEY* ►

LTHOUGH THE HEROES of the Trojan War were known to the
Middle Ages as dukes, counts, and knights, their histories
and personalities did not depend on Homer but rather on
Ovid, Virgil, Statius, Dictys, Dares, Benoit, and Guido.[1]
The medieval *Iliad* was the *Pindarus Thebanus de bello Trojano,* a synopsis of the Greek epic in eleven hundred wretched Latin hexameters.[2]
A few true lines of Homer were known, as they were to Dante, from
quotations in Horace or Cicero, but the original epics on which Homer's
great reputation among the ancients rested seemed hopelessly lost. Petrarch tells in his letters about his lifelong search for a manuscript of
Homer and the eventual gift of one from Sigeros. The Latin prose translation of Homer, commissioned by Boccaccio[3] and executed by Pilatus,
filled Petrarch with "pleasure and joy";[4] but he undoubtedly read it, as

[1] Homer, *Ilias,* ed. T. W. Allen (Oxford, 1931), I, 203–4; A. J. B. Wace and F. H.
Stebbing, *A Companion to Homer* (London, 1926), pp. 226–29. We possess information about
Byzantine Homeric scholars like Arethas, Tzetzes, Moschopolos, Planudes, Thomas Magister,
Triclinius, Michael Psellos, but only the commentary of Bishop Eustathius remains. It was
once thought that Homer was read in ninth-century Germany, but this theory is no longer
accepted; see Ernst von Leutsch, "Homeros im mittelalter," *Philologus,* XII (1857), 366–68.
P. M. Marty's assumption that Walafrid Strabus owned and read a manuscript of Homer is
seriously questioned by Georg Finsler, *Homer in der Neuzeit* (Leipzig and Berlin, 1912), p.
475.

[2] The text can be found in *Poetae Latini minores,* ed. E. Baehrens (Leipzig, 1881).

[3] *Lettere delle cose familiari,* ed. G. Fracasetti (Florence, 1892), I, 560; IV, 90; V, 303;
Pierre de Nolhac, *Pétrarque et l'Humanisme* (Paris, 1892), pp. 341–45; A. Hortis, *Studi sulle
opere latine de Boccaccio* (Trieste, 1879), p. 502.

[4] *Lettere senili,* ed. G. Fracassetti (Florence, 1892), I, 326–27. The opinion that Petrarch
read classical literature for undermeanings is advanced by Gustav Koerting, *Petrarca's*

83

he read the *Aeneid,* to find the moral meaning. Pilatus' rendering was followed by several other attempts at translation by Italians who had some Greek; yet it was not until Angelo Poliziano, the "Homeric Poet," set himself to complete the Latin version of the *Iliad* begun by Carlo Marsuppini that Homer began to be read in the West.[5]

As his *Ambra* shows, Poliziano had substantial knowledge of Greek and Greek literature, but like Petrarch he read classical authors for their ethical undertones. In a preface to Plato's *Charmides,* Poliziano praises the Christian implications of Hermes' remarks to Odysseus and Diomedes' prayer to Athena;[6] in his "Oratio in Expositione Homeri" he describes the epics as absolute expositions of vices and virtues, exact mirrorings of universal humanity. For him Homer's term for "essence of air" is "Olympus," and he finds in the device on Achilles' shield a complicated allegory. He also advises the Venetians at his lecture to learn the perfect literary interpretation of Homer from the Greek allegorizers, Dio Chrysostom, Metrodorus of Lampsacus, Crates, Zeno, and Heraclitus of Pontus.

The first editors of Homer, Chalcondyles and Acciaiuoli, may have accepted Poliziano's recommendation because they furnished the Florentine edition of 1488 with the discourse on Homer by Dio Chrysostom, the biography of Homer ascribed for so long to Herodotus, and the *Life and Poetry of Homer* of the pseudo-Plutarch. The same retinue of Greek biographers and explicators was retained in Latin dress when within the first decades of the sixteenth century the Greek text was translated into that language. Between 1500 and 1505 Homer's *Iliad* was supplemented with poetic accounts of the war at Troy by Quintus Smyrnaeus, Colluthus, and Tryphiodorus, and in 1517 the commentary of Didymus was added. The allegorical readings suggested by some of these exegetes were greatly supported in 1521 by the publication of Porphyry's *Homeric Questions* and *Cave of the Nymphs.* This series of Neo-Platonic readings was followed in 1531 by the anonymous *Moral*

Leben und Werke (Leipzig, 1878), pp. 474–78, 651–54, and is sustained by Petrarch's remarks on the allegory in Homer in his oration at Rome and the annotations he wrote in his manuscript of Pilatus' prose rendering; see *Scritti inediti,* ed. A. Hortis (Trieste, 1874), pp. 320–21 and P. de Nolhac, "Les scholies inédites de Pétrarque sur Homère," *Revue de Philologie de Littérature et d'Histoire Anciennes,* XI (1887), 97–118.

[5] Ficino, who gave Poliziano his Homeric title, describes his Latin version, which got no farther than Book Five, as "so good one did not know whether or not the original was better"; *Opera omnia* (Basel, 1576), p. 618.

[6] Poliziano, *Opera omnia* (Paris, 1519), I, cxxii, verso; see Jacob Mahly, *Angelus Politanus* (Leipzig, 1864), pp. 97–100; Isidoro de Lungo, *Fiorentia* (Florence, 1897), pp. 116–23; Pietro Micheli, *La vita e le opere di Angelo Poliziano* (Livorno, 1917), pp. 24–27; and Finsler, *Homer in der Neuzeit,* pp. 34–38.

Interpretations of the Wanderings of Odysseus, in 1542 by the massive commentary of Bishop Eustathius and the *Homeric Commentaries* of Proclus, and in 1554 by the *Homeric Allegories* of Heraclitus of Pontus. With this apparatus in print and generally in Latin, Renaissance men were able to read the *Iliad* and the *Odyssey* as sagely as their grandfathers read Virgil and Ovid.[7]

Although fragments of Greek interpreters who used allegory to defend Homer against the charges of impiety levelled against him by the Platonists could be read in familiar Greek and Latin authors, it was in Heraclitus' long but still incomplete allegorization of the epics that men of the sixteenth century found both theory and example.[8] Heraclitus was born in the Christian era, but he was confused with his better, Heraclitus of Ephesus, and thought to be a contemporary of Socrates. This false identification seemed reasonable enough because the *Republic* contained most of the charges against Homer that Heraclitus pretended to refute. He attempted no feints but met the Platonic complaints head-on by stating openly that if the epics did not have hidden meanings Homer was the most blasphemous of men. The real accusation of impiety in Heracli-

---

[7] The earliest Homeric allegorizer is the pre-Socratic Theagines of Rhegium, who explained the quarrel of the gods in the twentieth book of the *Iliad* as a lesson in physics. Poseidon (essential water) opposes Apollo (essential fire), and Hephaestus (earthly fire) stands against Scamander (earthly water). Hera, or air, is properly cut through by Artemis or moon, whose name means "air-cutter." Hermes, or wisdom, fights Leto, or forgetfulness; and Ares, or foolishness, is routed by sagacious Athena. This allegory attributed to Theagines is preserved by Porphyry, see *Quaestiones Homericarum,* ed. H. Schrader (Leipzig, 1880), p. 241. It is also repeated in the pseudo-Plutarch, *De vita et poesi Homeri,* in *Moralia,* ed. D. Wittenbach (Leipzig, 1832), V. 2, p. 399. See also P. Decharme, *La critique des traditions religieuses chez les Grecs* (Paris, 1904), pp. 273–75; J. Pépin, *Mythe et allégorie* (Paris, 1958), pp. 97–98; F. Wehrlie, *Zur Geschichte der allegorischen Deutung Homers in Altertum* (Leipzig, 1928), pp. 89–91. The allegorical interpretation of the same passage was used in 1517 to illustrate the moral mode of reading Homer by Erasmus' friend Lodovico Ricchieri, who repeats from the pseudo-Heraclitus, the pseudo-Plutarch, or Eustathius the early Greek underreadings of the revolt of the gods against Zeus, of the adultery of Mars and Venus, and of the fable of Argus. He also knows Julian's moralization of the legend of Castor and Pollux: *Lectiones antiquae* (Lyons, 1560), II, 555–57. Poliziano seems not to have heard of Theagines; his knowledge of Metrodorus may have come from the *Ion;* and his acquaintance with Zeno and Crates from either Dio Chrysostom (*Orationes* LIII, 4–5) or the pseudo-Heraclitus (Heraclitus of Pontus, *Allégories,* p. 27).

[8] A *Peri apiston,* much later than the first-century Heraclitus, was ascribed to him and printed with his *Allegories* in the Renaissance. It is a series of chapters on individual myths and follows the euhemeristic method of Palaephatus. Orpheus and Hercules did not really descend into Hell; but when they returned from arduous adventures, men said "they had been through Hell." The modern version of this text is reprinted in *Mythographi Graeci,* ed. N. Festa (Leipzig, 1902), III. 2. 73–87. The attack on Homer, as men of the Renaissance knew, went as far back as the so-called descent into Hell of Pythagoras described by Diogenes Laertius (VIII. 21), and everyone had known of Zoilus from Ovid's *Remedia amoris* (365–68) if not from more recondite sources. Heraclitus disposes of Zoilus by calling him a "Thracian slave" and, hence, degrading him socially.

tus' opinion was not to be levelled at Homer but against the shallow, uneducated, not "truly purified" readers of poetry who are unable to follow "the lead of the epics towards holy truth" (1–3). Plato and Epicurus are in Heraclitus' words "enemies of those who have taken the ablutions" and, consequently, understand how these poems, or "gatherings of allegories," must be read.

The *Iliad* begins, of course, with the bad shooting of Apollo, who hits dogs, mules, and men by the score but not the hated Agamemnon, who had offended his priest. The foes of Homer pointed scornfully at the absurdity of this episode, but Heraclitus allegorizes the god's bad aim in physical terms. The Greeks were camped near a sea-bog and were, consequently, liable to summer plague because of the sun's rays. Plagues, he explains, manifest themselves by first striking down animals and common people. This plague is a nine-day fever and is terminated by Achilles, pupil of Aesculapius the physician, who is assisted by Hera, or a change of air (63–68). Homer's account of the conspiracy against Zeus of some of the major gods also shocked the pious, but not Heraclitus, the scientific expounder. Zeus, or fire, is naturally opposed by Hera, or air; Poseidon, or water; and Athena, or earth. The conspiracy is betrayed by Thetis, or Providence, who is aided by her manifold powers, or many-armed Briareus. From this poetic event, Heraclitus assumes Thales and Anaxagoras got the basis of their philosophical systems, just as Epicurus, the ingrate, got his theory of pleasure from Odysseus' initial speech to Alcinous (39–41). As he looked through the *Iliad* Heraclitus found a spring myth in Hera's seduction of Zeus, a creation story in Zeus' seemingly brutal punishment of Hera, and "philosophical riches" in the ungodly battle of the gods, which is for him actually a fatal conjunction of planets, a conflict of vices and virtues, or, to credit Theagines' early reading, a struggle between the four elements (52–58). The essays of Dio Chrysostom[9] and Plutarch[10] which can be

[9] The allegorical readings of Homer found in every edition as their endorsement Chrysostom's criticism of Plato's criticism and a recounting of the interpretive methods of Crates, Heraclitus, and Zeno as well as that of Antisthenes (Xenophon, *Symposium* III. 6) and Persaeus (Cicero, *De natura deorum* I. 14–15). Chrysostom states that there is a question whether Homer erred in his poetical presentations or really intended, "after the custom of his age," to transmit theories "about the phenomena of nature in fictional form."

[10] For the author of the pseudo-Plutarch's *De vita et poesi Homeri* (see note 7), the genius of the poet resides in his ability to "exhibit one thing by another" (70). He conveys his wisdom in "dark sentences" and "mythical expressions," but this procedure permits those "who desire to know" to be led "by the pleasures of the intellect" to the discovery of truth. "For what is stated directly is not valued, but indirection stimulates" (92). The gods of Homer are much more than they seem and are given bodies so men can comprehend them (113). The adultery of Mars and Venus is read as an allegory of Harmony, and seen as the

found in most sixteenth-century editions of Homer firmly supported the allegorical interpretations of the pseudo-Heraclitus. Further service was given the notion of a concealed meaning by the methods of the highly regarded Plotinus[11]—methods which were fully reflected in the Homeric analyses of his pupils, Porphyry and Proclus.

Though they only contain allegorical fragments, the *Homeric Questions* of Porphyry were only known to the Renaissance in the epitomized Vatican text, a deficiency somewhat remedied by the light thrown on the *Odyssey* in his fully developed *Cave of the Nymphs*. Proclus' commentary on the *Iliad,* excerpted from his discourses on the *Republic,* was in Latin in 1542 together with the unknown allegorizer's *Moral Interpretations of the Wanderings of Odysseus* and was, consequently, available to men who could not read Greek. His critical effort is devoted to resolving the contradiction between Plato's praise of poets in the *Phaedrus* and his disapproval of Homer in the *Republic.* Proclus assumes that Socrates' basic objection to the *Iliad* arose from Homer's assigning human attributes to purely intellectual powers; but this could hardly be a valid objection since Homer, like Plato himself, used myth to shroud truth, filling his fable with "traces of mystical discipline" in order to stimulate a higher contemplation in his readers. Simple minds, Proclus proposes, prefer literalness; but Homer's mysterious meanings are for godlike intelligences, enabling them to penetrate to the limits of nature. With this hypothesis in mind he unfolds a deeper meaning in each of Homer's difficult episodes. When nothing arcane can be found he follows

---

source of Empedocles' philosophical theories (101–2). The combat of the gods, the seduction of Zeus by Hera, and her punishment by Zeus are interpreted traditionally (96–97).

[11] When one looks at the *Enneads* (V. 8. 6.), translated for the Renaissance by Ficino, one finds the allegorical process working hard because Plotinus believes that all of men's artistic creations were reflections of divine truth and thinks that the Egyptians were wise to use pictures that exhibit "the absence of discursiveness in the realm of the intellect" in order to arrive at precise knowledge. Sculptors and men of letters knew the divine soul required a receptacle "serving like a mirror to catch its image." In the legend of Cronus, or the Intellectual Principle, Plotinus sees the god looking up to Uranus, or the Absolute, and down to his son Zeus, the All-Soul (V. 8. 3). Zeus looks up to both gods (V. 5. 3). Cronus is said to devour his children because the Intellectual Principle wishes to contain ideas and let none of them descend into matter, or be nourished by Rhea (V. 1. 7), whose sterility is suggested by her entourage of eunuchs (III. 6. 19). A philosopher's effort to stay in the realm of the intellect is allegorized in the myth of Narcissus, who was enchanted by "copies," or by Odysseus, who sailed home discontent with Circe and Calypso, "the delights of sensation" (I. 6. 8). Epimetheus, by rejecting Pandora ("all sensual gifts"), symbolizes those who would remain in the realm of the Intellect; but the rescue of Prometheus by Hercules indicates he was fettered with external bonds of his own creation (IV. 3. 14). Plotinus gives a great amount of attention to the Aphrodites of the *Symposium* (III. 5. 1–9; VI. 9. 9) and to the confusing legend of the Celestial and Infernal Hercules (I. 1. 12; IV. 3. 27, 32).

the advice of the great Alexandrian editor Aristarchus and permits Homer to explain Homer.[12]

When Proclus looked beyond the lines of the *Iliad* he saw cosmological propositions in the Homeric myths. The chaining of Cronus is the binding of the material to the "intelligible," and the emasculation of the god symbolizes the evolution of first causes into secondary manifestations. The expulsion of Hephaestus is a parable of sensible creation, whereas the conflict of the gods is a description of the generation of secondary causes. In essence the gods are unity, although the causes emanating from them are often contrary to one another. Many gods are one and the same with Zeus; but others, the multiple Apollos, Poseidons, Hephaestuses, clearly are not, and from this diversity dissension arises. Because of this dissension Homer's gods, to the distress of the friends of Homer, seem to be evil causes as well as good ones; but the distinction between good and evil is a human discrimination and by no means divine. There is good in evil, evil in good. The evil events related in the *Iliad* are generally not heaven-sent but the outcome of human depravity. Some of them demand a very subtle interpretation. When, for example, the gods laugh at the embarrassment of the embracing Venus and Mars trapped under the web of a cuckolded Vulcan, they are actually rejoicing because they themselves are really assisting Vulcan, who represents pure thought, which is static and thus lame, in the creation of the universe. The so-called lubricious Homeric account of Hera's seduction of the marriage-tired Zeus is likewise a creation allegory: Original Reason seeks union with the One, and by this sexual act Hera portrays the joining of the Inferior to Order and Unity.

When philosophy does not help Proclus to disclose the second meaning of Homer, he falls back on a comparison of literals. Achilles' savage mistreatment of Hector's corpse yields no deeper philosophical comprehension; hence, Proclus informs the reader that military customs of the Homeric age demanded that a victor mutilate his enemy's body. Eventually he manages to make his allegorical case against the Platonic opponents of Homer by finding parallels with the three stages of the life of Plato in the three major divisions of the *Odyssey* and by arguing that of the three types of poetry—the divine, the didactic, and the imitative —Plato disapproves only of the last, because it is "conjectural and imaginative." But the commentary of Proclus was a candle in the sun compared to that of Eustathius, Bishop of Thessalonica.

[12] The text may be found in Proclus, *In Platonis Rem Publicam Commentarii*, ed. W. Kroll (Leipzig, 1901), I, 69–180.

The oceans of information with which Eustathius surrounded the Homeric poems contained grammatical instruction, etymological discourses, cross-references to Greek and Roman literature, historical evidence, and what appears to be his own sometimes sensitive analyses of character and episode. To provide himself with erudition he turned to almost five hundred early authorities, many of whom owe their meager survival to one of his citations. Although his sources are not always named, it is clear that the bishop overlooked no etymological explanation, no moral or physical allegory, and no euhemeristic conclusion that had come down to him. Some of these explanations may be original, but there is no way to judge Eustathius' personal attitude toward this subtle type of interpretation. In the "Prooemium" to his commentary on the *Iliad* Eustathius states that Homer invented some of his fables but that "others are purely allegories." He observes that on occasion Homer wrote in myths invented by his predecessors, "but there the allegory does not concern Trojan affairs but what the first composer intended."[13] Some scholars, he hastens to add, "and Aristarchus is one of this number,"[14] think Homer means exactly what he says.

Like Cornutus, Eustathius cannot silently pass over the meaning of a proper name or a euhemeristic possibility. Eustathius rationalizes the statement in the twentieth book of the *Iliad* about the miraculous fecundation by Boreas of Erichthonius' horses by relating it to the sexual activity of all animals in cool weather (1205. 40). The influence of Palaephatus' method appears in Eustathius' explanation of Deucalion's story. Survivors of floods, he observes, are always surprised to discover that others have also escaped. When they notice that stones alone are unchanged by roiling water they assume that the other survivors were produced from these stones, because they also believe that Heaven can change men into stone (23. 27–24. 4). Some of Eustathius' allegorical readings are unattributed but clearly traceable;[15] others are not.[16] Many

---

[13] Eustathius, *Commentarii ad Homeri Iliadem* (Leipzig, 1827–29), I. 27–2. I.

[14] *Ibid.,* 3. 22. There are in Eustathius at least seventy references to Aristarchus, the Alexandrian editor who divided the epics into books and even estimated the number of troops in each army (190. 40). Nettled by allegorizers and perhaps annoyed by his predecessor, Zenodotus, who emended or elided Homeric passages which were impious, Aristarchus insisted on absolute literalness. "Thanks to an inborn inclination to lying," he says of the allegorists, "they put aside the literal for a moral, physical, or historical meaning." On occasion, Aristarchus, if his remarks are faithfully repeated by Eustathius, skates close to allegory to get out of trouble (3. 22; 40. 38; 426. 30–31; 614. 5–7).

[15] Eustathius knows Democritus' physical explanation of ambrosia, Crates' allegory of Agamemnon's shield, and Heraclitus' exposition of the plague or bad shooting of Apollo.

[16] Some of the equivalents more difficult to work out are the symbolism of Zeus, who is fate (612. 33–35), the circle of heaven, *Anima Mundi,* air, prudence, mind-turning-in-on-it-

of the interpretations are traditional in part but have new twists and turns that may be original with this commentary.[17] Often, however, Eustathius, like a good medieval preacher, sees a sound moral parable. When, for example, Dionysus is chased into the sea by Lycurgus, the careful reader is advised thereby to temper his wine with water (626. 21).[18] In similar fashion the reader learns that women are the cause of wars when Aphrodite takes Ares by the hand (1244. 40), or he gets instruction in oratory when Priam pleads with Achilles in the *Iliad*'s final book (1353. 35). With Eustathius' folios before him, a sixteenth-century reader of Homer would find the *Iliad* almost as full of hidden meaning as the Bible.

II

It was, however, only the troublesome places in the *Iliad* that required an allegorical apology; the whole of the *Odyssey* was explainable in the elucidating second sense. The *Iliad*, Eustathius wrote, "is august, sublime, truly heroic," whereas the *Odyssey* is "the real product of Homer's genius and filled with instruction for men" (4. 36–39). In announcing this opinion Eustathius was following a pattern marked out by generations of pagan and Christian readers of Homer who competed with each other in following the travels of Odysseus, or Everyman, as he wandered from temptation to temptation, or didactic experience to didactic experience, through the Mediterranean Sea of human life. Clement of Alexandria, Augustine, the orthodox, and the heretical saw in the *Odyssey* not only an account of Christian progress but also something reminiscent of the life of Christ.[19] By the fifth century the relationship

---

self (128. 23–28; 203. 20–26), and the intelligence which enables men to live well (196. 37–39). As ether, Zeus is hot and dry and incompatible with Hera, who is warm and moist; they agree in that they are air, but disagree in that they are different qualities of air. They are reconciled by Hephaestus, or heat; no other god could effect this reconciliation (150. 39–152. 1; 608. 8–11).

[17] The gathering of the gods at the beginning of the fourth book of the *Iliad* may, according to Eustathius, be an astrological conjunction, but the golden floor and the cup of gold carried by Hebe suggest serenity. The cup is the sun which draws ambrosia or humidity from the earth to feed the planets (435. 31–436. 32; 438. 14–21; 446. 31–37; 448. 7–8), and when Athena descends, Homer intends her to be seen as a comet. Eustathius adopts Heraclitus' understanding of the real meaning of the conspiracy against Zeus but appends others. The three opposing elements may be suppressed by Order in their assault on the *Anima Mundi,* or they may be checked by Order and Time in their rebellion against Life (122. 47–123. 24; 124. 12–16; 1194–97).

[18] Zenodotus, distressed by this event told in *Iliad* VI. 130–36, changed Homer's "frightened Dionysus" to "angered Dionysus" because gods could have no fear.

[19] Hugo Rahner, *Greek Myths and Christian Mystery* (London, 1963), pp. 286–390.

between the two heroes is so well established that Maximus can use the adventure with the Sirens as a pulpit *exemplum*: Christ tied Himself to the cross as Odysseus did to the mast to avoid the "desires of pleasure" in order that "all men might be saved from shipwreck in this world."[20] Bishop Fulgentius, writing about six hundred years before Eustathius, follows the same procedure and finds "stranger" in Odysseus' name; "wisdom is, indeed, a stranger from the affairs of this world," he concludes, "but it enables a pious man to escape from the Sirens whose song is death."[21]

The allegorizations of the *Odyssey* are almost always centered on the adventures related by the man of Ithaca for the entertainment of Alcinous and his court; they are intended to emphasize the moral meanings of the fight with the Cicones, the adventures with the Lotos-eaters, the Cyclopes, Aeolus, the Laestrygonians, Circe, the Cimmerians, the Sirens, Scylla and Charybdis, and Calypso. Certain of these adventures had been expounded by earlier Greek experts in hermeneutics, but the pseudo-Heraclitus surpassed them all in maintaining that the *Odyssey* was "a vast allegory," teaching the avoidance of vice and its conquest. He begins, unlike many Homeric allegorizers, with the first book of the *Odyssey* and finds in the intentions of Telemachus an allegory of the development of intelligence in a young man whose ship of life is fitted by Noeman, or Prudence, and has Athena at its helm. The tale in the fourth book that Menelaus tells of his wrestling with Proteus is translated into physics—the lion is ether, the dragon is earth (61–64). Eustathius,

---

[20] Maximus, *Homiliae, PL* LVII. 339.

[21] Fulgentius, *Opera,* ed. R. Helm (Leipzig, 1898), p. 48. In a curious version of the redemption of Achilles by Odysseus found in the *Gesta Romanorum* (CLVI), the gloss explains that "Paris is the devil; Helen, the human soul, or mankind; Troy is Hell; Odysseus, Christ; and Achilles, the Holy Spirit." It is no wonder that the Sirens appear in the Purgatorio (XIX. 10–24) and are interpreted by Daniello as "symbols of corporeal pleasure and other vain delights," whereas Odysseus is found wandering in the Inferno (XXVI. 90–142) "to gain experience of the world and of human vice and virtue." The character of polytropic Odysseus moved in two directions during the Middle Ages because men who relied on the word of Aeneas, Ovid, Statius, and Dares knew hardly how to describe him. In his *Metamorphosis Ovidiana moraliter* (Paris, 1515), the medieval allegorizer Bersuire follows Odysseus, "a just and prudent man," as he overcomes Polyphemus (who is spiritually blind), visits Aeolus, "devil king of the proud," subdues Circe, or "worldly prosperity," with the wand of virtue, and returns to Penelope or chastity (pp. 92–95v). Bernard of Silvester, while not praising Odysseus for his moral efforts, lays bare the real meaning of his adventures as Aeneas repeats them; see *Commentum super sex libros Eneidos Virgilii,* ed. W. Riedel (Greifswald, 1924), pp. 20–23. One need only remember that Chapman, who sought in allegory the "Soule" of a poem, saw "over-ruling Wisedome" and "the Mind's inward, constant, and unconquered Empire, unbroken, unaltered with any most insolent and tyrannous inflictions" in Odysseus; see Chapman's *Homer,* ed. A. Nicoll (New York, 1956), II, 4–5.

faced with the same story, sees Proteus as primitive matter or as a euhemeristic and generalized figure of wizards like Skymus or Philip of Syracuse. The incident can also be resolved into a practical parable of the rules of friendship, because Proteus tests Menelaus; had Menelaus similarly tested Paris, the Trojan War would have been avoided (1503. 7–30). As others before him, Heraclitus uncovers the Empedoclean doctrine of harmony in Demodocus' ballad of the adultery of Venus and Mars, but the story may also be an emblematic veiling of the nature of ironworking. Ares, or iron, can be softened by Hephaestus, or fire, with the aid of Aphrodite, or artisan grace (69).

The anonymous *Moral Interpretation of the Wanderings of Odysseus* describes each episode in the hero's narrative to Alcinous as a symbolic trial of or obstacle to a morally educated man. The Cyclopes are representations of savage and inhuman customs contrary in every respect to natural reason; when Odysseus comes to his senses and avenges himself on them, he discovers how blind he himself has been.[22] Eustathius states that the Cyclopes have one eye to indicate they have only animal souls; hence, having no insight, they are useless when blinded (1622). The *Moral Interpretation* describes the visit to Aeolus' den as suggesting the variant possibilities of any human action; but Heraclitus, considering the same event, finds it only a representation of the year and its months, or twelve children (71). In the famous sojourn with Circe, to which all interpreters ascribe lavish ethical meanings, Heraclitus hears a conflict of conscience in the dialogue with Hermes; Odysseus is talking to himself, and the disenchanting moly is the symbol of human reason (72–73). Eustathius thinks that the sorceress is only the vice of gluttony, or the pleasure of taste, which produces obesity and dullness; consequently, her symbolic animals, the hogs, never look to heaven (1659. 10–19). In the land of the Cimmerians, according to Eustathius, Odysseus entered Homer's "philosophy of symbols," and as a competent allegorist the bishop uncodes each of them (74); on the other hand, in *The Moral Interpretation* the same adventure shows "how righteously a man must live in order to emerge from the shadows." For Eustathius, Scylla is arrogance, and her dogs, shamefastness

---

[22] Besides the edition of 1531 in Greek by V. Opsopaeus and C. Gesners' Latin translation of 1542, this work has been edited by J. Columbus and published at Stockholm in 1678 and at Leyden in 1745. It appears to be unknown to Homeric scholars, but its Greek would suggest a late Byzantine origin. Since it is a short work with headings referring to each adventure, I shall not give page references. The "Protheoria," followed by eleven sections, states that all poetry has noble meaning which the poet wishes his readers to deduce from the literal.

(1714. 47); but the moral interpreter sees in the dangerous sea-crossing the colliding passions drowning both body and mind. The Sirens, in Eustathius' euhemeristic imagination, may be no more than some Greek seaman's recollection of a sailors' whorehouse, though morally they symbolize the allurements of the voluptuous life. The hero stops the ears of his companions with the wax of philosophy, informing other leaders by this cautious act how they should be careful of their subordinates' welfare. Odysseus listens to the songs of the Sirens "to teach us" that Sirens are likely to sing to us but that we should never invite them into our bodies; nonetheless, the bishop adds, "it would be sensible if philosophers permitted a little of the Sirens' sweetness to seep into their prose" (1707. 40–1709. 30). Calypso gets a great deal of Eustathius' attention. She is the daughter of Atlas, or Providence, and her father has taught her astronomy, a science in which she instructed Odysseus. She is, moreover, the emblem of the body in which Odysseus, or the soul, reposes; hence, her name translates as "she who hides." Like human flesh, her island is hot and moist, continually washed by seas of passion (1389. 42–65). Odysseus refuses her godlike gift of immortality because it would nullify his active but human pursuit of virtue (1709. 2). He learns how alien she is to his ambitions when Hermes, or Reason, urges him to leave her for the intelligible world, for Penelope, or Philosophy (1389. 46–1390. 2). We understand this significance of Penelope when we see her weaving and unravelling her web like a logician making and destroying syllogisms (1437. 19).

All of these competent allegorizers said something occult about the return to Ithaca but none of them is capable of finding in a few lines of verse all that Porphyry can draw out of the *Odyssey* XIII. 102–12 for his essay on *The Cave of the Nymphs*.[23] The seaside cave that shelters Odysseus is, for Porphyry, the dark world of matter whither the souls or nymphs descending enter by the northern gate of life to depart for immortality by the gate at the south. The few Homeric hexameters enclose the Neo-Platonic doctrine of generation, and Porphyry admittedly builds on a lost allegory by Cronius, reminding his readers that Numenius also considered Odysseus a wanderer over the dark sea of being, who finds "harbor where storms and seas are unknown." After perusing this symbolical translation of Homer's charming description of Phorcy's cavern, a man of the Renaissance would have some inkling of

---

[23] The Greek text may be found in Porphyry, *Opuscula*, ed. A. Nauck (Leipzig, 1886); it has been translated by Félix Buffière, *Les mythes d'Homère et la pensée Grecque* (Paris, 1956), pp. 597–616.

the explication of the "Sacred Marriage" read by Porphyry at the Feast of Plato;[24] however, he might have some difficulty in reconciling this Porphyry with the one who criticized Origen's compatriots for attributing all sorts of arcane meanings "to things Moses said plainly."[25] The Odyssean allegory composed by Porphyry is mentioned approvingly by Eustathius, who recommends it after he has removed "certain of its subtleties." Sustained by the symbolic caves of Plato and Aristotle,[26] it is undoubtedly responsible for the numerous anagogical holes and grottoes that are found throughout the landscape of Renaissance poetry.

III

The positive moral interpretations of the adventures of Odysseus which the Renaissance inherited from antiquity did much to stabilize the saintly status of the hero whose reputation had been dubious since the earliest times.[27] When Lodovico Dolce reduced the *Odyssey* to ottava rima in 1573, he wrote an allegorical preface for each section;[28] in 1549, Simon Lemnius prefaced his translation into Latin hexameters with an original poem supplying the moral reading of each major event.[29] The learned mythographers collected or invented double readings of Odys-

---

[24] In Porphyry's "Life of Plotinus," prefaced to the *Enneads*, one reads the following anecdote. "I read at the Feast of Plato a poem on the Sacred Marriage, and as I discussed its fable, according to mystic and hidden senses, someone said, 'Porphyry is a fool.' Plotinus then said to me in a way that all heard, 'You have shown that you were at one and the same time a poet, a philosopher, and a priest.'" The episode was known to the sixteenth century in Ficino's translation of Plotinus' *Opera* (Basel, 1580), p. B5.

[25] Eusebius, *Historia ecclesiastica, PG* XX, 566–67.

[26] Aristotle's not-so-well-known cave is described in Cicero's *De natura deorum* II. 37.

[27] W. B. Stanford, *The Ulysses Theme* (Oxford, 1954). The moralizations discovered by the Renaissance were undoubtedly helped by the sympathetic treatment by Ovid in the *Metamorphoses* and *Heroides* and the dignified portrait by Statius in the *Achilleid*. The hostile party which found comfort in the Odysseus of Virgil and Dictys of Crete may have secured additional support from the Odysseus described by Philostratus in his *Heroes of the Trojan War,* a book Latinized by Stefano Negri in the early part of the sixteenth century.

[28] According to Dolce, *L'Ulisse* (Venice, 1573), Calypso is a libidinous woman who does not hesitate to trap worthy men; the visit of Athena to Telemachus tells us about the promptings of the Holy Spirit; Odysseus' resistance to Circe is a lesson in continence.

[29] Lemnius states in the prefaces to *Odysseae libri XXIIII* (Basel, 1549) that true virtue is never overcome by pleasure (Lotos-eaters), is always opposed to vice (Aeolus). He adds that it is not enough to be brave in battle (Cicones). It should be noticed that, with the exception of Servius, the Virgilian commentaries read by the Renaissance are generally silent on this matter. While relating some amazing tales about Odysseus, Servius, *Commentarii in Virgilium* (III. 628) praises him for his constancy in adversity, his revenges on those who injured him, and his ability to overcome strength with wiles. Commenters on Ovid see in the trials of Odysseus the ultimate test of prudence and temperance and make a great deal of the adventures with Circe and the Cattle of the Sun; see Nicolas Renouard, *XV Discours sur les Metamorphoses d'Ovide* (Paris, 1614), p. 239, and N. di Agostini's edition of Ovid, *Le Metamorphosi* (Venice, 1533), p. 154.

seus' wanderings when they related them to the general reading public of the sixteenth and seventeenth centuries. The process of allegorization begins as early as Boccaccio's *Genealogy of the Gods,* where the attention of the reader is directed to the encounter with Aeolus, or God. Boccaccio states that the winds, or the concupiscible appetites, are enclosed in an oxhide, or virile age, and fastened with a silver wire of virtue, or divine love; hence, when Odysseus' companions, or the senses, unloose the wire, they are driven into the ocean, or Hell, far from their homeland, or Peace.[30] The popular Renaissance mythological authority Natale Conti makes much of the allegory of the *Odyssey* because "it expresses the whole course of human life and gives its readers encouragement in adversity."[31] He observes, for example, that those companions of Odysseus who succumb to anger, sorrow, or the enticements of an effeminate life disappear from the poem as adventure follows adventure; consequently, each episode of the poem holds a lesson for the wise reader. The affair with the Cyclopes shows the importance of temperance and prayer; that with Aeolus warns against avarice and lax leadership; that with the Sirens, who are illicit pleasures, proves that reason should deafen one to temptation. By his return to Ithaca Odysseus demonstrates that a wise man, patiently enduring calamities and bridling fleshly desire, will eventually live in "his true fatherland, sharing with other faithful men in the councils of God." Continuing this exposition Conti also finds the etymological, moral, and physical meaning of the *Odyssey* hidden by Homer in "the tents of fiction," so that "they would be spared the corruption of vulgar understandings and preserved for the good reader in the highest purity."[32]

The second readings in Homer, perceived by his Greek exponents and accepted and enlarged by his Renaissance students, probably stimulated those fictional expansions of individual episodes written during the sixteenth and seventeenth centuries. The *La Circe* of G. B. Gelli, which appeared in 1549[33] and became rightfully popular, was succeeded by similar works of less merit, like Ciro Spontone's *Hercole defensore*

[30] Boccaccio, *Genealogie deorum gentilium libri,* ed. V. Romano (Bari, 1951), p. 575.

[31] Conti, *Mythologia* (Padua, 1616), p. 493.

[32] *Ibid.,* pp. 305–9. Conti begins with a physical explanation of the Circe episode, which is incorporated with an etymological analysis of her name and that of her island. She is subsequently (p. 543) connected with animal heat, whereas Odysseus, temperance or the middle way of Aristotle (pp. 552–53), can always steer between moral dangers like Scylla and Charybdis (p. 550).

[33] In Gelli's ten dialogues Odysseus tries to convince his former companions, who are now anything from oysters to elephants, that their human condition was better. He has success only with the elephant, who was the philosopher Aglaphemus, when he convinces the animal that only man can know the First Cause. He explains his ill-luck to a rather pleasant Circe by arguing that the others "did not esteem their nobility" when they were men. As

d'Homere in 1595[34] and Fortunio Liceti's *Ulysses apud Circen* in 1636.[35] The tone of all these enlargements suggests that every literate man of this era was informed about the allegorical nature of the *Iliad* and especially of the *Odyssey*. When Ascham wanted to draw a warning picture for the Englishman about to take ship for Italy, he could find no better whetstone on which to sharpen his analogues than the travels of Odysseus.

For, he shall not always in his absence out of England, light upon the gentle Alcinous and walk in his fair gardens full of all harmless pleasures; but he shall sometimes fall either into the hands of some cruel Cyclopes or into the lap of some wanton and dallying Dame Calypso and so suffer the danger of many a deadly den, not so full of perils to destroy the body as full of vain pleasures to poison the mind. Some Siren shall sing him a song, sweet in tune, but sounding in the end to his utter destruction. If Scylla drown him not, Charybdis may fortune swallow him. Some Circes shall make him of a plain Englishman a right Italian. And at length to Hell or to some hellish place is he likely to go from whence is hard returning although one Ulysses and that by Pallas' aid and good counsel of Tiresias once escaped that horrible den of deadly darkness.[36]

Almost any edition of Homer used by Ascham would have supported his allegorical inclination, but in 1583 Jean de Sponde published a text which was almost modern in most respects and was often praised for its lack of moral annotations. None of the ancient allegorizers are

animals, giving no thought to their divine nature, the former companions, consequently, have more bodily pleasures; Gelli, *La Circe* (Milan, 1804), p. 137.

[34] In this book published at Verona, Hercole Bottrigano lectures his companions on the value of the *Odyssey* in showing "the worth of religion, the constant presence of God, what man owes God, and what man may expect from God." He is given to etymological analyses: nectar is ne + kteino or "to kill" and ambrosia is a + brotos or "deathless." Nepenthe is "the eternal light"; Athena, the guardian angel (pp. 40–45). The companions who stay with the Lotos-eaters are Odysseus' senses; the Cyclopes depend only on Natural Light (pp. 69–73). Odysseus' desire to return to Ithaca is the desire of all men to return to their Creator (p. 83). Circe represents the sun and heat (pp. 91–93) and the moly, which subdues her, is the "universal incorruptible element" as well as an experiment in alchemy. The colors of the moly, black and white, show the effect of the active virtue of heat on passive moisture which results in dryness and whiteness, the tint of new generation. Mercury is sent with the flower because mercury is used to extract natural virtue "from the center of the universe" (pp. 147–57).

[35] This rather charming jeu d'esprit was published at Udine and presents Odysseus guided by the Cumean Sibyl as he walks through Circe's garden, where even the flowers, which can understand Latin but speak their own blossom tongue, are formerly good men transformed by the witch. The Sibyl identifies them and tells their histories. Stupid or immoral men have become insects or lesser animals. Circe informs Odysseus that she has altered people according to the mythological, physical, or moral rules of allegory.

[36] Ascham, *The Scholemaster*, ed. Arber (London, 1927), pp. 72–74. O. Gifanio, whose edition of Homer appeared at Basel in 1572, states in his preface that the *Iliad* is for the instruction of soldiers, the *Odyssey* for that of travellers. F. Porta in his Geneva edition of 1609 writes (sig. iii–iv) that one is to learn patience, constancy, and high-mindedness from the *Odyssey*. Women are to find in Penelope instruction in modesty and conjugal love.

included in his critical apparatus, although he reprints the *Ilias Latina* and the *History* of Dares the Phrygian in an appendix and notices an occasional euhemeristic reading[37] or recalls that some episode has a moral or physical interpretation without setting it down. Before it is assumed that this edition broke the back of the allegorical obsession, it must be remembered that this was the text from which Chapman made his translation. There is no doubt that Chapman read Homer as occultly as Ascham, and while he found little to encourage him in de Sponde's marginalia, he may have learned the nature of the editor's creed from the preface.

Poetry, de Sponde states, is a solid branch of human knowledge and of enormous value to the commonwealth. To support this statement he summarizes the symbolism of the myth of Amphion and invites "hieroglyphic" authors among the heathen to testify to transmitted wisdom about the "One Power" which enlivens all men. While these well-known experts are speaking, de Sponde brings in Christian witnesses like Eusebius, Clement, Justin, Basil, and Cyrillus, who add their recognized convictions. Early poets, de Sponde asserts, were often kings and philosophers, moved by the "One Power" to lead their readers to Him. As a result of this inspiration they used their poems to teach fortitude, temperance, liberality, clemency, integrity, fraternity, justice, and prudence, and recommended excellent remedies for the subjugation of all the contrary vices. Among these poetical teachers of mankind, Homer is first. Nowhere could one find a better example of a virtuous man than Achilles, of a prudent man than Nestor or Odysseus, of a chaste woman than Penelope.

De Sponde traces the origin of poetry to the singing of the angelic choirs at the end of the sixth day of Creation. Human poetry was somewhat delayed, but as soon as man had an alphabet he wrote poetry, which, contrary to the opinion of some experts, was prior to oratory. "Poetry is God's first gift to man and man's first response to God." Pure song, contaminated before the Flood, was preserved by Noah but dissipated by the dispersal at Babel. Though preserved in its pristine state by David and Solomon, poetry has flowed since its origin through filthy and poisonous sewers; hence, the reader must attempt to penetrate to its deeper, purer meanings as he has learned to do when his Bible speaks metaphorically of "the Lion of Judah" or of "the serpent in the wilderness," or relates truth upon truth in the Song of Songs. Mysterious meanings of the same nature are to be found hidden in pagan literature.

[37] Homer, *Quae extant omnia* (Basel, 1583), p. 132.

Orpheus describes the Mosaic Creation in his "Hymn to Night." The Christian struggle of the Sun (Son) with the world is described in Apollo's killing of the Python. The Greek poets refer to wisdom as "the bread of Heaven," and Christ declared, "I am the bread of life." Castor and Pollux are the premonstrative pagan counterparts of John the Baptist and Christ.[38] Although de Sponde omitted the customary allegorical readings from his footnotes, his preface leaves little doubt about his personal attitude toward the true nature of the Homeric poems.

The allegorization of Homer's poems lasted until late in the eighteenth century,[39] but the obsession with second meanings did not prevent the seventeenth century from discovering some sound intents and wise methods of literary scholarship. In 1640 Leo Allacci, a distinguished teacher of Greek, investigated the claims of various cities to be the birthplace of Homer and won fame for his *De patria Homeri*. The more exact and careful histories of Tanneguy LeFèvre, J. H. Boecler, and other students of Greek literature brought out new information about the epics and were aided by special studies like the essays on Homer's nepenthes written by Pietro Lasena in 1624, by Pierre Petit in 1689, and by G. W. Wedel in 1692. With monographs of this nature, modern classical scholarship began, and its eventual dimensions are indicated by Everard Feith's *Antiquitatum Homericarum libri IV* (Leyden, 1677) which illuminated the poems with chapters on Greek theology, ritual, law, games, food, and other topics.

IV

Serious studies of the culture of Homer's age and of his epics were, of course, sometimes pricked on by the traditional search for evidences

---

[38] *Ibid.*, pp. 9–28. Chapman is clearly aware of hidden meanings when he makes his translation: see G. de F. Lord, *Homeric Renaissance* (New Haven, 1956), pp. 33–126. Sandys indicates his knowledge of the Homeric allegories in the notes to his translation of Ovid's *Metamorphoses*; Bacon knows the meaning of the Sirens in *De sapientia veterum*, XXXI; and Ross knows and invents even more in the *Mystagogus Poeticus*. It is worth noticing that Homer was defended against Plato's charges by G. Paquelin in his *Apologeme pour le grand Homère contre la reprehension du divin Platon sur aucunes passages d'iceluy* (Lyons, 1577). Homer's life was compared with that of Moses to show they were almost the same person in an anonymous *Discours en forme de comparaison sur les vies de Moyse et d'Homère* (Paris, 1604).

[39] Madame Dacier did not hesitate to publish the Homeric allegories in her edition; and the contemporary *L'Omero Toscana* (Lucca, 1703), of Bernardino Bugliazzini furnishes an allegory for each book. Most of Bugliazzini's symbolic equations are traditional, but he also invents a few novel ones: the nymph Ino is the Intercession of Saints, Nausicaa shows the dangers of clandestine marriage; Alcinous demonstrates the ephemerality of the happiness of monarchs, etc. As late as 1784, T. F. Benedict went over the whole matter at some length in his Leipzig published *Interpretationem allegoriae Homericae de errore et precibus incipit*.

of the visit of one of the epic heroes to the author-scholar's native village. In 1625 Lorenzo Pignoria wrote *L'Antenor* to prove by literary and antiquarian evidences that the hero of that name was the founder of Padua. Conviction that real historical identifications would be euhemeristically uncovered for each one of Homer's great names died hard in the seventeenth century. As early as 1593 Reinier Reineck, one of Raleigh's major authorities, proved to his own satisfaction that after Odysseus had wandered through Sicily, Italy, Spain, and Germany, where his adventures occurred, he was finally received by Idomeneus, not Alcinous, in Crete and returned by him to Ithaca. "We must rely," Reineck writes, "on solid sources and put aside the fabulous material added to fact by Homer in his noble poem."[40] Bochart, depending on his Phoenician hypotheses, pointed out a town by the significant name of Circello on the west coast of Italy; hence, it is not astonishing to him that the Phoenician word for "witch" is "latim" and that this whole area abounds in poisonous herbs. Sailing southward from this place, Odysseus came, he supposes, to Mola di Gaeta where the Auruncians, or Laestrygonians, were ruled by Lamus, a name derived from "laham" or "lahama," Phoenician for "to devour." The Cimmerians (Phoenician "camar" or "cimmer," meaning "to blacken") lived at Cuma, and the Sirens dwelled in Capri near the Sirenusae. To Bochart's mind, the whole course of the *Odyssey* took place along the shores of Latium and Campania.[41] The exaggeration of this euhemeristic form of historical inquiry resulted in Francesco Bianchini's theory that the whole Greek pantheon was some sort of secret history, in which Zeus was the king of Ethiopia; Juno, the king of Syria; Neptune, the ruler of Caria; and Apollo, the ruler of Assyria. This exaggeration reached an apex in the first quarter of the eighteenth century with the fantastic historical discoveries of Herman von der Hardt, professor of oriental languages at Helmstadt.[42]

[40] Reineck, *Historia Julia sive syntagma heroicus* (Helmstadt, 1593), I, 546–48.

[41] Bochart, *Opera omnia*, III, 587–92.

[42] Francesco Bianchini, *La Istoria Universale provata con monumenti e figurata con simboli de gli antichi* (Rome, 1697). Von der Hardt's obsession, which eventuated in innumerable publications, was that Greek literature is a secret account of historical events (most of them rather minor) that had been lost in the passage of time. Using both his imagination and Greek texts, he uncovered the truth. He looks through the *Odyssey* in his *Aenigmata prisci orbis: Jonas in luce in historia Manassis et Josiae, ex eleganti veterum Hebraeorum stilo solutum aenigma. Aenigmata Graecorum et Latinorum ex caligine Homeri, Hesiodi, Orphei . . . enodata* (Helmstadt, 1723), to disclose that Odysseus was Thesprotus of Pandosia, who fortified Mt. Hypatus, or the Trojan Horse, from which he led sorties; he then marched through Greece, establishing Thesprotian colonies in various places. Homer concealed this history in verse to baffle the kind of stupid folk who read badly and only accept the literal. As an example of Homer's technique, Von der Hardt observes that Homer pretends Circe's island is near Italy; whereas, it was actually off Colchis. Thesprotus did not go there, but went rather to Cirrha in Colchis, a place famous for the sort of dense wood

While some Renaissance students of Homer sought to understand him better by improving their knowledge of Greek history and literature and while others were attempting to decipher his verses for further information about pre-Periclean Greece, a third group of readers was finding in the *Iliad* and the *Odyssey* those evidences of universal Christian wisdom that they had also uncovered in Plato, Seneca, Orpheus, Virgil, and other Greek or Roman authors. A case in point is furnished by the *Noctes solitariae sive de iis quae scientifice scripta sunt ab Homero in Odyssea* (Venice, 1613), of J. B. Persona, who used texts from the epic for occasional essays on why children resemble their parents or why women talk so much but who was really engaged in proving Homer's proto-Christian information. He discovered the Greek's awareness of an eternal, perfect, creating, unified God,[43] who is omnipresent, omniscient, and possessed of an unopposable will.[44] He is pleased that Homer knew the soul to be separate and immortal;[45] while not denying that much of this doctrine could have come to Homer via the natural reason, he suspects most of it did not. A companion to Persona's book, the *De theologia Homeri*,[46] was written by Nicolaus Bergman in 1689 and may have stimulated Johannes Roth of Wittenberg to publish in 1704 his better controlled and almost modern analysis, *De philosophia Homeri*. Roth, unlike Bergman and others, did not see Homer's theology as despoiled or spoiled Judaism but as evidence of early Greek phenomenological speculation.

Toward the middle of the seventeenth century Jacques Hugues, who used up a good part of his life finding Christian prophecy concealed

---

Odysseus found round Circe's palace. Thesproteans were enslaved in this place, and the so-called seductive efforts of Circe really symbolize the attempts of the leaders of Cirrha to get an alliance with Thesprotus. The moly was not a magic plant but the symbol of Thesprotian armed might. Odysseus' children by Circe represent the colonies established by Thesprotus near Cirrha. The stag killed by Odysseus symbolizes Thesprotus' capture of Bulis; the Laestrygonians are the Leukastrians; the Cyclopes are the Oukalikkians. Some samples of Von der Hardt's other discoveries can be indicated by title: *Mythologiae Graecorum detecta* (Leipzig, 1716); *Proteus cum Phocis illustrata* (Helmstadt, 1719); *Aureum vellus Argonautarum ex Orphei thesauro . . . detectum* (Helmstadt, 1715); *Hercules ex Carcharia* (Helmstadt), 1719; *Arion citharoedus a delphine in mari servatus in veteres poetas et historicos pro rebus Jonas . . . illustrandis* (Helmstadt, 1719); *De Rhea Cybele magna Deum matre* (Helmstadt, 1720). All these books uncover lost history.

[43] Persona, *Noctes solitariae*, pp. 44–9.

[44] *Ibid.*, pp. 74–77.

[45] *Ibid.*, pp. 292–304. Lipse, in his *Physiologia stoicorum,* had earlier pointed out Homer's almost Christian understanding of Providence, the problem of evil, and the existence of demons (*Opera* IV, 548, 554, 561).

[46] Bergman points out Homer's knowledge of God's existence, essence, perfection, simplicity, immutability, invisibility, incorruptibility, eternity, omnipotence, omnipresence, omniscience, goodness, holiness, and justice with line by line references to the two epics.

in the *Aeneid,* supplemented his Roman researches with a hard look at the *Iliad,* the *Odyssey,* and the myths to be found in each epic. Surmising that the recorded fall of Troy was a historical conflation of the Babylonian and Roman captures of Jerusalem, Hugues, consequently, has no problem in letting the facts fall as he chooses. The judgment of Paris, or the temptation of Eve, sends Helen, or "incarnate divinity," to Troy, or rather to Jerusalem. Tiresias, or Abraham, is described as blind because he predicts the coming of Christ but never sees Him. Given these impressive discoveries, it becomes even clearer to Hugues that Cassandra, who predicted the fall of Troy, is Jeremiah. The gods and heroes of Homer are by deed or word proved to be Jesus Christ under a Greek varnish. Jason, for example, is not only Jesus but also the Holy Ghost, the Virgin Mary, the twelve Apostles, and the whole Christian Church. Achilles of Skyros becomes Jesus of Syria, and the identification is etymologically rational. Homer calls Achilles "the Aeacidian," which is the same as "the Ioachidian," and states that he is the son of Peleus, a name invented from "palaios," the Greek word for "old." When all of these facts are pulled together by Hugues it can be seen that Homer is announcing that Achilles is truly "the son of old Joseph." But Homer was not the only ancient to foresee the career of Christ. Catullus predicts the marriage of Joseph and Mary in his poem on Peleus and Thetis; though prophet Ovid appears to be writing about Ocyrhoe in *Metamorphoses* II. 635–60, he is really foretelling the mission, miracles, death, and resurrection of Jesus. According to Hugues' intuitions John baptises Christ when Achilles is dipped in the Xanthus; the Triumphal Entry is foreshadowed when the unarmed Achilles, going to marry Polyxena, is wounded by Paris, or the Pharisees. Helen, bride of Menelaus or the Jews, and carried off by Paris, or the Pharisees, is Christ, who is also Hercules and Adonis. If the latter comparison is correct, Venus is plainly the Mater Dolorosa.

In Hugues' mind the Jovian expulsion of Hephaestus is the Pentecost, and Thersites is Saul Tharsites, opponent of Achilles-Christ and Odysseus-Peter, whose conversion is predicted when Hector is pierced by the spear of Achilles, which, like the cross of Christ, no other man could lift. Castor and Pollux are Luke and Paul, brothers of Helen and, hence, brothers in Christ.[47] Odysseus, when he carries off the Palladium and the arms of Achilles, is Peter bringing the cross and keys to Rome. His name can be broken into "ode" + "eusous" or "singer of Jesus," and his wife

[47] Hugues, *Vera historia Romana, seu origo Latii vel Italiae ac Romanae urbis* (Rome, 1655), sig. B-B,v.

Penelope is the Church, whereas her suitors are heretics. Homer, Hugues supposes, foretells the catacomb worship of the early church when he describes Odysseus' stay in Calypso's cave. But Hugues can read the experience with Circe even more deftly. Circe is the Lutheran Church which is frustrated by the magic moly, or the "grace of God," and the weapon of Odysseus, or the Church's censure. The Protestant animals recover their human form, or faith, but drunken Elpenor is simply sent to Hell.[48] The reactions of the seventeenth century to Hugues' discoveries cannot be estimated. Nicolaus Bergman, who had no difficulty in finding Moses comforting Homer and who clearly had no ability to laugh at himself, described Hugues' book as "a piece of suave insanity." A few other solemn Germans, Protestants all, made humorless assaults on the *Vera historia Romana*.[49] No one else seems to have read prophecy on such a grand scale in Homer, but the search of the epics for the Mosaic message continued to be pressed on high academic levels.

Zachary Bogan, fellow of Corpus Christi, classical scholar, subscriber to Dickinson's theory that Joshua was known at Delphi, and a man mindful of Clement's description of Plato as "Moses Atticans," put together by 1658 and published at Oxford a massive compilation of parallel passages with the title *EBRAISON: sive comparatio Homeri cum Scriptoribus Sacris quoad norman loquendi*. Bogan places quotations from Homer and other poets side by side with verses from the Bible. In Genesis 28:20–21, Jacob says, "If God will be with me and keep me in the way I go . . . I shall come again to my father's house in peace." This verse is remembered in *Iliad* X. 284–85, when Diomedes invokes Athena to "follow with me now even as you followed with my father, the good Tydeus." Isolated comparisons of this nature hardly make Homer speak Hebrew, but as Bogan heaps the instances up, the hypnotic effect of so many similarities is appalling. Proofs of fact are added to these numerous verbal echoes. The "strapping daughter of Antiphates" who comes down to the spring Artacia in *Odyssey* X. 103–11, is Rebecca at the well as obviously as Proitos' wife Anteia's passion for Bellerophon (*Iliad* VI. 160–99), is the Homeric version of Joseph and Potiphar's wife. After mentioning other pagan loan legends of this nature, Bogan shrewdly

---

[48] *Ibid.*, pp. 138–48.
[49] Bergman, *De theologia Homeri* (Leipzig, 1689), p. A2; the nature of the humorless assault can almost be sensed in the titles of two of the major critiques: Eberhard Roth's *De ludicra Jacobi Hugonis deliratione bello Trojano* (Jena, 1672) and the academic oration of Johann von Seelen of Rostoch, "Schediasma philologico-sacrum quo Homerus passionis Christi testis a Jacobo Hugone productus rejicitur," in *Miscellanea* (Lubec, 1734–39).

places Homer's observations about Jehovah in an appendix, "lest I offend the minds of good men."[50]

Not to be outdone by an Oxford professor, James Duport, Master of Magdalene College, Cambridge, brought out in 1660 an extended demonstration of Homer's Hebraic education. The *Homeri gnomologia* announces the superiority of Zion to Helicon, Christ to Apollo, David to Pindar, Paul to Seneca, and Solomon to Homer and urges its readers to be Homerians, Aristotelians, and Ciceronians but Christians before anything else. Duport cannot put Homer "on the same spiritual level" as the Major Prophets; but he regards Homer's ethical doctrines, the consequence of his Hebrew studies in Egypt, as worthy to be compared and contrasted with their Old Testament counterparts. Duport is certain that Homer is vaguely remembering the Garden of Eden in his description of the Gardens of Alcinous and the impious intentions of the builders of Babel in his myth of the assault of the Giants and the Titans on Olympus. He does not find it difficult to date the fall of Troy because Jeptha's sacrifice of his daughter is recalled in Homer's legend of Agamemnon and Iphigenia. This discovery proves for Duport that Homer could not have lived before the reign of King David. Homer's Old Testament studies are, in the mind of the Cambridge don, the prime cause of Plato's malice towards him. Hebrew wisdom made the epics too profound, too full of religious mystery for an ordinary Greek like Plato. Although Duport has fathomed these mysteries, he does not expound them but contents himself with assembling the biblical quotations he has found in Homer. Like Bogan he works his way line by line through the two epics to crowd the margins of his pages with telling references to Scripture. For Duport *Iliad* I. 5, "and the will of Zeus was being fulfilled," is a reworking in Greek of Psalms 33:11 and Proverbs 19:21. Entry after entry of this sort enables Duport cogently to display Homer's great dependence on the Old Testament.

The efforts of these British philologians were consonant with the historical attempts of Vos, Bochart, Owen, Stillingfleet, and Gale and helped prepare the way for Huet's revelation of the Hebraism behind all Hellenisms. The efforts of all these scholars are responsible for Gerard Croese's *OMEROS EBRAIOS: sive historia Hebraeorum ab Homero conscripta,* a work of more than six hundred pages, which could be bought in Dordrecht in 1704. Its compiler, who was rather famous for his dislike of Quakers, thought that although Jews always held them-

[50] Bogan, *Ebraison,* p. A₃.

selves separate and aloof, Gentiles had intimations from the earliest times of Jewish doctrines. He advances the hypothesis that exiled Canaanites, or the Phoenicians of Bochart, spread the Jewish dogmas, which were absorbed by primitive Greek poets among the Pelasgians. From these men and from the living Hebrew tradition, Homer, Hesiod, Pythagoras, and Plato learned all that they were later to express in their own individual ways. The earliest Greek tragedians, for example, people their plays with characters who are patient or filled with pity. These are virtues, Croese insists, that were unknown to the Greeks but had been inculcated in the Jews by Jehovah. He regards the epics of Homer as continuous borrowing from Scripture and describes how "the great mystagogue" hides much of his wisdom under the names of gods and heroes but gives himself away by writing in an un-Greek language and using a Hebraic syntax. At first Homer's topics seemed as non-classical as his language until Croese discovered that he merely translates Hebrew proper names into Greek, retaining without linguistic alteration those of Hebraic origin like Poseidon, Hephaestus, Odysseus, Atrides, Telemachus, and Agamemnon.[51]

It is also obvious to Croese that Homer did not reproduce Old Testament events in the Mosaic chronological order; sometimes, as in the case of the fifth book of the *Odyssey*, he slips in an episode of his own invention. He takes issue with scholars like Feith who attempt to learn more about Greek rites, precepts, politics, and military science in order to understand Homer. Such notions are both ridiculous and inept. One should read Homer for sacred Hebrew history. Homer, as Strabo states, was from Smyrna, and he certainly lived after the time of Solomon; hence, he not only had Jews for neighbors, but his age was also the one in which the Jews began to trade with other peoples in their area. Homer, consequently, had every opportunity to talk to Jews and to assimilate their religious culture; moreover, his name is Hebraic and is derived from "omer" or "orator."[52] But other relationships between Greeks and Jews cannot be overlooked. At that time the Idumaeans and Egyptians were flourishing, and both groups, like the Cabiri and Curetes, had absorbed Hebrew lore because the Jews had become so religiously lax that they allowed their holy books, formerly withheld from the Gentiles, to be read by anyone. As a consequence of this failure of cult among the Jews, the Idumaeans were well versed in Hebrew theology and history; Homer, Lycurgus, Pythagoras, Plato, and others, if

[51] Croese, *Omeros Ebraios*, pp. 17–25.
[52] *Ibid.*, pp. 56–57.

not instructed by direct divine methods, could have learned from them. Hebrew words and turns of phrase stud the writings of all the Greeks and are even found among the Latins. "There are many proper names in Ovid's *Metamorphoses* that are Hebraic; Orpheus is from Ouraph and Eurydice from 'aur dachava,' or 'musical song.' "[53]

But for Croese there is no need to push hard the investigation of these Homeric origins; Homer's *Odyssey* betrays Homer. On several occasions Odysseus doubts his own existence, and once he refers to himself as "Noman." His wife is not Penelope; his son is not Telemachus; and his home is not Ithaca at all but Mesopotamia. The fall of Troy is frankly the destruction of Sodom and Gomorrah, just as Odysseus in Calypso's cave is Lot and his fearful daughters. When Odysseus expresses his desire to see his wife, it is Lot symbolically regretting his incest. Books One and Two of the *Odyssey* recount the calling of Abraham, the promise of a son, and the banishment of Ishmael. Isaac's sacrifice is the subject of Book Three, and the finding of Rebecca as well as the birth of Jacob and Esau are told in Book Four.[54] In Books Six, Seven, and Eight Jacob arrives at Laban's house, converses with Rebecca, and they are married.[55] The Gardens of Alcinous are once again converted into Eden, and Demodocus' ballad of Mars and Venus becomes the Homeric version of the history of Samson and Delilah. Croese completes his exhibition with an extended account of Hercules and Samson. Hence, we never learn what mysteries are still concealed under the literal of the remaining books of the *Odyssey*. Actually, we do not know whether Croese or his publisher tired. No matter what the reason, the eighteenth century had other things to do besides adding Homer's *Odyssey* to the canon of the Old Testament.

[53] *Ibid.*, pp. 143–46.
[54] *Ibid.*, pp. 295–386.
[55] *Ibid.*, pp. 555–629.

V

◆ THE SYMBOLIC WISDOM OF THE ANCIENT EGYPTIANS ◆

MUCH OF THE HISTORY, moral doctrine, natural science, and theology concealed by Homer in the lines of the *Iliad* and the *Odyssey* had been learned during his student years in Egypt. But he was not the only Greek to owe matter and method to the Egyptians. Solon, Thales, Plato, Eudoxus, and Pythagoras had travelled to the Nile to hear the lectures of Chonuphis of Memphis, Sonchis of Sais, and Oenuphis of Heliopolis; in fact, if Plutarch is right, Pythagoras, whose precepts are "not unlike the writings called hieroglyphs," was particularly admired by his teachers and imitated "their symbolism and occult teachings."[1] But for Christians Moses was more important and ancient than Homer; he, depending on the authority consulted, was instructed by the Egyptians or instructed them.

The historian Diodorus Siculus[2] and the geographer Strabo associate the Hebrew lawgiver with Mercurius, Minos, Lycurgus, Amphiarus, Orpheus, Musaeus, Zamolxis, and other leaders and prophets of various shades of respectability. Strabo talks like a premature Father of the Church when he describes Moses as a priest who held part of lower Egypt before he migrated to Judea with others who worshiped a god not represented in "Egyptian fashion" as an animal or in "Greek fashion" as a man. The disciples of Moses defined God as "one thing alone encompassing us all, the land and sea, the thing we call sky, or cosmos,

---

[1] Plutarch, *Isis and Osiris,* 354–55.
[2] Diodorus, *Bibliotheca* I. 94.

or the nature of all." Leaving Egypt, they settled in Jerusalem, a place selected for its unattractive and, consequently, unenvied natural situation. There they lived righteous lives of self-restraint in hopes of blessing and observed a ritual that oppressed none with "expense, divine obsessions, or absurd troubles."[3] The testimony of this pagan Greek was pleasing, but Jewish evidence was naturally surer and better.

Acts 7:22 relates that Moses was "instructed in all the wisdom of the Egyptians," and St. Paul's contemporary, Philo Judaeus, clarifies the Scripture by listing the subjects in which Moses was tutored and by adding that he also learned "the philosophy conveyed in symbols and displayed in the so-called holy inscriptions."[4] The Chaldeans taught him astrology, and from the Greeks, says Philo remembering his own Alexandrian education, he had the regular school courses. Philo's coreligionist Joseph ben Matthias, also known as Flavius Josephus, would probably blame Hellenistic superficiality for Philo's higher regard for style than for historical accuracy. In his controversy with the grammarian Apion, a learned anti-Semite, Josephus demolishes the factually erroneous biographies of Moses by Manetho, Chaeremon, and Lysimachus, turns his critic's scandalous anecdotes against him and the Greeks, and offers historical proof that Moses was the eldest of philosophers, the one from whom later thinkers derive their systems. Even the Egyptians, he pauses to observe, regard "the man as divine and wish to claim him as one of themselves."[5]

The testimony of pagan and Jew was gladly accepted by Clement of Alexandria, who abridges Philo's *Life of Moses,* embellishing it with a lengthy hexameter extract from *Exodus,* a play by the Hebrew tragic poet Ezekiel.[6] Origen, admitting that Moses may have heard "a somewhat ancient doctrine and transmitted it to the Hebrews,"[7] insists that he lived before Inachus and was acknowledged by the Egyptians to be "a man of great antiquity."[8] Celsus had objected to the allegories read by Christians into the Pentateuch, so Origen informs him that Moses "carefully introduces in every part of his five books language of two-fold meaning."[9] The venerability of Moses is substantiated by Eusebius, who turns to the history of Artabanus for true biography. Moses was

---

[3] Strabo, *Geography* XVI. 35–39.
[4] Philo, *Vita Mosis* I. 21–24.
[5] Josephus, *Contra Apion* I. 279–86, 290–300, 309–11.
[6] Clement, *Stromateis* I. 23.
[7] Origen, *Contra Celsum, PG* XI, 696–97.
[8] *Ibid.,* col. 1040–41; see Cyrillus of Alexandria, *Contra Julianum, PG* LXXVI, 524–25.
[9] Origen, *PG* XI, 692–93.

adopted, not found in the bulrushes, by Merris, wife of Chenepres—Epiphanius has it as Thermuthin, daughter of Amenophis[10]—who named him Mousos, or Musaeus as the Greeks render the name. Mousos not only instructed Orpheus but was the inventor of many things. "For these reasons Moses was beloved of the multitudes, and having discovered the hieroglyphics he was deemed worthy of divine honors and given the name of Hermes." As Eusebius notices, Moses' linguistic improvisation was also reported by the historian Eupolemus.[11]

The evolution of the alphabet was a matter of national contention in antiquity;[12] but the Renaissance, with some dissent, was inclined to agree that Hebrew, the pure language of the Hereafter, was not only the mother of tongues but also the first to be written.[13] Although many men of the sixteenth and seventeenth centuries could read Hebrew, no one could fathom its Egyptian daughter set down in symbolic pictures. Nevertheless, the obelisks brought to Imperial Rome had always claimed the attention of the curious. Since they could not be deciphered these needles of stone were assumed to be documents deep in secret. Diodorus Siculus, who lived in the first century before Christ, informed his contemporaries and later on men of the Renaissance that Egypt had a sacred as well as a demotic script.[14] This script did not express concepts by joined syllables "but by means of the significance of the objects which had been copied out and by the figurative meaning which practice had

---

[10] Epiphanius, *Adversus haeres, PG* XLII, 735.

[11] Eusebius, *Evangelicae praeparationis libri XV*, 431; see also 87–95, 419–20. Joseph, Moses' great precursor in Egypt, is also the subject of inquiry. Firmicus Maternus (*De errore* XIII, 1–3) relates that temples were erected to him so that the children of Egypt could be taught distributive justice; to make his worship more effective, he was given a name, which "being dead he could not prevent." The name was Serapis and was etymologically based on his descent from Sara or "Sarras pais." Isidore of Seville (*Etymologiae* VIII, 84–86) thinks that Apis was a King of Argos, who died in Egypt and whose remains were placed in a "soros"; hence "Soros apis." Augustine goes into this problem in *De civitate,* XVIII. 5. In the *Historia Ecclesiastica PL* XXI, 532, Rufinus, relating the destruction of the Temple of Serapis at Alexandria, ascribes its origin to the worship of Joseph.

[12] Various heroes and heroines were honored as inventors of the alphabet. Plato (*Phaedrus* 274e–275b) says that Theuth, an old god of Naucratis to whom the ibis is sacred, discovered letters; Tertullian (*De coronis, PL* II, 87) attributes them to Mercury; Pliny the Elder mentions Mercury as a surmise of Aulus Gellius, and adds Menos of Egypt on the authority of Anticlides (*Naturalis historia* VII. 56). Hyginus (*Fabulae* 277), Quintilian (*Institutio oratoria* III. 7, 8), and Cassiodorus (*Variae* VIII. 12) endorse the claims of Mercury, who got the idea of letters from watching flying flocks of cranes over the river Strymon. Augustine (*De civitate* XVIII. 37) writes, "Moses learned Egyptian wisdom . . . yet not even the wisdom of the Egyptians could be antecedent in time to the wisdom of our prophets, because even Abraham was a prophet, and what wisdom could there be in Egypt before Isis had given them letters."

[13] D. C. Allen, "Some Theories of the Growth and Origin of Languages in Milton's Age," *PQ* XXVIII (1949), 5–16.

[14] Diodorus, *Bibliotheca* II. 81.

impressed on the memory." To men of the Nile a hawk stood for "swiftness" and a crocodile for "evil"[15] Tacitus adds to this information by describing the Egyptians as preserving the most ancient of human records in "thought symbols" represented by animal figures;[16] Apuleius' romantic hero, visiting in Alexandria, is shown a priestly book written in unknown letters, "wholly strange and impossible to be read by the profane."[17]

What Greek and Latin historians had to say about the hieroglyphics sacred to the Egyptians was given emphasis when the battered old general Ammianus Marcellinus described the obelisks covered with birds and beasts, "some not of this world," as preserving the memory of Egyptian achievements and registering the vows of kings, "either promised or performed." Individual characters, he stated, stood for nouns, verbs, and whole phrases. "By a vulture they represent the word *nature,* because no males are found among these birds . . . and under the figure of a honey-making bee they indicate a king because he should have both sweetness and acuteness." Ammianus describes the obelisk brought to Rome by Constantine, which the Renaissance could see in the forecourt of St. Peter's; but even more teasingly he supplies a Greek translation made by Hermaphion of the hieroglyphics on another obelisk which had been moved and placed before the Lateran in 1586 by Pope Sixtus V.[18] These pagan elucidations of the symbolic inscriptions of the Egyptians stirred the imagination of scholars of the sixteenth and seventeenth centuries, but the most impressive explanation, and one closer to truth, was furnished by Clement of Alexandria.

In the sixth book of the *Stromateis,*[19] Clement describes a hieratic procession in which hieroglyphic symbols are ceremoniously displayed, but his reader is prepared to watch this parade by a description of the modes of Egyptian symbolism in Book Four, the longest essay on the sacred writing known before the rediscovery of the *Hieroglyphica* of Hor Apollo. "The truly holy Word," Clement writes, was *hidden* to the Egyptians, *veiled* to the Hebrews. "Only the consecrated were allowed access."

Now those instructed among the Egyptians first learned that form of Egyptian letters which they called Epistolographic; second the Hieratic practised by sacred

---

[15] *Ibid.,* III. 4; see also Herodotus, *History* II. 36.
[16] Tacitus, *Annales* XI. 14.
[17] Ovid, *Metamorphoseon* XI. 22.
[18] Ammianus, *Rerum gestarum libri* XVII. 4. 6–11, 14–23.
[19] Clement, *Stromateis* VI. 4. 35.

scribes; and lastly, the Hieroglyphic, of which one kind is literal by the first elements and the other symbolic.

Clement supplies examples to illustrate his classifications. The sun is represented by a circle, a hawk, or a beetle; the moon by an ibis; the other planets by bodies of serpents. The lion means "strength"; the ox, "husbandry" and "food"; the horse, "fortitude" and "confidence"; and the sphinx, "strength" plus "intelligence." These symbols could be formed into expressions like one in the temple Pylon at Diospolis, where a boy, an old man, a hawk, a fish, and a crocodile could be translated as "Oh, you who are born and die, God hates impudence." The conclusion is apparent.

All then, in a word, who have spoken of divine things, both Barbarian and Greeks, have veiled the first principle of things, and delivered the truth in enigmas, and symbols, and allegories, and metaphors, and similar tropes.[20]

But the probable Christian tone half-heard in Clement's excursus is made more clear when Rufinus subsequently discovered a cross in the alphabet of Egyptian symbols and learned that it meant "vita ventura."[21]

Knowledge of the history and religious philosophies of Egypt, which were undoubtedly extensively concealed in the unfathomable hieroglyphic, increased as men of the Renaissance read the allusive passages in Herodotus, Pliny, Lucian, Plutarch, Diodorus Siculus, and Strabo and picked up crumbs of information from Latin men of letters like Tibullus, Propertius, Ovid, Claudian, and Apuleius. Raleigh's chapters on the history, religion, and customs of Egypt, drawn partly from Annio, whom he knew to be spurious,[22] or second-handedly from Cedranus or Glycas, who were quoted in the *Chronicles* of Krentzheim, Angelocrator, Buenting, and others, seem practically fictional when compared with the early eighteenth-century *Origines mundi* of Nicolas Gurtler or the fantastically learned *Aegyptiarum originum et temporum antiquissimorum investigatio* of Jacques Voorbroek. But Raleigh lived far away from Rome, the true center of the new excitement.

In October, 1587, the obelisk which had been restored and placed before the Vatican was crowned with a cross, and the occasion was marked with a great religious ceremony and the reading of poems by forty-five poets.[23] The elegant Latin poet Pietro Angelio Barga not only

---

[20] *Ibid.,* V. 4. 19–21, 7. 41–42.

[21] Rufinus, *Historia, PL* XXI, 537.

[22] Raleigh, *History* II, 59–60.

[23] For a description of the occasion see P. Galesini, *Ordo dedicationis obelisci quem S.D.N. Sixtus V. Pont. Max. in foro Vaticano ad limina Apostolorum erexit* (Rome, 1586);

composed verse for the event but also wrote a *Commentarius de obelisco* in which he talked about the making and makers of obelisks, their religious significance, and, drawing on pagan and Christian sources, the rationale of the hieroglyphics.[24] Michele Mercati seconded Barga's account by publishing in 1589 in Rome a solid study of Egyptian learning and religion, the *De gli obelischi di Roma*. He declared that God had imparted both language and writing to Adam, who transmitted this skill to his descendants. Writing was, consequently, not invented by Moses because Abraham certainly knew how to write, and Mercati had seen Mexican inscriptions in the Vatican Library as inscrutable as Egyptian hierograms. If Moses was instructed in Egyptian lore, Egypt must have had written records before the Hebrews came into the land. Mercati draws heavily on Clement's description of Egyptian symbolism, which he sees revived in his own day by the *Emblemata* of Signor Alciati; but his ultimate authority is "Horo Egitto," whose book had been the cherished lexicon of Renaissance symbolists for more than eighty years.[25]

The *Hieroglyphica* of Hor Apollo, a supposed priest of Egypt, was found in 1419 in the Levant by an associate of the antiquary Niccolo Niccoli. Copies of this manuscript had a wide circulation among the learned. In his annotation on *Ennead* V. 8, where the hieroglyphs are explained, Ficino reveals he has read "Horus'" book which supports Plotinus' conjecture that hieroglyphs were pictures of the Platonic ideas. This curious dictionary of symbols was printed in Greek in 1505, and there were at least thirty reprintings with Latin, French, Italian, and German parallel versions before the century ended. Six further editions, each more scholarly than its predecessor, were finished before the mid-seventeenth century. The vogue of this work was certainly promoted by the bronze enameled tablet adorned with hieroglyphs and embossed silver figures that Cardinal Bembo purchased from the locksmith who secured it during the sack of Rome in 1525. The relic known as the Bembine Table was subjected to several attempts at an interpretation before it was stolen again in 1630.[26] But the *Hieroglyphica* of Hor

---

the poems of the celebrating poets were gathered in *Carmina a variis auctoribus in obeliscum conscripta* (Rome, 1586). The obelisks described in prose and illustrated by woodcuts were a regular feature of the guides to Rome and of the various historical descriptions of the city so regularly written, revised, and reprinted throughout the Renaissance. In the *L'Antichita di Roma* (Rome, 1588), pp. 137–43, of Andrea Fulvio one can find an account of them and of the ceremony attending the consecration of the Vatican obelisk.

[24] Barga, *op. cit.* (Rome, 1586), p. 27.

[25] Mercati, *op. cit.*, pp. 86–130.

[26] Montfaucon, *L'Antiquité expliquée* (Paris, 1719–24), II, 331–42.

Apollo was a principle stimulus to the renewed interest of the Renaissance in symbol and allegory.

The *Hieroglyphica* not only reinforced the belief that hidden meanings or lost secrets and histories were to be found in the records of the ancients but also presented the Christian world with an Egyptian Book of Creatures. The hexameral commentaries of the Church from the time of St. Basil and St. Ambrose had expounded the inner significances of each creature as it emerged from God's mind during the divine week. St. Augustine, in spite of his half-affection for the literal, had supported this symbolic methodology even for sacramental use.

Moreover, if for the administration of the sacraments, certain symbolisms are drawn, not only from the heavens and stars, but also from all the lower creation, the intention is to provide the doctrine of Salvation with a sort of eloquence, adapted to raise the affections of those to whom it is presented, from the visible to the invisible, from the corporeal to the spiritual, from the spiritual to the eternal.[27]

Not too long after St. Augustine voiced this opinion, St. Eucherius, following the advice offered by Cassian in his collation with Nestros,[28] produced in his *Liber Formularum Spiritualis* a work that is the ancestor of the symbolic books of creatures written by St. Isidore, Bishop Marbode, St. Hildegard, Rabanus Maurus, Vincent of Beauvais, all medieval bestiaries and lapidaries, and books of a similar nature that flooded the Renaissance.

St. Eucherius' *Liber*, which has been described as "a dull and desultory dictionary of metaphors," is composed of eleven fascicles providing the Christian meanings of divine names, the members of God's body, heavenly creatures, earthly creatures, animals, appellatives, human organs, words, Jerusalem, and numbers. By scanning its registers a reader learned that the eagle represents a saint; the ostrich, a heretic; the raven, a demon; the pelican, Christ; and the dove, the Holy Spirit. The cock, master of doorways, is a holy preacher, "who among the shadows of this our life looks toward the coming light."[29] Eucherius always shored up his analogues with Bible references, but because of

[27] Augustine, *Epistolae, PL* XXXIII, 210.

[28] Cassianus, *Collationes, PL* XLIX, 962–63. Cassian actually lays down the principles of the later four-fold interpretation. Theoretical knowledge can be divided into historical and spiritual knowledge; and spiritual knowledge can be subdivided into tropology, allegory, and anagogics. Historical knowledge concerns things completed and visible; allegorical is predictive; anagogical relates to the secret mysteries of Heaven; and tropological is moral. St. Eucherius, who made a digest of some of Cassian's writings, mentions these divisions but does not follow them in his own speculations.

[29] Eucherius, *Liber formularum, PL* L, 729.

long usage he was able to define an emblematic creature as a lexicographer defines a word. For Augustine, Christ's exhortation, "Come with me and I shall make you fishers of men," implied that the world was a wild ocean swarming with sinful fish. Somewhat earlier, St. Martin of Tours, pausing by a river bank and watching birds diving for fish, observed to his disciples that the birds were demons "lying in wait for the feckless, taking the ignorant, and devouring them."[30] As a result of this custom of comparisons, Eucherius can be dogmatic in his equation: "Fish are sinners." Christian metaphors of this nature, known to the Renaissance through the good offices of the Middle Ages, were clearly at home in ancient Egypt, thanks to Moses, instructor or instructed.

The *Hieroglyphica* of Hor Apollo, rendered into Greek by Philip, demonstrated in its 189 entries the similarity between pagan and Christian interpretation of the book of creatures. Some of the paragraphs give the sign and its hidden meaning. A pig symbolizes a pernicious man; a weasel represents a weak man; a swan stands for a musical old man. In most cases, the philosophical undermeaning is supplied with its natural symbol: death is an owl; love, a snare; work, a bull's horn; a king, a serpent; and a great king, a snake biting its tail. Few of these equivalents could be found in the Bible by interpreters who maintained that all material symbols should have scriptural authority, but some of them had a Christian coloration. In the first century Clement of Rome pointed to the phoenix as the sign of the resurrection of Christ and, hence, of human immortality. This first of Christian symbols was accepted by later allegorists, who saw a connection between it and the fact that the Virgin, during the Flight into Egypt, took refuge in the Temple of Heliopolis.[31] The Egyptians, according to the *Hieroglyphica,* used the phoenix in their inscriptions to represent the soul and the eternal renewal and restoration of all things.[32] Be this as it may, the influence of Hor Apollo

[30] Sulpitius, *Epistolae, PL* XX, 181–82.

[31] Clement of Rome, *Epistola I ad Corinthios, PG* I, 260–65. By the twelfth century this belief is firmly encysted in the minds of men; hence, Hugo of St. Victor, a master of symbolism, can write: "The whole visible world is almost a book written by the hand of God; it was created by Divine Power and each single creature is almost a letter not invented by human agreement but established by the Divine Will for the manifestation of the invisible wisdom of God. If an illiterate looks on an open book, he sees the forms of the letters, but he cannot read. The man who sees only the outsides of the creatures and does not realize what there is of God in them is as dull as an animal; he knows the outside but not the inner meaning. The spiritually gifted man, who understands all things, considers the beauty of the outward form, but also perceives in the inner nature the marvellous wisdom of God." *Didascalion, PL* CLXXVI, 814.

[32] I have followed the edition of Francesco Sbordone, *Hieroglyphica*, Naples, 1940. There is an excellent English version by George Boas in the *Bollingen Series,* XXII, New York, 1950.

on Renaissance art and letters was both immediate and intense.[33] It established the vogue of the emblem-book and is one of the stimulating forces behind the universal passion of these centuries for symbolic representations. The obsession with these arcane devices is found on all sides and is institutionally represented by the establishment of the Academy of Inscriptions, originally founded to supply by its researches learned ornamentations for the pleasure of the Sun King and his court.

One of the immediate effects of the enormous popularity of the *Hieroglyphica* of Hor Apollo was the compiling of symbolic lexicons, which attempted to bring together a world of interpreted representations. The first dictionary of this nature was the *Hieroglyphica sive de sacris Aegyptiorum literis commentarii* of Piero Valeriano Bolzani, classical scholar, local historian, and defender of priestly beards, the virtues of lightning, and the discomforts of the literary life. Valeriano's compendium, which brought together the hidden meanings of almost all things beneath the sun, was collected from Egyptian, Greek, Roman, and Christian origins. Though it was the work of a lifetime, it was more distinguished by its scholarship than by its good sense. It was, however, immediately popular, and there were at least seven editions—the latter ones fattened by editorial annexes—before the final printing of 1678. The Latin of the original version was turned into French in 1576 and 1615 and into Italian in 1602. So that the original folio of almost one thousand pages could be always consulted by eager mystagogues, it was reduced to nearly pocket size by Heinrich Schwalenberg in 1592 and later reprinted in this form.

In his dedication to Cosimo de'Medici, Valeriano describes his joyous labors in collecting and discovering these mysterious, lost meanings from the writings of Egyptians, Greeks, Romans, and barbarians. He remembers his dinner conversations with Cardinal Bembo about the obelisks at Rome and the current movement among Roman leaders to rescue from the lime-burners' kilns ancient monuments no more worthy to be destroyed than the statues of Michelangelo Buonarroti in St. Lorenzo. He imagines a connection between the form of writing used by

---

[33] Besides Boas' preface one can consult Karl Giehlow, "Die Hieroglyphenkunde des Humanismus in der Allegorie der Renaissance," *Jahrbuch der Kunsthistorischen Sammlungen der allerhochsten Kaiserhauses,* XXXII (1915), 1, 1–218, which points out the influence of this work until the publication of Valeriano's *Hieroglyphica,* and L. Volkmann, *Bilderschriften der Renaissance* (Leipzig, 1923). See also D. C. Allen, "Ben Jonson and the Hieroglyphics," *PQ,* XVIII (1939), 290–300; K. Dannenfeldt, "Egypt and Egyptian Antiquities in the Renaissance," *Studies in the Renaissance,* VI (1959), 7–27; and D. C. Allen, "The Predecessors of Champollion," *Proceedings of the American Philosophical Society,* CIV (1960), 1, 527–47.

the Egyptians and that employed by antediluvian men, who inscribed figures of animals or other things on columns of brick or stone in order to preserve the occult wisdom of poets, philosophers, and historians. The fame of the wise Egyptian priests gained them clients like Pythagoras, Plato, and Moses; oddly enough, the *modus interpretationis* of the hieroglyphics in which the hierarchs concealed their learning was not unlike that of the allegories used by Moses, David, the Prophets, and Christ. The same type of metaphoric expression was also employed by the Apostles, lest God's word be scattered before dogs and hogs. "Antiquity concealed science both human and divine, wrapped as it were in things which the most skillful among them used by custom in enigmas." Valeriano admits to no blame for attempting to decipher the messages of the past; he regrets only that his interpretive learning is inferior to that of his predecessors, Poliziano, Crinito,[34] and Beroaldo.[35]

This dedicatory letter to the great Duke of Florence is succeeded by eighty-three sections in which the significances of animals, birds, fish, insects, plants, metals, types of men, parts of the human body, human creations or ceremonies, and other phenomena are mystically read with authoritative quotations and footnotes. More than two hundred authors, ranging alphabetically from "Absinis rhetor" to Zoroaster and chronologically from the Bible to Jacob Ziegler, are wrung out to provide these references and allusions. Each specific section is individually dedicated in a head note proclaiming the special secret virtues of the creature under discussion. The lion begins the book, and a letter tells Cosimo that no one has written about this animal better than the priests of Egypt. "Few men have been more learned in the secrets of nature than they and have more diligently explored the essential being of creatures." Cosimo is reminded that lions or lion heads are frequently seen in antique monuments or in hieroglyphics and that lions are the symbols of magnanimity, bodily and mental power, the sun and the earth, reverence for parents, courage, petulance, lust in love, eloquence, vigilance, domination, clemency, vengeance, the flooding of the Nile, and "many other things." Homer, Lucretius, Aristophanes, Pausanias, Eucherius, Dio Chrysostom, Callimachus, Euripides, as well as the reverses of coins of the Antonines and Trajan, are among the documents providing the authority.

[34] Poliziano's interest in symbolism has been recognized in the chapter on Homer. Crinito, author of the popular *De honesta disciplina,* inserted several papers on symbolism in this gathering and an essay on Egyptian hieroglyphics that might be the first on this subject.

[35] Filippo Beroaldo, an associate of Poliziano, wrote the frequently reprinted *Symbola Pythagorae moraliter explicata.*

By swallowing Hor Apollo and every discernible interpretive metaphor or symbolic implication in hundreds of Greek and Latin texts, Valeriano fills his volume with a menagerie of hieroglyphic creatures from land, sea, and air.[36] The second part of the *Hieroglyphica* begins with an address to J. J. Fugger, "maecenas of the learned, comparable only to Cosimo of Florence." The German merchant prince is rewarded with flattery for gathering a fantastic library and subsidizing the studies of men like Jerome Wolf. Valeriano also gives him "an explanation of what the priests of Egypt meant by their hieroglyphics of the human body . . . so that he will know they were not just superstitiously given to the veneration of animals. . . . Man also furnished them with . . . hieroglyphics and sacred letters since each part of him is mysterious." Hence, after Fugger knew that one head meant "prince," "divinity," "providence," "posterity," and "Rome," he was provided with the Valerianian interpretation of two heads, three heads, four heads, five heads, and seven heads. Valeriano then descends slowly but symbolically down the body to the fingers and to the things the fingers make and carry. The hieroglyphic dictionary ends in a kitchen garden, where a final cabbage is turned, on the counsel of Pliny, Cicero, Beritius, Varro, and Nestor, into an arcane sign standing for "confused pleasure." But Valeriano had immediate imitators.

The *Hieroglyphica* of Celio Agostini Curio, editor of Bembo and historian of the Saracens, was appended to the 1567 edition of Valeriano. It is a modest collection of about ninety hieroglyphs missed by Valeriano, who had seen the hidden meaning in Isis, but overlooked Eneph, plumed god of Egypt, Pan, Osiris, Pluto, Silenus, Vulcan, Hercules, Prometheus, Mercury, Argus, Endymion, Fidus, Hecate, Diana,

---

[36] Some of the letters in Valeriano's alphabet, besides the lion, are the elephant, rhinocerus, bull, horse, dog, ape, monkey, deer, ant, beetle, hedgehog, pig, goat, sheep, ram, wolf, hyena, lynx, bear, panther, tiger, ass, mule, camel, rabbit, weasel, beaver, fox, mouse, cat, serpent, basilisk, viper, salamander, dipsas, hydra, stork, crane, ibis, vulture, eagle, phoenix, pelican, owl, crow, sparrow, pigeon, dove, swallow, goose, peacock, partridge, nightingale, ostrich, wasp, bee, dolphin, crocodile, tortoise. The generic category of fish, for example, provides the following meanings: profane and abominable, flesh and spirit, purification, loss and gain, silence, hate, divine versus human, carnal desires, sound friendship, an uncultured man, a cookshop, souls, innocence, demons, pagans, ignorance, waters, the Goddesses Facelitis and Atargatis. An obelisk before the temple of Saïs, or Minerva, displayed an infant, an old man, a falcon, a fish, and a hippopotamus all in descending order. The translation is, given Valeriano's lexicon as guide, simple, for here is "demonstrated the fragility of human life, which turns from childhood into age and again into childhood. The falcon is God and, consequently, love and vital life, divine in us. The fish is hate and death together, for the sea has branded them with ruin and destruction. The hippopotamus that kills its father to enjoy its mother is impudent violence. This is the *concordia discors* of the bodily complexions, so that when disuniting, one displants and destroys the other with violence and death follows" (Valeriano, *Hieroglyphica*, p. 219v).

Astrea, and other gods and goddesses, besides girls with "their hair standing upright" and girls with "shaved heads." Books of this sort did not satisfy the hieroglyphic hunger of the century but stimulated it. J. Van Gorp, an odd scholar of Holland, proposed in his *Hieroglyphica libri XVI*, published in 1580, that Dutch was the matrix of all languages and that hieroglyphics were the alphabet of all primitive societies. The professional heralds were delighted by the discovery of a new form of metaphorical thinking, one which put a certain amount of backbone in their habitual tasks. One of them, Pierre L'Anglois, happily expanded the hint of the Egyptologists in his 1584 *Discours des Hiéroglyphes Aegyptiens,* which took the whole art of symbolic representation back to the Pharaohs. Stimulated by the attempt of Pignoria to translate the so-called Bembine Tables, Michael Maier wrote an *Arcana arcanissima; hoc est hieroglyphica Aegyptio-Graeca* in 1614 in which he conjectured that these signs, incorporating both ethical and physical lore occultly expressed, were invented at the moment when the world of civility was undergoing catastrophic religious and political change. Those entrusted with the preservation of the esoteric wisdom of their age, he imagined, were probably threatened with death if they revealed it; hence, they wrote it down in symbols that only a few could read.[37] These students of the hieroglyphics reflect the symbolic trend of the later sixteenth century, which made it almost impossible to discuss the things of this world without alluding to their symbolic meanings. Authors of books like Simone Maioli's *Dies caniculares* or the series of encyclopedic natural histories which began to appear in 1602 from the editorial rooms of Ulisse Aldrovandi would not think of omitting the symbolic values of the creatures any more than an heraldic expert like Reusner or Typoest avoided the evidence of ancient Egypt or Greece in recording and expounding their truly medieval art. But one of the largest accumulations of hieroglyphic material after Valeriano's primary effort was the *Electorum symbolorum et parabolum historicarum syntagma* of Nicolaus Caussin, which appeared in Paris in 1618.

Father Caussin's publication contained the texts of Hor Apollo, a summary of Valeriano's definitions, the hieroglyphic documents from Diodorus Siculus and Clement of Alexandria, the symbolic *Physiologus* then ascribed to Epiphanius, the *Aenigmata* of Symposius, and about one thousand new symbolic equivalents to be added to those found in Valeriano's *Hieroglyphica*. At the turn of the century the witty Tommaso

---

[37] Maier, *Arcana* (Oppenheim, 1614), p. 29.

Garzoni in his treatise on the professions of the world had given a chapter to the "professors of Hieroglyphics,"[38] an open indication that the passion for this matter was by no means limited to a minority of scholars. Caussin's original contribution to this book carries the modest title of *Polyhistor Symbolicus* and brings together protases and substantiating apodoses from the world of Greek and Latin literature. Following this conventional rhetorical practice, the hieroglyphical meaning of the universe and its parts flows from page to page, encompassing the ancient gods, men both good and bad, human rites, birds, animals, fish, serpents, insects, plants, minerals, and manufactured items. According to Aelian the sick peacock, symbolic bird of pride, feeds on the healing flax root, thus lending meaning to the former wearing of linen by penitents. Just as linen root cures the peacock, so penitence brings health to the proud. One example of this nature hardly suggests the overwhelming conviction of Caussin's torrent of quotation and commentary.

In addition to practical symbolic equations Caussin put together some prefatory essays on the hieroglyphic art. He admits that Moses was instructed by the Egyptians in mathematics and music but assumes he could write because Abraham, who learned astrology in Egypt, wrote; in fact, writing was a gift of the Divine Light to Adam, and hieroglyphics, often cabalistic in nature, are found even in septentrional regions. After running through the usual classical accounts of the broken coin or the tessera, Caussin defines a symbol as a sign somewhat obscure but figuratively significant because of the natural relation of its terms. The term is for him the generic cover for enigmas, emblems, parables, and hieroglyphs, but he understands the last to be artificially agreed upon signs. Caussin's attempt to rival or complete Valeriano was followed by Marcus Wendelin's emblematic rifling of 385 authors and by similar symbolic compendia compiled by Jacques Masen and Filippo Picinelli; but these "professors of hieroglyphs"[39] were children, hardly knee-high to Athanasius Kircher, whose assault on the translation of the hieroglyphic inscriptions of Egypt began in 1636.

[38] Garzoni, *La piazza universale di tutte le professioni del mondo* (Venice, 1601), pp. 243–45.

[39] Wendelin called his book, printed at Frankfort in 1623, *Admiranda Nili, commentatione philologica, geographica, historica, physica, et hieroglyphica ex 318 autoribus.* Masen's *Speculum imaginum veritatis occultae* (Cologne, 1664), contains classifications and explanations of various categories of symbols with numerous examples in each group. Picinelli's *Mondo simbolico* (Milan, 1635), is drawn mainly from emblem-writers, who are each carefully acknowledged. The compiler bows to the great symbolographers like Govio, the Tassos, and others and writes one of the fullest theoretical accounts of emblems. He proceeds, after the manner of Valeriano and Caussin, to provide a symbolic dictionary, beginning at the top of the chain of being and descending link by link.

II

Kircher, whose studies of Egyptian history, religion, and culture and whose translations of all known Egyptian documents appeared in magnificently printed and illustrated folios during the middle years of the seventeenth century, had a modest predecessor in Lorenzo Pignoria, who published the *Bembine Tabula* in 1605. This impressive objet d'art, then in the museum of the Duke of Mantua, had been copied in a series of copperplates by Vico of Parma and published in Venice in 1600. The plates had caused some stir, and Marcus Velser, discoverer and publisher of part of the celebrated *Peutinger Tabula,* had urged Pignoria to reprint the Vico plates with an explanatory text. Pignoria was a poet in both Latin and Italian. He would later annotate Alciati's *Emblemata* and Tasso's *Jerusalem Delivered* as well as write the first study of the Magna Mater, letters on symbolism, and an account of the ancient murals at Rome. The *Vetustissimae tabulae aenae sacris Aegyptiorum simulachris coelatae accurata explicatio, in qua antiquissimarum superstitionum origines . . . enarrantur,* which appeared in Venice in 1605, was his first work and it won him immediate acclaim.[40] Pignoria, who would eventually own a widely admired museum, had already learned the value of antiquarian objects as illustrative and explanatory documents; hence, the services of the artist brothers Johannes Theodore and Johannes Israel de Bry were engaged to furnish his text with helpful engravings.

Pignoria did not share the symbolic passion of Valeriano, Caussin, or Kircher; his method in examining the *tabula,* he stated, would be *"non allegorikos,"* meaning by this expression that he would write no interpretations which could not be supported by classical texts, carved gems, coins, statuettes, and inscriptions. There is no twisting of evidence, no unsustained and uncritical use of the interpreter's bare intuition. Although he cannot at times separate the representation from the hieroglyphic inscription, Pignoria managed to identify most of the Egyptian gods and goddesses on the *tabula,* supply their histories or accounts of their cults, and indicate their symbolic creatures or signs. He has no farfetched theories about the philosophical meaning of the *tabula,* but his learned moderation, rare in his time, was not adopted by other "professors of hieroglyphics."

---

[40] The Frankfort edition of 1609 was titled *Characteres Aegyptii,* and the Amsterdam reprint of 1669, which included other writings of Pignoria and an account of his life by J. P. Tomasini, was named, probably thanks to Kircher, *Mensa Isiaca.*

The modest approach of Pignoria can be fully appreciated by turning to the first syntagma of the third folio of Athanasius Kircher's *Oedipus Aegyptiacus,* where the greatest of seventeenth-century polymaths puts his imagination and immense erudition to work on the *Bembine Tabula.* By 1652, when this vast study was available, the original *tabula* had disappeared from the Duke of Mantua's museum and Kircher had only the Vico copper plates to read. He assumes that the *tabula* is anterior to the time of Cambyses and contain the summation of Egyptian theology as set down by the "hieromantics." Like Pignoria, Kircher agrees that it is a *mensa sacra,* but unlike Pignoria, he does not conclude with this fairly sound idea. The *Mensa Isiaca,* as Kircher names this *tabula,* can be divided into suites of triads based on the central Egyptian theosophy of Father, Power, and Mind, or faith, truth, and love, with their presiding daemons. Kircher, by this time long practised in reading hieroglyphs, searches out in the course of a hundred pages the various trinities—those of Hecate, Serapis, Osiris, Horus, or East, Fontana, or West, Pandochea, or North, and Thaustica, or South—that spring from the Egyptian theories of the nature of the *Anima Mundi.* He is able by this means to discourse on each square inch in the *tabula* as he follows the chain of ideas from God down to matter. But this is Kircher in mid-course and at the peak of his renown; naturally there was a beginning.

Kircher took the whole world of knowledge as his province, but his interest in the hieroglyphics and in matters Egyptian was stimulated by his youthful study of the Coptic language, a tongue hardly known in Europe until Fabri de Peiresc, the generous French patron of scholars, became interested in that language and promoted its understanding by securing manuscripts from Egypt and subsidizing their study. He gathered from North Africa Coptic versions of the Evangels, the Psalms, and the liturgies of Basil, Gregory, and Cyril;[41] when another shipment of similar manuscripts was captured by pirates, he negotiated directly with the Pasha of Tripoli for its recovery.[42] In 1650 he employed Claude Saumaise, Milton's Salmasius, to study the language;[43] shortly after this date, Pietro della Valle bought a Coptic-Arabic dictionary manuscript, invaluable to a student of this unknown language, and brought it to Rome. But Peiresc could not obtain the use of this dictionary for Saumaise, who was both Protestant and anti-Roman, so it was turned over

[41] P. Gassendi, *De vita Peireskii* (Hague, 1655), pp. 152, 186.
[42] *Ibid.,* pp. 205–6: see C. Saumaise, *Epistolae* (Leyden, 1656), p. 176.
[43] Saumaise, *op. cit.,* pp. 132–33, 156–62.

to Father Kircher, who was twenty-eight and at that time ignorant of this language.[44] The Pietro della Valle manuscript became the basis of Kircher's first important publication, the *Prodromus Coptus* of 1636.

The *Prodromus Coptus* is a sometimes incorrect but not unimportant grammar and vocabulary preceded by a preface which is five times larger than the book it introduces. In this introduction Kircher states his belief that Coptic is a degenerate form of Egyptian demotic and announces his program as an intending Egyptologist. He proposes to reconstruct the earliest form of Coptic, compile a thesaurus of the language, and translate all the Roman obelisks. He must first demonstrate that old Coptic and Egyptian demotic—the hieratic could not degenerate—are the same. The proof is plain enough. Coptus, a city known to Pliny, Pausanias, and Plutarch but now "hardly found in ruins," gave its name to the language. At first its inhabitants—it was second only to Thebes—worshiped animals as the Egyptians did, but they were converted to Christianity. As a consequence of this change of religion, the original Egyptian language, corrupted elsewhere by the inroads of Islam, was immaculately preserved in Coptic monasteries, which became centers of culture and the originating places of Christian missions to India and China.[45]

Kircher's linguistic demonstration of his thesis is based on the uniqueness of Coptic, which he proves at great length by showing that words shared by other oriental languages are not to be found in it. On the other hand, the one authentic old Egyptian phrase, the "Tsaphnath phanehh" of Genesis 41:45 is clearly the same as Coptic "Psontom phanech." Admitting that he is not yet perfect in the old language of Egypt, Kircher reveals that he is already studying Egyptian hieroglyphic inscriptions about which he has a definite theory. He regards these inscriptions "not so much as writing but rather as symbolic representations of sublime theosophy expressed through signs universally intelligible." With this announcement Kircher falls into line with the symbolistic conviction of the seventeenth century, that mystery inhabits anything that is ancient and that a learned interpreter can explain, or at least half-explain, whatever lies beneath the surface of things. So that men of his age could be prepared for his later efforts, Kircher provides them with "a specimen of hieroglyphic interpretation."

[44] Kircher, *Prodromus Coptus sive Aegyptiacus* (Rome, 1636), p. 5. Saumaise, whose writings after 1630 indicate that he had made progress in learning Coptic, lost out to Kircher with a grace that was unusual for him: see Saumaise, *op. cit.*, pp. 177–78.

[45] Kircher, *Prodromus*, pp. 7–16.

Figure 1

In order to have an available text Kircher selects a figure from the published *Bembine Tabula* (Fig. 1), which Pignoria had temperately described as "a scarab with the head of Osiris." This man-bug, accompanied by a winged sphere, has a crescent enclosing a *t* on its head, an epaulet of concentric circles on its shoulder, and an inscribed tablet in its foreclaws. Studying this figure, Kircher finds six "universally intelligential" symbols: the scarab, or "the world"; the head of Horus, or "the reason or sun governing the world"; the concentric circles, or "the superior heavens"; the crescent, or "the moon of Isis"; the cross within the crescent, or "flux and reflux, generation and corruption, the mixing of elements, the disunited universe held together by love." Love is also expressed by the inscription on the tablet in the scarab's claws, which Kircher reads as the Coptic word "philo." The supreme symbol in the motif is the winged sphere, which as sphere symbolizes the universe but as a winged sphere "the union through 'philo' of the upper and lower worlds." Since the Copts were Christian, it is not difficult for Kircher to assume that ancient Egyptians had some awareness of the Christian revelation; hence, he associates the beetle with Christ, the winged sphere with God, and the "philo" with the Holy Spirit. The transliteration established, the door to Egyptian metaphysics opens. The winged sphere is the *Anima Mundi* or "Hemephta," the supreme intellect. The body of the scarab is "the world machine," or Osiris. The concentric circles are "the celestial spheres" and "the heavenly genii." The head remains the sun, or Horus, and the crescent, the moon, or Isis. The cross and "philo" are the elements, the higher world joined to the lower by love or by the daemons who unwind the chain of being. This foretaste of Kircher's allegorical approach must have whetted the appetite of Renaissance men intrigued by symbolic analysis.[46]

Kircher's second contribution to the art of Egyptology was the *Lingua Aegyptiaca* published in 1644, which is della Valle's Coptic-Arabic lexicon with an appendix of ten essays on Egyptian subjects.[47] This work, however, shrinks before the first of Kircher's great compendia of symbolic interpretations, the *Obeliscus Pamphilius* of 1650.[48] In this work the varied erudition of the author is spread over an area vast in time and space, and it is clear from the style that Kircher triumphs in a

[46] *Ibid.,* pp. 238–77.

[47] The titles of the essays are: On the Egyptian Language and Alphabet, On the Coptic Church, Coptic names of God, The years and months in Coptic, The numerals and ordinals with some Coptic mathematical propositions, Egyptian astronomy, Egyptian weights and measures, Egyptian animals, Egyptian herbs and plants, Egyptian city names in Coptic, Egyptian philosophical terms. These essays are followed by an inventory of Arabic and Egyptian manuscripts brought to Rome by Raymondo. This same year of 1644 saw the first printing of J. B. Casalio's *De veteribus Aegyptiorum ritibus* at Rome. Casalio admits he lacks Kircher's Egyptian learning and relies heavily on his *Prodromus Coptus.* He writes sections on Egyptian idolatry and its dissemination, on the various gods and customs of Egypt, and on hieroglyphs and Egyptian symbolism. There is a chapter on obelisks, which are thought (p. 8) to be astrological in purpose. All that he knows about hieroglyphs, he garners from Clement, Diodorus, or Porphyry; hence, this matter probably came to him through Van Gorp or Kircher. He states there were three languages in Egypt: Coptic or demotic, hieratic for sacred matters, and hieroglyphics, which express things in characters (pp. 31–43). He publishes, probably for the first time, a number of antiquarian objects of Egyptian provenience.

[48] Though it is not explicitly stated, the fact that Kircher's introduction to this volume is followed by letters from Angeloni, Casalio, and Agostini, famous Roman antiquarians, all certifying that the obelisk is carefully published, suggests that Kircher had been subject to voiced criticism. This suspicion is supported by the fact that a series of well known orientalists and two Maronites from Lebanon also testify that his Hebrew, Arabic, and other Semitic quotations are correct. The great outcry against Kircher came in the next century when he was attacked for various faults. Louis Picques said Kircher knew only a little Latin and Greek besides his mother tongue (an obvious slander); see C. E. Jordan, *Histoire de la vie et ouvrages de M. la Croze* (Amsterdam, 1741), pp. 291–92. The great antiquarian, Abbé Bernard de Montfaucon, who gives a full account of the *Bembine Tabula* (*op. cit.,* II, 331–42), complains Kircher is halted by no enigma; "he explains all." In his supplementary second volume (pp. 196–98) he accepts Kircher's suggestion that Coptic is a corrupt form of the ancient spoken language of which the written form has been lost. In an almost prophetic fashion for 1724, he thinks that the hieroglyphics will not be deciphered until one discovers a parallel inscription in Greek. As late as 1763, Abbé Barthélemy complains of Kircher's useless and boring erudition, which has made men doubt his plain wisdom. He observes that Kircher's translations of hieroglyphic documents have succeeded only in delaying their decipherment; see Barthélemy, "Sur la langue Cophte," *Mémoires de l'Académie des Inscriptions,* LVII (1773), 388–89. For other comments on Kircher as an Egyptologist see: C. G. Blumberg, *Fundamenta linguae Copticae* (Leipzig, 1716), p. 29; P. E. Jablonski, *Pantheon Aegyptiorum* (Frankfort, 1750), I, 274; C. H. Tromler, *Bibliothecae Copto-Jacobiticae specimen* (Leipzig, 1767), p. 22; G. W. Leibnitz, *Opera* (Geneva, 1768), V, 296; and, of course, J. B. Mencken, *De charlataneria eruditorum* (Leipzig, 1715), pp. 38–39.

sure success. He begins by dating this obelisk, recently removed from the Coliseum of Caracalla to the Agonale Forum, in the reign of Soth, son of Menuphta, or in 1366 B.C.[49] The subject of the inscription on the obelisk is sun-worship, and the obelisk was dedicated to Hemephta, one of Kircher's favorite Egyptian deities. He describes all the obelisks at Rome, dates them, discourses on their substance, transportation, and erection. Their inscriptions are all in hieroglyphs, which were invented by Hermes Trismegistus, who lived after the Flood and instructed the Egyptian Misraim in priestly duties and in making inscriptions on stone. The later priests of Egypt intended to keep the meaning of the hieroglyphs a secret, but by the time of Joseph's Potiphar (who was, by the way, a priest) revelation had lost its former sanctity. The cult of the true God, based on Noah's sermons, had been replaced by myths like those about Osiris and Horus. Then magic, demon-worship, oracles, and idol-adoration took the place of religion, and the theological doctrines promulgated by Hermes were totally obscured.[50]

Kircher now feels required to write about the nature of the hieroglyphic symbols prescribed by Hermes in order to prevent his pristine religious knowledge from being debased. To this end he combs the ancients and moderns for definitions of symbols because the priesthood has always hidden its divine knowledge under rhetorical clouds. Moses, Pythagoras, Plato, Dionysius the Areopagite, St. Augustine, and other Fathers of the Church used symbols because an open exposition of the nature of things is always unpleasing to God. Rabbi Ibn Ezra, who is supported by Rabbis Eliezer and Juda ben Levi, held that Adam was tutored in the use of symbols by the angel Raziel, who lessoned him in both the natural and supernatural. Kircher agrees with Valeriano and earlier authorities that the Egyptians based their alphabet on the postures of animals. When Hermes saw a crane cross its knock-kneed legs with its neck and bill to preen its tail feathers, he saw the original form of the alpha, or *A*. But the wise priests of the Nile used other types of letters besides those derived from creatures; there are, as well, the symbolic or gnomic letters of Hor Apollo, the mixture of simple and symbolic letters, and the purely symbolic alphabet.[51]

Having reminded his readers that they almost innately recognize a bare sword as "danger," a lyre as "harmony," or a set of scales as "justice," Kircher proceeds to inform them about the meaning of definite

[49] Kircher, *Obeliscus Pamphilius,* pp. 65, 103.
[50] *Ibid.,* pp. 93–100.
[51] *Ibid.,* pp. 104–32.

hieroglyphs. In some inscriptions from Egypt there are characters resembling the profile of a bird's head; this is, of course, the representation of the lowercase sigma (ꝺ) and should be read as such. A twisting serpent is, therefore, a zeta; when the same serpent coils and crosses the coil with its tail, it becomes a theta and also stands for "Toth." After these linguistic premises, Kircher pauses to discuss at great length the physical and metaphysical mysteries concealed under the divine veil of Egyptian mythology, a digression followed by "hierogrammatisimi," of twenty creatures such as dogs, cats, scarabs, and hawks, commonly observed as signs in Egyptian inscriptions with the keys to how they should be translated. The crocodile, for example, stands for the ineffable nature of God because it is without a tongue; the crocodile also represents solar movement from east to west (especially when it is found bearing on its back a boat containing the sun), the land of Egypt, the river Nile, and, as in the *Bembine Tabula,* the humid property in substance or the lunar genii of humidity necessary in the generation of things.[52] Once he has established the meaningful equivalents of these frequently observed hierograms, Kircher is ready to make a line for line translation of the obelisk.

Kircher's confidence in his readings of hieroglyphic inscriptions is as robust as his findings are profoundly wrong and foolish. It never occurred to him or to any other seventeenth-century man that the Egyptian inscriptions on stone were as mundane as any contemporary monuments. For example, a cartouche on one face of this obelisk actually transliterates as Greek "autokrator," but Kircher renders it, "Osiris is the source

---

[52] For many of his Egyptian illustrations but not for his account of the Egyptian deities and their Greek manifestations, Kircher depends on the *Thesaurus Hieroglyphicorum ex museo J. G. Herwart ab Hohenburg* (Munich, 1610). This series of engravings consists of two large folding plates of murals with ten cuts of their detail. It reproduces five of the Roman obelisks in detail and numerous other objects of Egyptian origin. Among the latter is a figure of Anubis, which Kircher explains in his section on the dog as hieroglyphic sign (*ibid.,* pp. 292–97). The dog head of the god stands for "sagacity"; the sphere he holds in his hand is "celestial discipline." In the original *tabula* the deity has a phallus that touches the ground, but Herwart's illustrator removed this *mentula maxima* and neatly girded the loins with a toga. Unaware of this artistic interpolation, Kircher observes that "the girded loins of the god are the sign of his mental fecundity," committing an unconscious pun. The plates in this book are explained in J. F. Herwart ab Hohenburg's *Admiranda ethnicae theologiae mysteria propalata* (Munich, 1623), and the author becomes by his interpretations a great precursor of Herman von der Hardt. The murals, he decides, which have figures at the center, represent the earth surrounded by points of the compass and winds, because all mythology is a secret naval history. The nymphs in the *Odyssey* are ships; Scylla is a port; Polyphemus is a ship; Mars is a rude black form of magnet stone; the myth of Bacchus' birth is an enigmatic account of the invention of the compass. The two Herwarts were clearly mentally disturbed, but they managed to inaugurate the great eighteenth-century controversy over which civilization invented the compass.

of all fecundity and vegetation; the holy Mophta draws this power of generation from the sky into his realm."[53] A second example transliterates into Greek as "Kaisar Domitianos Sebastos," and goes on to indicate that Domitian ordered the obelisk and had the inscription cut at Rome. With his mind intent only on higher matters, Kircher reads a noble but somewhat confused Egyptian pronouncement: "The four-powered beneficial guardian of celestial generation, dominator of air, through Mophta commits benign aerial humor to Ammon, most powerful of inferiors, so that by images and fitting ceremonies it is potently expressed."[54] The monumental mass of religious philosophy that Kircher read into these inscriptions undoubtedly gave him the courage to continue his unswerving effort to unveil the primal doctrines, known to Adam and Moses, in these antique symbolic inscriptions.

Two years after the publication of the *Obeliscus Pamphilius,* the *Oedipus Aegyptiacus; hoc est universalis hieroglyphicae veterum doctrinae temporum iniuria abolitae instauratio* appeared in four folios of more than two thousand pages. This paper edifice was dedicated to Ferdinand III of Austria, whose praises are proclaimed in poems and eulogies written in twenty-six different languages. The twenty-sixth encomium is a hieroglyphic inscription written by Kircher and engraved on an obelisk erected in Volume One at signature **********3r. Kircher compares, without repeating a symbol, the Austrian Osiris with Hermes Trismegistus, Horus, Mophta, "the archetype of mental operations, the divine legislator, and the Genius Agatho." This feast of praise is followed by a "Propylaeum Agonisticum" addressed to critics who have complained that Kircher is laboring at an impossible task, scanted by ancients and shunned by moderns. Admitting that there are difficulties, Kircher announces his intention of employing his God-given talents in order to explain the symbolical inscriptions and the allegorical representations of the ancient Egyptians. He denies that linguistic changes make the task of decipherment and interpretation impossible; the same process did not hinder those scholars who rediscovered the ancient literary glories of Greece. Having dismissed his louder critics as either obscurantists or anti-intellectuals, Kircher writes a full history of the religion, culture, and politics of Egypt.

Deeply versed in the lore of the Arabs and the Jewish rabbis, Kircher has better success at describing the withering away of the original theology than had most of his predecessors. Adam, according to

[53] Kircher, *Obeliscus Pamphilus,* p. 557.
[54] *Ibid.,* p. 559.

Rabbi Moses of Egypt, was born of parents descended from the moon and was himself a priest and prophet of the moon, urging men to worship the planet until corrected and shown the true way by Seth. Nonetheless, men continued to worship the stars, and in time Adam, Eve, the serpent, Cain, and Seth were transformed into gods, a theology carried by Cham into Egypt where there was a continual fragmentation of the idolatrous pantheon attended by constant ritualistic degeneration. Kircher delights in unwinding the holy confusions to demonstrate how Eve became Tellus, Niobe, Vesta, and Isis and how Adam was transfigured into the consorts of these goddesses. He describes, and in this he anticipates the eighteenth-century scholar Caspar Hartzheim,[55] the penetration of Egyptian idolatry into the surrounding world; the Hebrews first took over the adoration of fire, then that of Theraphim, Baalim, Baelphegor, Beelzebub, Beelsephon, Baalgad, Thammuz, Apis or the Golden Calf, Astarte, Chemos, Moloch, Dagon, and numerous other gods of Egypt in their neighborly manifestations. The religious world, Kircher thinks, was "Egypt's ape"; hence, the gods of the Greeks and the barbarians can all be traced to Cham's version of Adam's heresy.

The second part of this masterwork is first given over to a larger account of symbolism than Kircher had written before. After recording five standard ancient definitions of *symbol,* Kircher supplies "the true, the strict definition." A symbol is "the significant sign of a hidden mystery," and its nature is "to lead our minds through meditation on certain similarities to the comprehension of something much different from the thing presented to the external senses, the nature of which can be said to be transcendent or hidden as obscured by a veil."[56] Perhaps this formula is made clear when in succeeding essays Kircher discusses emblems, impreses, enigmas, riddles, parables, and other rhetorical phenomena. These discussions bring Kircher to a history of the spoken and written language, and, after presenting the claims of the inventers of various races nominated by a score of ancient and Renaissance experts, he assigns the primacy to the kind of Hebrew that was divinely taught to Adam while he was being angelically instructed in theology, philosophy, medicine, astrology, chemistry, mathematics, and law. All languages are descended from Hebrew, the essential tongue in which each noun contains in its very letters the distinguishing qualities of the

---

[55] Hartzheim turned through the Bible and discovered exactly one hundred places where paganism had crept into the text and had to be extirpated by allegory. He published his results at Padua in 1731 under the title *Explicatio gentilium fabularum et superstitionum quarum in sacris scripturis fit mentio; vario hinc inde sensu, praeter literalem, ut allegorico, morali, anagogico exornata.*

[56] Kircher, *Obeliscus Aegyptiacus,* II, 6.

thing it designates. The Hebrew alphabet known to the Renaissance is, of course, modern; but Kircher, who reprints the famous altar inscription from the base of Mt. Horeb, does not have much difficulty in reconstructing some of the letters of the original alphabet.[57] When technical problems of this nature have been resolved, Kircher composes a "Sphynx Mystagoga," a title he found pleasing, in which he stores, as he puts it, "the enigmatic speaking of Chaldeans, Egyptians, Hebrews, and Greeks as well as the allegorical knots, as presented to Oedipus, of the fables of Orpheus, Homer, the Pythagoreans, and the Platonists loosened by mystical, physical, ethical, and anagogical interpretation."

The first peoples to use mysterious utterance were the Egyptians; but the Greeks learned the art from them, and Kircher summons Palaephatus and Diodorus Siculus to reveal the history behind the myths of Homer and the Greek stories of the gods and heroes.[58] The cryptic statements of Zoroaster, the Orphists, the Pythagoreans, and, of course, Hor Apollo are turned over on their backs for the wisdom they conceal —which is sometimes Christian. The disturbing moments in Homer's epics, like the conflict of the gods or the assault of the Titans on Olympus, are conventionally expounded; the interpretive advice of Proclus about the proper reading of celestial fornication and animal metamorphosis is seriously restated.[59] To Kircher's mind these shadowing allegories were as divinely granted to the poets as they were to the Hebrew prophets.[60] To demonstrate this supposition properly, he concludes this discourse with mystical, physical, and anagogical readings of the Cronus-Zeus myth, the rape of Proserpine, and the story and nature of Apollo.

Kircher's massive account of ancient symbol and allegory wanders into a dissertation on the Hebrew and Arabic cabalas and is followed by a treatise on Egyptian cosmology based once again on the Horus-headed scarab of the *Bembine Tabula*. Kircher, it may be remarked, never refrained from repeating himself. The *Oedipus* then supplies the Renaissance symbolist with accounts of the hieroglyphic mathematics, mechanics, medicine, chemistry, magic, and theology of the ancient world and particularly of Egypt. With the learning of three folios soundly digested, the reader is prepared for the ultimate volume in which all the obelisks, besides the Pamphilian, plus the inscriptions on mummy cases, canopic jars, lamps, amulets, and other Egyptian objects are patiently

---

[57] *Ibid.*, II, 42–122.
[58] *Ibid.*, II, 124–7.
[59] *Ibid.*, II, 129–80.
[60] *Ibid.*, II, 189–93.

translated. Unexhausted by this tremendous effort, Kircher returned to his task in 1661 with the *Obelisci Aegyptiaci nuper inter Isaei Romani rudera effossi interpretatio hieroglyphica*. It is clear from this contribution to learning that whatever archaeologists dug up, Kircher immediately transcribed. In 1676 the *Sphinx mystagogus*, interpreting all inscriptions seen after 1661, was added to Kircher's Egyptian shelf. This two-foot row of volumes, profusely illustrated, not only emphasized the common theory that pagan as well as Christian documents yielded concealed meanings but suggested once again that the true religion was more widely spread than men had supposed.

In the first volume of the *Oedipus*, Kircher pointed to parallels between the customs of China and those of ancient Egypt. Both civilizations were supported by a caste system, and in each the upper caste, Egyptian priests and Chinese literati, employed hieroglyphics to shield the precious wisdom that they alone possessed.[61] The Chinese hieroglyphs differed from those of the Egyptians in that the Chinese symbol for "sun" meant "sun," whereas the Egyptian scarab symbol does not mean "sun" but rather "those secret and mysterious operations of that planet which foster growth and generation."[62] Kircher returned to this Egypto-Sinological theory and enlarged it in 1667 when he retired from his linguistic, historical, mathematical, and physical studies long enough to write his impressive *China illustrata*.

Kircher does not pretend to be a Sinologist; he is only writing a book about China. He claims no proficiency in the Chinese language but relies on Father Michel Boym, an indefatigable Jesuit missionary, who became an eminent authority on Chinese and had earlier contributed the Chinese eulogies of the Austrian Emperor to the *Oedipus*. Since he was no authority (in fact, he had never been east of the Danube), Kircher did not hesitate to propose that ancient China was instructed by ancient Egypt. His hypothesis is based on that sound historian Herodotus. When Cambyses invaded Egypt he smashed the images of the gods and cast down the obelisks. He killed the bull Apis with his own hands and drove the priesthood, wise with the learning of a thousand years, into exile. As the priests fled eastward, Kircher tracks them in their wanderings through the Arabian desert, into the plains of India, and finally to the far, far land of China. His imaginative pursuit of the Egyptian priests as they crossed the borders of China was aided by the little he knew about the Chinese language, for, as might be logically expected, many of its ideograms seemed to him to be rough forms of the Egyptian

[61] *Ibid.*, I, 398–402.
[62] *Ibid.*, III, 10–13.

hieroglyphs. Kircher wisely made no attempts to find linguistic connections between the two languages about which he knew nothing; nonetheless, he was firmly convinced that China was culturally influenced by Egypt.[63]

When Kircher advanced this theory that China was the heir of Egypt, he was stepping squarely into the raging seventeenth-century chronological controversy about the age of civilizations. His theory was promptly attacked by an English heretic, John Webb, who argued in *An Historical Essay Endeavouring a Probability that the Language of the Empire of China is the Primitive Language* (London, 1669), that China had a high culture before the confusion at Babel; in fact, he eventually argued that Noah built the ark in China and settled in that country after the Flood subsided. As a result of this fortunate postdiluvian event, the Chinese speak a language that is as close to the primitive language of Adam as is likely to be found.[64] Webb's arguments are almost as scholarly as Kircher's and nearly as sound.

Kircher's binding of Egyptian symbols, each of which is supplied with one or more equivalents authorized by other pagan or Christian texts, into philosophical allegories of a confused but esoteric nature was in keeping with the Renaissance's faith in the hidden meaning. There were some objectors to his methods and results, but for the majority of concerned people he had solved the riddle of the Sphinx. In 1704, for example, when the antiquarian J. P. Rigord published the hieroglyphics found on an Egyptian ceinture, he had no difficulty in making out the meaning of the mythical representations because he had Kircher's discoveries to help him; but he invited other Egyptologists to advise him on the inscriptions, which were "not Punic, Coptic, or like those on the *Bembine Tabula.*"[65] Some years later, Melchior à Briga made a Kircherian rendering of some hierograms on an Egyptian statue at Rome and praised the brilliance of the Jesuit master's theories of interpretation, which should be taught in the better universities.[66] Briga had hardly printed this suggestion when Pierre D. Huet restated Kircher's Sino-Egyp-

---

[63] Kircher, *China illustrata* (Amsterdam, 1667), pp. 151–54, 233–35.

[64] Webb held that the Egyptians invented their symbols for concealment, the Chinese theirs for communication (pp. 151–52). See also D'Assigny's essay in his translation of P. Gautruche, *The Poetical Histories* (London, 1671), pp. 154–83 and John Marsham, *Chronicus Canon* (London, 1672), pp. 38–39. In his *Essay towards a Real Character* (London, 1668), p. 12, Bishop Wilkins doubts whether or not the contents of hieroglyphical inscriptions are even worth knowing.

[65] "Lettre de Monsieur Rigord Commissaire de la Marine aux Journalistes de Trévoux sur une Ceinture de Toile trouvée en Égypte autour d'une momie," *Mémoires pour l'Histoire des Sciences et des Beaux Arts* (Trévoux, 1704) pp. 978–1000.

[66] Briga, *Fascia Isiaca statuae Capitolinae nunc primum in lucem edita* (Rome, 1716).

tian hypothesis in his book on ancient commerce. He added other comparative details of religion and culture to Kircher's proofs but agreed that the common use of a symbolic language was the best indication of the colonization of China by Egyptians.[67] The truly eminent orientalist Etienne Fourmont[68] came to the support of the Kircherian notion with his thesis that the nongods Hermes and Osiris carried the pure, original religion to India, a country which was only a stone's throw from China. Although expert orientalists—Renaudot, Freret, and Du Halde—were making discoveries that undermined Kircher's theories, he had many disciples;[69] in fact, William Warburton,[70] who had to prove Kircher wrong in order to establish his own hypotheses about the influence of the Egyptians on the Jews, was among his first serious critics.

Various studies of Egypt's symbolic language and occult theosophy preceded Warburton's attempt to explain the hieroglyphic writings. Thomas Burnet, who recorded a jaunty conversation in Eden between Eve and Satan, presumed that all orientals—Egyptians, Babylonians, Ethiopians, Brahmans, and Chinese—wrote symbolically about "physiology, theology, ethics, history, and politics" in "animal forms, parts of the body, and mechanical implements."[71] Protestant Herman Wits, no partisan of Catholic Athanasius Kircher but even more restrained in his esteem for the anti-Hebraists Spencer and Marsham, is ready to believe in Egyptian symbolism even though he fiercely denies that the Jews learned anything from them.[72] Other experts wrote on special aspects of Egyptian religion and its relation to that of the Jews and the Greeks,[73]

[67] Huet, *The History and Commerce of the Ancients* (London, 1717), p. 25.

[68] *Réflexions critiques sur les histoires des anciens peuples* (Paris, 1735), I, 145–46, 353–56.

[69] Kircher's symbolic methods are responsible for the commentaries Alexander Gordon, Secretary of the Society of Antiquaries, wrote on some inscriptions in *An Essay towards Explaining Hieroglyphical Figures on the Coffin of the Ancient Mummy belonging to Capt. William Lethieullier. An Essay towards Explaining the Ancient Hieroglyphical Figures on the Egyptian Mummy in the Museum of Dr. Mead* (London, 1737). They also stand behind Dominique Reverend's *Lettres à Monsieur H*** sur les Premiers Dieux ou Rois d'Egypte* (Paris, 1733) and Christian Herzog's *Essay de Mummio-Graphie* (Leipzig, 1718).

[70] Kircher is attacked as "bewildered" and his works as "visionary." He "steered at large," Warburton writes, through a half dozen folios with the writings of the later Greek Platonists and the forged books of Hermes, which contain a philosophy not Egyptian, "to explain monuments not philosophical"; *The Divine Legation of Moses Demonstrated*, ed. R. Hurd (London, 1837), II, 44.

[71] Burnet, *Archaeologiae philosophicae . . . libri duo* (London, 1733), pp. 117–19; the book first appeared in 1692.

[72] Wits, *Aegyptiaca et Dekaphulon; sive de Aegyptiacorum sacrorum cum Hebraicis collatione libri tres* (Amsterdam, 1696), pp. 87–92.

[73] There were numerous special treatises such as Matthias Bax, *De Busiride* (Leyden, 1700), which attempts to identify this villain after refusing to accept him as the Mosaic Pharoah because he lived at the time of Joshua or Amos. Bax decides that since the Nile was

but the old view that the Greeks learned their Judaism in Egypt was changing. When William Jameson, lecturer in history at Glasgow, wrote his *Spicilegia antiquitatum Aegypti atque ei vicinarum gentium,* he took up the question of Homer's Egyptian education and pointed out there was no evidence supporting it at all. When he talks about Egypt in the *Odyssey*—the allusion to the Pharos in Book Four, for instance—Homer shows himself ignorant of things Egyptian. There are those who think that he learned about the Hereafter, its rewards and punishments, from his years in Egypt, but what ancient does not speak of this matter. "In truth no one save a man flatly stupid or without hope would deny that after death there were rewards and punishments."[74] But this statement was made in 1720, and even at this late date not every man had the common sense of a learned Scot.

once called the Sirin, the name is "Bos Siris" or "Nile Bull," which is, of course, the crocodile. A similar special study of the Magna Mater which supplanted that of Pignoria was Heinrich van Bashuysen's *De Iside magna dearum matre* (Zerbst, 1719).

The question of Joseph as Apis is the subject of Peter Schroer's *De Serapide Aegyptiorum Deo Maximo* (Bratislava, 1666), which attacks the theory of Firmicus Maternus, Cornelius à Lapide, De Sponde, and Kircher that Serapis is from the Greek *Saras + apo.* The name really means "bull face," and bull figures have a different symbolism from that associated with Joseph. Schroer is forced to explain why the oracle of Serapis, according to Suidas, once told an Egyptian king, "First God, then the Word and Spirit with him are all one," an utterance his predecessors thought more worthy of Joseph than Serapis. "The devil," says Schroer, "has often spoken pious oracles." He agrees with Macrobius that Serapis is the sun. The matter now seems to have rested as the subject of a special study until 1694 when Johannes Cnoblach wrote his Wittenberg study, *De Apide bove atque idolo Aegyptiorum,* which is mainly about the god and his cult and expresses doubts about a connection with Joseph; however, the doubts are not pressed.

In 1700, the Dutch scholar Jacob Trigland published his *De Josepho Patriarcha in sacris bovis hieroglyphico* at Leyden, and once again the fat was in the fire. Trigland mentions the general knowledge of the major Jewish heroes among the Gentiles; Trogus, Strabo, and other authorities have heard of Gideon, Joshua, and Moses. He feels that Joseph was equally known. In Egypt the symbol of Apis is a scarab rolling a ball of earth containing a seed, which is a way of stating that Joseph by word of mouth rolled round Jewish doctrines. The descent of this doctrine to the Greeks and then to the Romans is evidenced when Ovid puts the Hebrew account of Creation, the patriarchal tradition, and the Mosaic history in his *Metamorphoses.* Apis with the sun and the moon between his horns and a hawk on his back is clearly the emblem of Joseph, whose father and mother were the sun and moon, who wore the horns of wisdom, and whose name "by the laws of hieroglyphics" is expressed by a hawk. Apis, Trigland discovered by reading in Herodotus, had thicker hair than other bulls, and full hair is an old symbol of those who differ from others in righteous thoughts and actions. Other classical authorities support this assumption. Ammianus Marcellinus reports that Apis could predict future events, a talent which links him with Joseph. Tacitus associates the Egyptian god with Aesculapius, and medicine is associated with Joseph in the biblical account. Actually, the Joseph-Apis relationship is plainly signified when the Israelites worshiped the golden calf.

[74] Jameson, *Spicilegia* (Glasgow, 1720), pp. 452–58.

VI

THE MIDDLE AGES, hardly knowing the name of Homer, much less the true contents of his epics, knew, however, that he furnished the poetic stimulus that produced the *Aeneid* of Virgil. The almost saintly, certainly prophetic, Virgil was not only credited with miracles worthy of a white magician[1] but was assumed to have buried in his great poem wisdom lost to the memory of man. In the character of Aeneas he had created an epic figure who wandered more surely and wisely than Odysseus along the symbolic path of mortal existence. At each stage in his progress the grave hero exemplified both the decisions and the actions wise men should imitate. Besides reading the text of the *Aeneid* medieval men could follow the life of the perfect poet in the biographies attributed to Donatus, Philargyrius, Servius, and Focas Grammaticus.[2] The fate of his younger contemporary, Ovid, was somewhat different. Until the Renaissance when his life was written by Pietro Crinito[3] and Giglio Giraldi,[4] Ovid's career

---

[1] Domenico Comparetti, *Vergil in the Middle Ages,* trans. E. F. M. Benecke (London, 1895); J. W. Spargo, *Virgil the Necromancer* (Cambridge, Mass., 1934). A correction and augmentation of Comparetti by V. Ussani appeared as "In margine al Comparetti," *Studi Medievali,* n. s., V (1932), 1–42.

[2] *Vitae Vergilianae,* ed. J. Brummer (Leipzig, 1912). In the preface to Suetonius, *Reliquiae* (Leipzig, 1860), the editor August Reiffersheid makes a strong case for Suetonius' authorship of the life attributed to Donatus.

[3] Crinito, *De honesta disciplina* (Lyons, 1554), pp. 463–69.

[4] Giraldi, *De poetarum historia dialogi decem* in *Opera omnia* (Leyden, 1696), II, 224–31. In 1556 M. T. Porcacchi wrote a "La vita di Vergilio" for the Italian translation of Daniello and Lori.

was known mainly through his highly autobiographical poems and the *De Vetula,* which Richard de Fournival claimed had been found during the reign of Vastasius in the poet's tomb at Colchis. This fourteenth-century hoax describes Ovid's long pursuit of an unattainable woman and concludes with his abandonment of "sweet sin" so that he might prove through astronomical, historical, and physical speculations that there is one God, who took human flesh to show his creatures the proper way to live.[5] However, by the time this romance had been composed the poetry of Ovid had already inspired a host of secular poets,[6] and his *Metamorphoses* had been revealed to have Christian significances.

Because of this medieval interest the *Aeneid* and the *Metamorphoses* were handed on to the Renaissance with allegorical commentaries as authoritatively pious as those on Scripture. In the case of the *Aeneid* the commentaries were more venerable and, hence, more impressive. Some of the Renaissance editions of Virgil's *Opera* reprinted only the metrical and grammatical observations of Junius Philargyrius and Valerius Probus, but most editions surrounded the text with the fourth-century remarks of Maurus Servius Honoratus and of his younger contemporary, Tiberius or Aelius (the sixteenth century was not sure of the praenomen) Donatus. As time passed, each editor added his own views to these and often added those of his approved predecessors as well.

In the proem to his commentary Donatus asks the reader to be aware of an august figure masquerading as Aeneas, the figure "in whose

---

[5] Fournival, *La vielle ou les derniers amours d'Ovide,* trans. Jean Lefevre; ed. H. Cocheris (Paris, 1861). Roger Bacon comments on this work in a serious fashion in *Opus maius,* ed. J. H. Bridges (London, 1900), I, 263–67; see also Paul Klopsch, ed., *Pseudo-Ovidius De Vetula* (Leyden, 1967).

[6] Of the many articles and monographs on the medieval Ovid, the following are very helpful: Karl Bartsch, *Albrecht von Halberstadt und Ovid im Mittelalter* (Quedlingburg and Leipzig), 1861; H. Sedlmayr, "Beitrag zur Geschichte der Ovidstudien im Mittelalter," *Wiener Studien,* VI (1884), 142–58; G. Paris, "Chrétien Legouais et autres traducteurs ou imitateurs d'Ovide," *Histoire littéraire de la France* (Paris, 1885), XXIV, 455–525; L. Sudre, *Ovidii Metamorphoseon libros quomodo nostrates medii aevi poetae imitati interpretati sint* (Paris, 1893); M. Manitius, "Beitrage zur Geschichte des Ovidius und anderer romischen Schriftsteller im Mittelalter," *Philologus,* Suppl. VII (1899), 723–67; E. K. Rand, *Ovid and his Influence* (New York, 1928); L. K. Born, "Ovid and Allegory," *Speculum,* IX (1934), 362–79; F. W. Lenz, "Einführende Bemerkungen zu den mittelalterlichen Pseudo-Ovidiana," *Das Altertum,* V (1959), 171–82; S. Battaglia, "La tradizione di Ovidio nel Medioeva," *Filologia Romanza,* VI (1959), 185–224; Franco Munari, *Ovid im Mittelalter* (Zurich, 1960); S. Viarre, *La survie d'Ovide dans la littérature scientifique des XIIe et XIIIe siècles* (Poitiers, 1966). A series of papers in the *Atti del Convegno Internazionale Ovidiano* (Rome, 1959), pp. 159–216, should be consulted: V. Ussani, "Appunti sulla fortuna di Ovidio nel Medioevo"; A. Monteverdi, "Aneddoti per la storia della fortuna di Ovidio nel Medio Evo"; P. Lehmann, "Betrachtungen über Ovidius im Lateinischen Mittelalter"; P. Fabbri, "Ovidio e Dante"; and G. Brugnoli, "Ovidio e gli esiliati carolingi."

honor this poem was written";[7] but his annotations are as literal as those of Aristarchus on Homer. He scrupulously omits any moral or physical form of interpretation. Servius belongs to a different sect. He begins his observations by stating that Virgil's intent is to imitate Homer and praise Augustus by lauding his ancestors,[8] but he has hardly said this before he introduces the very important word "polysemus" into the critical vocabulary of Europe.[9] He adorns his commentary with historical explanations,[10] but he also pauses over the allegorical translation of the myths of Apollo, Deucalion, and Prometheus.[11] Interpretation of this sort reveals why Liber and Ceres are known as "clarissima mundi"[12] and permits Servius to see the chariot of Cybele as significantly as if it were the one described by Ezekiel.[13] In Hercules' taming of Cerberus, Servius discloses a moral meaning that impressed the Renaissance.[14] Yet Servius is not always an allegorizer; when he comes to the myths of the Sirens,[15] Daedalus,[16] and the Gorgons,[17] he speaks like a disciple of Cornutus. Whereas Servius offers the students of the *Aeneid* the opinions of a schoolmaster, Fabius Planciades Fulgentius, who wrote during the chaotic fifth century, reports what Virgil, who visited him in a vision, said about the true meaning of his epic.

Fulgentius, famous for the *Mythologiarum libri tres,* printed as early as 1498, became more celebrated when his *De expositione Virgilianae continentia* appeared in 1589 and was subsequently included in many editions of the *Aeneid.*[18] Since it was an age in which man could scarcely depend on man, Fulgentius leaned heavily on supernatural inspiration. The Muse Calliope helped him in his explanation of ancient myths; hence, Virgil comes to his aid when he explains the *Aeneid.* In a

---

[7] Donatus, *Interpretationes Virgilianae,* ed. H. Georg (Leipzig, 1905), I, 1. On the general problem of this commentary consult E. K. Rand, "Is Donatus' Commentary on Virgil Lost?" *Classical Quarterly,* X (1916), 158–64.

[8] *Commentarii in Virgilium,* ed. H. A. Leon (Gottingen, 1826), *Aeneid* I. *praef.*

[9] *Ibid., Aeneid* I. 1.

[10] *Ibid., Aeneid* I. 292; III. 274; V. 45, 556; VI. 69, 230; VII. 170; VIII. 672. All of these references and others are pointed out by J. W. Jones, Jr., "Allegorical Interpretation in Servius," *Classical Journal,* LVI (1961), 217–26.

[11] *Ibid., Bucolics* V. 66; VI. 41.

[12] *Ibid., Georgics* I. 5–7.

[13] *Ibid., Aeneid* III. 113.

[14] *Ibid., Aeneid* VI. 395.

[15] *Ibid., Aeneid* V. 864.

[16] *Ibid., Aeneid* VI. 14.

[17] *Ibid., Aeneid* VI. 287. The Heidelberg edition of 1589 contains Fulvio Orsini's annotations on Servius plus some allegories of his own.

[18] Fulgentius, *Opera,* ed. Rudolf Helm (Leipzig, 1898), pp. 83–107. For an account of the work see Armand Gasquy, *De Fabio Planciade Fulgentio Virgilii Interprete* (Berlin, 1887). I quote from Helm although the less available text of Van Staveran seems better.

letter to "a reverend deacon," which introduces the *De expositione,* Fulgentius confesses that he had searched all Virgil's poems for their "physical secrets." He found in each eclogue a hidden lesson in human conduct and saw great pedagogical worth in the *Georgics,* but to him all poetry is surpassed by the sage and serious *Aeneid.*

In the vision Virgil appeared to Fulgentius with "a mouth full of the Ascrean stream" to explain that the first lines of his epic really mean "strength and wisdom" afflicted by fate but not overcome through weakness. This is the dominating theme of the whole poem. Birth and the dangers attending birth are symbolized by the great storm; hence, Juno, presiding goddess of parturition, aided by Aeolus (Greek "enolus"), or "destruction of life," brings to pass the tempest that wrecks the fleet. The seven escaping ships represent a favorable, symbolic birth-number. At first, Aeneas, the new-born infant, fails to recognize his mother or communicate with his companions. He listens with pleasure to music as infants do to the lullabies of nurses. In the second and third books the symbolic child attends to childish stories and encounters the Cyclops, whose single eye may be understood as the irrational nature of childish pride. When Anchises dies and is interred at Drepanum (Greek "dremipedos"), or "bitter child," the event represents a young man's liberation from parental control.

Freed from paternal restraint Aeneas, who is now "youth," leaps into the life of passion personified by Queen Dido, but he is rescued from impending ruin by Mercury, who is once again "intelligence." It is important to notice, Fulgentius explains, that love dies, as it always does, in ashes. Safe from disaster, the youth Aeneas can engage in manly games. While he is engaged in these legitimate masculine endeavors, the ships are set afire (Beroe's name means "order of truth"), an episode allegorizing the violent customs of young men. Eventually, Aeneas is ready for Apollo, or "study," but first he must bury Misenus (Greek *mise + enos*), or "hating praise." The funeral signified for Fulgentius "that when one reflects on future events, one penetrates the obscure and secret mysteries of wisdom." The golden bough is naturally "learning," and its possession enables Aeneas to discover "the secrets of knowledge" in Avernus. Cerberus stands for "the trickery of law"; Dido portrays "lust destroyed." At this point in the exposition, Virgil, unaware that he is not yet in Dante's Inferno, remarks:

If in the midst of so many Stoic truths I had not also tasted something Epicurean, I would not have been a pagan. The knowledge of the whole truth is not given to anyone except you for whom the Light of Truth shone. I was brought into your book as a commentator; I came not to discuss what I should have known, but rather to shed light on what I did know.[19]

Among the things known to Virgil was that the death of Caieta meant the overcoming of "fear of masters"; he knew, too, that when Aeneas disembarks on Ausonian shores, youth is ended, and Lavinia, or "laborum via," must be taken in marriage. The lady is rightly called "daughter of Latinus" because labor hides ("latere") in many places. Aeneas seeks out Evander, or "good man," for counsel and straps on armor forged by Vulcan, or "deliberation." In Book Nine Aeneas finally fights Turnus, or "violent mind," whose closest friend is Messapus, or "hater of speech," and whose sister is Iuturna, or "destruction." At this part of the *Aeneid* the revelation of its meaning ends, but Virgil may be allowed a final exposition.

Turnus had Metiscus as his first charioteer, Metiscus, or the Greek for "drunkenness." Drunkenness brings madness of soul. Then destruction comes. For this reason Iuturna is said to be immortal and Turnus mortal, because madness of soul is quickly ended, whereas destruction is everlasting. Hence she drives his chariot around, that is, for a long time she keeps it in flight. The wheels represent Time, so Fortuna is said to be a wheel, the constant revolution of Time.[20]

II

The other famous medieval commentary, the *Commentum super sex libros Eneidos Virgili* of Bernard of Silvester, though known to Salutati and Landino, was not published in the Renaissance;[21] nonethe-

[19] Fulgentius, *Opera,* p. 103.

[20] *Ibid.,* pp. 106–7.

[21] The bad Paris manuscript, which stops at VI. 636, was edited at Griefswald by W. Riedel in 1924 and is the only text that is now in print. In the preface, Bernard states that Virgil writes "sub integumento" and explains that "integumentum" is "involucrum" and means the wrapping of truth in fable. M. D. Chenu has discussed these terms in *"Involucrum: Le mythe selon les théologiens médiévaux," Archives d'histoire doctrinale et littéraire du moyen age,* XX (1956), 74–79. Bernard's allegory, as we have it, seems far more sophisticated and completely rounded out than the *De expositione* of Fulgentius. Bernard also, recognizes Virgil as quasi-Christian and is guided in his allegory by a conviction that "from the day he was given speech and led out through the door of curiosity, man conversed with the Tempter." He also believes that "a nature divine and pleasing to God because of its inborn grace can belong to the elect"; hence, Virgil has merit. One gets the impression that Bernard was aware of predecessors like Macrobius, because he too reads the symbolical meaning of pagan deities on several planes. Apollo is sometimes the sun and sometimes divine or human wisdom; Jupiter is sometimes fire and sometimes the supreme god; Venus is both carnal desire and the "concordia mundi." These multiple interpretations or "multivocationes," as Bernard terms them, govern the exposition of the *Aeneid.* Aeneas is, therefore, "the human spirit" and the child of Anchises, or body, and Venus, or concord. The storm is the surging of passion and the ship of Aeneas represents the soul. The fleet of seven ships are

less, the earliest humanists had the habit of allegory and could read the
Aeneid under the proper lamp. Petrarch, influenced by the text of Fulgentius, read the epic morally to Francesco d'Arezzo and expounded
Aeneas' departure from Troy to St. Augustine in the *Secretum*.[22] Aeneas'
inability to understand what was happening when he was accompanied
by Venus and his awareness of true reality once she had departed made
it plain to Petrarch that Venerian activities blind men to the divine
vision. "You have discovered," St. Augustine exclaims, "light in the
clouds; for in poetic fictions there is truth to be glimpsed in little
glimmers." Other allegorical readings of Virgil find their way into
Petrarch's *Rerum memorandarum libri*,[23] but it is clear from his preserved manuscript of Virgil that Petrarch was continually supplying
the margins of the text with moral gleams.[24] His perception of these
lighted cracks in the clouds was also shared by Boccaccio and find their
way into his mythology, but they were still bright when the fifteenth-
century humanists carried the text of Virgil, adorned with glosses and
commentaries, to the printers.

The early editions of Virgil's *Opera* are the most profusely anno-

---

the five senses plus the powers of action and rest. The lost companions are human faults put
aside by reason, study, and doctrine. The sea cliffs are sloth. The cloud enveloping Aeneas
when he comes to Carthage is ignorance, for the ruler of the city is Dido, or libido. The
whole allegory can be summed up in terms of the five ages of man. The first book is infancy;
the second is boyhood; and the third is adolescence. Youth with its foolish fancies is
expounded in the fourth book, whereas the fifth book shows the virile age of man. The sixth
book—the almost line by line explication occupies pages 28–115 of Riedel's edition—provides
an allegorical equivalent for almost everything up to line 636. Once we assume that the cave
of the Sibyl is Theology and that the golden bough is Philosophy, all the other personages
and episodes can be logically translated.

In the *Polycraticus*, John of Salisbury uses Bernard's method for his brief exposition of
the *Aeneid*. "Under the cloak of poetic imagination in his *Aeneid*, he subtly represents the six
ages of life by dividing his work into six books. In these, imitating the *Odyssey*, he seems to
represent the origin and progress of man." There is a demonstration of how Virgil understood every philosophy; hence, it is not until Book Four that his allegory has much to do with
the journey of Aeneas. See *Polycraticus*, ed. C. C. I. Webb (Oxford, 1909), 816ᶜ–818ᵇ; 820ᵃ⁻ᵉ.
Like both the commentators Dante picks up the same idea in the *Il convito*, IV. 26. 8–13, stating that the fourth, fifth, and sixth books are about manhood and its qualities. Restraint is
illustrated by the abandonment of Dido; lovingness, by the commending of the aged Trojans
to Acestes and the instructing of Ascanius and the other young men; courtesy, by the treatment of the corpse of Misenus; and loyalty, by Aeneas' keeping his promises to the contestants
at the games.

[22] Petrarch, *Opere*, ed. Emilio Bigi (Milan, 1966), p. 590.

[23] Petrarch, *Rerum memorandarum libri*, ed. G. Billanovich (Florence, 1943), pp. 51–52,
141, 175.

[24] Pierre de Nolhac, *Pétrarque et l'humanisme* (Paris, 1892), pp. 103–35. Petrarch's
manuscript of Virgil can be examined in superb reproduction in the *Francisci Petrarcae
Vergilianus Codex*, eds. Giovanni Galbiati and Achille Ratti (Milan, 1930). The most
impressive of Virgil studies is Vladimiro Zabughin, *Vergilio nel rinascimento Italiano da
Dante a Torquato Tasso* (Bologna, 1921), a work on which I have leaned heavily for
bibliographical comfort.

tated classical texts the world has ever seen. Each ten lines of the *Aeneid* is surrounded by hundreds of lines of exposition. But there were other helps, too. Although a life of Virgil had been composed in the fourteenth century by Sicco Polenton and exists in many manuscripts,[25] it was not published. However, the lives by Donatus, by Servius, and by the newly discovered Probus are to be found in most Renaissance editions as well as the authentic Appendix and other dubious shorter pieces such as "Hortulus," "In Maecoenatis obitum elegia," "De vero bono," "De ludo contra avaritiam et iram," "De horae," and "De venere et vino." With the Venice *Opera* of 1471 the so-called Thirteenth Book by Maffeo Vegio begins to be a regular part of the *corpus criticus*; in fact, it was regarded as so important that Jodocus Badius Ascensius wrote a commentary on it for the Paris Virgil of 1500.

Vegio, whose *De educatione liberorum et eorum claris moribus libri sex* was a popular pedagogical treatise, describes the surrender of the Rutuli, the burial of Turnus, the betrothal of Aeneas and Lavinia, the death of Latinus, and, finally, the apotheosis of Aeneas after three years of happy kingship. Without question, Vegio, who read the *Aeneid* as the pilgrimage of a divinely guided man, was displeased with Virgil's abrupt ending. The ultimate event in the life of a good man is its conclusion; hence, in the last lines of his continuation, Venus begs Jupiter (who had it in mind right along) to promote the soul of doomed Aeneas to a star. The congress of gods agrees; even Juno adds her vote. Venus descends and bears "the happy soul" skyward. The new ending is nearly Christian and accords with Vegio's expressed opinion that if explained according to reason, the *Aeneid,* with the exception of the perverse Fourth Book, "hides under the ornament of poetic figment the highest mysteries of philosophy." And what are the natures of these mysteries? Vegio sums them up.

Through the person of Aeneas, Virgil wishes to show a man provided with all virtues in both adversity and prosperity. In the character of Dido he admonishes women to live according to reason so that they may desire praise and fear infamy which ends in a sad death. . . . Therefore, Virgil and the others who use this mode of writing should be accepted and commended for their merit by all good and learned men, because we are taught by them how best to live according to virtue and flee from viciousness.[26]

[25] Polenton, *Scriptorum illustrium latinae linguae libri XVIII,* ed. B. L. Ullman (Rome, 1928), pp. 73–90. Although Polenton mentions the "philosophical" meaning of several myths in his life of Ovid (pp. 44–45), he says nothing about an allegory in the *Aeneid.*

[26] Vegio, *De educatione liberorum et eorum claris moribus libri sex,* eds. Mary W. Fanning and Anne S. Sullivan (Washington, D. C., 1933, 1936), pp. 83–90. The text of Vegio

Though Vegio's final book was added as early as 1471, the first publication of the *Opera* was possibly the Strassburg edition of 1468 (?) and certainly the Rome edition of 1469. Servius' commentary published separately in Rome in 1470 (?) was published with the Virgilian text in Calderini's Venice version of 1482. When Landino edited the Florence edition of 1487/88, Donatus' commentary was added to that of Servius, and all these commentators were brought into one volume with the Venice *Opera* of 1489. Antonio Mancinelli's remarks on the *Eclogues* and *Georgics,* separately published in 1490, became part of the critical apparatus in the Venetian edition of 1493. Toward the end of the 1480s the observations of Pomponio Leto (Sabinus), who wrote a biography of Virgil, were published without his permission and promptly repudiated.[27] His authorized commentary began to be published in the 1544 edition of Virgil long after he was dead. With the opening of the sixteenth century other scholars—Scoppa, Barland, Datho, Ricchieri, Melanchthon, Valeriano—added their commentaries to those traditionally printed. As the years passed, the roster of Virgilian scholars grew longer and longer.

III

The most impressive and influential of the fifteenth-century Virgil scholars was Christoforo Landino, a member of the magic circle of Florentine Platonists, led by Ficino and sponsored by Lorenzo de'Medici. After publishing in the 1470s an Italian translation of the elder Pliny, which proved his skill in Latin, Landino edited in 1481 the *Divina Commedia* of Dante and in 1482 the poems of Horace. Both editions were supplied with full commentaries that are superb, considering the times. In 1487–88, Landino published the text of Virgil, and in *prohemiums* to each of the three major poems—all addressed to Lorenzo's son Piero—explained, among other things, his plans for a scholarly edition. At the end of the *prohemium* to the *Aeneid* he reminds the Medici that he has already explained "the inner sense" of the epic for the benefit of the learned in the two final books of the *Quaestiones Camaldulenses.*[28] In the projected edition he proposes to omit the "philo-

---

with its translations by Thomas Twyne and Gavin Douglas are reprinted in Anna Brinton, *Mapheus Vegius and his Thirteenth Book of the Aeneid* (Palo Alto, 1930). Professor Brinton (pp. 27–28) supplied the quotations on Vegio's attitude towards Virgil.

[27] Zabughin, *op. cit.,* I, 89–90 states that Calderini's commentary on the Virgilian *Appendix* in the Venice publication of 1482 was by Pomponio Leto.

[28] Virgil, *Opera,* C. Landini Prohemium (Florence, 1487), sig. B.

sophical interpretation" and devote his commentary to grammatical and rhetorical matters. Although he occasionally refers the readers of the text to his earlier philosophical explanation,[29] he is in the main faithful to his announced plan.

The *prohemium* makes it plain that the *Quaestiones Camaldulenses* were known to the Florentine Academy—and undoubtedly to other learned Italians—long before 1487; however, the date of the first publication of the book is obscure, and there may have been editions as early as 1480. The first edition dated with certainty is that of 1505. The *Quaestiones,* which of course depend for their form more on Cicero than on Plato, were reprinted separately on several occasions and were appended as the *Allegorica Platonica in XII libros* to the Basel editions of the *Aeneid* in 1577 and 1596. This title is misleading because Landino, like most of the earlier allegorizers, did not get beyond Book Six. But the two discussions of Virgilian allegory with which the *Quaestiones* concludes are actually practical demonstrations of the philosophical theory presented in the two first books.

The disputations take place in the Monastery of Camaldoli at the invitation of Abbot Mariotto Allegri, who invites the audience to dinner at the conclusion of each day's conversation. The date is said to be 1468, and the principal speaker and leader of the group is the famous scholar, philosopher, and architect L. B. Alberti.[30] The discourses of Alberti are regularly interrupted by the great Lorenzo with a question or comment inaugurating or permitting a transition from one topic to another. Alberti, who announces that he has read the yet unpublished treatises of Ficino on the immortality of the soul, is presumed to be expressing in some degree the ideas of the master; hence, Giuliano de'Medici, Marco Parenti, Pietro and Donato Acciaioli, Alamanno Rinuccini, Antonio Canigione, Piero Landino, and even Marsiglio Ficino, other Florentines

---

[29] *Opera* (Venice, 1491), pp. 76, 124v, 127, 174. In these places (*Aeneid* I. 36; III. 7; III. 94; V. 505), he refers to his allegorical reading of the passage. See E. Wolf, "Die Allegorische Vergilerklärung des Cristoforo Landino," *Neue Jahrbücher für das Klassische Altertum Geschichte,* XXII (1919), 453–79.

[30] There is no question that Alberti, like Vegio and Landino, on some occasions saw the world through allegorical lenses. In his *Apologi* (written out according to his own statement between December 16 and 24, 1437) he puts together a hundred fables and supplies each with a "senso morale." This collection, printed at Venice in the *Opusculi morali* of 1568, (pp. 384–94), is pedagogical and aimed at young people. In one of the fables a ship, learning of the metamorphoses of Aeneas' ships, sinks itself in hopes of also becoming a sea-nymph. The moral of the fable is succinctly stated: "Half-baked ambition results in great falls." Alberti's skill at allegory can be further observed in his allegory of the sea of life and how men contend with it in his essay on Fortune and Fate; see *Opera inedita,* ed. G. Mancini (Florence, 1890), pp. 136–43.

in the assembly, hang on his words and, with the exception of Lorenzo, are generally silent. The disputations are dedicated to "the glorious and most invincible" Federigo, Duke of Urbino, who is fulsomely praised— not that Lorenzo is overlooked—for coming closest of all modern men to the ideal expressed by Virgil in the character of Aeneas.[31]

The two first disputations circle round the virtues of the active and the contemplative life and the definition of the *summum bonum*. In them Landino attempts to evolve a philosophy acceptable to social man; and though he does not find all he wants in Plato, Plato is the best philosopher he knows. Man, he believes, is fitted to act rightly and seek out the truth because, unlike animals, man has reason which enables him to discover the good practices necessary to familial and then to civic life. Contemplative life is not separable from active life; while Landino has the highest regard for contemplation, he feels that it is often another way of hiding one's light under a bushel. A Phidias who does not work in gold and ivory is worthless. "Hercules was wise, but not wise for himself and aided all mankind with his wisdom." The really wise man is, therefore, self-dedicated to humanity.

Now the possession of a mind, "an eternal mind," is the hallmark of man; hence, speculation is to the mind as food is to the body. Without contemplation any action is likely to be absurd, but contemplation is best expressed in virtuous activities. Society's end is the preservation and tranquillity of man; hence, only the mind free of bodily contagion can achieve this calm stability. The mind must, consequently, dominate the body. If it does not, it is like yoking a race horse and a donkey. Once this control is effected, the mind can perceive the *summum bonum*.

The *summum bonum* is man's proper good, but it is not exactly transcendent although it identifies itself, as it is identified, with God. Consequently, man's true origin is suggested by the activity of the mind, or understanding, in the attainment of godliness. The most noble idea entertained by the mind is that of God, and the *summum bonum* inheres in this conception. A knowledge of divine things delights the mind, and the absolute is so conjoined to the reason that it is impossible to think of one without thinking of the other. In this experience objectivity and subjectivity are erased in each other. When knowledge and will are likewise the same, beatitude is achieved. The mind is, of course, more pure than the will; nevertheless, they too cannot exist apart. Like most of the philosophers prior to him, Landino cannot develop a satisfactory

---

[31] *Allegorica Platonica* in Virgil, *Opera* (Basel, 1577), pp. 3030–31, 3046–47.

explanation of morality on a transcendent basis; he believes, nonetheless, that given a proper conjunction of all these human qualities, morality will emerge as spontaneously as poetry does. Guided by this conviction, he turns through Virgil looking for moral rather than for scientific meaning.[32] But the prelude to what he discovers in Virgil is his theory of allegory.

Among the prefatory essays to his edition of the *Divina Commedia,* Landino wrote a discourse on the nature of poetry and the divine and ancient origin of poets. Much of this material reappears in the *Quaestiones* devoted to the *Aeneid* because it forms the foundation for his belief in the moral undermeanings. Poetry, he holds, cannot be a liberal art because it is superior to all arts of human origin. "God is the greatest poet, and the world is his poem"; hence, from the beginning of things poets knew what God wished and described His mysteries to all peoples. The ancients realized this when they made Apollo, "intending by this name the highest God," chief of the Muses; in fact, they represent by this fiction the true God directing the nine choirs of angels. The poet, like the philosopher, is God-inspired, and we may turn to Plato to understand how this occurs and how we may increase the divine spirit animating us. We learn from the Greek that before we descended to our bodies, our souls contemplated God, His wisdom, justice, harmony, and beauty. We saw all of this as if in a mirror as we supped on the nectar and ambrosia of divine knowledge. After leaving the celestial mansions our souls were drenched in the Lethe of forgetfulness, and we have now lost this knowledge without which we cannot return to our true home. To recoup our loss we must follow justice and participate in both the active and contemplative life. To engage in the former we must pursue the moral virtues; the latter is reached through religion and the intellectual virtues. The first rung on the ladder of return is meditation on natural things, which is a form of imitation. Shut in the prison of the body, our ears do not hear the harmony they once did, but it is approximated by the poetical and musical genius of men. The concord of voice and music is a lesser form of imitation; but there are those, more grave in judgment and stirred by a divine spirit—poets like Dante—who reveal to us the deep sense of their minds. Landino, invoking divine aid, proposes to interpret Dante by opening not only the "natural sense" but also the allegorical, tropological, and anagogical senses. "Because they

[32] The best analysis of Landino's Neo-Platonic system is found in G. Saitta, *Il Pensiero,* I, 490–506.

have a great consonance between them, we shall call them all allegorical."

What Landino states in his Italian preface to Dante he repeats more fully and with firmer emphases in his two allegorical essays on the first six books of the *Aeneid*. He recalls the allegorical biblical exegesis of Abraham's nocturnal meditation in the fields to supply his reading of Virgil with traditional authority,[33] but he takes the objections of his potential detractors[34] in hand as soon as the discussion begins. Landino admits that he is afraid of falling under the censure of some men who judge all by "their own imbecility" and say that Virgil intended only to please the lazy ears of his hearers and that "we have willfully imagined all the things we say." But a poet, who reports what men have done, known, and contemplated, has something larger than the literal in mind because, Landino explains, poetry raises these matters, which seem humble, to a hidden excellence. The explicator or auditor who notes the "grave error" and is stimulated by it comes not only to a knowledge of high hidden matters but also derives great pleasure from the fable.[35] These secret flowings forth from the celestial fountain take place when the poet is wrapt in a divine madness, so that when the ecstasy departs he is himself amazed and astonished at what he has written.

Landino proposes to reveal only what has been darkened by "the style and figure of allegory,"[36] and he constantly inveighs against forced interpretation. He will leave "vain double meanings and empty fables" to sophisters[37] because he is convinced that the best allegory is obtained without forcing.[38] Occasionally Landino states that some passages, such as Aeneas' farewell speech to Dido, are rich in allegorical possibilities,

---

[33] Virgil, *Opera* (Basel, 1577), p. 3022. For much of my information I have relied on the unpublished Johns Hopkins dissertation, "Cristoforo Landino's Allegorization of the *Aeneid*" by Thomas Stahel, S.J.

[34] In his *Lectiones subsicivae*, Franciscus Floridus Sabinus thinks that in some of his writings other than his Virgil Landino pushed allegory too far. Nonetheless, he holds that those who read poets literally do them a great injustice because it is clear on the face of things that they intend double meanings and that a search for these meanings is a source of delight. To deprive poets of allegory strips them of ornament and shows that such a reader is the "inept of the inepts." Sabinus complains, however, that one must read poets in terms of a tradition; failing to do this is Landino's great mistake. He is himself a disciple of Palaephatus and Fulgentius and, guided by them, finds Homer and Ovid filled with allegory. He is also somewhat of a euhemerist and uncovers the story of two kinds of astrologers in the myth of Daedalus and Icarus: the father practised a moderate astrology; the son went too far. Sabinus' book is reprinted in J. Gruter, *Lampas sive fax artium liberalium* (Frankfort, 1602), I, 996–1223.

[35] Landino, in Virgil, *Opera* (Basel, 1577), pp. 3001–3002.

[36] *Ibid.*, p. 3051.

[37] *Ibid.*, p. 3036.

[38] *Ibid.*, p. 3024.

but he restrains himself.[39] He further demonstrates his control by limiting himself to a consistent moral reading, announcing this theory at the beginning of the last disputation, where he repeats the criticisms of some learned men whom he had converted to his interpretation of the *Aeneid*.

They contend that these readings should not be based on Ethics (as we argued at some length) but on Physics. Desiring to defend this view they advance certain writers who lived shortly before our time and who are by no means unlearned who interpreted some passages both intelligently and acutely to demonstrate that the nature of things is set forth in these places. We would not deny that there is much that can be conveniently and accurately allegorized in this manner. You will remember, as we said yesterday, that Virgil, because he found several classes of gods among the primitive theologians, frequently recounted things that could be applied to moral living, the forces of nature, and the pleasure of the auditors. We, however, desire to know the thought and plan with which the writer undertook the work; hence, I think we must consider why the whole work was undertaken, because it was written for a reason of some sort and not for something else. . . . Who does not see that what Virgil wrote was directed at the proper conduct of life and the *summum bonum*. He did not write to express the power of nature, but, on the contrary, the poem follows a free and continual discourse condemning vice, extolling the beauty of virtue, and commending the search for truth. A few things, added for the sake of ornament and delight, are derived from Physics.[40]

[39] *Ibid.,* p. 3032.

[40] *Ibid.,* p. 3029. Virgil's medieval repute had depended to a large degree on the adventual prophecy found in the fourth eclogue. In his notes on this poem Landino associates the whole theme with an unconscious knowledge of the coming of the Christ-child; nevertheless, he reads "tuus iam regnat Apollo" as a direct reference to Octavius. Pomponio Leto reads "Iam redit et virgo" simply as an allusion to the departure of Justice, Piety, and Faith from an earth made intolerable by wickedness and fraud. In his commentary on the eclogue, separately published as *Bucolicorum Vergilii expositio potissimum allegorica* (Antwerp, 1544), but written, of course, in the fifteenth century, Juan Luis Vives urges the literal-minded to be silent because the whole poem is about Christ. The "virgo" is the virgin changed by Virgil to Justice, or rather to "the great justice of Christ." "Te duce" implies the cleansing of original sin and so does "solvent formidine." "At tibi prima puer" refers to the rule of Christ on earth, or the church; hence, "Nec magnos" implies that Christians need not fear earthly monarchs. "Iam simul heroes" are the Apostles and other believers, but "Pauca tamen subeunt" suggests that men "filled with old error" cannot accept Christ's doctrine. "Celestial beatitude" and "the perfect Christian" is the proper comment on "Hinc ubi iam firmata virum," and the expectancy of men, angels, even of the earth itself, is found in "Aspice venturo." When the poet writes, "O mihi tam longae," he means it would require more than one lifetime to explain the deeds of Christ.

In his commentary Piero Valeriano, the great Renaissance symbolist, completely omits the Christian interpretation of the fourth eclogue. Mancinelli contents himself with writing that some people, St. Gregory for example, read the poem as prophecy. He hastens to point out that Virgil could not have known about Christ, because he died twenty-six years before the Incarnation. It is possible, he adds, that Virgil simply used the phrases of the Sibyl about Christ in his praise of Augustus and Pollio. Jodocus Badius Ascensius begins his commentary on the eclogue by stating that the poem is the subject of controversy. Some think it is a prediction of the birth of Christ; others deny this because it was written too long before the Advent. "My opinion is that the poem speaks and sings of Christ, but it is by an ignorant poet who thinks the happy age of the Advent was spoken of the time of Augustus, hence, he

Landino's search for the true meaning of the *Aeneid* was controlled
by several premises. In the *prohemium* he compares the poem to Xenophon's life of Cyrus, which simply provided the best possible example of

says, 'And now comes the last age of the song of Cumae,' repeating the prophecy of the
Cumean Sibyl about Christ." With this premise in mind Badius takes every opportunity to
write a Christian gloss. When, for instance, he comments on "Ordo est," he writes, "All this
squares with the Advent, but since the poet did not know Christ, he talks, as far as I can see,
about Caesar's progeny." The other early Virgilian commentators on this poem, Calderini,
Datho, Beroaldo are silent about the allegory.

In his commentary on the *Bucolics,* printed at Lyons in 1554, Richard Gorraeus notes that
it is thought that Virgil "filled with the Holy Spirit" wrote this poem, "a prophecy of the
Advent." In 1570 Michael Barth reports in his Leipzig printed *Bucolica commentarii* that not
all men will agree with him, but he thinks that Virgil got this prediction from the Sibyl and,
unaware of its true meaning, applied it to Pollio's son. Virgil, he says in Jerome's words, was
"a Christian without Christ." To this end, he remembers that when Virgil was asked how
long he expected his poems to endure, he replied, "Until a virgin has a child." Virgil's
"statement meant that the poems would last forever," but Barth, whose chronology was a
little weak, adds, "That night Christ was born."

The question of the nature of the eclogue continued into the seventeenth century.
Albericus Gentilis, the famous Oxford professor of law, in a *Lectionis Virgilianae variae
liber* (Hanover, 1603), quotes Augustine and Jerome on Virgil's Christian doctrine and is
convinced of the Erythrean Sibyl's prophecies. He thinks that Virgil and the Cumean Sibyl
got their information from her (pp. 58–62). Guillaume de Oncieu accepts the same theory in
his *Colloquia mixta* (Geneva, 1620), pp. 24–25. Huig de Groot also thinks that Virgil got his
prophecy from the same sources but holds that God permitted such a prophecy not to confirm
the pagan religion but rather to overthrow it; see *De veritate religionis Christianae*
(Leipzig, 1709), pp. 199–200. In 1627, the same year that de Groot's book first appeared, the
renowned Daniel Heinz also stated that Virgil read the Sibylline books before writing the
eclogue; his comments are found in his *Aristarchus sacer, sive ad Nonni in Johannem
metaphrasin exercitationes* (Leyden, 1627), p. 650.

August Buchner, Professor of Poetry at Wittenberg and a contemporary of Heinz,
discussed the whole problem in an academic oration. He admits, after quoting Eusebius at
length, that the pagans had prophets like Hermes and the Sibyls who predicted the coming of
Christ; but he points out that Tertullian, Cyprian, and Minucius Felix, all of whom knew
Virgil's eclogue, did not regard it as prophecy. Since he was a pagan Virgil could not have
known the adventual prophecies of Amos or Isaiah; moreover, if the Sibyl knew of the
Incarnation, she was inspired by demons. He points to "tuus regnat Apollo" as a pure pagan
emphasis and concludes that there is nothing in the eclogue that could not come from a pagan
source. The famous "Iam redit et Virgo" is an obvious reference to Astrea. He ended his
lecture, however, by hoping that Virgil would be given a place in the New Jerusalem so he
might sing of Christ instead of Trojan Aeneas. The "Oratio de quarta Virgilii ecloga" is
published in his *Orationes academicae* (Dresden, 1682), II, 165–98. Buchner was, of course,
engaging in the great controversy about the authenticity and inspiration of the Sibylline
books. The controversy rocked the century and would require a monograph to describe. See
H. Leclercq, "Oracles," Fernand Cabrol and H. Leclercq, *Dictionnaire d'archéologie
chrétienne et de liturgie* (Paris, 1963), XII. 2, cols. 2209–2244.

But one more sceptical account, that of Frederick Benedict Carpozov, may be mentioned.
In 1669 he published his *De P. Virgili Maronis ecloga quarta* and devoted the opening pages
to this matter as a prelude to his case against the Sibyls. He claims to have no interest in
those who think Pindar better than David, or Ovid superior to Job, but he cannot endure men
who say that the Sibyls or some other pagan writers testified about divine matters and have
the same worth as sacred authors. Others have shown the weak spots in Seneca; hence, he
will point them out in Virgil, who was, indeed, an artist, "but at the farthest possible distance
from the Christian religion." He inquires why Horace's "Tutus bos etiam rura per ambulat"
and his "tua Caesar aetas/Fruges et agris rettulit uberes" have not been read as prophecies
of the Advent.

a ruler; in contrast, Virgil's poem was an example to all mankind regardless of rank, age, sex, or condition. In it the reader would find all vices castigated and all virtues praised so that Aeneas represented the most perfect man and the unique exemplar able to instruct man in the proper conduct of life. Thanks to the rediscovery of Probus' biography of Virgil in his century, Landino had evidence that Virgil was a follower of Plato. Furthermore, Landino believed that Virgil stood on the threshold of the Church. "O divine intellect! O man most excellent among the choicest men, most worthy the name of poet! Although not a Christian, all he wrote is similar to Christian truth."[41] The almost Christian Plato lent the light of his inspiration to the almost Christian Virgil, but the ultimate ground of Landino's conviction is found in Dante, who, for more than one reason, chose Virgil to be his guide through Hell.

> For as I omit that which Servius, most eminent of grammarians . . . said about single places in this poet, so I am silent about the remarks of Macrobius, an excellent Platonic philosopher. I shall say naught of the pertinent things written by St. Jerome and St. Augustine, for have we not among our own people Dante, a serious writer learned in all things? It is he who imagined, when he crossed the whole universe from Tartarean depths to heavenly heights, that this man was his guide. Seeking the *summum bonum* of men with unquestionable genius, he selected for imitation only the *Aeneid*. It seems that he takes little from it; but if we look more carefully, he never puts it aside. Are not those things right in the beginning about the middle age of life, the wood, the three beasts, the summit of the mount lit by the rays of the sun taken from thence? I leave out other things so hidden in Dante's poem that they cannot be seen except by a few, and they very learned. He elected Virgil to be his leader when he considered those things that concerned the *summum bonum*. . . .[42]

Subscribing to a conviction that the difficulties involved in allegory lend authority to what is said and trusting that his interpretive endeavors will incite "more learned men" to find greater things in the *Aeneid*,[43] Landino began to decipher the poem. Like the pseudo-Plutarch he found in Virgil a master of all human knowledge who had realized that the Egyptian wisdom found in Homer was not unlike that of the Platonists. This perception moved Virgil to portray in Aeneas what Homer had

---

[41] Landino, in Virgil, *Opera* (Basel, 1577), p. 3023. Landino's perception of Virgil's Platonism is somewhat in advance of his time. It is rather interesting, however, that Landino having preferred a Platonic to a Stoic reading of the *Aeneid* should also be aware (pp. 3051–52) that Virgil accepted Chrysippus' immanent god rather than Plato's transcendent deity. He points out, nevertheless, that Virgil's notion of Providence coincides with that of Plato.

[42] *Ibid.*, pp. 3029–30.

[43] *Ibid.*, p. 3002.

found in Odysseus. The character created by Virgil was that of a man who gradually purged himself of many great vices, learned the marvellous ways of virtue, and, in spite of obstacles, reached his *summum bonum,* a feat which no man can achieve without wisdom.[44]

"Transferring" (Landino's favorite word for "allegorizing") Troy into the emblem of man's first age, "when reason sleeps and the senses reign," he discriminates between the careers of Paris and Aeneas in the city of the sensations. Aeneas, guided by his mother, the celestial Venus, escapes the conflagration, but Paris, abusing the right goddess and following the earthly Venus, perishes.[45] Aeneas gathers his family (strength of soul and the virtues) and makes ready to fly, but Anchises, or "bodily sensuality," refuses to leave pleasure and must be carried out on the strong part of the soul.[46] Aeneas' weeping as he leaves Troy simply suggests that though he is continent, he is not yet temperate.[47]

The continent man comes first to Thrace, which can be understood as the kind of avarice which delights in acquisitions, but then he goes promptly to Delos to consult with Apollo or wisdom. He is here informed that the Trojans must seek their original home, and this advice, while subject to an historical reading, also means they must live according to the soul's nature. Given this equivalent, it is natural that Anchises would fail to realize that Italy, or the *summum bonum,* is intended by the oracle. Italy is "where the soul governs the body," but Crete, whither they come through the senses' blunder, is a state "in which all things look toward the body."[48] In Crete, Aeneas has no success, and he departs when the Penates (reason, intellect, and understanding) support the oracle.

Piloted by Palinurus, "libido," the wanderers easily take the wrong course and arrive at the Strophades, which is the kind of avarice that withholds help from those who need it. This type of greed is symbolized by the Harpies with fair, hypocritical faces and foul feces.[49] Again consulting with reason or Helenus, Aeneas learns that he must reach Plato's third order of virtue, that belonging to purged souls, or he will never come to Italy.[50] Informed by the prophet he avoids Scylla, or "lust," and Charybdis, or "greed," sees "tyranny" and "tyrants" person-

[44] *Ibid.,* p. 3004.
[45] *Ibid.,* pp. 3006, 3009.
[46] *Ibid.,* p. 3008.
[47] *Ibid.,* p. 3009.
[48] *Ibid.,* p. 3012.
[49] *Ibid.,* p. 3013.
[50] *Ibid.,* pp. 3015–16.

ified in the Cyclops and Laestrygonians, and finds haven in Sicily, which was once joined to Italy and is consequently the lower level of the soul. At this symbolic place Anchises, or "sensuality," dies; but it is logical that Aeneas cannot proceed to Italy until the funeral rites are performed.[51]

Buffeted in the storm raised by Aeolus (the appetites) at the behest of Juno ("love of human affairs which hinders our knowledge of the divine"), the Trojans are saved when Neptune (the superior reason) lifts his head above the seas and restores them to tranquillity. If "Italy is the figure for the contemplative life," then "Carthage is the figure for the active life." Carthage is on an inlet because no man is a continent but rather an island, separate and torn by the surges of ocean.[52] Aeneas' experience in Carthage is, consequently, an education in kingship. He first ascends a high place to signify that a ruler must have a speculative vision of things. What he views from here is the pattern of a republic, and republicanism is personified in Dido.

All this is concerned with civic life because Virgil wishes to express what I said shortly before, that republics which grow from small beginnings are better in these than in their end. Therefore, he shows the Queen in the beginning temperate in all things; but very shortly, smitten by love, she slips little by little from temperance to continence. Next, overcome by love, she becomes incontinent; and, finally, she declines into the highest intemperance.[53]

Her natural lusts supported by Anna's arguments based on the prospects of pleasure and hope, Dido consummates her union with Aeneas in a cave, "which represents those who have restricted their souls to corporeal and corruptible matters."[54] From Aeneas' side the liaison indicates that the most excellent of men are sometimes deflected from a right course by ambition; nevertheless, when he is able to distinguish the true from the false, Aeneas decides to leave secretly for fear Dido will not let him go. "The inferior reason, which is properly personified as a woman, tries to keep an excellent man in civic life and turn him aside from desired contemplation." Although Dido calls it marriage, Aeneas is not "married" to Dido anymore than we are married to mortal things; so he may be said not to fly from activity but to withdraw from it.[55]

Pursuing his metaphor of the inferior reason as feminine, Landino

[51] *Ibid.*, p. 3018.
[52] *Ibid.*, pp. 3019–23.
[53] *Ibid.*, p. 3026.
[54] *Ibid.*, p. 3027.
[55] *Ibid.*, p. 3032.

interprets the firing of the ships while the men are at the games as the ease with which this lower reason is charmed by the senses when separate from its superior director. The lower reason almost perishes in the flames of desire but repents when the higher reason comes with the speed of the racing Aeneas and Ascanius, and the passionate fire is quickly extinguished. Subsequent to this near disaster Neptune, or reason, promises that all of the Trojans except Palinurus, or appetite, will reach Italy; hence, Palinurus, hopelessly blinded by the seas, has to be lost. "It is necessary for rational appetite to seize the tiller and resist pleasures. . . . Aeneas comes to Italy; he would never have done so with Palinurus at the wheel." The ships enter the harbor where Aeneas anchors them as he had done at Carthage, but there is a difference. At Carthage the harbor appeared tranquil, but the ships were not safe from the storms of civil life; now "the habit of virtue is so firm that Aeneas would not leave his proposed life."[56]

The remainder of Alberti's discourse as presented by Landino depends on the famous sixth book,[57] where the commentator finds the fullest expression of Platonic idealism. The Sibyl or "the thought of God" dwells in a cave indicating "that truth lies hidden." Nearby is the temple of Apollo built by Daedalus, whose flight through the air suggests there can be nothing earthly "in the mind borne towards contemplation." The doors of the temple are adorned by representations of vices, and the Sibyl rightly warns Aeneas not to contemplate them. Placed in the forecourt of contemplation, he asks to be taken to the underworld. Landino, as at other moments of this discussion, provides a learned account of both the Hebrew and Greek conceptions of Hades, but Plato's philosophical interpretation of the underworld is his congenial topic. It is essentially a Platonistic-Christian description of the descent of the soul, but, somewhat like Christ's descent, it is guided by wisdom, or the Sibyl, and signified by the golden bough, which suggests the ability of knowledge to nourish knowledge. The beginning of this search for truth is symbolized in the burial of Misenus, a man who put aside solid truth to chase after empty glory.

The allegorical abstractions that crowd the entrance to Hell permit Landino to summarize his interpretive concepts.

With amazing judgment Virgil expresses what follows about the entrance to Hell. If he agrees with the opinion of Plato, on whom he depends, he is describing

[56] *Ibid.*, pp. 3033–34.

[57] The explanation occupies *ibid.*, pp. 3035–53; I shall, consequently, only annotate direct quotations.

the descent of souls into their bodies; it is manifest that the soul, which up till then was free of all these evils, falls into them by the body's contamination. Now it feels all those disturbances. It is torn with weeping and cares; it fears impending dangers; it experiences sickness and labor; it is vexed by hunger and need; it is oppressed by all the calamities enumerated by Virgil from which, absent from the body, it was once free.[58]

The encountered monsters enforce this reading. The Centaurs, offspring of Ixion, were first imbued with humanity but finally descend to savagery. The Hydra is "sophistic deceit." The Chimera is "wrath"; the Gorgons "the charms of passion"; Geryon is "the weaker part of the soul which governs all of the vicious man." Each of the famous rivers has a moral meaning, and the Styx, or "the sadness attendant on committed sin," is crossed only by the boat of "voluntas" steered by Charon, or "free-choice." Aeneas, safely on the other bank "after a long conflict between reason and appetite," is brought to contemplation. Here he is confronted by Cerberus, whose three heads symbolize the Earth and its three parts. "If Cerberus is the Earth, who does not realize that our poet wished to express in his barking the insatiableness of the body?"[59]

In Tartarus Aeneas is taught by the Sibyl about all the vices he must avoid so that, purified of them, he may enter the Elysian Fields. Lorenzo, who is Baptista's only interrupter, breaks in at this point to observe that while Virgil was being clarified, "You were at the same time leading into a discussion of our own city's divine poem." Now Lorenzo knows what Dante meant. First there is the descent to the underworld; then one emerges to find no other way to Heaven than through Purgatory. Baptista congratulates him for recognizing in Dante "all these carefully hidden matters"; then he continues to demonstrate how Virgil hides "a knowledge of things in Heaven" under the fiction of the Elysian fields, where Aeneas visits with those "who religiously led the life of contemplation and justly led the active life." All these men are worthy of returning to Heaven, the place of their origin. He has now illuminated the dark places in the *Aeneid* in enormous detail; so he concludes with advice to its readers.

You have seen, unless I err, a long journey filled with difficulties and wanderings, but one in which a man, amorous of virtue, finally attains his desired end. Through many mishaps and trials Aeneas has finally arrived in Italy, his quiet home. If we will imitate him, freeing our soul from bodily banes and refreshing it at

[58] *Ibid.,* p. 3043.
[59] *Ibid.,* p. 3046.

virtue's clear fountain, we shall lead happily the same life while we are still in the flesh; and when, flying from thence, they return to their origin, we shall enjoy it forever.[60]

With this, says Landino, Baptista concluded his interpretation.

The two discourses on the first half of the *Aeneid* are solidly anchored on the Christian Platonism of the Florentine Academy and are, consequently, both metaphysical and moral. But Landino is not unaware of the other modes of symbolic reading that tradition had lent him; and, as he moves from line to line of the epic and inspects it in detail, he often sees meanings of other sorts. He is aware of the various astrological readings of myths and of stellar episodes in the *Aeneid*, whose hero left Troy when Venus was conjunct with Jupiter in Libra.[61] He pauses time and time again over the etymological significance of proper names. Aeneas, for example, derives his name from "aenos," or "praise."[62] He knows many of the conventional allegorical equivalents for the sea,[63] the wood,[64] and Jupiter's Golden Chain,[65] equivalents hallowed by continuous Christian usage. The commentary is further adorned with erudite essays on purely historical or scientific matters. There are scholarly accounts of the Penates,[66] the Harpies,[67] the Greek classification of the gods,[68] the nature of bees,[69] and the phenomena attendant on the rainbow.[70] Many of these points are rehearsed again in his nonallegorical edition of Virgil and provide a model for sixteenth- and seventeenth-century editors. It is clear that after the publication of the *Quaestiones Camaldulenses,* men would find it difficult to read the *Aeneid* as nothing more than the master poem of Latin paganism.

IV

It must be admitted, however, that not all of Landino's ideas were unique. He was in some things simply in the current of humanistic theory. As early as January, 1427, Filelfo wrote to Cyriacus of Ancona

[60] *Ibid.,* p. 3051.
[61] *Ibid.,* p. 3005.
[62] *Ibid.,* p. 3007; see also pp. 3001, 3013, 3022, 3033, 3034, 3038.
[63] *Ibid.,* p. 3020.
[64] *Ibid.,* p. 3025.
[65] *Ibid.*
[66] *Ibid.,* p. 3012.
[67] *Ibid.,* p. 3013.
[68] *Ibid.,* p. 3021.
[69] *Ibid.,* p. 3026.
[70] *Ibid.,* p. 3021.

and reported as common opinion that Virgil wrote the *Aeneid* to instruct magistrates. He imitates Homer's *Odyssey,* says Filelfo, and praises Augustus in Aeneas, but more than this he demonstrates, through the wisdom and virtue of his hero, both the active and the contemplative life in order to mark out the way to the *summum bonum.* Since Nature expects man to think before acting, the first six books are about the contemplative life and prepare the reader for the active life revealed in the latter books in which Aeneas, or Justice, overthrows Turnus, or Injustice. In this he is superior to Homer, who wrote the *Iliad* before the *Odyssey.* With his eye on Fulgentius or Bernard of Silvester, Filelfo finds in the first five books allegories of infancy, boyhood, adolescence, youth, and manhood; but almost with the unborn Landino in mind, he urges Cyriacus to read the sixth book as Pythagoras or Plato would. The wisdom and prudence taught by Virgil is, he thinks, valuable for men in civil life, but it pales before celestial truth which is the highest wisdom.[71] When Jodocus Badius Ascensius, professor turned printer, wrote a preface for the Paris Virgil of 1507, he repeated the allegory of Filelfo about the five ages, but he read the sixth book more in the manner of Landino. "Old age warned by death," though the soul is not yet separated from the body, descends into Hell as an act of spiritual meditation.[72] Commentaries of this nature and the reprinting of Landino's allegories until almost the end of the sixteenth century firmly placed the moral reading of the character of Aeneas in men's minds; in fact, even Melanchthon, who is disturbed by Virgil's paganism and complains that he permits the gods to govern things, is ready to admit that Aeneas is the pattern of a virtuous man.[73] The central nature of all Aeneas' virtues was within two decades brought into total focus by Girolamo Balbi, a pupil of Pomponio Leto and, ultimately, Bishop of Gurck.

Balbi's real purpose in composing the *De civili et bellica fortitudine liber ex mysteriis poetae Vergilii nunc depromptus* (Rome, 1526), a book addressed with lavish compliment to Pope Clement VII, was to urge the spiritual and temporal leaders of Christendom to smash the Turks and free the republics of Europe "from the danger that hangs over them." To develop his moral theories he draws on a score of Greek and Latin poets, but it is Plato and Aristotle—not the erroneous Seneca

[71] Filelfo, *Epistolarum libri sedecim* (Paris, 1513), pp. 4v–7. See also Coluccio Salutati's letter to Giuliano Zennarini in *Epistolario,* ed. F. Novati (Rome, 1891), I, 306–7.

[72] Virgil, *Opera omnia* (Paris, 1507), p. **4v. This preface might have appeared as early as the 1503 (?) Strassburg Virgil which I have not seen.

[73] Virgil, *Opera . . . Vergilius Philippi Melanchthonis scholis doctissimis illustratus* (Cologne, 1545), p. A2.

—who supply him with ideas coinciding with those of Christian doctrine. Though Pindar and Claudian furnish an occasional illustrative quotation, it is the *Aeneid* which is constantly rifled to illuminate what the philosophers, the Hebrew prophets, and the Apostles have written. Balbi recalls the praise of Homer voiced by Plato, Plutarch, and others, but Virgil, likewise, is no narrow poet but a philosopher whose verses conceal all knowledge. "Therefore, let us listen to Maro philosophizing about fortitude, a virtue once held in such great esteem, that those who had it the most were called heroes and venerated as demigods, obtaining the superior places in the Elysian Fields."[74]

If men, Balbi says, would adjust their thoughts and acts to the image of the Divine Mind (Plato's Idea), they would find nothing to condemn in a well-lived life. A proper love of glory is reasonable; even those philosophers who write to the contrary always sign their books. But true glory does not reside in popular esteem; in fact, its basis is fortitude, which was once thought "the only virtue" as Apollo's address to Iulus (IX. 641) makes clear. Without fortitude, the mean between fear and audacity, one can have no virtues. Turnus' state of conflicting emotions (XII. 666–68) symbolizes the need for a middle way. Man is, consequently, both a potential brute and a potential angel, and he can go in either direction (VI. 542–43, 567; VII. 17–18, 191). As Anchises told Aeneas (VI. 730–34), the soul is divine in origin, nevertheless, brutes are superior to men in sight, hearing, and smell (II. 664–66). "Both Platonic and Christian philosophers describe man's double nature, inferior in one aspect, superior and divine in the other."[75] Hence, man's virtue may be shown in both contemplation and action.

But virtue is not *a natura* (the absurd theories of Stoics and Epicureans set aside) as the affections are; hence, restraint, exercise, and training are necessary to its growth. "Under the cover of words and in oblique figures, Maro reveals this secret of philosophy decorously, when, in the first book, he shows reason, or Aeolus, confessing that his power is based on Juno, or the senses."[76] No mortals except the unnatural Apathes of Ethiopia are without affections, but their control is another matter and in the gift of reason. The whole doctrine is skillfully allegorized by Virgil in his description of Aeolus' kingdom (I. 53–63) and may be clarified by other Virgilian descriptions (III. 29; II. 774; IX. 66) of the physical signs of lack of control.

[74] Balbi, *De civili et bellica fortitudine*, p. A4v. I am following the text seriatim, supplying the references from the *Aeneid* for Balbi's direct quotations.
[75] *Ibid.*, p. C1.
[76] *Ibid.*, p. C3.

The sensitive part of the soul is possessed by two powers, desire and anger. The nature of desire is carefully anatomized in Dido's conversation with herself (IV. 534–37), but both powers are equally based on joy, libido, "which calls itself 'hope,'" sorrow, and fear. Although astrologers are inclined to derive these dispositions from planetary influences, they actually come from the two levels in man's nature. Fear, for instance, can be good (II. 726–29) or bad, when it arises from ignorance (X. 843) or results in suicide (VI. 435–36); but its opposite, recklessness, is always to be condemned (V. 376–78; XII. 14–15). Anger, like fear, is also an ambivalent affection; if just and moderated it is proper to man, but otherwise it actually lessens fortitude rather than augmenting it (IX. 757–61). In his description of the enraged Turnus, Virgil provides, according to Balbi, a symbolic representation of anger.

> Driven by fury from his whole face ardent
> Sparks shoot; from his keen eyes fire gleams;
> Just as a bull, before battle begins, utters
> A fearful bellowing; and gathering rage in his horns,
> Tries the stout trunk of a tree, or lashes the wind
> With blows, or commences the fight with scattered sand.
> (XII. 101–6).

Balbi, after listing remedies for anger, which can, in time, develop into a form of envy called "hate," a passion well-known to Virgil, comes to fortitude and discriminates between its military and its civil manifestations. The former is by no means inferior to the latter; in fact, there is a domestic version of fortitude which makes for household harmony. The true virtue is often defined or described in the *Aeneid:* when Ascanius is lectured on valor (XI. 435–40); when, early in the epic, Aeneas fled from Thrace, "symbol of cupidity"; when Turnus in scorn taunts the Trojans (IX. 603–10). In the opening pages of his book Balbi had called fortitude "the pristine virtue"; in the closing paragraphs,[77] he takes a lesson from the pseudo-Albericus and describes her as a goddess invoked under other names by early leaders of men. Using "Virgilian colors," he views her enthroned with Justice and Prudence on either hand. Her four followers—Endurance, Perseverance, Generosity, and Patience—serve her. Each of these symbolic personages finds her identifying lines in Virgil's epic. Having seen the goddess, one should avoid, as Turnus and other opponents of Aeneas fail to do, her false semblances. If one recalls the exhortation of Pallas, son of Evander, "Gods do not attack; mortals, we are driven by mortals," (X. 372–76) and

[77] *Ibid.,* pp. LIV–L4.

realizes how luxurious and enervated the Turks are, the duty of the Christian is obvious.

Balbi's search for moral and psychological meaning in the *Aeneid* was paralleled in a limited way by Sebastiano Regoli, a somewhat younger Italian contemporary, whose *In primum Aeneidos Virgilii librum ex Aristotelis de arte poetica et rhetorica praeceptis explicationes* was eventually published in 1563 in Bologna. Regoli, Professor of Literature, acknowledges his debt to his teacher Achille Bocchi[78] and refers to Landino's *Quaestiones,* which he, like all men of his generation, had read. There is no indication in his book that he intended to go beyond Book One, and his commentary, which embraces historical material and poetical cross-references as well as allegory, is probably from his classroom lectures, which certainly must have covered at least the first half of the epic.

Summarizing the experiences of Aeneas in a sentence which would leave Cicero short-winded, Regoli urges his readers to see in the hero a man blessedly at the summit of praise; he has reached felicity by virtuous action, which it was the duty of the best ethnic poets to describe. Poetry, he maintains, must serve politics, "queen of all arts," by marking the way to virtue; just as the physician conceals the bitterness of a draught in something sweet, so the poet "with sweetness of speech and joyful imitation instructs men in what is right and good though it may seem to them hard and difficult."[79] Following in Landino's footsteps, he interprets Troy as the first age and as voluptuousness, seeing in Aeneas and Paris cultivators of the proper and of the indecent Venuses. Juno is again ambition, who wishes to deflect Aeneas from the life of contemplation, whither he will disembark after he has overcome many hardships and difficulties.[80] Regoli, having accepted the traditional theme of the *Aeneid* and having several hundred pages at his disposal, does not

---

[78] Achille Bocchi (Bocchius) was a friend of Giglio Giraldi who referred to him as Phileros and caused a later confusion among early biographers. His most impressive work was the *Symbolicarum quaestionum de universo genere libri quinque* (Bologna, 1555), a collection of 151 emblems with verse explications. Like other emblematists he was clever at converting the myths into allegories and was aided in his efforts by Fulgentius, Martianus Capella, Proclus, Porphyry, Plotinus, Eustathius, and the pseudo-Heraclitus. In the 1574 edition (p. 119) the 65th *Symbol* is an etching of a statue of Hercules, who is "the true image of wisdom." His purloining of the golden apples from the dragon is symbolically analysed. The dragon is wicked desire, and when it is dead, a triple glory results. Anger is destroyed; desire and slothful love perish. Hercules' garments signify strength of mind; his club means power. "Who conquers the senses is victor."

[79] Regoli, *In primum . . . explicationes* (Bologna, 1563), pp. 10–11. Numerals in text refer to lines in Book One of the *Aeneid.*

[80] *Ibid.,* pp. 24–25.

hesitate to supply allegorical explanations for each episode in the first book of the epic.

Virgil, in a poetical aside about Juno's case against her spouse, mentions "the honors paid kidnapped Ganymede" (28); so Regoli identifies Ganymede, explains Jupiter's connection with the eagle, and brings in the euhemerists' explanation of the event as well as Xenophon's allegorization. He etymologizes Ganymede's name as "bringer of counsel" and provides the allegory: "Prudence rejoices in counsel which is born of the pure mind; therefore, Jupiter takes it to himself and embraces it and furnishes it with entertainment because prudence thus has a tranquillity of mind free from external care."[81] In a similar fashion Regoli repeats Landino's interpretation that Aeolus represents both the inferior mind and prudence, which controls the winds of perturbation moved to conflict by Juno, or the desire of ruling. He disagrees with this interpretation. Aeolus lives in a cave, or the human breast, which is filled with affections disturbing the mind, the true reading of the first verses (52–55); however, when Virgil writes, "In his high citadel Aeolus sits, scepter in hand, taming their passions" (56–57), Landino's translation is proper.[82] This conclusion enables Regoli to support Landino's doctrine that Neptune is the higher or divine reason.[83] But Regoli does not limit himself to matters of this sort, and, while he can find "understanding and knowing" personified in Triton and Cymothoe[84] or an allegory of prudence in Aeneas' arrival in port,[85] he can also pause over the etymology of Deiopea's name as well as the meteorological significances of the nymphs attending Juno, or air.[86]

Landino had so completely filled the *Aeneid* with allegory and symbol that there was little original explication remaining to be done, and most Virgilian scholars turned more and more to historical explanations of the epic. K. Willich traces Virgil's debt to Homer, the geography of the *Aeneid,* and similar scholars' topics in his *De consilio et scopo Aeneidos Virgilianae* (Frankfort, 1551). Similar problems of a historical or philological nature were investigated in the sixteenth century by Francesco Campani, G. Leonberger, O. Toscanella, B. Maranta, and others. The historical, philological, and literary study of Virgil, originating in the sixteenth century, flowed like a gathering torrent into

[81] *Ibid.,* pp. 74–75.
[82] *Ibid.,* pp. 111–15.
[83] *Ibid.,* pp. 175–76.
[84] *Ibid.,* p. 184.
[85] *Ibid.,* p. 191.
[86] *Ibid.,* pp. 136–39.

the next age. In 1604 a superb commentary based on comparisons and illustrations from all classical literature was published in Lyons by J. J. Spanmueller as the *Symbolarum libri XVII*. Separate monographs, pointing the way to nineteenth-century scholarship, also began to appear. Castalio wrote on hot and cold drinks in Virgil, and Eysson concentrated on nut-bearing trees mentioned by the Roman. Slowly but surely allegory begins to fade out of the *apparatus criticus,* but it is sometimes remembered in prefaces.

De Sponde had written about the traditional allegorical interpretations in the prologue to his edition of Homer, and in the same way the eminent Frederick Taubmann wrote a preface to the *Ciris* in his Wittenberg text of Virgil, posthumously published in 1618. Recalling the demonic contamination of biblical episodes, he showed the likenesses and unlikeness of various myths to their prototypes in the Scripture.[87] But allegory, disappearing from professional classical texts, was revived in vernacular commentaries when the *L'Opere di Virgilio Mantoano* was published in Venice in 1576. The *L'Opere* provides the Latin text and surrounds it with an Italian commentary. Carlo Malatesta wrote on the *Bucolics*; Filippo Venuti on the *Georgics*; and Giovanni Fabrini supplied an enormous scholium for the *Aeneid*. Neither Malatesta nor Venuti inclines toward symbolic reading; the famous fourth eclogue is subjected only to a historical and grammatical analysis. Fabrini is of a different breed from his associates and in addition to an "Ordine delle parole," an "Espositione delle parole, delle favole, dell'historie, e luoghi grammaticali," and a "Luoghi rettorici" furnishes the reader with a "Sensi fisici, allegorici, e morali."[88]

Fabrini's allegorical commentary, which concentrates its full attention on the first six books of the *Aeneid,* is essentially a translation paraphrase of Landino. At times it is close enough to be almost a literal rendering, but like other similar performances it is naturally redundant and prolix.[89] Often Fabrini adds nothing more to his great predecessor than words, words, words. He also had his eye on Landino's Dante

---

[87] Virgil, *Opera omnia*, ed. F. Taubman (Wittenberg, 1618), "Ciris," pp. 7–8. In this edition each poem of Virgil is separately paged.

[88] There were editions in 1588, 1604, 1615 and as late as 1710. In the Venice 1615 edition, allegory is found on pages 2v, 4v, 6–7, 8–8v, 12, 14, 21, 25, 26, 57–57v, 58, 59v–60, 64–64v, 67–68, 71–71v, 73v–74, 77–79, 83v–84, 96–96v, 118–18v, 121v–22v, 139–39v, 141, 142, 144, 146, 147, 151–51v, 152v–53, 154–54v, 157v–58, 159, 159v–60, 164v–69v, 173–73v, 174v, 181–81v, 182–83, 194–94v, and 208–208v. The last two references are the only allegorical commentaries on the second six books.

[89] Fabrini, in Virgil, *L'opere* (Venice, 1615), p. 67v should be compared with Landino in Virgil, *Opera* (Basel, 1577), p. 3009, or Fabrini, *op. cit.* p. 71 with Landino, *op. cit.,* p. 3011.

commentary, and where Landino pointed to the similarities in Virgil, Fabrini finds Virgilian analogues in Dante. Landino had defined Thrace as avarice, Juno as ambition, and Troy as pleasure; these, says Fabrini, are the three beasts seen by Dante.[90] The lioness is pleasure; the wolf, avarice; the lion, ambition. But the commentary of Fabrini, though an Italian rendering of Landino, is something more than this. A great number of Greek and Latin authors are brought in to add greater emphasis to what Landino had said, and Fabrini sometimes goes to the earlier allegorical or euhemeristic commentaries for comfort. At times, as in his lengthy remarks on VI. 14–39, he is impressively learned and original.[91] There are occasions too when he embroiders on his master.

When he ascertained the meaning of Cerberus, Landino identified him as "the three-nooked earth" which, in the end swallows all. The barking represents a desire for food, drink, and sleep, desires without which meditation is impossible; hence, the demands of body need to be met moderately. To support this advice Landino calls not on Diogenes but on Epicurus, whose temperance he praises. Taking his cue from Landino's commentary, Fabrini extends the idea in his own way.

According to my opinion, they gave Cerberus three heads to signify the natural and necessary needs without which one cannot live or do anything. They are hunger, thirst, and sleep, which are in the body and bark round the mind never letting it rest unless it satisfies them. This is true because when the body is hungry, thirsty, or sleepy it can do nothing and must first satisfy these needs before doing anything else. Therefore, Aeneas, who has now entered the Inferno, that is contemplation, being troubled by natural and necessary needs must look after them before contemplating. The Sibyl, who is counsel, gives Cerberus a bone and puts him to sleep. With this Virgil teaches that it is not wrong to attend to natural needs up to a certain point. Who denies necessities to nature discovers in the end that he has done wrong and must obey. With all of this, however, it is virtuous to virtuously and voluntarily deprive onself of necessities in order to please God for charitable or penitential reasons. And to show then that Nature requires only a little, Cerberus is put to sleep with a simple bone because when nature is hungry, she asks no more than bread, and when she is thirsty, she is content with water, and when she is sleepy, a little hut will do. Epicurus, who places the highest good in pleasure, did not seek any spice other than hunger and thirst because one made eating pleasant and the other sweetened drinking.[92]

Although there are many allusions to the allegory in Virgil during the seventeenth century and it is obvious that the *Aeneid* was read for

[90] Fabrini, *op. cit.,* p. 2v.
[91] *Ibid.,* pp. 142v–44.
[92] *Ibid.,* p. 166.

other purposes besides literary delight, the full-scale allegorization of the epic terminates with this Italian translation and augmentation of Landino's century-old interpretation. Hugues, who did such a fine Christian analysis of Homer, did not, of course, slight Virgil, or for that matter, Ovid, finding in the voyage of Aeneas the journey of Peter via a ship (the Church) from Antioch to Rome. Whenever Aeneas prays or sacrifices, Hugues finds the first Pope at his religious rites and duties, but he can go beyond this and discover in Romulus and Remus the figures of Peter and Paul and in the founding of Rome, the establishment of the Roman Church.[93] His allegorical approach and results were heavily censured, but he would find a true disciple in the cryptic Herman von der Hardt of the next century. Although they were erudite, both these men are on the lunatic fringe of interpretation and as far from the fixed tradition as the literalists.[94]

[93] Hugues, *Vera historia Romana* (Rome, 1655), pp. 129–45, 169–77. On pp. 97–101 he sees the destruction of Troy as that of Jerusalem under the Babylonians or the Romans and argues that if Aeneas can be understood as Peter and Lavinia as the Church, then Turnus stands for the heathen who will be converted to Christianity. He prepares his readers for all of this by stating Noah to be Prometheus whose chaining in the Caucasus is Noah's sorrow for the separation from his son Japheth. The eagle that ate his liver is either "sorrows and cares" or the Roman military eagle or the wind Aquilo which carried his son away. Saturn is, naturally, Adam and Eve is Ops; the devoured children are recollections of the eating of the forbidden fruit, the reason that all the sons of Adam perished (pp. 14–16).

[94] Hugues' analysis was criticized, always solemnly, by Joannes Böck in *De bello Troiano praecipue Jacobo Hugoni . . . opposita* (Jena, 1672), and Matthias Linck in *De bello Troiano in qua contra omnes fere historicos ostenditur, Trojam in illo bello quod decennale putatur, minime a Graecis flammis ruinisve fuisse deletam* (s.l., 1674). Böck attacks the Catholic censor who had passed such a silly book and makes mock of Hugues' belief in the divine inspiration of the Sibyl and Virgil. "The word of God is not some fabulous poet's" (p. 2); nonetheless, he thinks highly of Duport's *Gnomologia,* because it not only shows that "the Gentiles had some knowledge of God but is also a morally useful book" (p. C4). Linck points out that Jerusalem can hardly be Troy because, if one believes the Homeric legends, Troy either never existed or was completely destroyed by the Greeks. He inclines to the opinion of Dio Chrysostom that none of the events recorded in the *Iliad* really took place and that the Greeks finally withdrew and lost part of their fleet. Linck supposes that Priam ruled happily and Hector after him; both kings sent Trojan colonies into Greece, France, and Westphalia. In due course, Troy was destroyed by an earthquake followed by a flood. This rejoinder is a fine example of the pot making sport of the kettle.

Herman von der Hardt, unwilling to see a mystery shirked, published a series of pieces at Helmstadt between 1739–40 in which the hidden history in Virgil was displayed. The titles are enough: (1) *Prooemium in Botanica et Bucolica Virgilii, hortulans Tityro, Alexi, et Sileni;* (2) *P. V. M. dulcia arva Q. Varus literatissimus bellorum dux in Octavi Caesaris Augusti Romana curia excellens;* (3) *P. V. M. Deus Pan sylvarum et pastorem numen . . . O. Caesar pro paronomasiae divinitate;* (4) *P. V. M. famosa Amaryllis marmorae Roma, Maecenate, Vero et Pollione in Caesarea Romana curia;* (5) *P. V. M. fatidici poetae Alexis;* (6) *P. Virgilii Silicernum;* (7) *Musa Virgilii Augusta patula fagus duodecim frondium.*

VII

≈ UNDERMEANINGS IN OVID'S
METAMORPHOSES ≈

THE RENAISSANCE INTERPRETATIONS of the *Metamorphoses* are in some respects quite different from those of the *Aeneid* or of the Homeric epics. The allegorizers of Homer had a long and sacred classical tradition to guide them. The Virgilian moralizers, with only Fulgentius and perhaps Bernard of Silvester behind them, had no store of ancient or medieval interpreters to lead the way. Ovid, however, came into the hands of Renaissance editors with the blessings of many medieval commentaries; in fact, it could be said without too much fear of contradiction that the Middle Ages invented the theory that the *Metamorphoses* of Ovid was capable of allegorical exposition. One supposedly early summary of the fables, the *Narrationes* of Lactantius or Luctatius Placidus, was unknown to the Middle Ages but was reverently printed and reprinted in the Renaissance because the author was confused to his advantage with the Church Father of similar name.[1] He was clearly a Christian,[2] but he is unmentioned

---

[1] The text of the *Narrationes* may be found in *Metamorphoseon libri XV*, ed. H. Magnus (Berlin, 1914) and in D. A. Slater, *Towards a Text of the Metamorphosis of Ovid* (Oxford, 1927). A study of the *Narrationes* has been made by Brooke Otis, "The *Argumenta* of the so-called Lactantius," *Harvard Studies in Classical Philology*, XLVII (1936), 131–63. See also Ursula D. Hunt, *Le Sommaire en Prose des Métamorphoses d'Ovide dans le Manuscript Burney 311* (Paris, 1925). The notion that more was to be found in Ovid's poem than met the eye was suggested by many men before the twelfth century, and he was pillaged for matter as early as the time of Dracontius. There is of course the well-known poem "On Books I am Accustomed to Read" by the eighth-century Theodulf of Orleans, who suggested that "a great deal of truth hides under the covering of falsity." See Theodulf, *Carmina*, ed. E. Dümmler (Berlin, 1881), p. 543.

[2] In the *Commentarios in Statii Thebaida et commentarium in Achilleida*, ed. R. Jahnke (Leipzig, 1898), p. 229, Lactantius, to whom the work is assigned, states that it was always customary to call the highest power "God" as did Orpheus and Moses, Isaiah, and other

until the fourteenth century.[3] As he moved through the *Metamorphoses* he epitomized each tale in prose, in this way setting the fashion for a consecutive but separate commentary. His procedure was followed by Arnulph of Orleans, who adds a moral explanation to each summary.[4]

priests of "the Great God." It might be assumed that the extant commentary on Ovid may once have been as full as that on Statius.

[3] The fourteenth-century humanist Coluccio Salutati frequently quotes from Lactantius Placidus' commentary on Statius in his *De laboribus Herculis,* but there is no evidence he used the *Narrationes.* D. A. Slater, *op. cit.,* pointing to the fact that the earliest manuscript of the Ovidian summaries is dated 1462, thinks the earlier dating is suspicious; Ghisalberti (see note 4 below), however, is inclined to date the knowledge of this work at least a century earlier.

[4] A text of Arnulph with prefatory material and commentary has been published by F. Ghisalberti as "Arnolfo d'Orleans, un cultore di Ovidio nel sec. XII," *Memorie del Reale Instituto Lombardo di Scienze e Lettere,* XXIV, 4 (1932), 157–234. Ghisalberti finds that Arnulph depended on Fulgentius, the three Vatican mythologies (*Scriptores rerum mythicarum Latini tres Romae nuper reperti,* ed. G. H. Bode, Celle, 1834), and Albericus of London. He also used Servius' commentary on the *Aeneid.* In his opening commentary on V. 1 (p. 212) Arnulph states he will explicate according to the moral, historical, and allegorical methods: "Modo moraliter, aut historice, aut allegorice exponamus." By "historical" he seems to mean euhemeristic, and he either states that "this is true history" or explains the myth by converting the gods and goddesses into kings and queens or great men. By "moral" he means both moral and physical, and he usually gives equivalents: Y is "heat"; Z is "ambition." When he turns to allegory he often calls his interpretation "allegorice" or writes, "allegoria est" before he puts his equivalents in motion. An example is his reading of the myth of Orpheus, X. 1 (p. 222). Following his commentary through the first four books of the *Metamorphoses* (pp. 201–12) one can see something of his method.

The Creation account is like that of Moses, and so is Prometheus's forming of the first man. Prometheus, however, was a wise man who went into the Caucasus to study the nature of man, which is that of an earthly body and the soul. The latter is indicated when he urges men to look at the sun's course. The vultures devouring his liver are the cares that eat the student. The giants are earth-lovers and tyrants. Deucalion and Pyrrha are physical allegories, suggesting that females are born when the female sperm is superior; males, when the male sperm dominates. The Python is false credulity; Apollo is truth. Io is loved by Jupiter because God loves virgins. Argus is the world; Mercury is "eloquence." Aesculapius is from Greek "hard making," or the third branch of medicine, which is surgery; hence, he is the son of Apollo, or "wisdom," and Coronis, or "mortality." Jupiter, King of Crete, loved Europa, daughter of the King of Phoenicia; his eloquent son Mercury lured her to the seashore, and Jupiter carried her off to Crete in a ship with a bull figure-head. The dragon teeth sown by Cadmus, who invented writing, are the letters of the Greek alphabet, and the five surviving warriors are the vowels. Atlas, King of Libya, being unable to resist Perseus, retired to the mountain which bears his name and studied the procession of the signs of the zodiac. The comment on Ceres and Proserpine (pp. 213–14) will show his full-scale approach, but the myth is of course not Ovidian.

Ceres, "creans res," is the earth whose daughter is the moon, closest planet to the earth. Proserpine comes from "pro," "serpo," and "pis" because she creeps near the earth. Seeking her daughter, carried below, Ceres became thirsty and at the house of Mesies drank from a stream and was derided by Mesies' son who was changed into a lizard. Ceres, or the earth in dry summer, seeks her moon daughter, or moisture gone below; since in summer, the superficial damp of earth hides in its veins. Hence, coming thirsty to the house of Mesies means the season of autumn in that Greek "mese" becomes Latin "medium." There is also a vein in the forearms called "mese." Mesies is, then, autumn between summer's heat and winter's cold; the stream is the rains soaking the earth but not helpful to growth as those of spring with which creation begins. Autumn's moisture

This twelfth-century *Allegoriae super Ovidii Metamorphosin* was paralleled in the next century by the *Integumenta Ovidii* of John of Garland,[5] which was succeeded by the verse and prose *Allegorie librorum Ovidii* of Giovanni del Virgilio,[6] the friend of both Dante and Mussato. This

creates certain sprouting and abortive things that do not grow and only last for a short time. These things are Mesies' sons, autumn growths, which are so small and degenerate they seem to ridicule the earth. Earth, therefore, changes them into lizards and lizards, like autumnal growths that do not last after autumn, hide in winter, but in spring both growth and lizards appear again.

Alexander Neckham, who lived in the generation between Arnulph and John of Garland, applies allegories to fables related in his *De naturis rerum,* ed. T. Wright (London, 1863). Discussing the sowing of the dragon's teeth he writes, "Under the fables of the poets lurks some moral lesson; therefore, the fabulous Ovidian metamorphosis of snake's teeth into armed men, who attack and destroy each other with wounds, teaches that not only quarrel and combat but also spiritual death arise from poisonous detraction" (p. 189). The poet likewise conceals moral instruction about the evils of hunting and the importance of seeing wisdom naked and unadorned in the myth of Actaeon (p. 217). A much more literary treatment of the myths, with allegorizations borrowed rather completely from Fulgentius, was written in hexameters by Baudri de Bourgueil in a lengthy poem beginning ominously "Abscisis ipsum genuisse virilibus aiunt." See Bourgueil, *Les oeuvres poétiques,* ed. P. Abrahams (Paris, 1926), pp. 273–303.

[5] The *Integumenta super Ovidium Metamorphoseos* of Joannes Anglicus (John of Garland) has been edited by Fausto Ghisalberti and was published in Milan in 1933. It is written in Latin verse and in some of its interpretations follows those of Arnulph of Orleans. Garland observes that the fables hide truth, real history, and accounts of human manners in order to preserve them for future generations. These fables are "velamen" or "integumentum" (pp. 39–40). The fable of Semele is about the effect of wine; Narcissus is a youth desirous of glory (pp. 48–49). Cerberus is the earth, as his three heads suggest, and his subjection by Hercules demonstrates that the custom of virtue can master horrible things (p. 52). Ceres is the crops; Proserpine, the seed; Pluto, the earth (p. 57). The historical, physical, and moral methods of reading are applied to the fables, but not many fables are read in more than two ways.

[6] The earliest study of Giovanni del Virgilio is P. H. Wicksteed and E. C. Gardner, *Dante and Giovanni del Virgilio* (Westminster, 1902), which contains a brief account of his allegorizing of Ovid. The Ovidian commentary was more fully studied in C. Marchesi, "L'allegorie ovidiane di Giovanni del Virgilio," *Studj Romanzi,* VI (1909), 85–135. Records from the archives of Bologna for 1325 mentioning Del Virgilio's lectures on Virgil, Statius, Lucan, and "Ovidius Maioris" are appended to G. Lidonnici, "La correspondenza poetica di Giovanni del Virgilio con Dante e il Mussato, e le postille di Giovanni Boccaccio," *Giornale Dantesco,* XXI (1913), 205–43. The text of his Ovidian allegory was published by Fausto Ghisalberti in "Giovanni del Virgilio espositore delle *Metamorfosi,*" *Giornale Dantesca,* XXXIV, n.s. IV (1933), 3–110.

Taking his text from Ecclesiasticus 47:15–17, "Repletus es [impletus est] quasi flumen sapientia et terram rexit [retexit] anima tua et replesti in comparationibus enigmata et ad insulas [longe] divulgatum est nomen tuum," which he can divide into the efficient, material, formal, and final causes, Del Virgilio equates each division with the life and works of Ovid. His allegorization of the *Metamorphoses* consists of 796 verses, summarizing the work and sometimes briefly indicating the interpretation. The deeper understanding is fully revealed in the accompanying prose commentary, which, as Ghisalberti finds, depends at times on Arnulph of Orleans or John of Garland. The bases of the readings are spiritual, moral, physical, and euhemeristic. A few examples will suffice.

The Giants have men's faces but no reason; hence, they represent men proud of their wealth and disbelieving in God. Io was a prostitute redeemed by Divine mercy, who, moralization must certainly have influenced the manner in which Petrarch and Boccaccio read classical myths of the Roman poets. Shortly the *Ovide Moralisé* by some anonymous Minorite not only converted the *Metamorphoses* into French verse but also supplied it with a metrical reading consonant with Christian thinking.[7] The numerous other medieval allegories of Ovid's witty legends, such as the *Fulgentius metaforalis* of John Ridewall,[8] the well-known Vatican mythologies,[9] or the fifteenth-

---

becoming virtuous, brought religion to Egypt, was made a goddess, and wedded to Osiris. Chiron was a physician both for men and horses and was made into a heavenly sign to symbolize the immortal fame of wisdom. Cadmus was a philosopher, who sent his disciples to Greece to dispute with a certain wise man, called "the serpent." Those who are said to have died lost the dispute. When Cadmus first hurls a stone at the serpent the act represents a poor question, which brought no result. When he uses his javelin it was a stronger question, but the serpent protected itself. Finally, pressing the point home, he won with the strongest question. The armed men who spring from the earth are ignorant errors, which Cadmus has scattered through the earth, but which his wisdom, thanks to Pallas, finally eradicated. The five survivors are naturally the vowels. When he arrives at the tenth book, where the labors of Hercules are only alluded to by Ovid, he devotes his whole discussion to the moral evaluation of the work of "the virtuous man" whose stepdame is Juno, or "the active life."

The universal respect for the interpretive approach to Ovid of men like Giovanni del Virgilio is attested to by a contemporary like Richard of Bury, who writes in the *Philobiblon,* ed. E. C. Thomas (Oxford, 1960), p. 125, as follows: "All the varieties of attacks directed against poets by the lovers of naked truth may be repelled by a two-fold defence: either that even in an unseemly subject-matter, we may learn a charming fashion of speech, or that where a fictitious but becoming subject is handled, natural or historical truth is pursued under the guise of allegorical fiction."

[7] The *Ovide Moralisé,* which stands behind so many medieval texts and commentaries, is an octosyllabic poem in about seventy-five hundred lines. An edition was undertaken by C. De Boer who was eventually aided by Matina G. De Boer and Jeannette T. M. Van't Sant; it has now been completed after more than a quarter century of effort and published in the *Verhandelingen der Koninklijke Akademie van Wetenschappen: Afdeeling Letterkunde, n. r.* XV (1915), 1–375; XXI (1920), 1–395; XXX (1931), 1–303; XXXVII (1936), 1–478; XLIII (1938), 1–429. Each episode in the *Metamorphoses* is recapitulated and supplied with a Christian allegory. The poem was originally attributed to Philippe de Vitry by P. Tarbé in *Les Oeuvres de Philippe de Vitry* (Reims, 1850). Gaston Paris in "Chrétien Legouais et autres Traducteurs ou Imitateurs d'Ovide," *Histoire Littéraire de la France,* XXIX (Paris, 1885), 455–525, made an impressive case for Chrétien Legouais, a Minorite. Paris' theory was accepted by F. E. Guyer, "The Influence of Ovid on Crestien de Troyes," *Romanic Review,* XII (1921), 97–134, 216–47 and by F. Zaman, *L'Attribution de Philomena à Chrétien de Troyes* (Amsterdam, 1928), pp. 15–30. Doubts are cast on the attribution made by Paris in A. Thomas, "Chrétien de Troyes et l'auteur de *l'Ovide Moralisé,*" *Romania,* XXII (1893), 271–74, and by De Boer, *op. cit.,* I, 9–11. J. Engels, *Etudes sur l'Ovide Moralisé* (Groningen, 1945), p. 62, simply walks the middle way to conclude that the author of the work was "an anonymous Minorite." It should also be noted that there was also a prose version of the poetical text discovered by Ernest Langlois and described in his "Une rédaction en prose de *l'Ovide Moralisé,*" *Bibliothèque de l'école des Chartes,* LXII (1901), 251–55. Jeannette Van't Sant has edited a manuscript of the work in her *Le Commentaire de Copenhague de l'Ovide Moralisé* (Leyden, 1929).

[8] Ridewall's *Fulgentius metaforalis,* brilliantly edited by Hans Liebeschütz and published at Berlin and Leipzig in 1926, is a fine adjustment of the pagan divinities to the Christian vices and virtues. The god or goddess is pictured and the picture learnedly explained, but each one is associated with a quality either good or bad. Saturn is prudence; Jupiter, benevolence; Juno, memory; Neptune, intelligence; Pluto, providence.

[9] The almost wittily titled "Vatican Mythologies" were put in print in the third volume of Angelo Mai's *Classicorum auctorum e Vaticanis codicibus editorum* Tomus I–X (Rome,

century *De archana deorum* of Thomas Walsingham[10] continued the symbolic exegesis. None of these allegorizations was printed during the sixteenth or seventeenth centuries, but their general direction was effective beyond belief and was first concretely presented to Renaissance readers of Ovid in the published moralizations of the Benedictine Pierre Bersuire and the Franciscan Petrus Lavinius.

Sometime prior to 1515/16 Friar Conrad Dollenkopf of Heidelberg wrote to Master Ortwin Gratius to tell him about his progress in theology at the university. To add spice to his studies he mentions that he is attending lectures on poetics and doing well in the subject.

1828–38). The text is rather badly copied and was somewhat improved when Georg Bode brought out his *Scriptores rerum mythicarum Latini tres Romae nuper reperti* (Celle, 1834). A modern text is clearly required and plans for it are described in Kathleen O. Elliott and J. P. Elder, "A Critical Edition of the *Vatican Mythographers,*" *Transactions of the American Philological Association,* LXXVIII (1947), 189–207.

The first mythology, divided into three books, contains 234 myths, beginning with that of Prometheus and concluding with that of the Pleiades. There is no systematic plan, although almost all the Ovidian myths are recounted. There is an occasional etymology and a few rare euhemerisms but no other interpretations. See R. Schulz, *De mythographi Vaticani primi fontibus* (Halle, 1905). The second mythology opens with a "prooemium" drawn from Isidore reviewing the origins and spread of idolatry. It has no allegorical material, but its accounts are longer than those in Vatican I. It begins with the chief gods and goddesses and traces their descendants; then it takes up lesser deities, giants, Titans, demigods, and heroes. Its sources have been studied by F. Keseling, *De mythographi Vaticani secundi fontibus* (Halle, 1908).

The third mythology is clearly later than the first two in composition and far more interesting and fuller in content. After a "prooemium" on the origins of idolatry and on the meaning of gods' names, there are sections on Saturn, Cybele, Jupiter, Juno, Neptune, Pluto, Proserpine, Apollo, Mercury, Minerva, Venus, Bacchus, Hercules, Perseus, and the Zodiac. Each deity is treated at some length; the work is better organized and more richly annotated than previous mythologies. It is perhaps because of these qualities that Boccaccio appears to have used this mythographer. In most cases the physical or moral allegory of the myth under scrutiny is related, and the pagan pantheon is carefully revealed *in bono* and *in malo*. It is now rather probable that this mythology was written by Albericus of London and that the *Libellus,* circulated during the Renaissance under his name, is actually a fourteenth-century epitome of this work with additions from Bersuire. On this problem see Fausto Ghisalberti, "Mitografi latini e retori medievali in un codice cremonese del sec. XIV: Fulgenzio, Alberico, Giovanni di Virgilio, Folchino de Borfoni," *Archivum Romanicum,* VII (1923), 95–154; A. Warburg, *Gesammelte Schriften* (Leipzig, 1932), II, 471, 627; Eleanor Rathbone, "Master Alberic of London, Mythographus Tertius Vaticanus," *Mediaeval and Renaissance Studies* I (1941–43), 35–38; R. Klibansky, E. Panofsky, F. Saxl, *Saturn and Melancholy* (Cambridge, 1964), pp. 172–75. Robert Raschke, *De Alberico mythologo* (Bratislava, 1912), still has virtues as a source study.

[10] The *De archana deorum* by the fourteenth-century Benedictine Thomas Walsingham is divided into fifteen books and follows the Ovidian myths through the whole of the *Metamorphoses.* At the beginning of each book Walsingham lists the "principal fables," summarizes each fable briefly, and provides a line-tag locating it in Ovid's text. He then offers moral, physical, and sometimes Christian readings of the fable. He uses Bersuire, Arnulph, Vaticanus Tertius, and John of Garland among later sources and quotes frequently from Fulgentius and Martianus Capella. See the edition by Robert A. van Kluyve (Durham, N.C., 1968).

> I already know by rote all the fables of Ovid in his *Metamorphoses,* and these I can expound quadruply—to wit, naturally, literally, historically, and spiritually— and this is more than the secular poets can do.

To indicate his own virtuosity he describes with pleasure the ignorance of another student in the technique and enumerates biblical passages casting light on events in the myths of gods, goddesses, and heroes. He is downcast because modern poets are such literalists and do not understand "allegorizing and spiritual expositions"; he can make this complaint without blushing because he has had expert instruction. Dollenkopf writes:

> I lately bought a book composed by a certain English Doctor of our Order, Thomas of Wales by name; this book is all written about Ovid's *Metamorphoses,* explaining each story allegorically and spiritually, and its profundity in theology passes belief. Most certainly the Holy Spirit has inspired this man with so great learning, for in this book he sets forth the harmonies between the Holy Scriptures and the fables of the poet.[11]

Dollenkopf had laid out his money for the *Metamorphosis Ovidiana moraliter a magistro Thoma Walleys . . . explanata* in the Paris editions of 1509 or 1511 or in the Lyons edition of 1513. This moralization of Ovid was composed in the fourteenth century by Pierre Bersuire[12] and intended as the fifteenth book of his allegorical compendium of all philosophical, natural, and theological doctrines. Sections of it were severally published during the sixteenth century and were brought together in the three-volume Antwerp *Opera* of 1609 as *Reductorium morale, Reductorium morale super totam Bibliam,* and *Repertorium vulgo dictionarium morale.* The moralization of the *Metamorphoses* found shelter in none of these versions and enjoyed a separate life.

---

[11] *Epistolae obscurorum virorum,* ed. and trans. F. G. Stokes (Hew Haven, 1925), pp. 343–45.

[12] Fausto Ghisalberti has edited the first part of Bersuire's moralization and extracts from the second part in "*L'Ovidius Moralizatus* di Pierre Bersuire," *Studi Romanzj,* XXIII (1933), 5–136. J. Engels has also issued the first part as P. Berchorius (Bersuire), *Reductorium morale, liber XV, Cap. i., De formis figurisque deorum* (Utrecht, 1962). The Badius Ascensius text, attributed by him to Thomas Walléys, was restored to Bersuire by Benoit Hauréau in "Mémoire sur un commentaire de Metamorphoses d'Ovide," *Memoires National de France, Académie des Inscriptions et Belles-Lettres,* XXX (1883), 45–55. Earlier studies of Bersuire are C. Samaran, "Pierre Bersuire, Prieur de Sant-Eloi de Paris," *Histoire Littéraire de la France* (Paris, 1900), XXXIX, 259–451; Léopold Pannier, "Notice biografique sur le bénédictin Pierre Bersuire, premier traducteur français de Tite Live," *Bibliothèque de l'École des Chartes,* XXXIII (1872), 325–64; A. Thomas, "Estraits des Archives du Vatican pour servir à l'histoire littéraire," *Romania,* XI (1882), 181–87; F. Fassbinder, *Das Leben und die Werke des benedikter Pierre Bersuire* (Bonn, 1917); and J. Engels, "Berchoriana," *Vivarium,* II (1964), 62–124.

Attributed in medieval manuscripts to Johannes Gualensis, Nicolas Trivet, Robert Holkot, and John Ridewall, it was known to the Renaissance (because Jodocus Badius Ascensius used a certain manuscript) as the work of Thomas Walleys. It was first published in an epitomized and contaminated version in Bruges in 1484 as *Cy commence Ovide . . . son livre intitule Metamorphoses contenant XV livres particuliers, moralise par Maistre Thomas Waleys . . . translate et compile par Colard Mansion.* In 1493 Antoine Verard brought out in Paris a redaction of this version as *Bible des Poetes methamorphoses.* Caxton, Mansion's pupil and associate, translated it—he may have used Mansion's manuscript—into English as *Ovyde hys booke of Methamorphose,*[13] but never published it. Englishmen who only knew their own language were deprived of this informative interpretation, but those who had Latin could choose one of the five editions published in the first quarter of the sixteenth century.[14]

Relying on the advice of St. Paul and the allegorical customs of the biblical expositors, Bersuire announces in his preface that the poets who first invented fables wished some truth to be discovered under their fictions; in fact, Lucan is not thought to be a poet by some critics because he wrote only history. Under many myths there are natural truths, says

[13] Bersuire's *La Bible des Poetes* (Paris, 1531), contains a preface similar to the Badius Ascensius Latin issue, but the translator presents the book to Charles VIII, informing him he first expounds the fables literally, then morally and allegorically, "which is a thing not impertinent to do." The Pepysian manuscript of Books V–XV—all that remains of Caxton's translation—was edited in 1819 by George Hibbert and in 1924 by Stephen Gaselee.

[14] Badius Ascensius printed the *Moralitates Ovidii* in Paris in 1509, 1511, 1515, and 1523. The 1515 edition has been employed for these documentations. Ghisalberti holds there were three manuscripts of Bersuire's moralization. Manuscript A was written in Avignon; manuscript P in Paris; and manuscript W, used by Badius Ascensius, was copied and revised by someone other than Bersuire and attributed to Thomas Walleys. Manuscript A is simply a matter of hypothecation based on P and W. In the published version the preface is less full than in Ghisalberti's P, which relates the stay in Avignon, the return to Paris, and the rencounter with Philippe de Vitry, who, at this late date gave Bersuire the opportunity to peruse the *Ovide Moralisé.* The differences between the printed preface of the Badius Ascensius edition (fo. Iv–II) and the Ambrosian manuscript text published by Ghisalberti (p. 89) are important. The published text reads: Non moveat tamen aliquem quod dicunt aliqui fabulas poetarum alias fuisse moralizatas: et ad instantiam domine Iohanne quondam regine Franciae dudum in rithmum gallicum fuisse translatas: quia revera opus illud nequaquam me legisse memini, de quo bene doleo: quia ipsum invenire nequivi. Illud enim labores meos quia plurimum revelasset; ingenium meum etiam adiuvisset. Non enim fuissem dedignatus expositiones in passibus multis sumere et auctorem earum humiliter allegare. The manuscript follows this text with slight variants until "translatas," then continues as follows: quia revera opus illud non videram quousque tractatum istum penitus perfecissem. Quia tamen, postquam Avenione redivissem Parisius, contigit quod magister Philippus de Vitriaco, vir utique excellentis ingenii, moralis philosophie historiarumque et antiquitatum zelator precipuus et in cunctis mathematicis scientiis eruditus, dictum gallicum volumen mihi obtulit, in quo proculdubio multas bonas exposiciones tam allegoricas quam morales inveni, ideo ipsas, si antea non posueram, assignare cercavi.

Bersuire; under others, one seeks history. This matter is well understood. For his part he proposes to seek a confirmation of the mysteries of the faith in the morality of these human fabulations. He will spoil the Egyptians and collect grapes from thorns and honey from stone. Only rarely, Bersuire writes, will he mention the literal meaning, for he proposes to expend his labor on the moral and allegorical exposition of Ovid's *Metamorphoses*. He knows he is not the first to attempt this task. When he returned from Avignon to Paris, Philippe de Vitry had given him a book in French rime written for Jeanne, Queen of France. This manuscript, generally assumed to be the *Ovide Moralisé,* is presumed to have supplied some of the material found in Bersuire's post-Avignon versions; it is also obvious from textual similarities that he knew John Ridewall's *Fulgentius metamorforalis.* In the preface to the Badius Ascensius edition (where the reference to Vitry and the moralized Ovid do not occur), Bersuire acknowledges his debts.

But before I go to the fables I should say something about the forms and figures of the gods. However, because I could not find their images described or painted anywhere I consulted Francesco de Petrarca, a poet profound in learning and fluent in eloquence, an expert in all poetical and historical disciplines who described these prefatory figures in a certain work of his in elegant verse. I also went through the books of Fulgentius, Alexander, and Rabanus and drew from different parts the figures or images which the ancients wished to give these feigned gods for historical or philosophical purposes.[15]

The first part of Bersuire's *Metamorphosis Ovidiana Moraliter* is limited to the ancient pictorial representations of Saturn, Jove, Mars, Apollo, Venus, Mercury, Diana, Minerva, Juno, Cybele, Neptune, Pan, Bacchus, Pluto, Vulcan, Hercules, and Aesculapius. Fifteen of these descriptions are similar in content and sometimes in phrasing to the

[15] Bersuire acknowledges Petrarch's aid in his description of how the gods were represented. Since there is a section of this nature in the *Africa* (III. 138–262), Bersuire's knowledge of this work has been discussed. But the relation between Bersuire and Petrarch was more than that of poet and reader as the letters of Petrarch (*Delle Cose Familiari* IV, 475–97 and *Le Senili* II, 504) make clear. The connection was noticed early by de Sade in his *Mémoires pour la vie de F. Pétrarque* (Amsterdam and Avignon, 1764–67), I, 365; III, 546–55. See also E. H. Wilkins, "Description of Pagan Divinities from Petrarch to Chaucer," *Speculum,* XXXII (1957), 511–22. Petrarch's descriptions of Mercury, Pan, and Mars are very similar to those found in the first part of Bersuire's book, but the connection between the interests of the two men is absolutely proved by the allegorization of Apollo's attendant three-headed beast. E. Panofsky pointed out that the literal beast occurs in Macrobius, *Saturnalia* (I. 20); however, Petrarch (III. 160) was first to interpret the heads temporally as past, present, and future. Bersuire follows this reading (A6v). See *Hercules am Scheidenwege* (Leipzig and Berlin, 1930), p. 15. The custom of describing how the gods were graphically represented probably begins with Rabanus Maurus' etymological, physical, and euhemeristic commentaries on the gods in the *De universo, PL* CXI, 426–36.

Libellus assigned to Albericus, a fact possibly establishing an upper limit in time for that work. Bersuire has the long tradition at his fingertips and reminds his readers that the ancients thought of Saturn as time, Jupiter as ether, Juno as air, Thetis as water, Neptune as ocean, Cybele as earth, Apollo as sun, and Diana as moon. In addition they read each myth historically and naturally. He then turns to Saturn, drawing on *Vaticanus Tertius* and John Ridewall for much of his information.

The ancients, Bersuire continues, painted Saturn as a pale, sad old man holding a scythe in one hand as well as a dragon biting its tail. In the other hand he lifted his weeping children to his mouth and devoured them with his teeth. His head is helmeted, and he is covered with a cloak. The god is accompanied by his four children and his wife Ops. Before him was painted the sea into which his *virilia,* from which Venus was born, were cast. "I will now," Bersuire writes, "expound this myth literally, historically, naturally, and allegorically."

In the literal sense Saturn is a planet, the first, oldest, and slowest of the seven. The scythe signifies the curved course of a retrograde star. That he devours children makes clear that children born under Saturn rarely survive; Jupiter's castration of Saturn is another way of representing the tempering and moderating influence of this planet on an ascendant Saturn. Ops, of course, is the earth from whose body all things are produced. Naturally interpreted, Saturn is time and his four children are the elements. His castration by Jupiter, or fire, makes it plain how heat destroys all things born in time. In the same mode of reading, the swallowing of the children expresses the fact that time devours all things. The scythe makes equally clear time's curving back on itself, and the dragon reinforces this meaning. In a historical sense, Saturn was King of Crete. His brother, Titan, predicted that one of his sons would expel him from his throne; consequently, he advised Saturn to devour all of his sons and to save himself from this evil. So Saturn ate all his children except Jupiter because he did not think that the prophecy referred to his offspring by Cybele. Overthrown, he fled to Janus in Italy, where he instructed men in agriculture and for this benefit was elevated to the rank of a god and named Saturn from *"saturando."*

Adorning his allegorical reading of the Saturn myth with quotations from the Psalms, Isaiah, Ezekiel, Ecclesiastes, Kings, Job, and finally St. Jerome, Bersuire reads the myth *in bono* and *in malo. In malo* the legend signifies an important but wicked old prelate who has let his will be perverted through avarice. With the scythe of malice and the edge of rapine and bloody envy he cuts others. He can be said to eat his children because he confounds and weakens his underlings through his exactions. He is surrounded by dragonlike servants and officials who oppress his subjects; in due course, after devouring many victims, he takes Ops, or "riches," to wife. Sometimes a Jupiter, an underling more audacious and shrewd than the others, reports him to the Pope or the King, who see to it that he is cut off from power and deposed. It is just that the unjust be overthrown by someone on whom they preyed. Bersuire interprets the throwing of the *virilia* into the sea as the change of fleshly pleasure into salty bitterness.

Reading the legend *in bono,* Bersuire equates the Saturn who taught farming to the Italians with good prelates, eager to satisfy their subjects but also daring to chew up their bad sons for the sake of correction. These men are married to Ops, or piety and compassion, and nurture the poor with charitable gifts. They carry in their hands the pruning knife of justice, and their advanced age indicates mature discretion. When such a prelate is cut off by his son Jupiter, one perceives how a good prelate is molested by an ambitious underling. When good prelates castigate bad subjects they are always hated by other bad subjects who fear to be similarly devoured. They in turn attempt to castigate their fathers, the good old prelates, by expelling them from rule and prelateship and governing in their place.[16] In this manner Bersuire moves through his seventeen major and minor deities, pointing to the literal or astronomical, the natural or physical, the historical or euhemeristic, and the *in bono* and *in malo* allegorical meanings. Bersuire does not hesitate to pause over and speculate on details. Apollo's laurel symbolizes wise and learned men; his crow signifies the poor and destitute.[17] Venus, though not a figure of recommended virtue, is accompanied by the Graces, who are Faith, Hope, and Charity.[18] Pluto and his infernal associates are given the most space;[19] hence, when Bersuire emerges panting from the lower world, he has only a few lines of text left for Vulcan, Hercules, and Aesculapius.

In Bersuire's succeeding fable-by-fable commentary on the *Metamorphoses,* his slighting of the latter three "prefatae imagines" is rectified only in the case of the great Christian hero Hercules. Unlike so many medieval scholars, Bersuire was not too much given to repetition; hence, there is very little in the commentary that is not new and different

[16] Bersuire, *Metamorphosis Ovidiana Moraliter* (Paris, 1515), fo. II–IV.
[17] *Ibid.,* VII.
[18] *Ibid.,* VIIIv.
[19] *Ibid.,* XV–XVIIIv.

from the matter explaining the images of the first book. In the second part of the *Moralitates Ovidii,* Bersuire summarizes and elucidates each fable according to one or more of the four modes of interpretation. Proteus' transformations provide a theme for an essay on hypocrisy;[20] Atlas is the type of a good prelate and of Christ;[21] Callisto is changed into a bear because through her carnal submission she has put aside her rational nature for a bestial one. Her hooked paws symbolize perverse affection; her hairy hide, vile conversation.[22] *In malo* Actaeon is a usurer; *in bono* he is Christ.[23] Ceres is an eager priest; Proserpine, a girl instructed by her mother in piety; Pluto is, naturally, Satan.[24] The temptation of Adam by Eve is visible in the legend of Hercules and Deianira; but Hercules is also a good, wise priest, who fights against the lion of pride and anger, against the devil Diomedes and his horses of heresy, against multiple livings signified by Cerberus and Geryon, and against Cacus, who is, among other things, the Prince of Hell.[25] The attention Bersuire gives the demigod is equalled by that which he bestows on the hero Ulysses, whose non-Ovidian death at the hands of his bastard Telegonus demonstrates God's hidden Providence, which no one can escape.[26] There is little wonder that Badius Ascensius introduced this book as useful to preachers, who would find "faint copies of Christian ceremonies" (Saturnalia versus the Advent) in pagan festivals, and who, now that these "fabulous stories" had been morally altered, could themselves be metamorphosed into clever bees drinking celestial nectar from blossoms of the pagan sort.[27]

II

It seems natural that the first Ovidian work to come into print was the 1470 Cologne edition of the *De vetula;* but after this date Ovid's poetry was almost annually published in whole or in part. The so-called appendix, containing the "Consolatio ad Liviam," "De Nuce," "Epistola Sapho Phaoni," "Halieuticon," and "De medicaminibus faciei" was usually included in the *Opera;* though it is described as spurious in the

---

[20] *Ibid.,* XXVv.
[21] *Ibid.,* XXVII, XLVIv.
[22] *Ibid.,* XXIX.
[23] *Ibid.,* XXXV–XXXVI.
[24] *Ibid.,* Lv–LIv.
[25] *Ibid.,* LXXIIIv–LXXVIIv.
[26] *Ibid.,* XCVv.
[27] The preface addressed to Fr. Giovanni di Vepria is found in the 1509 edition.

1486 Venetian edition of De Novaria, it was not until Melchior Goldast's *Ovidii Nasonis erotica et amatoria opuscula* of 1610 that a serious attempt was made to eliminate the dubious poems from the corpus Calderini, who had edited Virgil, was one of Ovid's earliest Renaissance editorial sponsors, but among the more impressive and respected of his early commentators are Giorgio Merula, Paoli Marso, and Raffaello Regio. Regio, Professor of Rhetoric at Padua and quarrelsome editor of various ancient authors, saw his commentary on the *Metamorphoses,* which he claims he wrote as an adolescent ("quas adolescens composueram") but defended as a magnum opus, through the press in Venice in 1493. Regio's commentary incorporating the summaries of Lactantius Placidus was reprinted at least twelve times before 1510, when the commentary of Petrus Lavinius on the first book was added. Regio, Lactantius, and Lavinius remained together until the 1580s when this edition, which had sold fifty thousand copies before Regio died, lost its vogue and was replaced by other editions.

Regio's annotations are essentially expository and without allegorical content. It is clear, however, that he was aware of the presence of allegory because his implicit emphasis on the opening lines of the *Metamorphoses* is straightforwardly Christian. More than this, in the prefatory epistle to Francisco Gonzaga, dated in September of the year of publication, Regio mentions the proper moral understanding of the myths of Lycaon, Deucalion and Pyrrha, Daphne, and Phaeton. "The rest of them truly offer examples, not less charming than useful, of vices and virtues and are to be judged as more suitable for the conduct of human life than the contentious disputations of philosophers." Whether Regio is responsible for the later addition of Lavinius' commentary cannot be said, but there is no doubt that if he saw the Lyons edition where they first were printed, he would have been very unreasonable had he disapproved.

Petrus Lavinius, who furnished the "moralized and tropological" commentaries on some of the fables, is an elusive figure. His French name can only be conjectured, but it is clear that he spent his life at Lyons, where he was known as "a philosopher, poet, theologian, and the most celebrated preacher of God's Word." Sometime before 1512 he furnished "historical elucidations" and a poem in praise of the author for a Paris edition of Jean Lemaire de Belges' *Les illustrations de Gaule.* Two letters to the odd savant Henry Cornelius Agrippa are preserved. In one he expressed a desire to meet Agrippa on his next visit to Lyons; in the other (dated June 28, 1526) he seconds Agrippa's views on judicial astrology.[28] At the end of his Ovid commentary—he got as far as I. 339—he reports that he wrote all of it during the forty days of Lent; but since Easter has come, he has hardly time to breathe. The printers, however, were in a hurry to get what he had into print and carried off his manuscript, publishing it while he was engaged in other duties without giving him a chance for correction. "If ever the *Metamorphoses* of Ovid is returned to our hands, we shall, God willing, freshly pursue the revision of the whole work."[29]

In a preface which appears in the edition published in Lyons in 1510, but not in all later editions, Lavinius explains that while the testimony of pagan poets does not strengthen the truth, it helps to show what the truth is; moreover, it cannot be denied that under their poetical fables physical, tropological, and allegorical meaning hides. The same methods which have enabled theologians to untangle the metaphors, prosopopoeia, and tropologies of Ezekiel, Daniel, and the Apocalypse can be used in reading the pagans. After all, Lavinius declares, poets simply use words differently from other men, or cover a context with a fabulous veil, or hide the truth with a new way of speaking or figure of speech so that "the higher skill of men is exercised in seeking the truth and the minds of hearers are delighted by strange and never-before-heard innovations." Ovid, by his myths of transformation, teaches men to avoid brutish desires and vices; moreover, he is a sound moral adviser, and in his account of Creation, the age of gold, the Deluge, and the wars of the giants he changes very little of what the "legislator" Moses had set down in the Pentateuch. One wonders, writes Lavinius, knowing both Plato and Pythagoras were influenced by Moses, whether or not Ovid read Holy Writ in the Septuagint version.[30] With this standard conviction to guide him Lavinius turns to the text of his poet.

Lavinius' allegorization of the opening lines of the *Metamorphoses* is more an attempt to show Ovid's Christian background than to cover every legendary moment in the literal with sublime meaning. The open-

---

[28] Ovid, *Opera* (Lyons, s.d.), pp. 843–45.

[29] I am following *Metamorphoseos libri XV. In eosdem libros Raphaelis Regii luculentissime enarrationes. Neque non Lactantii et Petri Lavinii commentarii non ante impressi* (Milan, 1540), p. XXVII. Unconvinced by the second half of the title, I compared the texts with the Lyons editions of 1510 and 1519 and the Venice edition of 1527. The Lyons editions contain the observations of Joannes Baptista Pius, Lodovicus Rhodiginus, Joannes Theodorus Bellovacis, Janus Parrhasius, and Jacobus Bononsesis. The remarks of the latter two are slight; those of the first three are very slight. None of them touch on allegory. All are principally historical commentary or literary parallels. The remarks of Parrhasius are quoted at secondhand as if they were from conversations, lectures, or correspondence.

[30] *Ibid.*, sigs. A5v–A6.

ing lines of the poems are for Lavinius a clear testimony to ethnic scriptural knowledge, and Ovid's account of Chaos and the separation of the elements is Genesis converted into Latin verses. Consequently it is not amazing that Prometheus, or Providence, son of Japetus, or divine power, aided by Minerva, or "sancta sapientia," creates man of mud. The Trinity stands behind all these names and, as Lavinius observes, "You see aspects of truth hidden by a poetical mask." Under the "veil of winds" Ovid writes (57–66) about the creation of angels and the fall of the dissenting angels; but there is also a tropological and conventional reading associating Aeolus with prudence, and the winds with the conflicting passions. There is also a possible tropological exposition of the myth of Prometheus, the announcer of the Divine Word, whose wisdom and eloquence cleansed men filthy with sin. Minerva led Prometheus to Heaven just as prudence is pointed heavenward by a change of life and then rises to perfection through speculation. The stealing of fire from the wheel of the sun signifies both the illumination of man by God, the true sun, and the nature of eternity, which, like a wheel, has no beginning or end. The golden age is Eden and also Daniel's giant with the head of gold. The Olympian war with the Giants fits the story of Babel, whereas Lycaon is as plainly Cain as Deucalion is Noah. When Jupiter, disguised as a man, descends from Heaven to investigate the rumors of human wickedness (209–15), Lavinius writes an essay on the Incarnation, a subject "that Ovid had in mind." The story of Apollo, whose harp is the Cross, is easily converted into a "sensus phisicus" and a "sensus allegoricus." The three-headed python not only makes a perfect Satan, but also symbolizes the three angelic hierarchies that fell. The nine Muses, consequently but not unusually, become the nine choirs of angels harmoniously directed by the baton of Apollo-Christ.[31] The allegorical readings supplied by Bersuire and Lavinius for the *Metamorphoses* in Latin were

[31] Lavinius's commentary, alternating with that of Regio and the summaries of Lactantius Placidus, begins on p. Iv and concludes on p. XXIIv. It has a great number of points in common with its medieval predecessors; the commentary on Saturn (pp. VIII–IX) may be compared with Bersuire's analysis. Lavinius begins with the usual euhemeristic account and follows on with an astrological interpretation. He then picks up the seasonal symbolism of "Satur" + "annis" with his four children, Jupiter (summer), Juno (spring), Neptune (autumn), and Pluto (winter). Time, of course, devours all. But Saturn, son of sky and earth, is also Adam, who was made of earth by Heaven. Under both Saturn and Adam there was a Golden Age. Saturn married Ops, "omnibus opem ferentem"; whereas Adam married Eve, "mater cunctorum viventium." Saturn is always shown with a dragon, symbol of the Fall. Saturn was expelled from his kingdom by his son; Adam expelled his sons from their place of innocence and delight. Saturn ate his children, and Adam by his sin caused his children to be devoured by death. Both Saturn and Adam had the same children; because Abel is Jove, Seth is Neptune, and Pluto is Cain.

shortly imitated in the vernacular, a labor permitting men without classical education to grasp the hidden meanings.

In 1497 Giovanni Bonsignori's prose reductions of the *Metamorphoses,* made in the fourteenth century, were published in Venice as *Ovidio Methamorphoseos vulgare.* The same work, furnished with woodcut illustrations, was reissued in Milan in 1519. In 1533 with the prose summaries reworded and the illustrations revised, it became part of *Di Ovidio le Metamorphosi, cioe Transmutationi tradotte dal Latino diligentemente in volgar verso con sue Allegorie significatione e dichiaratione delle Fabole in prosa,* which was published in Venice. This publication contained a reasonably faithful verse translation of the *Metamorphoses* and a prose allegorization of the fables. The author of the translation and the allegories is not indicated but is thought to be N. di Agostini. The allegorizer, whoever he is, states his principles of interpretation in his "Proemio." He writes that although Ovid was a pagan, the reader will notice the similarities of the text to "our law" and particularly to the Old Testament. The Roman had no knowledge of the true faith but was, nonetheless, inspired and followed Moses step by step from the Creation to the Deluge. "Finally, there is not a single transformation which did not result from a disregard of God or from sin."[32]

There are more than 150 fables in the *Metamorphoses* which the commentator on this Venice translation subjects to allegorizations. In addition to these moralizations there are substantial essays, several pages in length, on Hercules, the Centaurs, and Ulysses. The commentator uses the word "allegoria" to designate a number of expository approaches. The allegories of the first book, as far as Apollo's wooing of Daphne, rely to some extent on the explications of Lavinius, and many of the subsequent expositions are repetitions and/or augmentations of Bersuire.[33] Many of the "allegories" are flatly historical, bringing in details from other sources. No mode of interpretation—moral, physical, astrological, or spiritual—is shirked. On occasion one interpretation openly contradicts another, presenting the figure in both a good and a bad light. The fable of Medea and Aeson is made into an allegory of the state of the human conscience before its Maker, but the next legend of Medea and Theseus illustrates the actions of a virtuous man molested by an evil person.[34] The fable of Niobe demonstrates, contrary to the

---

[32] Ovid, *Metamorphosi,* trans. Agostini (Venice, 1533), p. 2.
[33] The account of Ceres and Proserpine (*ibid.,* pp. 50v–51v) is an example of a direct rendering of Bersuire.
[34] *Ibid.,* p. 61.

reading of Bersuire, the nature of "pride in flesh"; and her seven sons are the hands, feet, eyes, and nose, whereas her seven daughters are the activities of those bodily members. Niobe's husband Amphion logically comes from the Greek "passions of the flesh." Latona, almost "Laterona," is "religion," whose children Apollo and Diana are "wisdom and chastity." When "religion" is scorned by "pride of flesh," her children subdue "the passions of the body" which, now lacking fleshly inclinations, becomes stone and weeps in penitence. Because of this alteration, the wind of the Divine Spirit transports her to the height from which all came, or to God "by whom we were created and to whom we return only through the way of *santa religione.*"[35]

The methods employed by this Italian commentator on the *Metamorphoses* were followed by other readers of Ovid during the middle of the century. Jacob Moltzer, who wrote a commentary on Boccaccio's *Genealogia* and edited Regio's Ovid at Basel in 1543, omitting the allegories of Lavinius,[36] notices the close parallels with Moses' history and makes proper etymological deductions.[37] He refuses, however, to accept the theory that the fable of Apollo and Daphne is, as some say, a veiled historical account of the relations of Augustus and Livia; "this is far too clever."[38] A few years later when Moltzer joined with Ubertino Clerici in an edition of the *Amatoria,* the latter indicates how completely the allegorical process infected the annotators of Ovid by announcing in his preface that "he would annotate for utility and not for ostentation." There are, he continues, "too many learned men who prefer enigmas to interpretations, and we shall leave them to their ambition."[39] In 1556 when Anneau added his translation of the third book of the *Metamorphoses* to Marot's translation of the first two books, he refuses to give

---

[35] *Ibid.,* pp. 74v–75, 78. Melanchthon's *Enarratio Metamorphoseon Ovidi,* while not incorporated in any Renaissance edition, shows he was ready to go farther with this poet than he did with Virgil. He describes the poem as a series of manifestations of divine benevolence and wrath, informing men that the world is not the product of chance but of divine power. These manifestations lead us, he says, to a "moral view of life." He attaches moral and physical readings to the myths of Creation, Prometheus, the Titans, Deucalion, Phaeton, Envy, the dragon's teeth, Actaeon, Semele, Venus and Mars, Medusa, Picus, Harpies, Cephalus, Pasiphae, Proteus, Hercules, and Orpheus. See Melanchthon, *Opera,* ed. G. Breitschneider and H. E. Bindseil, XIX, 502–64.

[36] Ovid, *Metamorphoseos,* eds. R. Regio and J. Moltzer (Basel, 1543), p. 12.

[37] *Ibid.,* p. 174.

[38] *Ibid.,* p. 24. He states in his preface to Jacob Spiegel his indebtedness to Boccaccio and agrees that the story of Creation came to Ovid from the Hebrews via the Egyptians and Greeks.

[39] Ovid, *Opera quae vocantur Amatoria cum doctorum virorum commentariis,* eds. J. Moltzer and U. Clerici (Basel, 1549), p. 3.

the alchemical readings[40] of the fables because he does not understand them. Nevertheless, he is forced to admit, "one should not explain a poet by the cold literal but rather seek a secret sense since all old religions are clothed in myth." Jupiter is for him the great of this world; the fable of Phaeton shows how to quell an upstart; and the myth of Europa relates how the second king of Crete won part of Europe from the kings of Asia.[41] In 1560, Antonio Tritonio brought out his allegorizations of the *Metamorphoses,* which were later incorporated in the *Mythologia* of Conti. The year 1563 saw the publication of Johannes Spreng's elegiac Latin verse epitome incorporating the allegories of the Ovidian fables, a book handsomely illustrated by the famous engraver Virgilius Soli.[42] Before some of these moral interpretations were printed the Rector of the Konigsberg Academy, George Schuler, a disciple of Melanchthon and a friend of Bembo and Aleandro, published his lectures on the poetry of Ovid.

Schuler's *Fabularum Ovidii interpretatio tradita in Academia Regiomontana* was first published in Wittenberg in 1555. Subsequent editions appeared in 1572 and 1575. In 1584 the work was published in Cambridge with the title *Fabularum Ovidii interpretatio, ethica, physica et historica tradita in academia regiomontana a G. Sabino et edita industria T. Thomae.* To make the rationale plain the Frankfort edition of 1593 appended Conti's essay on the value and use of fable. The observations of Schuler were still of enough interest to men of the seventeenth century to require an ultimate printing in 1699. Thomas, who edited and published the Cambridge edition, was a fellow of Kings and first printer to the University; his readiness to undertake this task

[40] The alchemistic allegorizations of Ovid are frowned on by Conti but were avidly read by these precursors of modern science. Manuscripts bearing the title, "Le Grand Olympe, ou philosophie poétique attribué au très renommé Ovide, traduit de latin en langue françoise par Pierre Vicot, prestre, serviteur domestique de Nicolas Grosparmy, gentilhomme normand et Nicolas le Vallois" were written and circulated during the sixteenth and seventeenth centuries and have been discussed by Paul Kuntze, *Le Grand Olympe, eine alchimistische Deutung von Ovids Metamorphosen* (Halle, 1912). This work is not to be confused with the French prose redaction, *Le grand Olympe des histoires poétiques du prince de poesie Ovide Naso en sa Metamorphose,* published in Lyons in 1532, 1537, 1538, and 1539. The author of this latter redaction observes that he is summarizing the fables "sans allegorie"; nonetheless, he urges the readers to derive honest instruction in the way of a good life from the legends.

[41] *Trois premiers livres de la Métamorphose d'Ovide* (Lyons, 1556); material derived from F. Hennebert, *Histoire des traductions françaises d'auteurs grecs et latins pendant le XVIe et le XVIIe siècles* (Brussels, 1861), pp. 113–20.

[42] *Metamorphoseos Ovidi, argumentis quidem soluta oratione, enarrationibus autem et allegoriis elegiaco versu expositae* (Frankfort, 1563).

could be an indication of solicitation resulting from an English interest in the hidden meanings of the *Metamorphoses*.

Schuler follows the usual method of proceeding through the *Metamorphoses* and lecturing extraneously on each important fable. He was widely read in the early Church Fathers; he quotes or refers to almost every important Greek and Latin author. In addition to the sort of erudition one would expect of a man of his generation, he also knows the opinions of the great humanists: Valla, Sadoletus, Campanus, Mantuanus, Camerarius, and Erasmus. He is rather silent, however, about the more obvious allegorizers of the *Metamorphoses* and of classical myth. He quotes from Palaephatus and from the allegories of Tzetzes, which he must have read in manuscript or in some secondary source; but in the main his acknowledged allegorizations probably come from contemporary printed scholia on Ovid and other classical texts. Erasmus is credited with understanding Cadmus' scattering of the dragon's teeth as the invention of the alphabet;[43] Melanchthon expounds the contention between Neptune and Minerva over Athens as proof that a proper state is based on civil arts;[44] and Vitus Winsheimus in a "certain speech" pointed out that self-admiration is absurd at any age, but particularly in adolescence.[45] But these observations are not always original with these men.

In his talks to his pupils about Ovid's poem, Schuler reminds them that proper names always have significant Greek or Latin meanings. Prometheus is one way of saying "Providence"; Philomela is the Greek word for "amiable." On occasion he follows the technique of medieval allegorizers and of Bersuire by describing how the deities were represented. The Parcae, he relates with his mind on Plato, are three women seated at equal distance on a throne; they wear crowns, are dressed in white, and turn with their fingers the adamantine spindle of Necessity.[46] The astrological mode of interpretation also comes into his lectures. Hermaphroditus is said to be the son of Venus and Mercury because when the latter planet is in the ascendant, it modifies the strongly masculine or feminine effects of the other planets.[47] The euhemeristic understanding of the myths is frequently brought out. Prometheus was an astronomer who went into the Caucasus to study the nature, orbit, and effects of the sign Aquila.[48] The physical wisdom behind myth,

[43] Schuler, *Fabularum Ovidii . . . interpretatio* (Cambridge, 1584), p. 101.
[44] *Ibid.*, pp. 214–15.
[45] *Ibid.*, pp. 119–20.
[46] *Ibid.*, p. 85.
[47] *Ibid.*, p. 150.
[48] *Ibid.*, p. 9.

Schuler proposes, can be found in the procreation of Bacchus. Semele is the earth, moist and rich for the growth of the grape; Jupiter is heat and the warm air, which not only brings the fruit to fullness but also assists in the fermentation of wine.[49] A subdivision of Schuler's physical interpretation is what might be called the psychological exposition, and Ovid's account of Envy, "an elegant Prosopopoeia," gives him an opportunity to explain to his boys how a meaning of this nature is poetically disclosed. The personification of Envy lives in a deep vale to make it obvious that people possessed by this disease are humble and have no confidence in themselves; this is because their blood is colder than normal.[50] But this interpreter's preceptorial emphasis is naturally on the moral or ethical reading.

The myth of Cadmus' sowing of the dragon's teeth evolved, Schuler suggested, from the true history of his scattering of dissent among the disinherited sons of the defeated King Draco, who formed a military alliance against him. Their political concord, brought to naught by Cadmus, provided a sixteenth-century lesson about the federations of princes. These diplomatic arrangements never endured, and in time all allies became enemies.[51] The rebellion of the Giants against Jove displays the nature of tyrants, of heretics, and of philosophers arrogant in their wisdom.[52] Lycaon not only personified impiety but also inhospitality of the sort shown by the city of Badius to Quintus Crispinus.[53] The romance of Pyramus and Thisbe is not pleasant or sad because it unfolds the sorry fate of young people who put their mutual sexual passion before their pious duty to their parents.[54] The account of gabbling Picus, according to Schuler, is Ovid's way of condemning inept and arrogant versifiers or so-called men of letters, who are ill-mannered and make themselves obstreperous to the learned. It also instructs youths who devote themselves to literature to follow in their writings, religion, piety, honesty, and virtue and not give themselves to scurrilities and blasphemy. "For the spirit of poetry, which is both divine and from God, should concern itself with matter pleasing to God; otherwise it is not holy, but profane; nor is it ethereal, as Ovid says, but comes from an infernal place."[55] With such an understanding of Ovid as Schuler pro-

[49] *Ibid.*, p. 111.
[50] *Ibid.*, p. 92.
[51] *Ibid.*, pp. 100–102.
[52] *Ibid.*, pp. 14–15.
[53] *Ibid.*, p. 23.
[54] *Ibid.*, pp. 138–39.
[55] *Ibid.*, pp. 188–89.

vided, the adolescents of Europe must have rushed into virtue totally unaware of the Roman's humanity and teasing wit.

From instruction of this nature, both in the schools and the universities, didactic graduates must have felt it their studious duty to convey the hidden wisdom of this poet to the less-learned general public. A feeling of this sort may account for the tendency that begins in the middle of the sixteenth century to translate in a moral fashion one of the myths of the *Metamorphoses* into the native language. An example of this sort in England is found in T. H.'s *The Fable of Ovid treting of Narcissus,* which appeared in 1560 and was an early product of what might be called "the Ovid industry." The poet turns the fable into poulter's measure and then presents the reader with a versified "moral thereunto, very pleasante to rede." The moralization is justified because Ovid did not write foolishly but with a "meaning straunge/ That wysdome hydeth, with some pleasaunt chaunge." The reader is urged to know "The thynges above as well as those belowe." The author, who has read Boccaccio and who quotes Ficino, not only finds the undermeaning to his central legend but also offers the conventional interpretations of the myths of Lycaon, Deucalion, Daphne, and Phaeton. In a sense T. H. sweeps the way for Arthur Golding's moralized and epistolatory prefatory poems to his 1567 translation of the *Metamorphoses,* and he furnishes illumination for William Webbe's evaluation of "Ovid most learned and exquisite Poet."

The work of greatest profite which he wrote was his Booke of Metamorphosis, which though it consisted of fayned Fables for the most part, and poetical inventions, yet beeing moralized according to his meaning, and the trueth of every tale beeing discovered, it is a work of exceeding wysedome and sounde iudgement.[56]

The Elizabethan attitude toward Ovid is not different from that of the Italians, whose public interest in the moralization of the *Metamorphoses* was both sustained and stimulated when Giovanni Andrea dell'Anguillara's Italian translation of the poem was published in Venice in 1563 with brief marginal moralizations of Gioseppe Horologgio. When the Venetian edition of 1571 appeared, the fuller allegorical commentaries of Francesco Turchi were added at the conclusion of each of the fifteen books. The two Italian allegorizers approached the fables with different interpretative purposes. After reading about Apollo's serpent

[56] *Of English Poetry, Elizabethan Critical Essays,* ed. G. G. Smith (Oxford, 1904), I, 238. For a bibliography of Renaissance English works based on Ovid see Douglas Bush, *Mythology and the Renaissance Tradition in English Poetry* (New York, 1963), pp. 310–39.

opponent, Horologgio found the python to be the symbol of a rich and vicious man who gave a bad example to the good and virtuous and, hence, was struck down by the arrows of divine tribulation. Turchi's reading is essentially physical, and he interprets the python as the moisture and slime left on the earth's surface after a flood, a dampness which will sicken men unless it is dried by the rays or arrows of the sun. If this drying occurs, as it does in Egypt, the fertility of the land is improved and the soil is more fruitful.[57] The myth of Niobe seems to Horologgio to be a lesson for the princes of the world, who proudly scorn religion unaware that they will be punished just as the wicked are but perhaps in a different way. Turchi sees in the story a not unlikely warning for all proud men, who will be deprived in due time of the objects of their pride; he also unfolds in the myth of Amphion, builder of the walls of Thebes, instruction in the value of speaking well, pronouncing sweetly, and talking with emphasis, a skill which turns men away from a wild and savage existence and into a quiet and civilized way of life.[58] When Medea rejuvenates Aeson, Horologgio discovers in the tale a message to those mature men who put aside their grave manners and slide into lasciviousness at the beckoning of an immodest woman. Turchi twists the legend another way to observe that Aeson was actually cleansed of his inveterate vices and reborn into virtue.[59] In many respects both of these moralizers are sometimes original in their readings, and the Italians, who purchased some seventeen printings of this excellent translation and abundant moralization between 1561 and 1624, were almost given free choice in how they might read the secrets of the Ovidian legends.

A few years after the moral annotations of Horologgio and Turchi were made available to Italian readers, Ercole Ciofani, a native of Ovid's Sulmona and a fine classical scholar, provided a possible counter-irritant in his *In omnia P. Ovidii Nasonis opera observationes* (Antwerp, 1575). When he turned in the course of his meditations to the *Metamorphoses,* Ciofani showed himself a careful reader of the ancient

[57] Ovid, *Le Metamorfosi,* eds. G. Horloggi, F. Turchi, and G. dell'Anguillara (Venice, 1584), pp. 13, 25.

[58] *Ibid.,* pp. 201, 228.

[59] *Ibid.,* pp. 240, 265. It should be observed that in addition to the moral readings supplied in Italian translations of Virgil and Ovid, other authors of Roman origin were not overlooked. Claudian's poem on Proserpine translated as *Il Ratto di Proserpina* by Giovanni Domenico Bevilacqua and printed at Palermo in 1586 was allegorized in a preface by Antonio Cingale. It should also be noted that other works of Ovid underwent the same allegorizing process. The editor of the Venice *Heroides* of 1583 describes the ethical value of the epistles, which are "the most moral of all of Ovid's poetry" and without any lubricious intent if they are properly read. One should consequently see an example of chastity in Penelope and learn the horror of incest from Phaedra.

euhemerists, whose rationalizations he reproduces with learned care. Atlas for him was simply an African king who worked out the principles of astronomy;[60] Orithyia was carried off by Strymon, son of Boreas;[61] Geryon was no monster but three brothers so agreeable in nature that they seemed to have one soul.[62] Hymenaeus, who gave his name to marriage, was such a beautiful boy that when pirates carried off the virgins consecrated to Ceres, they took him by mistake. Escaping while the captors slept and returning to Athens, he agreed—before he was very reluctant—to marry and in retribution dedicate his daughters to the goddess whose priestesses he had not been good enough to rescue.[63] Ciofani's account of Medea is almost directly from the ancient euhemerists.

Medea was the first person who could turn white hair black. Those men who chose to leave whiteheadedness she made appear dark-haired. She is also the first to have discovered the virtue of hot medicinal baths in which all willing could be cured, and these not in public but secretly so that the means would not be learned by physicians. To this end she employed a concoction and was called for that reason Parepsesis. Whoever used this was at once more agile and healthier, but whoever observed this got the impression that Medea cooked men in her kettle of concoctions. When Pelias, a weak old man, used the concoction, he was too far gone in the weakness of age and hence was consumed.[64]

Although Regio's edition of the *Metamorphoses* appears to have been the most popular Latin version, Ciofani's more coldly historical and cynical approach shows the direction in which professional scholars were beginning to move. Gregory Bersman, who revised Moltzer's text, carefully eschewed all second readings, but the custom of moralization was hard to escape. Jacob Spanmueller, who brilliantly provided elucidating scholia to Virgil in his *Symbolorum libri XVII* of 1599 and who had edited the *Tristia* and the *Ex Ponto* in 1610, published a *Metamorphoseon libris XV* in Antwerp in 1610. To a modern eye this is the finest series of annotations provided for Ovid by a scholar of the Renaissance because Spanmueller not only made use of all previous editors and commentators—Regio, Moltzer, Ciofani, Tritonio, Schuler, and others —but also added a large number of sound clarifications of his own. He also appears to have made a careful study of available manuscripts and

[60] Ciofani, *op. cit.,* p. 88.
[61] *Ibid.,* pp. 123–24.
[62] *Ibid.,* p. 178.
[63] *Ibid.,* p. 191.
[64] *Ibid.,* pp. 139–40.

selected, according to his own lights, the best readings; he further adopted the annotations of his predecessors with scrupulous caution and conscientiously acknowledged his debts to them by name. This scholarly approach (seen full-blown in his *Castigationes ad Virgili opera* of 1626) is not too usual in his generation; nevertheless, the old allegorical entanglements occasionally creep into his margins. The myth of Lycaon reminds him of Abraham's reception at Sodom and Gomorrah. "Is Ovid imitating this?" Certainly he is, "for the Gentiles knew many mysteries of the sacred books either through reading or hearing or through doctrine taught by the Chaldeans or Egyptians among whom the Hebrews lived."[65] With this conviction in mind, Spanmueller at times not only follows the custom of explaining a line physically or of offering an etymology of a proper name, but also pauses to point out something in the *Metamorphoses* which is derived from Scripture or from Christian rite. He does all of this sparingly, but he does it enough to be one of the two recent allegorical commentators—the other is Schuler—to be admittedly consulted for enlightenment by George Sandys, who also took most of his translated "Ovid Defended" from Spanmueller's "Dissertatio quarta: Eruditorum de Metamorphosibus Ovidianis testimonia."[66]

Spanmueller's rational edition of the *Metamorphoses* was hardly in the hands of booksellers before the *P. Ovidii Nasonis Metamorphoseon plerarumque historica naturalis moralis ekphrasis* of the historian, geographer, and naturalist Johann Ludwig Gottfried was published in Frankfort in 1619. The book is a prose summary of the *Metamorphoses* followed by an extensive book-by-book commentary. The interpreter informs the reader that he will not avoid historical, physical, and moral explications as far as they suit modern times and points to Fulgentius and Conti's commentaries as his great examples. As is the case of Sandys' subsequent edition a plate summarizing in picture the contents of each book precedes the texts. The moral readings outweigh all the others, although Gottfried provides occasional astrological and alchemistic allegories. The myth of Atalanta's race may be read chemically as the pursuit of Hippomenes, an alchemist, after the golden apples, or the Elixir. "Those who would philosophize in this fashion," Gottfried writes, "have my permission, but I shall not waste my gold, little as it is, on this Atalanta."[67] But the method followed by Gottfried (some of

---

[65] *Metamorphoseon libri XV,* ed. J. Spanmueller (Antwerp, 1618), p. 41. In a following note Spanmueller points out the similarity of Jupiter's descent in human form from Olympus and the Incarnation.
[66] Spanmueller lists his bibliography on p. 656; his "Dissertatio" is found on pp. 5–6.
[67] *Metamorphoseon . . . ekphrasis,* ed. J. L. Gottfried (Frankfort, 1619), pp. 253–54.

whose comments are found in Sandys) throughout his thick volume can be illustrated by his treatment of the legend of Pasiphae.

Pasiphae is "reason" married to Minos, or "justice," her proper virtue, but she deserts her lord for the pleasures of the flesh, symbolized by the lustful and furious bull. When the mind of man declines to lawlessness, what is begotten besides "obscene monsters"? Man is an ambiguous creature who should never relax his hold on the bridle controlling his brutish vices. The myth of this animal lover is, furthermore, a lesson to wives whose husbands are off with the army. Gottfried is hesitant to offer any modern illustrations; nevertheless, he reminds the readers of Ovid of the military experiences of Uriah and Agamemnon. Noble ladies married to great men are sometimes so carried away by passion that they give themselves like animals to other men who have nothing in common with them in either birth or rank. In a hieroglyphic sense the Daedalian labyrinth is the winding anxieties of life filled with deceits and frauds, difficult to escape and containing a deformed beast symbolic of all vices. The Minotaur, which devoured so many well-born and liberally educated Athenian youths and maids, primarily represents the pleasures of the stomach. The labyrinth can also be an emblem of the court, which has destroyed a great number of famous men like Thomas More and Thomas Wolsey.[68] This English example apparently did not appeal to Sandys, who like Gottfried and the classical interpreters also recognized in the labyrinth the tortuous course of human existence.

III

George Sandys' translation-adaptation and commentary on the *Metamorphoses* emerged from the long shadow cast by Golding's dull English version with its encysted moralizations. But if Sandys is to be judged as an interpreter as well as a first-class poetical renderer of the Latin, *The Third Part of the Countesse of Pembrokes Yuychurch*, published by Abraham Fraunce in 1592, must be regarded as his conspicuous English precursor. This pastoral invention is composed of poetical redactions of sixteen Ovidian tales recited by a series of nymphs and shepherds who wear the names of Damaetus, Fulvia, Alphesibaeus, Damon, Ergastus. Each of the verse renditions is followed by prose explanations pronounced by the learned and ingenious Elpinus. If one were given to etymologizing, as Fraunce was, one would translate this

---

[68] *Ibid.*, pp. 187–90.

unusual name as "the imaginer." With his eye on both Boccaccio and Leo Hebraeus, Fraunce opens his poetical commentary with a discussion of Demogorgon and his posterity. Aided principally by Conti and Schuler, as well as by their quoted authorities and by his own reading in classical authors or in contemporaries like Pontano[69] and Tasso,[70] he leads his gentle and noble readers through the romances of Pan and Syrinx, Jupiter and Io, Narcissus and Echo, Acis and Galathea, Proserpine and Pluto, Apollo and Daphne, Venus and Mars, Hermaphroditus and Salmacis, and, in fact through the truly grand amours of the fifteen books. In the course of his prose commentary which, like most commentaries, spatially exceeds the text it explains, he peeks into almost every corner of classical mythology fourfoldedly expounded.

In his first commentary on his prosy-poetical rendering of the first four hundred lines of Book One, Fraunce makes his confession of faith, which has a familiar ring about it. Both poetry, the speaking picture, and painting, the dumb poem, "cover the most sacred mysteries of auncient philosophie." Pythagoras, Plato in the *Phaedrus,* the *Timaeus,* and the *Symposium,* the Indians, Ethiopians, Egyptians, and Greeks all have wrapped up their secrets in such a fashion "as of the wise unfolder may well be deemed wonderfull." Solomon's Song of Songs is similarly "mystical and allegoricall." The reason for this concealment is plain because men's minds are moved, delight is stirred up, memory is confirmed, and thought is allured "by such familiar and sensible discourses to matters of more divine and higher contemplation."

He that is but of a meane conceit hath a pleasant and plausible narration concerning the famous exploits of renowmed Heroes, set forth in most sweete and

---

[69] *Pontano's Urania, sive de Stellis libri quinque* is the Renaissance source of a large amount of astrological interpretation. His account of Mercury, for example, explains his relation to Maia and his overcoming of Argus (pp. A2v–A4, B2). Similar allegories appear in Pontano's poem on Jove (B5), on Saturn (B6–B7v), and on the Council of the Gods (C1v–C3), as well as in those on the various zodiacal signs. (References are to the *Opera* [Venice, 1505].) The ever popular *Zodiacus Vitae* of Marcello Palingenio also contains various moralizations of Ovidian story.

[70] As Fraunce points out, Torquato Tasso was quick to notice a double meaning. In his "Il Gonzaga overo del Piacere Onesto," *Dialoghi,* ed. E. Raimondi (Florence, 1958), III, pp. 275–76, Agostin Sessa and Cesare Gonzaga discuss the separation of the waters at Creation. Sessa turns to Ovid (XIII. 906–65) for the myth of Glaucus' transformation and says: "Glaucus, who leaped into the sea, is the intellect, which descends into the body, where it mingles with the sensitive and vegetable souls on which the body depends. This can be compared with the mixing of spume and shell because shell signifies the sensitive soul in that sea shellfish are sensate. The vegetative soul is the alga, which is vegetable. The word 'spume,' then, probably denotes the highest act of the supreme force of the vegetable soul, which shares this power with the sensitive, in that Nature has placed the highest pleasure in the act of generation."

delightsome verse to feed his rurall humor. They, whose capacitie is such as that they can reach somewhat further then the external discourse and history, shall finde a morall sence included therein, extolling vertue, condemning vice every way profitable for the institution of a practicall and common wealth man. The rest, that are better borne and of a more noble spirit, shall meete with hidden mysteries of naturall, astrologicall, or divine and metaphysicall philosophie to entertaine their heavenly speculation.[71]

With this statement Fraunce sorts out the readers of Ovid on a social and intellectual basis. There are the obtuse, who read for pleasure; the substantial, who look for practical and political advice; and finally there are the university-educated aristocrats, who hear what the poet is saying. "That this is true," he continues, "let us make triall." The trial is further worth the effort because, as Fraunce states here and repeats elsewhere, many of these things "were taken (although in part mistaken) out of the sacred monuments of Moses."

Like John Ridewall and Pierre Bersuire, Fraunce describes how the ancients represented Saturn, Cybele, Pan, Jupiter, Apollo, and other divinities. He summarizes myths and in the case of Saturn, Jupiter, Prometheus, Scylla and Charybdis, Proteus, Ceres, Minos, and Rhadamanthus repeats the euhemeristic or "historical" explanations. Fraunce brings some of this matter into the light of fact by repeating the anecdotes of the satyr brought to Sulla, the Triton reported to Tiberius, and the mermaid seen by Theodore of Gaza. He also knows all other possible interpretations of designating symbols and curious interludes. The word "allegory," however, covers for him a multitude of meaning. "Allegorically," the Sirens "signifie the cosning tricks of counterfeit strumpets, the undoubted shipwrack of all affectionat yonkers."[72] "Allegorically, Prometheus is the fore-seeing and fore-knowing of things

---

[71] Fraunce, *The Third Part* . . . (London, 1592), pp. 3v–4. It should be observed that Fraunce is not the only Englishman to bring matter of this sort into the native language before Sandys' Ovid was in print. When Sir John Harington wrote his "Apologie of Poetrie" as a preface to his 1607 translation of *Orlando Furioso,* it is well known that he borrowed Leo Hebraeus' allegorization of the myth of Perseus. In the same way John Brinsleus' *Ovid's Metamorphosis* (London, 1618) follows the custom of locating the Christian analogues for the first twelve fables of Book One because (p. 2) the poets had these accounts of ancients, "who it is most like had seen or heard of sacred scriptures." When Thomas Lodge translated S. Goulart's *Commentaires et annotations sur la sepmaine de la creation du monde de Guillaume seigneur du Bartas* (Paris, 1583), as *A Learned Summary upon the Famous Poeme of William of Saluste, Lord of Bartas. Wherein are Discovered all the Excellent Secretts in Metaphysicall, Physicall, Morall, and Historicall Knowledge* (London, 1621) he carefully brought over all the allegories of his author on Bacchus, Ceres, Pandora, Latona, Orithyia, etc., and refers his readers to the mythologies (p. 61) of "Noel de Comtess, Lilius Giraldus, and Catari of the Images of the Gods."

[72] *Ibid.,* p. 22v.

before they come to passe (for soe the very woord importeth), as Epimetheus is the knowledge we get by the end and event of things already past and gone, whose daughter is Repentance."[73] "Allegorically . . . when in any mans action or nativitue Jupiter is predominant, then doth he controle Saturne."[74] "Allegorically," Polyphemus is a humble keeper of sheep, who loves "the Lady of milke," Galathea; since he knows the best places for milk, he does not wish her to come near Acis, "a river in Sicilia, whose naturall propertie was saide to be such as that it would drie up and consume milke."[75] But since Amarillis has poetically returned from Hell, Fraunce's general method of reading can be found in Elpinus' commentary.

Proserpine (from *proserpo*) is "the vertue of the earth" and is logically kidnapped in the fertile isle of Sicily, an event reported to Ceres by Arethusa, or "the vertue of the seede and roote." Pluto, or "earth from which mettals are digged," is also Divitas; hence, he is sometimes represented as blind to signify the common, unequal distribution of wealth. He is also pictured with keys because as "God of Ghosts," he locks the gates of Hell. He is shown on a throne with his dog Cerberus, who is the devouring earth, the sensual body of man, hunger, thirst, and weariness, or the manifold guilt of covetousness. Charon is joy and gladness, sage advice, or time. Chimera, otherwise a volcano in Lycia, an area made habitable by Bellerophon, is also "inordinate luste." Medusa is the personification of "lustfull beawty" overcome by Perseus, who is "celestiall grace and wisdome." Sisyphus has meaning *in malo,* but:

Others expound it so, as meaning by the stone, the studies and endevours of mortall men: by the hill, the whole course of mans life: by the hill top, the ioy and tranquillitie of the minde: by Hell, the earth and men on earth: by Sisiphus, the soule and minde of man, which included in this prison of the body; striveth and contendeth by all meanes possible, to attaine to eternall rest, and perfect felicitie: which some repose in wealth, some in honor, some in pleasure: all which having once gotten what they sought, begin againe as fast, to covet new matters, and never make an end of desiring: so that, he who first was wholly given to catch and snatch, being now growne to wealth, seeketh honor, and is as infinitely addicted to that vaine humor, as ever he was to the other miserable affliction.[76]

After this peroration Fraunce understands Tityus "physically" as "a stalke or blade of corne"; Tantalus is the pattern of "a covetous

---

[73] *Ibid.,* p. 9v.
[74] *Ibid.,* p. 7v.
[75] *Ibid.,* p. 21v.
[76] *Ibid.,* pp. 26–30v.

wretch," but, in his divine origin, could likewise stand for the sort of philosopher so intent on contemplation that he loses his goods, his wife, and his children; Triptolemus is the ship which brought corn to Athens; and the Danae may be unthankful minds, insatiable desires, the whole estate of man's perturbed life, or the "exchecquer or treasury of a prince." The Sirens who follow Proserpine, "which I had almost forgotten," are strumpets and wanton housewives who "folow riches and aboundance." With this large helping of exposition to whet their intellectual appetites, the aristocratic and the learned Elizabethans must have hungered for more. Sandys, who was a generation away, would satisfy their desires, and the great popularity of his Ovid indicates how keen they were.

The history of Sandys' translation of Ovid and its various publications, first, in the five-book version of 1621, next, in the complete translation of 1626, and last, in the standard Oxford edition of 1632 with the title *Ovid's Metamorphosis Englished, Mythologized, and Represented in Figures* is a minor bibliographical romance.[77] The finished edition with its heraldic frontispiece, its portrait of Ovid, and the symbolical summary plates at the beginning of each of thirteen books was reprinted in almost every decade until the end of the seventeenth century and is the triumph of Jacobean translation. Its engraved title page[78] displays, each in a corner, the figures of Jupiter, Juno, Ceres, and Neptune attended and interpreted physically or morally by symbolic creatures while Venus and Cupid oppose Minerva from lateral lozenges and Apollo straddles the arch of the entrance to the curtained Temple of Poetry. The governing motto "All comes from these" is further emphasized by a charioted Hercules (man drawn to the higher realms) at the

[77] R. B. Davis, "Early Editions of George Sandys' 'Ovid': The Circumstances of Production," *The Papers of the Bibliographical Society of America*, XXXV (1941), 255-76; J. G. McManaway, "The First Five Bookes of Ovids Metamorphosis, 1621, Englished by Master George Sandys," *Papers of the Bibliographical Society of Virginia*, I (1948-49), 71-82; R. B. Davis, *"In re* George Sandys' Ovid," *Studies in Bibliography*, VIII (1956), 226-30; R. B. Davis, *George Sandys, Poet-Adventurer* (London, 1955), pp. 198-226.

[78] The portrait of Ovid was based on a silver medal in Sandys' collection; it is unknown to modern numismatists. This and all the other plates were designed by Franz Klein of Rostoch, who came to England and did the walls and ceilings in Somerset House, Carew House, Holland House, as well as Charles I's great seal. The same plates were used in the first Paris printing, in 1637, of Farnaby's edition of the *Metamorphoses*. Klein subsequently did the plates for Marolles' *Tableaux du Temple des Muses*, 1655, and for Ogilvy's Virgil. Solomon Savery, who did the copperplates, was born in Amsterdam but emigrated to London in 1632, where his skills were variously employed. In the preface to the reader Sandys praises the "rare Workman" who made the plates and writes a brief account of the harmonious union of poetry and painting, "Daughters of the Imagination," feasting both ear and eye, "the noblest of the sences, by which the Understanding is onely informed and the mind sincerely delighted."

top of the design, whereas Ulysses with the moly of wisdom and love in an octagon at the foot of the plate restores to human shape men sunk into the bodies of swine. The translator, who probably composed the humanistic axiom which surrounds the Circean episode and significantly reads, "Affigit humo divinae particulam aurae," printed a suite of verses explaining "The minde of the frontispeece and the argument of this Worke." The elements, the poem remembers, were drawn into harmony by love; Pallas, who orders "our will, desire, and powres irascible," attires the mind with heroic virtues so that under her guidance men seek the way of Hercules to fame and glory. Forsaking "that faire Intelligence" and charmed by Circe's luxury, they follow "passion and voluptuous sense" and decline to bestiality. The theme was not invented but only given the poet, since

> Phoebus Apollo (sacred Poesy)
> Thus taught: for in these ancient Fables lie
> The mysteries of all Philosophie.

In the preface "To the Reader" Sandys, like so many explicators of the *Metamorphoses* before him, justifies the journey through the fables in search of "the mysteries of all Philosophie." He has searched many authors for news about the philosophical sense, which was encased in myth long before writing was known. Like the "sacred pen-men," early writers used allegory to express the works of nature, administer comfort in calamity, expel the perturbations of the mind, and inflame men to emulation by noble example, leading them "as it were by the hand to the Temple of Honour and Vertue." In the mythology he supplies, Sandys admittedly follows a variety of interpretive conceptions "where they are not over-strained" rather than curiously examining "their exact proprietie." In other words, he was certain that there was no unilateral reading of any myth or poetical text; all he asked was for the allegory to fit the tale or, as he puts it, "so as the principall parts of application resemble the ground-worke." But Sandys, who had traveled in both the Old and New Worlds, was fully aware of the other explorers of his time, who only wandered through the books of the past in search of the original truth. To this awareness he testifies:

I have also endeavored to cleare the Historicall part, by tracing the almost worne-out steps of Antiquitie; wherein the sacred stories afford the clearest direction. For the first Period from the Creation to the Flood, which the Ethnickes called the Obscure, some the Emptie times; and the Ages next following which were stil'd the Heroycall, because the after deified Heroes then flourished; as also the Fabulous, in that those stories convayed by Tradition in loose and broken Fragments, were by the Poets interwoven with instructing Mythologies, are most obscurely and perplexedly delivered by all, but the supernaturally inspired Moses. Wherefore, not without authority, have I here and there given a touch of the relation which those fabulous Traditions, have to the divine History, which the Fathers have observed, and made use of in convincing the Heathen.[79]

The dozen or more pages of commentary which Sandys supplies at the end of every book of his translation are the most readable discussions ever written on Ovid. The attractively turned out prose is interspersed with verse translations of illustrative passages from other works of Ovid and from the poetry of Lucretius, Virgil (whose *Aeneid* he once had hoped to translate), Lucan, Seneca, Manilius, Horace, Juvenal, Martial, Petronius, Ausonius, Claudian, Catullus, and Tibullus. Among the Greeks, Sandys quotes from Homer, Hesiod, and Orpheus, but, apparently having large Latin and small Greek, he bases his translations on Latin renderings. In addition he sometimes calls on the *Poemata* of J. C. Scaliger, the *Epigrammata* of Faustus Sabaeus, or the Latin verse of Alciati, Aeneas Sylvius, Claude Anneau, or Giovanni Pontano. There are some poetical insertions that seem to be original and should be added to Sandys' corpus. In one instance, when he quotes from Plato's *Republic* (452), he declares the statement "best apparelled in numbers" and proceeds so to do.[80]

The marginal comments with which Sandys supplies his text are of an explanatory and summary nature and are clearly from the Regio Ovid as revised by Moltzer. The interpretive appendices to each book of the *Metamorphoses* are sometimes rewritings (as in the first book) of Lavinius[81] and at other times of Schuler.[82] Among ancient mythographers, Sandys called on Apollodorus, Hyginus, Diodorus Siculus, and Palaephatus; among recent mythologists he used Giraldi, Conti, and the *Wisdom of the Ancients* of Francis Bacon. He has been said to have consulted almost two hundred authors,[83] but many of his seeming sources

[79] *Metamorphosis Englished*, ed. G. Sandys (Oxford, 1632). This conviction reappears elsewhere in the notes as, for example, in his first note on Chaos (*ibid.*, p. 19) where he writes, "And though by not expressing the originall he seems to intimate the eternitie of his Chaos; yet appears in the rest so consonant to the truth, as doubtlesse he had either seene the Books of Moses, or received the doctrine by tradition."

[80] *Ibid.*, p. 292.

[81] There are other examples, but a good one is the translation of Saturn as Adam and the account of the Four Ages by Sandys, *ibid.*, pp. 25–26; Lavinius on I. 113ff. in *Metamorphoseos* (Milan, 1540).

[82] See as one case Sandys, in *Metamorphosis Englished*, pp. 66–67; Schuler, *op. cit.*, pp. 63–7.

[83] Davis, *George Sandys*, pp. 218–19.

came to him secondhandedly, for Sandys, like Sir Thomas Browne or many other men of his generation, did not hesitate to steal another's stolen footnotes.[84]

Sandys' commentary, which embraces all the known types of readings, is actually a great variorum of adjusted and acceptable symbolism and allegory. The ordinary Englishman who had little or no Latin was made as comfortable in this matter as Continentals in the same predicament had been made by the Italian and French translators. Sandys' euhemeristic, physical, etymological, and moral readings are definitely conventional and often traceable. Prometheus is again Providence; the "celestial fire is his soule inspired from above."[85] Niobe is a historical queen who lost all her children in a plague and is also an example of the proud, who, contemning God and man and forgetful of human instability, "are reduced by divine vengeance to be the spectacles of calamity" and lacking the ability to support affliction are turned to stone, or "stupified with immoderate sorrow."[86] The coupling of Venus and Mars is both astrological and physical because Mars is hot and Venus is moist, "whereof generation consists"; but Neptune, or water, puts out the fire, or Vulcan. But adulteries, committed by even the greatest, are discovered in the long run by the eyes of the sun; this is the moral suggestion.[87] In addition to all this relatively traditional material Sandys, following the indication of his preface, looks for biblical proveniences.

Like many early Church Fathers, Sandys knew the true origin of pagan myth, the nature of its distortions, and the purpose of its invention. When Jupiter calls the council of the gods at the beginning of the poem, Ovid is suggesting that human affairs are governed by providence and not by chance, as Seneca supposed. However, the assembled deities were invented by "the Divell" to bring confusion and induce error.[88] Noah's Flood got converted by the demons into other deluges in all parts of the world, so that "even the salvage Virginians" have a legend about it.[89] The Hebrew hero of the episode was transformed, as all the historical readers assumed, into Bacchus.[90] The Giants of course are the sons of Seth by the daughters of Cain; Cain himself is the first Jupiter

[84] An example is Erasmus' allegorization of Cadmus' sowing of the dragon's teeth (p. 99), which might, of course, have been taken from Erasmus but more likely comes from Schuler (*op. cit.*, p. 101).

[85] Sandys, *Metamorphosis Englished*, p. 25.

[86] *Ibid.*, p. 222.

[87] *Ibid.*, p. 157.

[88] *Ibid.*, p. 29.

[89] *Ibid.*, p. 31.

[90] *Ibid.*, p. 109.

just as plainly as Tubal Cain is Vulcan, Jubal is Apollo, and Naamah is Venus.[91] The discovery of perverted Scripture in Ovid's first book prompts the disclosing of Christian doctrine elsewhere as in the story of Pasiphae, who is:

> The Soule of man inriched with the greatest reason and knowledge, by how much the body is more sublimated by the virtue and efficacy of the Sun. . . . This Soule espoused to Minos (Justice and Integrety) where carried away with sensual delights is said to forsake her lawful husband and to committ with a Bull; for so brutish and violent are the affections when they revolt from the obedience of Virtue, producing Minotaures and monsters by defaming Nature through wicked habit, and so become prodigious.[92]

The real virtue of Sandys as a spreader of the cult of second readings resides in what he adds to the conventional commentaries and from his relaxed rhetorical manner reminiscent of that of Montaigne or Burton. When he describes Ovid's cosmology, he calls on Copernicus and on Galileo's glasses to assist him.[93] A little later, remarking on the millionaire row where the major gods resided, he resorts to Tycho Brahe and Kepler for their theories of the Milky Way.[94] Medea's bathing of Aeson reminds him that the Germans have a bath "clarifying the blood and suppling the body"; but he has also heard of a "ridiculous Spaniard," who sought for a fountain in the West Indies "famous for rendring youth unto age, which is rightly ranked among incurable Diseases."[95] Orpheus' moving forest is repeated for him when William the Conqueror was deluded by the Kentishmen and "the usurper Macbeth by the expulsed Milcolmb."[96] The Scottish history comes in also when Sandys rereads the myth of Althaea and Meleager and relates from Buchanan's history the story of Duff, King of Scotland, who was wasting away "in a perpetual sweat," with a new and incurable disease.

> Insomuch as suspected to have beene bewitched, which was increased by a rumor that certain witches of the Forrest of Murry practised his destruction, arising from a word which a girle let fall that the King should dye shortly. Who, being examined by Donald, Captaine of the Castle, and tortures showne her, confessed the truth and how her mother was one of the assembly. When certaine souldiers being sent in search surprised them a rosting the waxen Image of the King before a soft fire, to the end that as the wax melted by degrees so should the King

---

[91] *Ibid.*, pp. 26–27.
[92] *Ibid.*, p. 289.
[93] *Ibid.*, p. 20.
[94] *Ibid.*, p. 23.
[95] *Ibid.*, pp. 257–78.
[96] *Ibid.*, p. 356.

dissolve into a sweat by little and little, and his life consume with the consumption of the other, as here is described in the death of Meleager.[97]

IV

The interest in the moral reading of Ovid, which was also stimulated to a large degree by the composers of mythographical handbooks and which found a place in studies of pagan theology like that of Maichin[98] or in parallel studies of the Bible and legend like the works of Bompart[99] or Ursinus,[100] was not alone satisfied with Sandys' ever popular translation and commentary. Before Sandys was in English print, Nicolas Renouard had issued in Paris in 1614 for the use of France his *Les Metamorphoses d'Ovide traduittes en Prose Francoise . . . Avec XV Discours contenans l'explication moralé des Fables.* This translation and commentary was reprinted at least thirteen times before it was replaced at mid-century by Pierre du Ryer's similar French translation and vernacular commentary.

In his amiable first essay to his discourses, Renouard praises Ovid for concealing "a treasure of wisdom" under the subtle veil of his transformations; were this not so, one would recoil from the kinds of love, sometimes chaste but more often incestuous, adulterous, perverted, or bestial, portrayed in his poem. But the ancients were inclined to convey by these myths some strange but true event or phenomenon of nature or a fine moral precept. The Greeks knew, and now the Italians, Spaniards, and Germans know, that under these colors may be found both philosophical secrets and philosophical instruction. Renouard pro-

---

[97] *Ibid.,* pp. 293–94. On June 26, 1636, Marcus Boxhorn (Boxhornius) delivered a series of three lectures, the second of which bore the title, "De Fabulis Poetarum: Lectiones ad Metamorphosin Ovidii." The purpose of ancient poets, he stated, is to teach by fable those who cannot otherwise be taught. "Just as God created what had never before existed, so the poet makes something of nothing." The great heroes—Hercules, Ulysses, Aeneas—probably never lived except in poet's books, "yet they have improved the desires and aspirations of ordinary men. Those who never reigned teach men to reign; those who never fought teach men to fight bravely; they teach men to counsel though they never sat in council; they teach men to lose what they never had, to keep what they never obtained, to defend what they never could lose; and, finally, since they never lived, they teach men to die." We should laugh at the *Metamorphoses,* but can we? "When we read about Lycaon, we should laugh or be horrified. We cannot be horrified because it could only happen in Lapland. We cannot laugh because he is the personification of a tyrant and those who have lived under tyrants know what it means." Boxhorn continues in this fashion to conclude that these fables had two purposes: that one might drink here both the science of nature and the theology of Gentiles. The oration is printed in *Orationes tres* (Leyden, 1686), pp. 23–39.

[98] See Chapter III, note 49.

[99] See Chapter II, note 61.

[100] See Chapter III, note 43.

poses then to relate the lines of the *Metamorphoses* to philosophical principles: the ideas of Plato, the harmony of Pythagoras, the fire of Heraclitus, the stars of Hermes Trismegistus, the numbers of Chrysippus, and the entelechies of Aristotle. To this end he likens himself to the commonplace example of the Renaissance bee, and, dividing each one of the fifteen discourses into chapters according to the number of impressive fables, Renouard proceeds to metamorphose the pollen of abuse into the honey of use. But he has not done all of his distilling without aid. Ariste, the "surname of one of the most learned men of the century" urged him to write the discourses and personally visits him from chapter to chapter to provide the proper insight.

Ariste does not differ from other expounders of the first book of the *Metamorphoses* in noticing behind it the same hand of Moses found in the doctrines of the Stoics, of Aristotle, and of Hermes Trismegistus. Prometheus is once again both Providence and an early astronomer; the four metallic ages are from the prophecy of Daniel; the Giants are the builders of Babel; Lycaon is a lesson in piety and hospitality; Deucalion is Noah; the python is the dampness and sludge of the Flood; the story of Daphne and Apollo shows that the sun makes trees grow and expresses the laurel virtue of virginity; the myth of Io warns virgins against the adulterous enticements of men. In most of these interpretations Renouard, as is his continued practice, supplies the historical truth or brings a parallel story from history to match the myth.[101]

Once the first book is traditionally explained Ariste sometimes becomes relatively original. The story of Pyramus and Thisbe is not only a warning to children who disobey their parents but also to parents who interfere in their childrens' amours.[102] The adultery of Mars and Venus may be astrological, but Venus' incitement of the Sun's five daughters should be seen as the effect of passion on the five wits of man.[103] Medusa is, among other things, the French Protestants; therefore Perseus is Henry of Navarre.[104] Minerva is true learning; Arachne is the finespun sophistries of men lacking firm doctrine.[105] The myth of Icarus demonstrates the arrogance of an astrologer who embraces fallacious views and suffers the shipwreck of his reputation.[106] Medea's ministrations to Aeson and Pelias is a lesson about seventeenth-century charlatans, who

---

[101] *Les Metamorphoses,* trans. N. Renouard (Paris, 1614), pp. 68–114.
[102] *Ibid.,* p. 116.
[103] *Ibid.,* p. 118.
[104] *Ibid.,* p. 130.
[105] *Ibid.,* p. 153.
[106] *Ibid.,* p. 181.

use an apparent miracle to ruin other clients.[107] The race of Atalanta and Hippomenes shows, first, the light-mindedness of young beauties who seek one amorous conquest after another. When Atalanta is finally won it is not Hippomenes' grace, nor his courage, nor the nobility of his birth, nor even the aid of Venus, but the charm of the apples of gold, which the poet curiously represents as a miracle. "It may have been so in his time, but it is not so today; the results are too common to be thought strange."[108]

Renouard's *Metamorphoses,* while preserving the moral method, tended to move towards more modern applications, to limit itself to fewer emphases, and to drop out the more outlandish readings taken over from the medieval explicators by the sixteenth century. The translation was usually accompanied by Renouard's original *Judgment of Paris,* his translation of Virgil's "Metamorphosis of Bees," and his rendering of the first book of Ovid's *Remedies* and of eleven of the *Heroides.* Appearing in 1619, the second edition was enriched with figures, which were repeated in later editions. In 1660 Renouard's French translation gave way to *Les Metamorphoses d'Ovide en Latin et François: Avec de Nouvelles Explications Historiques, Morales et Politiques sur toutes les Fables, chacune selon son sujet* of the playwright, translator, and historiographer Pierre du Ryer. Du Ryer made his living by his pen, and his plays are not much better than his translations of Greek and Latin authors; nevertheless his reputation, which must have been inspired by his voluminosity, brought his election to the Academy in the same class with Corneille. His edition of Ovid prints the Latin text alongside a French prose rendering with his explication at the foot of each myth. In most editions Renouard's *Judgment of Paris* and his verse versions of the *Heroides* (followed by the remaining nine in Du Ryer's prose) are appended. The book is further ornamented by a series of luxurious engravings, often copied or adapted for Banier's later text and translation.[109] Given all this goodness, it is not surprising it was still reissued as late as 1744.

[107] *Ibid.,* pp. 170–71.

[108] *Ibid.,* pp. 206–7.

[109] The illustrations in the Amsterdam edition of 1702 were, when acknowledged, engraved by Martin Bouche, Peter Paul Bouche, Philibert Bouttats, and Peeter Clouwet. The original designer is seldom indicated. Several are by Abraham van Diepenbeech or by Giulio Romano, and one carries an HA monogram and may be the work of one of the Aspers. Some seventy-seven of them were directly or closely copied by Pieter Stevens van Gunst or Philip van Gunst (they are difficult to separate) for Antoine Banier's *Les Metamorphoses d'Ovide en Latin, traduites en François avec des Remarques et des Explications Historique* (Amsterdam, 1732), although the title page assigns them to Bernard Picart "et autres habiles

Du Ryer naturally follows Genesis through the opening pages of his Ovidian commentary; once he enters the second book, however, he is, with obvious borrowings, on his own. Phaeton is the governor of a republic; the chariot of the Sun is the state; the monsters of the Zodiac are state ministers. This is the political meaning. The moral meaning is the traditional one of the disobedient child, whereas the physical meaning has to do with the vapors raised by solar heat.[110] Medea's myth tells one that the same medicine works differently on different constitutions; she personifies the sexual effect a young woman has on foolish old men; moreover, if one can think of Jason as symbolizing medicine, Medea stands for the caution a physician should have.[111] The myth of Hermaphroditus and Salmacis makes clear with what difficulty hard-working and puritanical young men escape the wiles of a voluptuous woman.[112] Although the conventional euhemeristic commentary, elucidated by similar histories, is still present in Du Ryer's expositions, the physical and spiritual meanings are almost silent, and the old-fashioned moral readings have been largely replaced by fairly trite and obvious observations on social and political conduct.

Banier's *Metamorphoses,* which charmed eighteenth-century French taste, is the stout plant grown from Du Ryer's frail seeds. Although he noticed that previous interpreters read Ovid according to their own thoughts or plans and found in his fictions "a mysterious obscurity" supporting physical, moral, chemical, or medicinal wisdom, Banier, looking toward a scientific tomorrow, read them as the history of the early world.[113] His opinion coincided in theory but not in performance with the indefatigable Herman van der Hardt, who in 1711 exposed the lost historical annals in Ovid's myth of the frogs and in 1739 the vanished events in the myth of Syrinx. But before Banier could express his doctrine, there appeared in 1684 and again in 1696 a sort of child's version of Ovid moralized. Francesco Bardi's *Favole d'Ovidio istorico,*

Maîtres." It is quite possible that the illustrations not taken over from Du Ryer's volume are by these men. A comparison of the engravings in Du Ryer's translation with those in Banier's indicates the following copies or near copies (book and fable are represented by roman and arabic numbers; hyphenated numbers are one plate): I. 3, 5, 6, 7, 8, 13, 15, 16; II. 1, 1a, 6-7, 10, 14; III. 1, 2, 3, 3a, 6, 7; IV. 3-4, 15; V. 4-5, 6, 8-9, 10; VI. 1-4, 5, 6, 10, 11; VII. 1, 2-4, 20-24, 25, 26; VIII. 1, 2, 3, 7-10, 11; IX. 1, 2, 3-4, 5-6, 7-10, 11; X. 1, 2, 4, 6, 7-8, 9, 10, 11, 12, 13, 14-15; XI. 1, 3, 7-9, 10, 11; XII. 4-7; XIII. 1-4, 5-8, 12, 13; XIV. 1, 3, 4, 6-7, 8-9, 10-12, 13, 14; XV. 1-8, 9.

[110] *Les Metamorphoses,* ed. P. du Ryer (Paris, 1660), p. 49.
[111] *Ibid.,* p. 218.
[112] *Ibid.,* p. 126.
[113] *Les Metamorphoses,* ed. and trans. A. Banier (Amsterdam, 1732), p. **3.

politico, morale con le allegorie[114] is actually a series of seventy-eight etchings illustrating eighty fables. Beneath each picture is a prose summary of the tale and its allegorical significance. The book could be slipped into the pocket and read as a boy ran.

The interpreters of Homer, Virgil, and Ovid, who exposed for more than two centuries the hidden meanings of these poets, were aided (as the earlier of them had been assisted) by the professional mythographers, who during the same two centuries put together the authoritative handbooks about the gods and heroes of Greece and Rome. The commentaries of the fifteenth- and early sixteenth-century editors of these poets flowed into the mythologies of Conti, Cartari, and the others. In due course the observations of these mythographers returned like the tide to wash imperiously over the margins of the seventeenth-century scholiasts on the *Iliad,* the *Odyssey,* the *Aeneid,* and the *Metamorphoses.*

[114] The moralizing tendency turns up, of course, in other places. In 1671 Frederick Hildebrand, rector of the school at Nordhausen, published in that city a *Centuria gemina epistolarum prior epistolas varii argumenti, altera fabulas ad moralia applicatas complectitur juventis.* The latter part (pp. 145–294) moralized, actually Christianized, a large number of Ovid's fables. Pasiphae is a soul married to Jesus, who forgets her spouse; Ulysses ties himself to the mast of Christ and stuffs his ears with Christian prudence against the songs of worldly pleasure; Atalanta is a faithful soul racing towards eternal salvation, distracted by the apples of ambition, pleasure, and honor cast in her path by Hippomenes, or Satan; Perseus' birth is that of Christ and his rescue of Andromeda the salvation of the soul of the Christian. As late as 1721, when Lucas Cuper wrote a preface to his *Paratitla tes Chronologias et historia sacrae a mundo condita usque ad ten Exodon Jisraelitarum ex Aegypto; profanum quae explicat prout desumpta ex libris Metamorphoseon Publii Ovidii Nasonia ad haec tempora spectat,* he follows the worn track. Like his master Huet, he knows many tongues, and this knowledge permits him to see Levi in Aeolus, Esther in Astrea, Sara in Asia, Dinah in Diana, Isaac in Inachus, Miriam in Minerva, Onan in Vulcan, etc. His method is very precise. Esther or Hadassah means "the highest star," such as the Nativity star (Esther, 4:16). This is enough to prove she is Astrea, but in addition there are words in Ovid's account of Astrea also found in Esther (pp. 73–74).

VIII

◆ THE ALLEGORICAL INTERPRETATION OF THE RENAISSANCE MYTHOGRAPHERS ◆

THE PROFESSIONAL MYTHOGRAPHER was a Renaissance creation, and the manuals he wrote were closely consulted by artists, men of letters, and all educated men. His primary sources were the literary texts of Greece and Rome, the earlier commentaries on these texts, the curious mythologies of the Middle Ages, and the newly discovered classical interpreters. From these works he gathered his raw material, which he classified and summarized. Although there are restrained exceptions like Giraldi, the force of tradition was too much for most of these compilers, and they found it impossible to avoid the euhemeristic, ethical, or moral readings of the Christian apologists and syncretists and of the symbolical and allegorical commentators on all ancient writings. Their readers found in their pages the same fascination with hidden meanings that impelled the scholiasts on Homer, Virgil, and Ovid.

By the middle of the sixteenth century the ancient mythographers Apollodorus, Hyginus, Antoninus Liberalis, and Cornutus had joined authorities like Proclus, Porphyry, Heraclitus, and Diodorus Siculus in the mythographers' libraries. An accomplished scholar like Natale Conti does not hesitate to cite Silenus of Chios, mentioned by Eustathius, and Pherecydes, known through Celsus. However, it was Apollodorus and Cornutus, assisted by Cicero's celebrated conversations *On the Nature of the Gods,* who furnished the warp for most mythographers' webs. The first author was available in print in 1555 and the second in 1563; Cicero's engaging little dialogue on religion was first published in 1471 and reprinted many times before 1500. These authorities and the allegorical commentary of Heraclitus gave men of the Renaissance solid training in the Stoic *modus legendi.*

II

A man of the Renaissance learned from Dio Chrysostom's *Discourse on Homer* that Zeno of Citium, founder of Stoicism, said that Homer must sometimes be read in accordance with "appearances" and other times as "truth." This literary means of judgment might have pervaded his *Homeric Problems,* a book known to Cicero's Epicurean spokesman, Velleius, who remembers that Zeno identified Zeus with æther and said that the names of the gods "have been assigned allegorically to dumb and lifeless things." Zeno's disciple Persæus, Velleius said, believed that great men had been deified and was dismayed that divine honors have been awarded "to mean and ugly things and the rank of gods to dead men."[1] Velleius, true to his master's prejudices, also talks about Chrysippus, the third in the Stoic succession,[2] whose allegorical anatomy of the Moirai based on the etymology of their names got him quoted by both Theodoretus[3] and Eusebius.[4] He made nature myths of Jupiter, Ceres, and Neptune, identified Jupiter with Necessity or Fate, and "attempted to reconcile the tales about Orpheus, Musaeus, Hesiod, and Homer with his own theology . . . so that he makes it appear that even the earliest poets of ancient times, who had no glimpse of these doctrines, were all Stoics."[5]

---

[1] Cicero, *De natura deorum* I, 14–15. Besides Seznec's book, *The Survival of the Pagan Gods,* trans. B. F. Sessions (New York, 1953), there are several other indispensable studies: O. Gruppe, *Geschichte der Klassischen Mythologie* (Leipzig, 1921); F. von Bezold, *Das Fortleben der antiken Götter im Mittelalterlichen Humanismus* (Bonn and Leipzig, 1922); and A. Frey-Sallman, *Aus dem Nachleben antiker Göttergestalten* (Leipzig, 1931).

[2] The second in the Stoic succession is Cleanthes, who wrote a "Hymn to Zeus" so Christian in theme and expression that it might have been sung in Augustine's City of God. He interprets mythology after the manner of the *Cratylus* (394a–422b). He looked for the represented natural phenomena in the names of the gods or in their Homeric qualifications. Apollo represents the sun because "sometimes it rises here and sometimes there" ("ap allon kai allon topon"). If report is correct he may have invented the allegorization of the Labors of Hercules: see Cornutus, *De natura deorum,* ed. F. Osann (Gottingen, 1844), 223.

[3] Theodoretus, *Curatio Graecarum affectionum,* trans. P. Canivet (Paris, 1958) I. 257–58.

[4] Eusebius, *Praeparatio evangelica* VI. 263.

[5] Cicero, *De natura deorum* I, 15. Apollo, Chrysippus thought, means that "the sun is not one of the many" ("a + pollon") "harmful manifestations of fire" (Macrobius, I. 17. 7). Plutarch (*Amatorius.* 757) is too religious for linguistic games but records that Chrysippus derived Ares from "anaires" or "cut-throat." As a priest of Apollo he had little tolerance for people who said Aphrodite was only "desire" and Hermes, "eloquence." "You surely will see

From the *Bibliotheca* of Apollodorus men of the Renaissance got a supply of learned but baffling information, without symbolic interpretation, about the Greek gods and heroes;[6] but if they required further understanding, they had only to listen to Balbus, who defended under Cicero's guidance the faith of the Stoic sect against the criticisms of Velleius the Epicurean and Cotta the Academic. It is probably the one time in unburned pagan literature that a quasi-Christian advocate is harshly but safely treated by pagan opposites. In the course of his defense Balbus, a Stoic of the old school, reveals a knowledge of Stoic exegesis. This is as it should be because Cicero knew that Balbus was an accomplished reasoner worthy of being compared with the Stoics of Greece.[7]

When his turn to talk comes in *On the Nature of the Gods,* Balbus announces that most of the divinities known to the Romans got their haloes as rewards for the benefits which they bestowed on men. Hercules, Aesculapius, Romulus, and Quirinus were deified for this reason alone. But Balbus also knew that myths, sometimes called "superstitions," grew, as Zeno, Cleanthes, and Chrysippus stated, from scientific attempts to explain the ordinary workings of the universe. There was, for example, an old Greek belief that Caelus was mutilated by Saturn and that Saturn was put in bonds by Zeus. At first this myth seems immoral, but it masks a clever idea. Fire, the highest element, does not require genitals in order to procreate. Balbus is also a sublime philologist and is able to find merits in the divine nomenclatures. Cronus got his name from "time"; Saturn ("satur + anni") is sated with years; the names of Jove and Juno come from "iuvare," or "to help." Neptune is "nare," or "to swim"; and Demeter is "earth-mother," or "Ge + mater." Once he has placed this evidence before his associates,

---

the abyss of atheism which engulfs us if we list each several god on the roster of emotions, functions, and virtues." According to Velleius, Chrysippus' pupil Diogenes of Babylon wrote a *Minerva* which offered a physiological explanation of the goddess' birth. The opinions on these matters of Crates of Mallos, master of the Stoics of Pergamus, were collected for the Renaissance in the Homeric allegory of the pseudo-Heraclitus (27), who relates that Crates saw a cosmic map in the ten circles and twenty bosses on the shield of Agamemnon (*Iliad* XI. 32–37). When Zeus threw Hephaestus from heaven it was an experiment in celestial mechanics enabling the god to determine the dimensions of the universe. Crates, according to Aulus Gellius (II. 25), adopted the "anomalistic" method of Chrysippus in opposition to Aristarchus of Samothrace's literal readings.

[6] In the preface (pp. x–xi) to his translation of the *Bibliotheca,* Frazer distinguished between the two mythographers of this name. The author of *On the Gods,* once in twenty-four books, now in slivers, was a firm allegorizer and his fragments may be consulted in C. Muller and T. Muller, *Fragmenta historicorum Graecorum* (Paris, 1841).

[7] Cicero, *De natura deorum* I. 6; *Brutus* 154.

Balbus can agree that allegory, once in the myths, has been perverted by time into old wives' tales.[8]

Cotta, a disciple of Carneades, looks coldly at any religion and is hardly contented by Balbus' assault on superstition. "These are the superstitions of the unlearned," he says in reference to the common myths, "but are the dogmas of your philosophers any better?"[9] Are those "allegorizing and etymological methods of expounding mythology" superior to bare tales themselves? Balbus' allegorical interpretation of the castration of Caelus, he goes on, implies that the "idiots" who invented these legends were also philosophers.[10] As for the meddling with significant names—it is not only dangerous but in a religious sense foolish. "What sort of interpretation can be gotten out of Vejovis or Vulcan?" The great Stoics, Cotta complains, wasted too much time on "rationalizations." But Cotta said all of this a generation before the birth of Christ; had he lived a little later, he would have been appalled at how far rationalization had pushed the universal lust for allegory and symbolism under the auspices of Lucius Annaeus Cornutus, not to mention Heraclitus.

Cornutus, or Phornutus as he was sometimes called in the Renaissance, was a Greek who came to Rome at the time of Philo Judaeus and St. Paul. He wrote a lost commentary on Virgil and a treatise called *The Hellenic Theology,* of which the extant *On the Nature of the Gods* is assumed to be a fragmentary and corrupt version.[11] His fame rests on the fact that he was the teacher of Lucan and Persius.[12] In the fifth satire of the latter he is revealed as a man of letters with a literary doctrine, qualities which do not appear in the compendium of Stoic allegory which the sixteenth century knew so well. In this inane volume, so often reprinted, names of gods and heroes are linguistically dissected for significances, and myths are scrutinized to uncover their moral or physical meanings. Everything is presented to stress the philosophical directions of Stoicism.

For Cornutus, as for most Greek symbolists, Zeus is aether, brother of Hera, or "aer." She rises from the earth; he descends; and

---

[8] *Ibid.,* II. 23–28.

[9] *Ibid.,* III. 16.

[10] *Ibid.,* III. 24.

[11] Decharme (*op. cit.,* p. 261) thinks his work is simply an anthology of the opinions of Zeno, Cleanthes, and Chrysippus, but Bruno Schmidt in his *De Cornuti theologiae Graecae compendio* (Halle, 1912) (pp. 44–50) argues for Apollodorus as his source.

[12] The relation between Cornutus and Persius is described in the *Vita Persii* found in most editions of the satirist.

from their fecundating union in mid-air, all is created.[13] The rebelling Titans represent diverse or contrary qualities of things, as is suggested by the name of the Titan Koios, a slip of the pen for "poios" or "of what sort?" Hyperion, on the other hand, gets his name from the fact he is at "the top."[14] Briareus, who helped the Olympians, symbolizes former times when the elements, or Giants, were contending for supremacy and Thetis, or Providence, called on this monster, whose name is derived from "airein," or "grasping" to put them in order.[15] For Cornutus, as for Cleanthes, Apollo is the sun and is born of Leto, or "lete," "oblivion"; because when the sun sets, night brings forgetfulness to men. His name may also be formed from "aploun," because he dissolves the shadows of night, or from "apoluein" because he "frees" men from disease. His father Zeus is pure fire, but domestic fire is called Hephaestus from "ephthai," or "kindling." Some say, Cornutus recalls, that Hephaestus is the son of Zeus and Hera; but others think that Hera bore him by parthenogenesis and point to the fact that flames fed by pure air become thicker. He is lame and walks with a stick because sticks are required to build fires; his fall from Heaven merely symbolizes lightning, man's first source of fire. He is married to Aphrodite in order to provide the animal heat required in her work.[16]

The vigorous virtue of Athena, Cornutus writes, is a symbol of the purity of abstract thought; nonetheless, Hermes is the Logos sent to men to make manifest the will of the gods. Hercules is also the personification of reason. His lionskin is a symbol of invincibility, but "it would also have been unseemly for such a great leader to wander about naked."[17] Cornutus has similar explanations of other Hellenic deities, but his account of Dionysus is a fine example of his allegorical technique. The god is doubly born to represent ripening of the grapes and their treading in the wine vats. Because men are stripped bare of all defenses under the influence of wine, the god of wine is always shown in the nude. To show that staggering drunks must be supported, he carries a thyrsus which ends in a point to warn men that drinking often ends in violence. In some accounts Dionysus is said to cohabit with nymphs to emphasize the necessity of diluting wine. The goat is his symbolic animal and the magpie his accompanying bird. The first indicates by its lascivious nature

---

[13] Cornutus, *Theologiae Graecae compendium,* ed. C. Lenz (Leipzig, 1881), p. 3.
[14] *Ibid.,* p. 30.
[15] *Ibid.,* p. 27.
[16] *Ibid.,* pp. 33–34.
[17] *Ibid.,* pp. 62–64.

the aphrodisiacal nature of wine; the second is an emblem of drunken chatter. In its tendrils and black berries his ivy crown recalls the grape. His flight with his nurses, his plunging into the sea to escape the violent Lycurgus, and his rescue by Thetis form an allegorical series. The nurses are the vines that suckle the grapes; Lycurgus is the vintner; and Thetis is sea water, usually mingled with wine as a preservative. When Dionysus is torn to pieces by the sycophants, the tearing of the grape bunches, which will be resurrected as wine, is intended.[18]

The Stoic rationalization of myth, which, as Balbus put it, had been debased into old wives' tales, found a ready reception among the medieval symbolists and allegorizers. However, the concern of antiquity with this matter does not end with Cornutus' account of the nature of the gods. Almost two centuries later the myths were raised to a higher understanding when Julian the Apostate attempted to revive old beliefs. Julian admitted that these legends were invented by a pastoral folk for the instruction of childlike souls and that poets converted them into fables which entertained "but conveyed moral instruction besides."[19] Because "Nature loves to hide her secrets and does not suffer the concealed truth about the essence of the gods to be flung in naked words to the profane," myths have serious philosophical value. Philosophers from Orpheus and Plato onward have used myth ethically, "not casually but of set purpose." There is an incongruous element in a myth, he thinks, which "warns us not to believe the bare words but to seek diligently for the hidden truth." The incongruous element is in the thought and not in the words, and Julian demonstrates how under "the guidance of the gods" there is something higher and graver in the myth of Dionysus leading the reader away from the "common euhemeristic explanation."[20]

In his "Hymn to the Mother of the Gods,"[21] Julian searches for "the original meanings of things" in the myth of Attis, which is intended "to remove the unlimited in man and lead him back to the definite." It is possible that Proclus, who lived a century later, read these remarks when he was inspired to say that myths stimulate the reader to seek the truth, to avoid superficial concepts, and to explore the obscure intentions of the original writers in order to learn "what natures and powers they intend to signify to posterity by mystical symbols."[22] But Sallustius, author of

---

[18] *Ibid.,* pp. 57–62.
[19] Julian, *Contra Heracleios* 206–7.
[20] *Ibid.,* 216c–221d.
[21] *Ibid.,* 169d–170c.
[22] Proclus, *In Platonis Rem Publicam commentarii* II. 108–9.

Concerning the Gods and the Universe and the close friend of Julian, is a proper exponent of the Emperor's idea.

When the Cynic Heracleios summoned Julian to a conference on these matters in A.D. 362, Sallustius, Prefect of the Orient, accompanied him and unquestionably read Julian's response to Heracleios and his hymn (both results of the confrontation) as soon as the ink was dry. Like his master, Sallustius knew that the old religion required philosophical reformation, but he likewise saw only superstition in Christianity. Foolish ideas, as he says, do not form the basis of a reasonable theology, which must rest on essential, bodiless divinities. To return to the old truths one must inquire why the ancients hid them in myths, "a question belonging to philosophy." Myths have many shades of understanding, but they inform men that "the gods exist, telling us who they are and of what sort," provided we are able to know. The very obscurity of myths and their seeming infamy and licentiousness are meant to teach the soul by their strangeness immediately to think, "the words a veil and truth a mystery."

Sallustius classifies myths as theological, physical, psychical, material, and combinations of these categories. He has almost no patience with material myths invented by "ignorant" Egyptians, who think the earth is Isis; moisture, Osiris; heat, Typhon; the fruits of the soil, Adonis; wine, Dionysus. "To say that these things, as also plants and stones and animals, are sacred to the gods is the part of reasonable men; to call them gods, is the part of madmen." The myth of Cronus is at once both theological and physical. A good example of the blended interpretation is found in the myth of the judgment of Paris.

> Here the banquet of the gods signifies the supramundane powers of the gods, and that is why they are together; the golden apple signifies the universe, which, as it is made up of opposites, is rightly said to be thrown by Strife; as the various gods give various gifts to the universe, they are thought to vie with one another for the possession of the apple; further the soul that lives in accordance with sense-perception (for that is Paris), seeing beauty alone and not the other powers in the universe, says that the apple is Aphrodite's.[23]

Before he attends to his full theological doctrine, Sallustius also offers a reading of the Attis myth which is less elaborate and different in some points from Julian's, but, nonetheless, echoes some of his phrases. Both

[23] Sallustius, *Concerning the Gods,* ed. and trans. A. D. Nock (Cambridge, 1926), pp. 3–11.

of these allegorists were unknown to the Middle Ages, but the late sixteenth century knew Julian; thanks to Naudé and Thomas Gale, the seventeenth century had a text of Sallustius.

III

It is no secret that Christianity made the majority of its early converts among women. The *paterfamilias* might be visiting the temple of Mars or Salus, but his wife and his daughters-in-law would be exchanging pious letters with St. Ambrose or St. Jerome. Gregory of Tours preserves the remarks of Queen Clotild to Clovis, who was reluctant to agree to the baptism of their firstborn son.

The gods whom you worship are nothing; they cannot help others or themselves because they are images made of wood, stone, or metal. The names you have given them are of men not of gods. Saturn was a man, fabled to have fled his son to escape being dethroned; Jupiter, a lewd practiser of debaucheries and unnatural vices, the abuser of his women relatives, could not abstain from fornication with his own sister, as she admits in the words "sister and spouse of Jove." What power had Mars or Mercury? They may have known magic arts; they never had the power of the Divine Name.[24]

St. Clotild had readily accepted the euhemeristic convictions of the Fathers; but Gregory, writing in the latter half of the sixth century, knew that there were other ways to look at the pagan gods. When he reaches the end of his history of the Franks, he recommends as the best instructor in elegance the curiously popular compendium of Martianus Capella.[25]

The *De nuptiis philologiae et Mercurii et de septem artibus liberalibus libri novem* was brought together sometime between 410 and 419 by a grammarian contemporary with the grammarian Macrobius. Both of these men had no prejudices against allegory; both were polymaths; both were converts to an esoteric philosophy; and both were indispensable authorities for the Middle Ages. Their books were also well thumbed by Renaissance readers. Macrobius, like Athenaeus, garnered learning for sheer joy, but sections of the *Saturnalia* describe the physical meaning of the divine myths, which is invariably betrayed by the etymology of the names of the gods.[26] Macrobius' theories of proper interpretation, un-

---

[24] *Libri historiarum X*, ed. B. Krusch and W. Levison (Hanover, 1951), p. 74. The Queen's outburst is echoed by Gregory of Tours, in the introduction to the *Liber Miraculorum, Monumenta Germaniae Historica*, I (1885), 487–88.

[25] *Ibid.*, p. 536.

[26] Macrobius, *Saturnalia*, ed. J. Willis (Leipzig, 1953) I. 17–24.

commonly close to those of Proclus and Julian, are found in that second Bible of medieval men, his *Commentarii in Somnium Scipionis,* where myth as an instrument of the philosopher is defended against the strictures of the Epicurean, Colotes of Lampsacus. Macrobius does not recommend all myths as philosophically acceptable. Those that charm the ear but contribute nothing to the enhancement of truth or the teaching of virtue are to be rejected. Of those that lead to right uses, only those the subject of which is true and decently related are admissible. Those in which the subject is untrue, or true but indecently uttered, are of no philosophical importance. But even the properly phrased myths are useful only for dissertations on the soul, daemons, or the lesser gods. When it is a matter of the First Principle of the Intelligence, which encloses all Ideas, these matters "which surpass discourse and human thought," it is necessary to seek out "images and examples."[27] What Macrobius meant by "similitudes et exempla" is never explained, but lack of explanation is a habit with exotic thinkers.

Only the first two parts of Martianus Capella's hierogamy fully feed the hunger of the allegorist. The book, which is in the tradition of Varro's disciplinary writings, although its literary form follows that of the Menippean satire, manages to outdistance its allegorical predecessors like the *Choice of Hercules* of Prodicus or the *Tabula Vitae* of the so-called Cebes. The limping Litae of Homer's *Iliad* and Parmenides' poem about his encounter with Queen Philosophy had sown allegorical seeds of vigorous growth. Philology adds together the numbers found in the letters of her name and that of her spouse, introduces the mystic theory of the upsilon, and restates various Pythagorean formulas to prove the divine nature of the marriage. The Orphic egg, the rites of Leucas, and other symbolical items are carried into the fete before her astral ascent to the circle of Juno, a divinity to be adored in silence. In the Milky Way, place of the blessed, she enjoys her apotheosis. All of this is part of the abracadabra of the Neo-Platonists and the mystery religions, and Gregory of Tours might well have spurned it. What he could not overlook was the minute symbolical evaluation of the attributes of the gods and the allegorizations of their myths, which appear not only in the two initial ceremonial books but also elsewhere when Martianus is discoursing on solid subjects like geometry.[28] The pagan pantheon might be filled with cancerous tales, but they could be cured with

[27] *Ibid.,* I. 11. 6–25.
[28] Martianus Capella, *De nuptiis philologiae et Mercurii,* ed. U. F. Kopp (Frankfort, 1836) 567.

explanation.[29] What Martianus failed to remark in his interpretations his medieval exegetes supplied or extended;[30] he also had a worthy successor in Fabius Planciades Fulgentius.

Sometime in the latter part of the fifth century or the first part of the sixth, the author of the *Expositio Virgilianae contentiae* gathered seventy-five myths together in a *Mythologiarum libri tres.* At least a dozen editions of the work were called for between 1500 and 1600, and the seventeenth-century compilers of mythographers' collections, Müncker and Van Staveren, included it in their volumes. When it was first published, the pious author was confused with Bishop Fulgentius of Ruspe or his biographer Fulgentius Ferrandus,[31] a misidentification which continued even after Francisco Modio had faulted it in the sixty-first epistle of his *Novantiquae lectiones,* published in Frankfort in 1584. The medieval renown of Fulgentius was immense. John of Salisbury, Henry of Hereford, Bernard of Sylvester—to name a few—leaned on his interpretations, and Remigius of Auxerre, who wrote a commentary on Martianus Capella, did not scant him. The width of his influence can be seen in a poem of the goliards, where the names and attributes of the horses of the sun are all derived from him.[32]

Dedicated to the Presbyter Catus, the opening pages of the *Mythologia* describe the composer's retreat to a hidden country villa at the time of a barbaric invasion. When peace is restored he wanders in the best medieval fashion through a meadow and espies a shady place under a tree. Resting here, he sleeps, but he first utters his impressions of the devastations of war in a series of trochaics. His old friend Calliope appears to him in a dream to tell him that the maidens of Helicon, once at home in Athens and Rome, have now moved to Alexandria; but even this formerly brilliant city has now sent Galen and his companions into exile. She is amazed that in these declining days Fulgentius still pursues the Muses. He assures her of his continued devotion, and she encourages him to write more poems. Fulgentius informs Calliope (and his readers)

---

[29] See him on Apollo (p. 212), Juno (p. 168), Jupiter (p. 32), and Vulcan (p. 49).

[30] There were commentaries on Martianus Capella by Johannes Scottus, Notker, Hadoardus, Gunzo, and Hucbald. That of Remigius of Auxerre has been edited by Cora E. Lutz, *Remigii Autissiodorensis commentum in Martianum Capellam* (Leyden, 1962).

[31] Gerard Vos is one seventeenth-century scholar who confused the two men, but Pierre Courcelle is still uncertain of the identification in his *Les lettres grecques en occident* (Paris, 1943), p. 206. The stylistic differences between the two men were pointed out in Rudolf Helm, "Der Bischof Fulgentius und der Mythograph," *Rheinisches Museum,* LIV (1899), 111–34, and M. Schanz, *Geschichte der romischen Litteratur* (Munich, 1914–20), IV, ii, 202.

[32] *Carmina Burana,* ed. A. Hilka and O. Schumann (Heidelberg, 1941) I. 2. 31 is based on Fulgentius' details.

that he plans to write a mythology, not one in which possible impossibilities are brought together, but one in which the poetical fittings of Hellas and her poets will be removed to reveal the underlying truth or mystical meaning. Calliope recommends that he use the comforts of Philosophy and Urania (to whom she introduces him), and that for relaxation from his serious studies he seek the aid of Satire. After a short explanation of idolatry (he repeats the ancient anecdote about the beginning of idolatry attributed to Diophanus of Sparta, the story of Syrophanus' statue to his dead son) he turns to his explanation of the myth of Saturn.[33]

Supporting Fulgentius' readings of the myths stands his great skill as an etymologist. In scores of instances he supplies the classical word or phrase behind the proper name, so that "nomen" becomes without any delay the same as "omen." Phaeton, thanks to this system, is from "phainon," Leda from "loide," and Ulysses from "olov xenos"; on the Latin side, Venus derives from "vana res"; Lavinia, from "laborum via"; and Vulcan, from "voluntatis calor." All of this philology is sound enough, but Fulgentius really triumphs in the allegorical interpretation of myths. Neptune is also called Poseidon because water reflects images ("poiounta eiden"), and he carries a trident because water is liquid, fecundating, and potable. He is married to Amphitrite, or "circumfusing three," to signify that water is found in the heaven, the air, and on earth. Proserpine, daughter of Ceres, or "joy in crops," symbolizes the roots serpenting through the soil. Mercury, or "mercium cura," has to do with business; his winged talaria mean "negotiations everywhere"; his caduceus represents the scepter of mercantile rule and its snakelike powers of wounding. In this manner the myths of Hercules, Endymion, Leda, and many other famous legends are unhulled; but Fulgentius' treatment of the story of Hero and Leander shows his approach to myth in full dress.

The third book of the *Mythologia* contains several accounts of ancient romances, and that of Hero and Leander reads in this fashion:

Love and danger are frequently companions, and while Leander, driven by Eros, the Greek for "love," swam toward his desired one, he did not know this. Some think he was called Leander from "lusin androgunon," that is "weakness of men." He swam at night, attempting risks in the dark. Hero is the symbol of Love. She bears a lamp, and what should Love carry but a flame to show the dangerous way to the yearning one. It is a flame quickly extinguished because young love does not endure. Finally, Leander swam in the nude because Love knows how to strip her disciples and throw them in a sea of danger. With the lamp out both found death in

[33] Fulgentius, *Opera,* ed. Rudolf Helm (Leipzig, 1898), pp. 3–80.

the sea. The significance of this is that the libido in both sexes dies when it is put out by the vapors of advancing years. They were, therefore, said to die in the sea just as if it were in the cold humors of old age. The little fires of heated youth chill in old age to a torpid lethargy.

A medieval monk with his mind on the *amor divinus* and a class of youths to instruct could hardly ask for a better reading of Musaeus' poem.

In Isidore of Seville sixth-century Spain furnished the early Middle Ages with a final encyclopedist whose compendium of information rivalled that of Martianus Capella.[34] A short section of the eighth book of the *Etymologiae* is called the *De diis gentium* and is filled with more than a hundred euhemeristic, moral, etymological, and physical accounts of ancient idolatry. The emphases are not out of order because Spain was still not a totally Christian country. In 572 the bishops attending the second Synod of Braga were urged to persuade their people to abandon the worship of idols. About the same time the Archbishop of Bracara in a "De correctione rusticorum" complains that godless men are still worshiped as gods.[35] The *Etymologiae* was printed at least ten times before 1500 and many times afterwards; hence, without probably intending to do so, St. Isidore supplied the next thousand years with an epitomized guide to symbolical and allegorical interpretation.

The mythological section begins by explaining that all pagan gods —Isis, Jove, Juba, Faunus, Quirinus—were formerly human beings. They were deified for merit: Aesculapius for medicine; Vulcan for ironmongering; Mercury for merchandising. Idols were first erected in Egypt to commemorate the dead, but demons persuaded men to venerate them. Certain of the Gentiles used significant names to express physical laws or to describe the nature of the elements in vain fables which were twisted by poets into histories of persons who were infamous or licentious. Saturn, for example, meant one "full of years"; if Cronus, or Time, devoured his children, it only meant that he swallowed his offspring, the years. Jove derived his name from "iuvare"; when he appeared as a bull and carried off Europa, it was in a ship of that name. His seduction of the Danae teaches that gold will buy the virtue of women. Neptune is "nube tonans"; Vulcan, "volans candor," and

---

[34] Isidore derived a great amount of information from Martianus Capella; see Jacques Fontaine, *Isidore de Seville et la culture classique dans l'Espagne Wisigothique* (Paris, 1959), pp. 969–70.

[35] O. Gruppe, *op. cit.*, p. 7.

"mors" is the root of Mars. Isidore, a master of the patristic allegorical methods, had little need for instruction in the art, but it is also clear that he had both Macrobius and Cornutus in his library.[36]

Martianus Capella, Fulgentius, and Isidore had medieval imitators,[37] but the original texts of these followers were not printed in the Renaissance. A poor exception is the *Libellus de imaginibus deorum,* which the sixteenth century attributed to the twelfth-century Albericus of London, author of "Vaticanus Tertius," from which this epitomized but highly influential pamphlet was derived. Unlike its source text, it is mainly concerned with the manner in which artists represented the gods, goddesses, and demigods of Greece and Rome.[38] In doing this it bridged the temporal distance between the *Imagines* of Philostratus and the *Delle imagini degli dei degli Antichi* of Cartari.

The compiler of the *Libellus* did not overwhelm his readers with symbolism and allegory as the true Albericus had done. The deities are described in proper posture with their designating implements, birds, beasts, and reptiles. Mars, one learns, is called Mavors from "mares vorans." Juno is the air. Mercury carries a reed pipe as a sign of eloquence. The section on Hercules, which dwarfs all the others, is closest to the real text of Albericus. The demigod's name comes from "herocleos" or "glory of strong men." In his victory over the centaurs he demonstrates the triumph of the virtuous soul over carnal concupiscence. Each one of the twelve labors is expounded in terms of a conquest of a virtue over some human weakness. In his final feat of taking the weight of the skies from the shoulders of the famous astrologer Atlas,

---

[36] Fontaine, *op. cit.,* pp. 944, 968.

[37] See Chapter VII, notes 1–10.

[38] Robert Raschke, *De Alberico mythologo* (Bratislava, 1912). The twelfth-century Byzantine Joannes Tzetzes followed a more sophisticated mode of allegorical interpretation than his European contemporaries. His *Allegoriae Homerica* was printed for the first time in F. Matranga, *Anecdota Graeca* (Rome, 1850), I, 1–295 and was generally unknown to Renaissance scholars, but a Greek-Latin text of his *Allegoricae mythologicae,* said to be extracted from the thirteen thousand line *Historiarum variarum chiliades* was published in Paris in 1616 as *Allegoriae mythologicae, physicae, morales.* I have been unable to find this text in that edited by T. Kiessling in Leipzig in 1826; in fact, the meters of the two texts are not the same. Kiessling bases his text on the one published by Nicolaus Gerbel at Basel in 1546 as an appendix to Lycophron's *Cassandra.* I have not been able to see this edition. In the 1616 text Tzetzes defines allegory as a form of eloquence, shading the real direction of thought and expressing the unexpected. He classifies it as elemental, spiritual, and a combination of both as found in the things of nature. He interprets the myths of the major gods as they express ideas about the elements, the human mind and heart, and the physical functions of man and his world. Cosmogony, he states, was first established by the Egyptians before the birth of Moses, and the Greeks had it from them. He hastens to add that none of these people got it as correctly as the prophets of the true God.

Hercules, himself learned in the way of the stars, attends what might be called the first astronomical congress.[39] But all the efforts of the Middle Ages to find meanings in pagan mythology, similar in nature but probably not so intense as those they found in the Scripture, helped sweep the way for Giovanni Boccaccio, the first of the systematic mythographers.

IV

In the sixth circle of the Inferno Dante is frightened by the sight of the Erinyes, and, as Virgil comfortingly takes his hand, the voice of the narrator is heard advising those of "sound mind to contemplate the doctrine hidden under the veil of mysterious verse."[40] The passage in the *Divine Comedy* closely coincides with the letter to Can Grande della Scala, where Dante, remembering Servius' remarks on Virgil's first line, describes his own poetry as "polysemos," or of several meanings, the literal and the allegorical or mystical.[41] Petrarch, son of Dante's fellow exile, loudly defended the theological worth of poetry in his famous apologetic letter to his monastic brother. To support his views—and he quotes St. Isidore—he sends one of his own allegorical bucolics with an explanation of what he intended.[42] There can be little question that Petrarch read the classics for symbolic meaning; but if there was a doubt, his letter to Aretino on the moral truths of the *Aeneid* would help dispel it. For Petrarch as for Fulgentius, Aeneas was "Man on the Way of Life." The storms endured are those of anger and desire, which can be checked by Aeolus, or reason. As the son of Venus, or pleasure, he is inclined to his mother's passions; when she meets Aeneas in the midst of the forest, Virgil is thinking of those middle years of life when men pursue pleasure more avidly. The garments of the goddess are girded so that, as pleasure, she may flee quickly; she is clad as a huntress "who

---

[39] *Auctores mythographi Latini,* ed. A. van Staveren (Leyden and Amsterdam, 1742), pp. 931–37. This famous work is a revision of Muncker's revision of Commeline's *Mythologici Latini* (Heidelberg, 1599); it also contains the texts of Hyginus, Fulgentius, and Lactantius Placidus. The *Libellus* attributed by the Renaissance to Albericus Philosophus was first printed in 1490 in Venice with L. Fenestella, *De Romanarum magistratibus*. There were subsequent editions of the two works, but the *Libellus* is usually found in the more congenial company of Hyginus. Liebschütz dates it at 1400 and thinks it derives from Bersuire; but since Wilkins shows it was used by Chaucer for his descriptions, it must be somewhat earlier; cf. "Description of Pagan Divinities from Petrarch to Chaucer," *Speculum* XXXI (1957), 511–22.

[40] *Divina Comedia* IX. 61–64.

[41] Dante, *Epistolae,* ed. P. Toynbee (Oxford, 1966), p. 173.

[42] Petrarch, *Lettere familiari* II. 486–96.

hunts the souls of us miserable ones." To charm and then smite her victims her hair is unbound and she carries a bow.[43]

About 1350 Petrarch's great friend Boccaccio was asked, through the offices of Donnino of Parma, to furnish King Hugo IV with a "genealogy of Gentile gods" and "an explanation of the meanings illustrious men found under the cortex of the fables." Protesting his lack of knowledge and skill, Boccaccio agreed to accept the commission so that the King might understand "not only the art of the ancient poets and the consanguinity of the false gods but the natural truths hidden with surprising art." The compilation of the *Genealogia deorum gentilium* required much of Boccaccio's attention for the remainder of his life.[44] The compilation, originally planned for thirteen books, finally included two additional books in which poetry was described and defended as a kind of theology. It is evident too that as Boccaccio came on new information or ideas, he inserted it in the margins of his manuscript, which, consequently, grew. In keeping with the traveler's metaphors of Virgil, Dante, and Petrarch, Boccaccio represented himself as an explorer of the lost land of myth.

In one section of the *Proem,* Boccaccio describes the spread of paganism which "blazed up on the Cyclades and other Aegean islands" during the youth of Abraham. This "foolishness" he proposes to follow as it wanders through mythological manuscripts as if he were a Marco Polo of libraries. He will carry out the King's wishes if mountain passages are easy, desert roads open, rivers fordable, and seas tranquil. He will succeed "if Aeolus . . . sends me strong winds and favorable from his cave, or if I may have on my feet the golden sandals of Argeiphontes." At the end of the preface he requests the help of the Christian God in the management of his boat. Keeping the navigation metaphor in mind, Boccaccio begins each book with an entry in his ship's log. In the second book he descends to Erebus; in the ninth he ascends Mt. Ida; he is at the Pillars of Hercules in Book Ten; and he is in the Polar Regions in Book Seven. In the last two books he represents himself as a sea-tired sailor ready to defend the purpose of his voyage and its possible success. It is then that he presents his theory of interpretation.

[43] Petrarch, *Lettere senili* I. 240–58.

[44] There have been several good accounts of the *Genealogia*'s history beginning with A. Hortis, *Studii sulle opere latine del Boccaccio* (Trieste, 1879), pp. 155–219. H. Hauvette, *Boccacce* (Paris, 1914), pp. 413–30; Cornelia Coulter, "The Genealogy of the Gods," *Vassar Mediaeval Studies* (New Haven, 1923), pp. 317–41; and Seznec, *op. cit.,* pp. 220–24. The text referred to is that of V. Romano (Bari, 1951).

Myths, according to Boccaccio's preface, are "polysemos" in understanding; Books Fourteen and Fifteen, though filled with other matter, explain what Boccaccio meant by multiple meaning.[45] Convinced that the first Christian emperor and Pope Sylvester had committed all opprobrious pagan literature to the flames, Boccaccio held that only the nobler kind, "wherein they exhibited the work of both men and nature . . . under an appropriate guise of myth and image," remains.[46] All literature, in Boccaccio's opinion, can be placed in four categories of which fiction-like-truth and fiction-like-history can be read in a second sense. Fiction-like-truth dresses "divine and human matters in fiction"; fiction-like-history (Aeneas in the storm) seems to be history, "but its meaning is much different." Boccaccio knew the mythographer Varro through St. Augustine and spoke of him in the *Proem*; now he expatiates on the Varronian modes of explication. "Physical theology is found in great poets, who conceal physical and moral truths in their inventions." The ancient theology should be called "physiology or ethology," according to whether the myths "embody truth concerning physical or human nature."[47] Sometimes, when Boccaccio takes his method to the myth, he finds nothing; but it is he and not the method that fails. Because of the manifold contradictions, he turns the Io-Isis myths over to "the experts";[48] at other times he leaves untwistable intricacies up to God.[49] He can compare himself to Argus, who once slept in all his hundred eyes. "What wonder, then, if I with only two eyes am overcome sometimes? Let my detractors interpret the myths I cannot, altering inadequate explanation and correcting what is based on error."[50]

If the author is a pilgrim he is also a genealogist descending a heraldic tree. Boccaccio looked for the founder of the pagan pantheon and identified him as Demogorgon, which is Lactantius Placidus' annotation on Statius' *Thebiados* IV, 516 ("triplicis mundi summum"). Theodontius, a medieval collector of classical detritus, who owes his immortality to Boccaccio, had promoted this slip of the pen to the father of the gods.[51] For Boccaccio, Demogorgon is a frightful deity living with his consorts, Eternity and Chaos, in a cavern at earth's center. From

[45] Boccaccio, *Genealogia* XV. 4.
[46] *Ibid.,* XIV. 14.
[47] *Ibid.,* XV. 8; XIV. 9.
[48] *Ibid.,* IV. 6.
[49] *Ibid.,* VII. 24; V. 1, 16.
[50] *Ibid.,* XV. 4.
[51] C. Landi, *Demogorgone, con saggio di nuova edizione delle Genealogie deorum gentilium del Boccaccio e silloge dei frammenti di Teodonzio* (Palermo, 1930). Lactantius' gloss reads, "Dicit autem deum demiourgon, cuius scire nomen non licet."

Aether, son of Demogorgon's child Erebus, springs a line of gods and heroes.[52] Of course there are confusions, but like mythologists before him, Boccaccio settles problems by assuming that there are several gods of the same name. There are a few divinities in the *Genealogia* known only to Boccaccio,[53] and there are occasional variations in the myths; Perseus, for instance, rides Pegasus,[54] and Bellona gets to be Minerva.[55] But considering the handicaps under which he labored, Boccaccio is amazingly correct.

Ordinarily, when Boccaccio is on the proper offshoot of the divine tree, the *Genealogia* provides a simple summary of the depending myths. But Boccaccio, who had acquired small Greek, makes an occasional stab at an etymology, which is sometimes correct.[56] On the other hand, Mors, eighteenth child of Erebus, gets his name from the fact that he bites, or from the bite of our first parents by which we die, or from Mars, or from "amarus," meaning "bitter."[57] His allegorical readings of myths are in keeping with the traditional theory. In his account of Demogorgon's eldest child Litigium, Boccaccio relates the several ways of reading the myth of Perseus' encounter with the Gorgon. It may be accepted as a historical event, or it may be read morally as a wise man's victory over sin; allegorically the myth may be understood as the soul spurning the mundane and rising piously to celestial regions; analogically the myth suggests Christ, conqueror of the princes of the world, ascending to his father. "These senses, though given different names, can all be called 'allegorical' . . . which comes from 'allon' which means 'alien or different' in Latin and signifies any sense not historical or literal."[58] Other moral or physical translations of myth—some taken from Fulgentius, Lactantius Placidus, Ugucio, Theodontius, or Pronapides, and some, mayhap, original—turn up throughout the *Genealogia;* but Boccaccio's reading of the Aeneas-Dido story is example enough.

The enemies of poets, Boccaccio recalls, object to Virgil because they hold that no wise man would ever tell Dido's story, which the Roman knew was not historically true. But Virgil had four reasons for so doing. First, like his master Homer, Virgil began in the middle of

[52] Boccaccio supplied a genealogical tree with his manuscript, and good examples of it can be found in E. H. Wilkins, *The University of Chicago Manuscript of the Genealogia deorum gentilium* (Chicago, 1927).

[53] *Ibid.,* I. 6; III. 22.

[54] *Ibid.,* X. 27.

[55] *Ibid.,* V. 48; IX. 3.

[56] "Phosphorus," *ibid.,* III. 22; "Strophades," *ibid.,* IV. 59.

[57] *Ibid.,* I. 32.

[58] *Ibid.,* I. 3.

things, and, wishing to have someone present to hear Aeneas' tale, made Dido his hostess "although she did not dwell then but many generations later." He also wanted to show how human passions are subdued. Boccaccio explains:

So he presents Concupiscence as Dido and the attracting power of Love armed with all that is needed; and in Aeneas, a figure ready for such acts and succumbing. But after showing the enticement of Lust, he demonstrates how we are led back to Virtue by bringing in Mercury, interpreter of the gods, to reprove Aeneas for his vanity and lasciviousness and remind him of glory. By Mercury, Virgil means the prick of conscience or the reproval of some eloquent friend which awakens us, sleeping in a bed of shame, and brings us back to the beautiful, straight path of Virtue.

Virgil also desired, Boccaccio continues, to praise the Julian gens by showing Aeneas scorning fleshly immodesty and female enticements. Lastly, in Dido's dying execrations, the Punic Wars and Rome's triumph are prophetically implied.[59]

V

Shortly after Boccaccio's *Genealogia* was available in print, his readers could scan the advice of Cornutus on the interpretation of myth. Certain that both Homer and Hesiod incorporated the science and philosophy of older and wiser men in their verse, Cornutus urges moderation in second readings and protests against Cleanthes' Herculean allegories. The exegete should not play with words or extract something too clever for the wits of an ancient philosopher from a myth.[60] Strange as these observations seem when voiced by Cornutus, they had the advantage of being overlooked since most Renaissance mythographers shared Ficino's belief in the divine mysteries found in these pieces,[61] an opinion supported by his worthy disciples, Pico della Mirandola[62] and Christoforo Landino.[63] Though Gianfrancesco Boccardo only rarely gets off the literal track in his *Deorum genealogiae* of 1498,[64] Pietro Montefalcio can

[59] *Ibid.*, XIV. 13.
[60] Cornutus, *De natura deorum*, pp. 45–46, 64.
[61] Ficino, *Opera*, p. 1537.
[62] Pico della Mirandola, *De hominis dignitate, Heptaplus, de ente et uno, e scritti vari*, ed. E. Garin (Florence, 1942), p. 580. In the *Heptaplus* Pico describes his theory of the three worlds from which all allegorical discipline is derived.
[63] We have seen Landino at work on Virgil; see the preface to his edition of Dante (Venice, 1578), sig. B3v.
[64] This is a five-book poem in hexameters expanding Hesiod; the author, a Salo schoolmaster, occasionally makes an etymological or allegorical comparison.

derive Vesta from "vi stando," Mercury from "medius currens," and Vulcan from "volcano."[65] In a generation or so experts like Antonio Cingale[66] would compose allegories to rival those of Fulgentius and Bernard of Sylvester, but Boccaccio's first sixteenth-century imitator, though a modest one, was Georg Pictor, a German scholar-physician.

Between the completion of Boccaccio's *Genealogia* and the 1532 publication of Pictor's *Theologia mythologica,* neither the science of mythology nor the allegorical rendering of myth sank out of sight. During these years Landino wrote his commentary and essays on the *Aeneid,* and Salutati, his *De laboribus Herculis.* Poliziano, Filelfo, and other humanists made fresh use of the mythology in their poetry but never forgot its subtler meanings. Late in the fifteenth century the pagan deities, often explaining their names and sometimes their other values, trooped into the *Elucidarius carminum et historiarum vel vocabularius poeticus* of Herman van Beek. During the next two hundred years this small onomasticon published in Holland in 1501 would widen to almost a thousand pages in the Oxford edition of 1670, "emaculated" by Nicolas Lloyd. In 1506 Raffaello Maffei of Volterra furnished his deceptively named *Commentariorum urbanorum libri triginita* with a section on pagan gods, and Jean Tixier de Ravisi, who listed gods under appropriate moral headings in his *Officina,* supplied brief biographies as headnotes for his alphabetical collections on them in the *Epitheta* of 1518. Few of these reference works were as complete as Pictor's volume, which proposes to expound the names, describe the appearance and significant symbols, and provide the allegory attending each antique divinity.

By his own admission Pictor draws his material from Albericus, Fulgentius, Isidore, Martianus Capella, Palaephatus, Cornutus, and other euhemerists, etymologists, and allegorists of classical and humanistic stripe. He never mentions Boccaccio, but he knows Theodontius'

---

[65] *De cognominibus deorum* (Perugia, 1525). Montefalcio is the first modern mythographer to classify the epithets applied to gods, and he makes an effort at unification, pointing out that Ops, Cybele, Rhea, Alma Mater, Mater Phrygia, Mater Idaea, etc., are the same goddess.

[66] In 1586 Giovanni Bevilacqua's translation of Claudian's poem as *Il Ratto di Proserpine* appeared at Palermo with Antonino Cingale's commentary. A disciple of Landino, Cingale would read ancient poetry, as he does the Bible, not with "lazy ears" but as deeply as he can. Allegories precede each of the three books of Claudian's poem. Pluto is a rich man whose conscience is obfuscated by transitory affairs. When Jove grants him Proserpine we see Providence dealing better with us than we suppose. Although Ceres has trained Proserpine well (witness her skill as a weaver), when she leaves her we are thereby warned not to leave virgins unprotected, seeing that Proserpine promptly goes out to gather flowers and slips incautiously into momentary and seeming delights.

comments from the *Genealogia*. He is especially attracted by the true meaning of proper names as invented by Greeks but preserved by the Germans with their Burgharts, Erharts, Gebharts, and other meaningful Christian appellations. As he writes his accounts of the fifty-seven higher powers known to the Greeks, Romans, Egyptians, and Syrians, deities that include Occasion, Favor, the twelve months, the nine Muses, the three Parcae, and the Harpies, he omits no rational etymology. Saturn gets his name from "satura"; Venus from "venustas"; and Minerva from "minitans armis." After the explanation of name, Pictor always offers, in the manner of Albericus whom he sometimes copies, a description of the artistic representation of the deity and a symbolical or allegorical exposition of the description. Hercules' name comes from "Hras kleos," or "praise of Juno"; but sometimes identified as the sun, his name may mean "aeris cleos," or "glory of air." He is represented in statues as a stern man clad in a lion's skin and holding three apples and the club with which he slew the dragon-custodian of the Garden of the Hesperides. His hands are calloused; his hair, disordered. The dragon, or "ever-watchful concupiscence," is destroyed by the club of "philosophy" and the apples of "control of rage"; "restraint of desire" and "conquest of voluptuousness" are thereby gained. The lionskin symbolized prudence, which contains the mad passions of the soul; the calloused hands stand for the patient virtue of labor which scorns ornament and colors. For all of this wisdom Pictor thanks Macrobius, Apuleius, Varro, Diodorus, Seneca, Plautus, Ovid, and Caelius Rhodiginus.[67]

In 1558 Pictor published *Apotheseos tam exterarum gentium quam Romanorum deorum libri tres,* which repeats some of the material of the *Theologia* but adds much that Pictor had learned in the intervening quarter of a century. The *Apotheseos* is a series of dialogues between Theophrastus and his pupil Evander about thirty-nine divine powers who are now properly divided into Magni Dei, Selecti, and Indigetes. The descriptions of the gods and goddesses are assisted by fairly crude woodcuts, but the same cut sometimes has to serve two deities, and toward the end of the book blanks are left for Volupia, Harpocrates, Angeronia, Osiris, Isis, and nine other divinities. Unlike the *Theologia,* which began with Janus, the *Apotheseos* starts with Varro's discriminations and a long lecture on Jupiter. Pictor represents the series of dialogues as a form of recreational pedagogy in his dedication to the "generous" Count Werner von Zimber. The interlocutors of the *Apoth-*

---

[67] Pictor, *Theologia mythologica* (Antwerp, 1532), pp. 37r–38r.

eseos follow Pictor's instructions, and Theophrastus cheerfully answers Evander's constant questions to provide him with the moral and physical values inherent in myth. At the end of the last book the *magister* concludes this exploration of paganism with a prayer to "the true and eternal God of all gods." While he was praying Pictor was undoubtedly collecting note slips for his *Pantopolion* of 1568, a treatise in which he personally defended "omnium deorum Deus" against the metaphysical strictures of the non-Christian philosophers.

Pictor's second mythology was preceded by *De cognominibus deorum* of Julianus Aurelius, the nom de plume of J. A. Haurech. This substantial study, the work of many years according to the preface, appeared with the 1543 Basel edition of Cornutus. Its composer excuses himself on the ground that Tertullian, Lactantius, and St. Augustine had busied themselves with pagan faiths and that recently Fulgentius and Boccaccio had followed the same course. If Augustine and Fulgentius, both elderly bishops, had studied mythology, he inquires, is there anything wrong with his attempt to sort out the various Jupiters and to record the fact that Diana, whose name may come from "duana" or "deviana," is also known as Opin, Trivia, Dictynna, Britomartis, and many other titles? First Haurech presents his readers with a euhemeristic theory of the gods, who, he is sure, were supported handsomely by cacodaemons in order to frustrate the contrary Christian convictions of Anaxagoras, Xenophanes, Plato, and Aristotle. Then Haurech, who knows Varro's distinctions, writes essays on the twelve great gods in two books and devotes a third section to lesser deities like Janus, Bacchus, and Pluto. There is little allegory save what enters in the course of expounding an etymology, but Haurech is far more learned than Pictor and is a worthy predecessor of Giglio Gregorio Giraldi, the first scholarly mythographer.

Since he was born of poor parents, Giraldi's struggle to obtain an education was the first act in a life of tragic experiences. He graphically describes them in the almost desperate *Progymnasma adversus literas et literatos* and in poems to Antonio Tebaldo and Celio Calcagnini. Although each one of his books must have cost him heroic effort, Giraldi managed to be the first to write a history of Greek and Latin poetry and to compose an account of the poets of his own time. His superior *Historia de deis gentium* was published in 1548 as a reference work for men of letters. It differs vastly from all medieval forerunners in that Giraldi, who had written treatises on sacrifices and on funeral rites, perceived certain unnoticed aspects of the religions of Greece and Rome, like local gods and those derived from human affection. This learned masterwork was also preceded by two trial flights, which were later incorporated in the *Historia,* the *De Musis,* completed in 1507, and the *De Herculis,* in 1514.

The *De Musis,* published in 1511, traces the development of the harmonious sisters from an original three or four with unfamiliar names and different duties until the occupants of the choir coincided in number with the nine spheres and Apollo was added as the tenth, or presiding Muse. Giraldi notices that even then the haunts of the Muses vary from account to account, as do their powers and rites. After writing a fully annotated section on each of the nine, he concludes his libellus with a study of Hercules Musagetes, the Odeum, and the Museum.[68] The *De Herculis,* which was not published until 1539,[69] had behind it the moral readings of Albericus, the Christ-Hercules comparison implied in the Inferno,[70] the three allegorical books of Coluccio Salutati's account of Hercules' labors, and a dialogue between a poet and theologian about the virtues of Hercules written by Marcus Marulic.[71] In his preface to Ercole d'Este, Giraldi tells him that as a boy, he himself wrote a life of Hercules in imitation of Plutarch's *Theseus,* "adding interpretations of the fables and histories or what the Greeks call allegories." He thinks that this was good enough for a child but not worthy of a man ("nec maturo satis homini dignus"); hence, he now proposes to supply a biography of this hero, whom he clearly regards as once having been a man on whose broad shoulders the Greeks loaded many a tall tale or historical happening thinly concealed.

Giraldi's general avoidance of the symbolical or allegorical readings, which enchanted him as a youth, is rather impressive since he published in 1551 *Aenigmata pleraque antiquorum explicantur,* a collection of some forty riddles including that of Samson-Hercules, and *Philosophi Pythagorae symbolorum interpretatio,* an attempt to make sense, even Christian sense, out of the Pythagorean prohibitions and admonitions. These books depended on what Giraldi could find in other authorities of a trustworthy nature and not in his own inventive mind. Thus,

---

[68] Giraldi, *Opera omnia* (Leyden, 1696), I, 555–68.

[69] *Ibid.,* II, 570–98.

[70] Inferno IX. 98–99. If the canzone "O alta prole del superno Giove" published by Curt Rothe, "Dante Dresdensia" *Deutsches Dante Jahrbuch,* XII (1930), 136–38 is Dante's, the overt connection between the two heroes is even earlier than has been supposed.

[71] In 1549 there was published in Venice a book with the title *Dialogo di Marco Marullo delle eccellenti virtu e maravigliosi fatti di Hercole, di latino in volgar nuovamente tradotto per Bernardino Chrisolpho.* I can find no information about the original.

they were fittingly companioned by the *Historia,* a work praised by
Joseph Scaliger, Claude Saumaise, Casaubon, and G. J. Voss and owned
by Montaigne, who complains in "Of a Defect in our Policies" about the
bad treatment accorded Lilius Gregorius Giraldus by Italy. The book
deserved its contemporary fame because, as Giraldi once again informs
Duke Ercole, it came into being because of all the errors he encountered
not only in reading the poets and viewing the work of painters, but also
in the mythological handbooks themselves. Too much emphasis had been
given the book of "Johannes Buccatius," a man studious and erudite for
his age but expressing himself better in Italian than in Latin and having
less than no Greek. The work of Boccaccio, says Giraldi, begins with the
error of making Demogorgon the father of all the gods. Unhappily, no
ancient ever heard of Demogorgon, let alone worshiped him; Boccaccio's primary deity was simply a misreading of "demiourgon," a word
used by Plato and other great men to signify "the highest God, Creator
of all."[72]

In the first *syntagma,* Giraldi relates that Gentiles were inclined to
worship God's creatures such as the sun and moon, or, like Euhemerus,
to assume that all gods had been men, or, like Diagoras, to deny the
existence of a deity. Although he regards as ridiculous the assumption
that Noah is Janus, and, consequently, does not subscribe to the beliefs
in Hebrew derivation of some of his prized patristic authorities, he
hastens to excuse the Jews from polytheism by repeating the conventional explanation of the plural "Elohim" of Genesis as "confirming the
mystery of the Trinity."[73] He inspects the notions of men of various
nations, including some from Germany, about a supreme God and col-
lects the views on the Absolute of scores of Greek and Latin philosophers and poets. In similar wise he presents the various ancient classifications of gods: the "consentes," "semidei," "selecti," "aeviterni,"
"indigetes," "divipotes," and "novensiles." He discovers and lists divinities based on human actions such as Truth, Hope, and Concord; he also
lists miscellaneous gods like Fever, Laughter, and Fear, and "dei to-
pici," or deities whose veneration was limited to a small or particular
geographical area.

Giraldi proceeds to classify the major deities into thirteen groups
based on their powers and functions, a method which enables him to fit
Venus, Cupid, the Graces, Vulcan, and Adonis into the same mansion. In
the fifth *syntagma,* he writes about Neptune and his various manifesta-

[72] Giraldi, I, 157.
[73] *Ibid.,* I, 4.

tions as Phythalmius Neptune, Aegaeus Neptune, or Canobus Neptune; then he surrounds the great god with lesser marine deities such as Phorcus, Glaucus, Portunus, and scores of Nereids. The Dioscuri are then introduced probably through their association with the Argonauts, and, finally, Giraldi writes about Aeolus and the winds in his charge. The adjustment of some divinities to their categorical companions is sometimes difficult to understand, and it is also true that Giraldi often gets lost in his notes and presents classical witnesses who contradict each other.

Though he is proud of his purely scientific approach, Giraldi is not loath to offer etymologies[74] or to reprint the allegorical readings of others.[75] He prides himself on the use of ancient texts, but he cites more recent allegorical mythographers like Martianus Capella,[76] Lactantius Placidus,[77] and Macrobius.[78] Sometimes he looks at the embossing on coins[79] or at a suite of classical descriptions[80] when he writes on the physical appearance of a god or goddess. There are times, however, when he simply copies Albericus, "a lower-class author in whom I have no confidence,"[81] or looks, as he does in his delineation of Fraud, at the account in "Dante Alligerio" or the scorned "Buccatio."[82] He frequently turns to Fulgentius, although he does not "wholly approve of what he says or how he says it";[83] on one occasion, having referred his readers to the allegory "concocted" by Fulgentius about Attis, he says that now that he has mentioned it, he will omit it.[84] In spite of these regular objections to the African allegorist, he sometimes must agree with him. It is obvious, for example, that the "cinthus" of Hyacinthus is the Greek word for "violet."[85] Proud as he is of his knowledge of truly ancient and authentic authorities, Giraldi, in spite of his protests, can quote the suspect. He is unable to make a break with the past; though he has reached man's estate, he cannot pass up a good etymology, a nice euhemerism, or a moral and physical allegory. Whenever he recalls something

[74] *Ibid.*, I, 5, 75, 158.
[75] Cornutus, of whose work he has a manuscript, on Jupiter (*ibid.*, I, 89–90) and pseudo-Heraclitus on Proteus (*ibid.*, I, 168).
[76] *Ibid.*, I, 77, 121, 160.
[77] *Ibid.*, I, 118, 131.
[78] *Ibid.*, I, 121, 123, 155.
[79] *Ibid.*, I, 123.
[80] *Ibid.*, I, 76–77, 86.
[81] *Ibid.*, I, 153.
[82] *Ibid.*, I, 37.
[83] *Ibid.*, I, 158.
[84] *Ibid.*, I, 142.
[85] *Ibid.*, I, 146.

of this nature, he shakes his head and puts down a footnote. His mythology is, nevertheless, a milestone on the road of classical scholarship; it is far better from a modern point of view than its very popular successor, the *Mythologiae sive explicationis fabularum libri decem* by Natale Conti first published in Venice in 1551(?).

Little is known about Conti besides his writings. He wrote a volume of Latin verse, which includes *Myrmicomachia,* or the *Battle of Flies and Ants.* He wrote a *History of His Own Times,* an account of the Turkish Wars, and translated into Latin selected works of Aristotle, Athenaeus, Menander, Plutarch, and other Greek authors. In its 1581 edition the *Mythologiae* was annotated by the famous editor of classical texts Frederick Sylburg. In 1583 Geofroy Linocier's treatise on the Muses and Antonio Tritonio's *Mythologia,* first printed separately in 1560, were added. Between 1600 and 1650, there were at least five Latin and five French editions because Conti's book was almost a mythological library by itself. Paolo Frambotti, who published the 1637 Padua edition, supplied a bibliography of worthy mythographers prior to Conti; in his mind they are Hyginus, Albericus, Sallustius (newly discovered and being edited by Leone Allacci), Fulgentius, Haurech, and Giraldi.

In his own bibliography of more than three hundred authors, among whom—to pull a few names from the *P*'s—are rare faces like those of Perimander, Phaestus, Phanodemus, and Phanodius, Conti lists only Hyginus from Frambotti's parade. Boccaccio and Giraldi, fellow countrymen and competitors, are unnamed in the bibliography and not mentioned in the text. Conti may have wished to seem completely independent of his predecessors, and in some respects he was. His system of organization is his own, although on occasion his immortals cluster in a manner which recalls Giraldi's arrangements. His knowledge of Greek and Greek authorities is clearly better than Giraldi's, and his translations into Latin appear generally to have been his own. On the other hand, he is not overtly writing a book for men of letters (although he certainly did) because he has been bitten by the same doctrine that Steuco and his successors were promulgating. No king had asked him to lift the myths to see what was beneath them, but that is one of his major purposes; he spends the first five chapters of Book One, which is a short history of pagan religions and religious rites, explaining his theory.

Conti subscribes to the belief that before the time of Plato, Greeks, who learned a venerable philosophy in Egypt, concealed this wisdom from *hoi polloi* in fables, which were in time twisted in the studies of lying poets into a "theology of fools." For this reason the earliest Church fathers cried out against those who transferred the worship of the true God to natural objects or pure fictions. Nonetheless, under these fables are philosophical teachings about natural forces, the movements of the heavens, and ethical conduct. He plans to do nothing with sottish or superstitious legends; he will interpret those which elevate mankind to the consideration of celestial matters, lead towards virtue, and discover natural secrets necessary to life. The explicator, Conti proposes, should be versed in ancient literature (and he eventually demonstrates his training in the rhetorical theories of Aristotle and Apthonius), and, like a good herbalist, should distinguish what is spiritually salubrious from what is not. Realising the essentially evil nature of man and wishing to teach the fear of God, the ancients invented fables, which instructed and morally disciplined men but also cheered and encouraged those of troubled hearts. Possessed by this intention, Conti cannot understand the literalists who deny the existence of hidden meanings which are "more divine" and worthy of knowing.

Were it not for the headings of each of the following nine books, it would be difficult to see a rationale in Conti's grouping of gods, goddesses, demigods, daemons, and heroes. One wonders why Hercules, the Harpies, the Gorgons, Medea, Pelops, and Atalanta were in the same society. But Conti is actually supporting the common notion that the Greeks and Romans had ideals similar to those of the Christians; hence, his first aggregation suggests a belief in one God; his second, a belief in a Hereafter; and his third, notions about the generation of men. The associates of Hercules teach that the best men pursued fame for the ends of justice and usefulness. The purely literal account of each mythological figure, profusely illustrated by references and quotations from Greek and Latin poets, is ordinarily completed with a moral, physical, or historical exposition, which is sometimes traditional, although Conti is not inclined to give credits in these sections. But to show his method in full scope, one may look at his history of Circe.

Homer, Hesiod, Dionysius of Miletus, Herodian, Apollonius of Rhodes, Pausanias, Ovid, Virgil, Pliny the Elder, Tzetzes, and Strabo are searched to provide information about Circe's genealogy, her murdered husband, her discovery of aconite and vervain, her residence in Tuscany or Colchis, her composition of aphrodisiacs, and her adventures with Odysseus. Her name means "to mix" and as daughter of Helios and Perse, child of Ocean, she mingles heat and moisture from which everything is generated. The four maidens who help her cull herbs are the elements. Since elemental things do not perish (although they change), she is said to be immortal. The idea of change is also signified by her transformation of men into animals. She dwells in Aea, designating the Greek plaintive outcry of those who are weary or ashamed. She cannot enchant Odysseus, who symbolizes the immortal soul gifted by God, but the companions of Odysseus, the body and its passions, are subject to alteration and destruction. It is possible that she is also the moon affecting by its powers the growth of plants and the course of fountains. In a moral sense Circe is simply animal pleasures, and men are transformed by her into whatever beast-passion dominates them. The ancients have wished, then, to advise men to govern themselves by reason and reason's copesmate, temperance.[86]

The last sections of most of Conti's legends conclude similarly. The myth of Pasiphae is historically the seduction of Minos' wife by General Taurus; morally it represents a soul abandoning its reason and beauty and receiving the form of an animal with the chaotic results symbolized by the windings of the Labyrinth.[87] Aesculapius signifies the healing power of the sun, which enables men to put off maladies as his symbolic serpent sheds its skin. His crow symbolizes prognosis; his cock, diligence in the care of the sick.[88] The congress of Mars and Venus only means that adultery is incited by a conjunction of these planets.[89] Saturn's expulsion from his realm shows that a wicked man cannot be happy for long.[90] Charon is the "joy" one has when, thanks to God's mercy, he passes through waves of trouble and dies certain of his innocence.[91] Jason's voyage, like that of Odysseus, is an allegory of man's life; listening to Medea, the Greek word for "advice," he avoids avarice and injustice, teaching men to fear and honor God and the kings of their lands.[92]

To make the interpretations of the myths easier for the average interested reader to finger, Conti's tenth and final book bears the title "That all philosophic teachings are contained in the fables." He apolo-

---

[86] Conti, *Mythologia* (Padua, 1616), pp. 307–9. By this date the *Mythologia* was illustrated as the earlier editions were not. Both Schoell and Seznec mention an edition of 1551, which is also the date given by A. Guillon in his account of Conti in the *Biographie universelle ancienne et moderne* (Paris, 1854). Various Italian encyclopedias date the first edition between 1561–64. I have never been able to find anything earlier than the Venice edition of 1568.

[87] *Ibid.*, p. 305.

[88] *Ibid.*, p. 198.

[89] *Ibid.*, p. 80.

[90] *Ibid.*, p. 64.

[91] *Ibid.*, p. 103.

[92] *Ibid.*, pp. 318–20.

gizes for composing this section by confessing that he will have wasted his labors unless he briefly summarizes what his earlier books contain. This admission is followed by a series of sententious theses epitomizing the metaphysical opinions of "Plato, Aristotle, Empedocles, Parmenides, Pythagoras, and others." The philosophical series begins with "That God created the world, which consists of universal matter and is, consequently, one, not many"; the series concludes "That after death each soul is punished according to the nature of its sins." Learning all of this from the Egyptian hieroglyphic texts, the Greeks converted it into Olympian fables, which have one or more plausible interpretations. The historical, moral, and physical translations provided by Conti enabled the allegorist to grasp the handle of meaning. To Christianize Conti's allegorical emphases, "Anonymous" adds to the exegesis by comparing Eden to the Garden of Adonis; Bacchus, Deucalion, and Janus to Noah; Japhetus to Japheth; Orpheus to Christ; Vulcan to Tubalcain; and Saturn to Adam. Tritonio concludes the complete editions by classifying the deities and heroes, as Tixier de Ravisi had done, under moral headings such as "Audacious," "Cruel," "Proud," "Envious." The search for the second, third, and fourth meanings, carefully played down by Giraldi, was firmly reestablished in the best ancient and medieval manner by this authoritative and immensely popular mythology.

In 1556 a very different book, *Delle Imagini de gli Dei de gli Antichi* of Vicenzo Cartari was published in Venice. Cartari lived between 1520 and 1570, but almost nothing is known about him and the bibliographical states of the volume he wrote. There were thirteen Italian editions, five French editions, a German edition, and an English translation by Richard Lynche before the seventeenth century ended. The Venice edition of 1556 is illustrated with a prefatory woodcut portrait of Cartari, but the 1571 edition is filled with eighty-five etchings of a very romantic nature by Bolognino Zaltieri. The same etchings appear in the Ziletti edition of 1580 and the very rare edition of 1587 by the same Venetian printer. Reversed and possibly redone, they were used in Antoine du Verdier's Latin translation of 1581; somewhat better copied by Paul Hachenberg, but not so well turned out as the originals, they were published as the appendix to the Frankfort reprint of du Verdier's text in 1687. More than 160 illustrations adorn most seventeenth-century editions, but these illustrations are rather crude. Some of them are new, but in general the illustrator simply breaks up one of Zaltieri's original drawings into component parts. The two figures of an original etching become in this way two separate illustrations. An attempt is made to flavor them with the spice of antiquity by inserting pertinent ancient coins or engraved gems as detail reproductions.

The original text of Cartari, which concludes with an essay on the Graces, remains constant, but the indices become more and more exact in order to enable the reader to use the book more efficiently. In the French version of du Verdier, published in 1606 and 1610, there are additions by the translator and Laplonce Richette. With the Padua text of 1615 Cesare Malfatti supplied what is called an "allegoric," and Lorenzo Pignoria, who explained the *Bembine Tabula,* adds learned emendations and annotations in a long appendix. This additional material appears in all subsequent Italian reprints but not in the Latin versions. The immense popularity of the *Imagini* is indicated by the accretions, but the bibliographical problems of the book are as yet unsolved.

The first publisher, Marcolini of Venice, prefaced the *editio princeps* with an address to the reader, where he pointed out that many men had written about the gods but no one before Cartari had described their statues or their other representations; hence, this volume should not only please the ordinary reader but be of great service to sculptors, painters, and poets. In the 1615 edition, this preface is replaced by one written by Pignoria, where man's superiority in joining his head and hands in the composition of "figures" is praised. Taking Hor Apollo as his most ancient point of departure, Pignoria praises the essays on analogy, or symbolic compositions, by Guido Pancirolo, Piero Valeriano, Andrea Alciati, Gabriel Faerno, Antonio Agostini, Fulvio Orsino, Abraham van Goorle, Joost Lipse, and other scholars who had published and explained antiquarian objects. Antiquarianism can hardly be said to begin with Cartari, but his volume of descriptions certainly was a telling stimulus to its advancement.[93]

It cannot be assumed that Cartari was an antiquarian in the seventeenth-century sense of the word; nor had he the pioneering instincts of Peter Apian, whose copied inscriptions, the *Inscriptiones Sacrosanctae Vetustatis,* were printed in Ingolstadt in 1534 and were liberally used in the *Imagini.* Cartari undoubtedly saw the reproduction of the symbolic ship in the Church of St. Agnes, to which he alludes in his section on the "Nave di Bacco,"[94] but it was not antique. His other references to plastic objects, such as the "Fidii simulacrum," are generally taken from the

---

[93] Because of its availability I have used the 1647 edition of Cartari's *Delle Imagini de gli Dei degli Antichi* reproduced by the Akademische Druck (Graz, 1963) for reference. I have seen six of the sixteenth- and seventeenth-century editions.

[94] *Ibid.,* p. 226.

work of Guillaume Du Choul on Roman religion.[95] His description of coins of Faustina to illustrate "eternity," Juno Lucina, and Concordia were all published by this French antiquarian.[96] The same may be said of his emblem for Macaria.[97] Sometimes he errs, as when he describes Concord as portrayed on a coin of Nero whereas it is really the reverse of a medal of Augustus on Du Choul's facing page.[98] His descriptions of a coin of Nerva[99] and of a Pax reverse[100] could, on the other hand, be from actual observation or from another publication. In the main Cartari's descriptions of antiquarian monuments are taken from sound classical authorities like Philostratus, Pausanias, and the elder Pliny.

Among his contemporaries or recent predecessors, Cartari draws on Alciati, Giraldi, and very heavily on Alexander of Naples or Alexander ab Alexandro, whose *Dies Geniales,* a suite of scholarly classical articles, appeared first in Rome in 1522. He also refers to Petrarch,[101] to Leo Hebraeus,[102] to Landino's commentary on the *Aeneid,*[103] to Alciati's emblems,[104] and to Giraldi.[105] Among the ancient mythographers, he used Apollodorus, Diodorus, Hyginus, Macrobius, Cornutus, Palaephatus, and Hor Apollo as well as the Christian revilers of myth, Lactantius, Firmicus Maternus, Arnobius, Tertullian, and Augustine. Among medieval experts, he leans most stoutly on Martianus Capella, but he has read Lactantius Placidus, Fulgentius, Eustathius, and Albericus of London. Boccaccio receives special attention. He says of Boccaccio's Demogorgon, "But I have never seen any ancient writer who speaks of him."[106] He mentions Boccaccio's comparison of the peacock of Juno to the rich and powerful of his day, "which could be said of many today."[107] Boccaccio and Fulgentius come together to furnish his description of Thetis,[108] but Boccaccio alone tells him why crowns of grass were sacred to

---

[95] *Ibid.,* p. 86, and Du Choul, *Discours de la Religion des anciens Romains* (Wesel, 1672), p. 30. The first edition of Du Choul is that of 1555. In the following footnotes the page numbers in parentheses refer to this work.

[96] *Ibid.,* pp. 12 (p. 128), 96 (p. 158), 283 (p. 27).

[97] *Ibid.,* p. 255 (p. 208).

[98] *Ibid.,* p. 169 (p. 16).

[99] *Ibid.,* p. 105.

[100] *Ibid.,* p. 168.

[101] *Ibid.,* p. 263.

[102] *Ibid.,* p. 272.

[103] *Ibid.,* p. 118.

[104] *Ibid.,* p. 196.

[105] *Ibid.,* p. 276.

[106] *Ibid.,* p. 12.

[107] *Ibid.,* p. 98.

[108] *Ibid.,* p. 138.

Mars.[109] On numerous occasions Cartari stands ready to repeat Boccaccio's allegorical or symbolic explanations. Pan's two horns symbolize "the courses and distances of the planets and their affect on the earth";[110] the Magna Mater's crown and scepter indicate "human riches and the power of kings";[111] the Sirens in meadows of scattered bones signify "the ruin and death brought by lascivious thoughts";[112] and Pluto's three-wheeled chariot is "a warning against the uncertainties of ambition."[113]

The *Imagini* opens with an essay on religion, which is, in Cartari's mind, an innate characteristic distinguishing men from beasts; but man, who had only to lift his eyes to the heavens to see the works of God, was so shortsighted that he mistook the sun, moon, and even animals for the ruling divinity. In fact as each nation, sometimes each man, selected a deity, polytheism, which embraced gods, demons, and heroes, spread beyond belief. In general, however, the great twelve, or the Consenti, were mainly worshiped, but every site on land or sea was said to have a divine spirit inhabiting it. In due course, although there were pagan objectors and the Hebrews, knowing the true God, were totally opposed, images of these gods were created and revered. Thousands of these figures were to be seen in the ancient world, and Lactantius attributed the creation of the first idol to Prometheus, a historical event which begot the myth that it was he who created the first man of mud. Plato, for Cartari, wrote the better explanation of the myth when he stated that Prometheus was Providence, creatrix of all, a goddess adored by antiquity in the form of a grave and governing mother.

The *Imagini,* each section of which is controlled by an etching or woodcut based on a classical literary description or on a published antiquarian object, begins with Eternity. The account of this primal being is succeeded by discussions of Saturn, Apollo, Diana, Jupiter, Juno, the Great Mother, Neptune, Pluto, Mercury, Minerva, Vulcan, Mars, Bacchus, Fortune, Cupid, Venus, and other gods and goddesses. Each major section is further divided in order to explicate a reconstruction of a statue, bas-relief, coin reverse, or other classical object in which the deity under discussion appears with identifying symbols or in association with other divinities. Cartari goes beyond the religious limits of Greece and Rome. The essay on Diana not only treats her triform

[109] *Ibid.,* p. 215.
[110] *Ibid.,* p. 74.
[111] *Ibid.,* p. 112.
[112] *Ibid.,* p. 132.
[113] *Ibid.,* p. 151.

nature but also describes her further manifestations as Isis and Dea Natura. Apollo is, consequently, related to Osiris, Adad, Adargate, Serapis, Aesculapius, Salus, and Hygeia; Mercury, however, is companioned with Concord, Eloquence, Sleep and Dreams, Anubis, and Hercules. In this fashion no deity is overlooked and the abstract divinities, handsomely remembered by Giraldi, attend the Consenti and demigods to provide painters and poets with a congregation of symbolic personifications.

Cartari's method is to weave together the mythic literary material with etymological, euhemeristic, symbolical, and allegorical expositions. He is an arranger and adjuster of what has been written and not an inventor of interpretation. He is actually the first modern to attempt the explanation of ancient works of art, and he uses learning to support what he says. His margins or his text usually credit his authorities. Fulgentius, for example, enables him to find the secret meaning for the three heads of Cerberus[114] and to spell out the etymology of the names of the Parcae.[115] The section devoted to Saturn is characteristic of Cartari's customary procedure.[116]

What Cartari has to say about Saturn comes principally from Macrobius, Pausanias, Eusebius, Plato, Ovid, and Martianus Capella. The exposition is introduced with lines from the eighth book of the *Aeneid* describing the westward flight of the dethroned king. Cartari relates the happy reception of Saturn by King Janus of Latium and the united rule of the two monarchs, which was of so much benefit to mankind that King Saturn was deified. Saturn's symbol is a scythe because he taught man the arts of agriculture; but he is also drawn as an old man, badly dressed, bareheaded, and about to devour a bundle containing his children. In this portrayal he stands for Time, or Cronus. He is old and ill clothed because Time is either eternal or began when all things were made out of Chaos and the measurable movements of the heavens commenced; hence, Saturn is also said to be the son of Uranus. Some think his shabby dress symbolizes the plain living of the Roman Republic and his uncovered head, the reverence of early Romans for open and undisguised truth. Cartari turns to the common myth of Saturn, Rhea, or Ops, and their four children and repeats the old allegory of the four elements devoured by time. He reprints Martianus Capella's

[114] *Ibid.*, p. 149.
[115] *Ibid.*, p. 162.
[116] *Ibid.*, pp. 14–20. Abraham Ortell's *Deorum dearumque capita e veteribus numismatibus* (Anvers, 1573) provides brief accounts of divinities represented on coins.

description of Saturn holding the "ouroboros" serpent, illustrated by Zaltieri, and adds his astrological explanation. He likewise describes two statues (one of which is reproduced) of the three-headed Saturn, who symbolizes past, present, and future. Platonists think Saturn is an allegory of the pure mind which finds a Golden Age in contemplation, but there is also an ancient picture of Saturn with tied feet to indicate the close relation between moments in time and the regular flow of causes according to natural law.

When Cesare Malfatti's "allegoric" was added to Cartari's text, it supplied an index to each drawing with an epitomized explanation of the artist's intent. Mercury is "to be seen with the caduceus, symbol of concord, unity, and peace, and with animals consecrated to him and signifying industry and vigilance in contracting and negotiating." In an adjoining woodcut Mercury stands with Minerva to represent the necessary union of "eloquence and prudence." Editions containing Malfatti's allegorical indices have Pignoria's appendix of annotations and additions, which are sometimes correctives and often augmentative and more definite. As an accomplished antiquarian Pignoria adds the gods of India, Mexico, and Japan to Cartari's gods of Greece and Egypt. Cartari's method had been anticipated by Albericus and Pictor, but he brought it to perfection and was one of the founders of the school of antiquarian interpreters which would flourish in the seventeenth century. As a symbolist and allegorist he steers between the sparingly careful approach of Giraldi and the carefree abandon of Conti. All three mythographers made such impressive advances over Boccaccio and his immediate successors that they dominated the field; no seventeenth-century scholar, man of letters, or artist could do without their mythologies.

VI

The vast success of Giraldi, Conti, and Cartari, especially of the latter two, made the publication of further mythological handbooks hardly worth the effort. In 1577 Stephen Bateman wrote *The Golden Boke of the Leaden Gods,* which moved from a pantheon of forty-odd pagan deities into secular ones beginning with the Pope and going on to heretics like the Anabaptists. Bateman describes how the god was represented and then writes a "signification." His representations are in the manner of Albericus and are usually translations from Pictor's *Theologia Mythologica* with an occasional addition from Cartari. The "significations" are drawn mainly from Pictor or from an authority described by him. Seventy years later Milton's "Chaplain Ross," brought out his *Mystagogus Poeticus,* a lexicon of mythology. Ross, whose *Pansebeia,* a history of world religions, is the target of a jesting, offhand allusion in *Hudibras,* supplied Christian allegorical interpretations for all of pagan mythology. Beginning with Achilles and concluding with Zetus, Ross uncovers a double handful of deeper meanings in every myth; but while he was opulently inventive, as Addison observed,[117] he drew heavily on the symbolic interpreters, stirring in their equivalents with those of his own concoction. After summarizing a myth he summons the "Interpreter" to supply an hors d'oeuvre of meaning in which he often finds a biblical story distorted or thinly disguised.

Shortly after Ross disclosed the heart of ancient legend, Pierre Gautruche, a Jesuit of Caen, finished in 1653 his *L'Histoire poétique, pour l'intelligence des Poètes et autheurs anciens,* which was turned into English by Marius d'Assigny as *The Poetical Histories.* Gautruche spent his first book on major and minor gods; his second, on demigods and heroes, the Trojan War, and the subsequent adventures of the Greek magnates; and his third, on honors rendered pagan gods. In the second book he places an essay on the truth of fable, in which he relates with examples the several Greek methods of seeking history or a moral and physical understanding of these myths. It was not, he writes, a consequence of popular error because the philosophers to whom "the truth of one God was evident" through the ministry of the Natural Light accepted these superstitions either "from a shameful fear of the common law or from a weak and detestable complaisance."[118]

In his translation d'Assigny adds to each chapter notes which are sometimes larger than the original text. To Book One he appended an essay on heathen deities mentioned in the Bible and those worshiped by the English. He contributes to Book Two famous pagans "not mentioned by Gatruchius" and a chapter on gods who were formerly men. There is a fourth book on "Roman Curiosities" and a fifth on Egyptian hieroglyphics in which he points out the similarities between Egyptian and Christian theology. Subscribing to the theory of the demonic perversion of the true belief, d'Assigny attacks allegorical readings.

For I look upon such Expositions as have been already given to the Fables of the Heathen Gods, as silly productions and groundless fancies of Religious Minds,

---

[117] Addison, *Miscellaneous Works in Verse and Prose* (London, 1726), I, 236–37.

[118] Gautruche, *L'Histoire poétique* (Caen, 1673), pp. 174–84. In his *Mythologia deorum et heroum* (Stargard, 1660), Heinrich Schaevius produced an onomasticon identifying geographical places, mythological figures, and historical moments in classical literature; there are no attempts at interpretation.

who have laboured to find in the ignorance of Paganism, the knowledge of the Gospel. In the contrivances and inspirations of the Devil, the sublimest Mysteries of Christianity. Such interpreters of the Poets, are near related to the wise Expositor of the Revelations, who would need declare the meaning of the Visions of S. John, by certain Characters found upon the back of some Fishes taken near the North Pole. The wit of Man may stretch out a comparison between Light and Darkness, between Virtue and Vice, between Christianity and Gentilism; but I see no reason to believe the latter was a favourer of the former.[119]

The efforts of Cartari and other mythographers to instruct the designers showed an impressive influence in Renaissance painting, but it can also be seen in the vogue of handsomely illustrated mythologies such as Michel de Marolles, *Tableaux du Temple des Muses* published in 1655 and in the subsequent parallel French translations and Latin texts of Ovid by Pierre du Ryer and Antoine Banier. The Abbé Marolles' book was commissioned by the Royal Councillor Jacques Favereau, who had in his cabinet a collection of mythological drawings by "the best masters." These drawings engraved by the Dutch artist Abraham Diepenbeek are the raison d'être for the *Tableaux*. Favereau, who died before he saw the book, was a poet and an antiquarian. Among other works, he brought together in 1613 a collection of French, Greek, and Latin verses by divers hands to celebrate the discovery of a statue of Mercury in the excavation for the Luxemburg Palace. The drawings turned over to Marolles by Pierre Favereau were sixty-eight in number and were intended, it can be gathered, "to represent the vices and virtues in the most famous of ancient fables." Sonnets of an allegorical nature were supposed to accompany each drawing, and Marolles preserves one of them on Proteus in his "advertissement." By way of a preface there is an allegorical explanation of the Temple of the Muses (the etching on the title page), which might be Favereau's; but his proposed intention to search "for the moral, physical, and political sense" of each myth was hardly pursued by Marolles.

The *Tableau* separates into seven mythological classifications, which would have startled any professional mythographer; they are: the origin of the world and creation, loves of gods and men, hunts and combats, twins and sea-gods, adventure in air and on water, events on earth, and death, mourning, Hades, and sleep. Each illustrative plate is followed by a highly literary prose description and the pertinent myth, which is annotated learnedly by the author of the prose. All of ancient literature is combed for information, and the mythologies of Albericus, Boccaccio, Eustathius, Fulgentius, Conti, and Giraldi are often con-

---

[119] Gautruche, *Poetical Histories* (London, 1672), pp. bI-bIV.

sulted. Marolles does not shun etymological considerations, and sometimes he supplies euhemeristic or allegorical explanations; but with the careful phrase "according to Phornutus" or "as Palaephatus writes," he detaches himself from responsibility. In this cautious manner Marolles differs from the Jesuit François Pomey, whose *Pantheum mythicum, seu fabulosa deorum historia,* cleared for publication by the provincial of Lyons in April, 1658, was published in the succeeding year.

The *Pantheum mythicum* became the mythological handbook of the following two centuries. The famous classical scholar Samuel Petiscus, engaged by the publisher to correct the sixth edition, advises the "Friendly Reader" that this book, deriving from Boccaccio, Giraldi, and Conti, was invaluable in the classical instruction of "studious youths." Translated into English in 1698 by Andrew Tooke, who was silent about the author of the original, it became known as *Tooke's Pantheon of the Heathen Gods and Illustrious Heroes* and was reprinted twenty-three times by 1771. It was published as "adapted for the use of students of every age and either sex" in America as late as 1859. The original seventeenth-century plates engraved by J. van Vianen were altered in later editions, but they followed the earliest designs in both their delineations of figures and their reproductions of numismatic reverses.

In his first five sections Pomey wrote about celestial gods, terrestrial gods, marine gods, infernal gods, and minor or miscellaneous gods. His last section, "De Diis adscriptis, seu indigetibus" is a discussion of demigods and heroes such as Hercules, Achilles, and Jason, the Egyptian divinities such as Osiris, Apis, and Serapis, and the "virtutes deae," Honor, Faith, Hope, Justice, Laughter, Fame, and Fortune. Most of the discussions are in the form of a dialogue between Palaeophilus, who asks questions, and Mystagogus, who furnishes the answers, which are supplied with learned footnotes and quotations from the classical poets. Palaeophilus, for example, looks at the second plate and inquires, "Who is this beardless unshorn young man, holding a bow and arrows in his right hand, a cithara in his left hand, crowned with laurel and dressed in shining gold?" Mystagogus responds, "It is Apollo," an answer producing further questions and replies that often border on lectures. But the *Pantheum* begins, as was the custom, with a colloquy on idolatry.

Pomey finds four reasons for the invention and dissemination of false gods. First, there was the folly of men who denied God, the true fountain of all good, in order to seek Him in muddy streams. After admiring some man for his physical beauty or intelligence, they respected him profoundly and, finally, worshiped him. Second, to flatter the conceit of a ruler, the commonality erected altars to him and burned incense to him as if he were a god. Third, many men too desirous of immortality left images of themselves in hope that their names would live in marble after they were dead. Fourth, men were made gods to perpetuate their reputations for excellence or usefulness. Ninus, in Pomey's mind, invented idolatry by raising a statue to his father Belus and decreeing its adoration. Other nations worshiped the elements, the planets, animals, birds, reptiles, and "though you may laugh," scallions and the portulaca. Worst of all, the Romans worshiped every god brought to the city until it was so crowded with divinities that they were forced to send them, as they did men, into the colonies.

Each section of the *Pantheum* opens with a symbolic explanation of the facing illustrative plate. Jupiter holds a scepter of cypress, the sign of eternity. Mercury's face is both black and white because he converses with celestial and infernal gods, and his wings are emblematic of the wings language gives to human thoughts. The symbolic explanation is ordinarily succeeded by the genus of the god or goddess, his or her deeds, lovers, and offspring. The etymological exposition of the deity's name is never omitted, and the rites are sometimes described. Although it was becoming unfashionable and was selectively omitted in later reprints, a "sensus fabulae" or a "sensus moralis" was appended to the chapters on Jove, Apollo, Bacchus, Mars, Juno, Minerva, Venus, Saturn, Janus, Vulcan, Vesta, and Proserpine.

Most of Pomey's allegorical readings are secondhand. Conti is responsible for those of a moral or physical nature; the investigators of the biblical basis of Greek myth—Huet owned a copy of Pomey's sixth edition—furnish the identification of patriarchal heroes. Jove, who is Abraham, is also air, fire, aether, Fate, and the *Anima Mundi*.[120] The fable of Mars and Venus shows the discovery of adultery by Divine Justice and the adulterers caught in a net of conscience.[121] Saturn is both Noah and time;[122] Janus, Noah and prudence;[123] and Vesta, fire and vital heat.[124] The exposition of the myth of Bacchus, which concludes with a temperance lecture and a summary of the symbolic qualities of inebriation to be seen in Bacchus' nudity, ivy crown, youthfulness, femininity, maskings, and hilarious mirth, begins with a solemn treatment of his other appearances as Moses and Nimrod.

[120] Pomey, *Pantheum mythicum* (Amsterdam, 1730), pp. 21–23.
[121] *Ibid.*, pp. 67–69.
[122] *Ibid.*, pp. 120–22.
[123] *Ibid.*, pp. 128–29.
[124] *Ibid.*, p. 142.

Nimrod Bar-Chus, or son of Chus, also takes his name from Hebrew "namur" or "tiger." Bacchus is also called "Nebrodes" or "Nimrod." Nimrod was "a great hunter," and this is implied in Bacchus' other name, "Zagreus." Bacchus and Moses are the same because they were both found in arks in Egypt, both had double natures, both were educated in Arabia, both were horned, both were connected with serpents, both drew water from a rock, and both opened ways through water; moreover, Orpheus called Bacchus "Mosen" and "Legislator." Such parallels lead Pomey to but one conclusion:

From this you may gather that the early architects of fables have taken matter very altered from Holy Scripture to stitch together their tales. So in Nonnus, Bacchus wrestling with Pallene and giving in is the story of Jacob wrestling with the angel. Similarly Pausanias recalls that the Greeks before Troy found an ark sacred to Liber, which when Eurypilus opened it and saw the image of Bacchus hidden within, he was immediately insane. This account is taken from first Kings where the Bethshemites are said to have been smitten by God because they looked curiously into the Ark of the Covenant.[125]

Gautruche's *L'Histoire* was the official mythological textbook in all Jesuit schools until the publication in 1705 of Joseph de Jouvency's *Appendix de diis et heroibus poeticis* as an addition to the Paris edition of Ovid's *Metamorphoses,* which, often printed separately and in translation, contended with Pomey's *Pantheum* for generations as the official guide to classical mythology. Father Jouvency does not shun the translation of the godly symbols, the moral and physical understanding of the myths, or the figurative Old Testament shadows cast by the pagan gods. In his final chapter he urges "the Christian expositor . . . to see what is hidden under the covering of fable and to bring forth truth involved in darkness" because, as he puts it, they must "turn the poison of impious antiquity into antidote." Jouvency had learned from Conti, whom he recommends, and from the seventeenth-century Christian seekers, especially from Thomassin, how the Light of Heaven shone on the human past. But the attitude towards the interpretation of classical literature and the Greco-Roman myths was shifting, and this turn in approach has a certain history.

VII

Although the majority of western explicators were intoxicated by the doctrines of nonliteral reading, there were men who were doubtful

[125] *Ibid.,* pp. 57–59.

of its value for the understanding of both sacred and profane texts. In 1530 Cornelius Agrippa, possessed of a mysterious sense of the cosmos and not at all averse to symbolism when it was astrologically engraved on talismen, wrote in the first modern anti-intellectual treatise about the fourfold and confused methods of the biblical exegetes. "This interpretive theology," he states, "consists only in liberty of speech and is wisdom separate from the Bible. . . . Everyone has the right to abound in his own sense . . . nor are we to believe all they say."[126] His contemporary and faithful reader François Rabelais, who consulted his personal copy of Hor Apollo when he explained the white and blue blazon of Gargantua, is as unfriendly to the allegorizers of Homer as Agrippa is to those of Sacred Writ.

> Do you believe upon your conscience that Homer, whilst he was couching his Iliads and Odysses, had any thought upon those allegories, which Plutarch, Heraclides Ponticus, Eustathius, Cornutus squeezed out of him, and which Politian filched from them? If you trust it with neither hand nor foot do you come near to my opinion, which judgeth them to be as little dreamed of by Homer as the gospel sacraments were by Ovid in his Metamorphosis though a certain gulligut friar and true bacon-picker would have undertaken to prove it if perhaps, he had met with as very fools as himself.[127]

Friar Lubin, the bacon-picker, is assumed to be Thomas Walleys, but the opinions of Agrippa and Rabelais about allegorical interpretations were supported by the leaders of the Reformed Church.

Luther's view on "these whores of allegory" is not so stout as his epithet might suggest; in fact, he is inclined to wobble. He confesses his early infatuation with allegory, although even in youth he thought it an empty speculation, mere froth compared to the literal. Nonetheless, he found it difficult to extinguish his fervid interest. History is the best form of theological exegesis, he insists, but "after this has been treated and correctly understood, one may turn to allegory as an adornment and flowers to embellish the account." Bare allegory has no virtues; even when it is properly pursued, one does best to follow the allegorical examples of the Apostles.[128] In his younger days he was impressed by the allegories of Origen;[129] but later he regarded them as so much "twad-

[126] Agrippa, *De incertitudine et vanitate omnium scientiarum et artium liber* (Leyden, 1643), pp. 287–88.
[127] Rabelais, *Gargantua and Pantagruel*, trans. T. Urquhart and P. Motteux (London, 1863), I, 96–97.
[128] Luther, *Works*, ed. J. Pelikan (St. Louis, 1955–64), I, 232–34; II, 68.
[129] *Ibid.*, II, 150–51; XXVI, 433.

dle,"[130] and he also finds the allegories of Augustine and Hilary on Creation simple "fabricating."[131] In his maturity Luther is ready to say that allegory is pleasurable, a series of pretty pictures which, like those of Apelles, merely approximate nature. In many places in his scriptural commentaries Luther emphasizes his conquest of his allegorical vice. Moses, he regularly repeats, writes history, not allegory.[132] This is all very well, but he can also find allegory in Genesis,[133] the Psalms, [134] and Galatians.[135] He even goes a little beyond this when he criticizes the vicious lives of the Germans by calling their attention to the traditional interpretation of Odysseus' visit with the voluptuous Circe.[136] But this is only a momentary weakness because in his commentary on Genesis 30:9–11, after pointing to the Turkish allegorizations of the Alcoran, Luther writes:

> For allegory is like a beautiful harlot who fondles men in such a way that it is impossible for her not to be loved, especially by idle men who are free from a trial. Men of this kind think that they are in the middle of Paradise and on God's lap whenever they indulge in such speculations. At first allegories originated from stupid and idle monks. Finally they spread so widely that some men turned Ovid's *Metamorphoses* into allegories. They made a laurel tree Mary, and Apollo they made Christ. Although this is absurd, nevertheless, when it is set forth to youths who lack experience but are lovers and students of literature, it is so pleasing to them at the onset that they devote themselves completely to those interpretations. Consequently, I hate allegories, but if anyone wants to make use of them, let him see to it that he handles them with discretion.

Melanchthon, the grave scholarly associate of Luther, while ready to practice a rhetorical form of allegory which he calls "mythologian," a form of euhemerism enabling him to understand the Cyclopes as a former barbarous people whose single eye symbolized their use of a shield with a loophole, is inclined to agree with Luther. He observes that the method has no value to the preacher, who should be clear in statement, and that it is particularly offensive when practiced by illiterates. When the Bible is seemingly allegorical, he finds the meaning so plain that no comment is required; but he sees a sound possibility in moral metaphors. A tyrant can be compared to the nature of a wolf or an

---

[130] *Ibid.*, I, 90, 97.
[131] *Ibid.*, I, 121.
[132] *Ibid.*, I, 5, 19, 132, 185, 188–89; III, 28.
[133] *Ibid.*, I, 87; III, 193; IV, 101.
[134] *Ibid.*, XII, 204.
[135] *Ibid.*, XXVI, 430; XXVII, 127, 324.
[136] *Ibid.*, IV, 208.

astute man to "a little fox."[137] Although a reasonably good aesthetician and a master of the *figura mentis,* Calvin espouses the same position. Playing with the Bible by turning the literal into allegory is bad practice, but even when there is scriptural allegory one should follow the custom laid down by Paul in Galatians, where the interpretation arises directly from the literal reading.[138]

Luther's opponent Erasmus, more radical in his theology than his adversary, makes a full statement of the theory in his *Ecclesiastae sive de ratione concionandi libri III.*[139] For Erasmus as for his classical models, allegory is a "translatio," an unfolded metaphor, a "perpetua metaphora," and it may be accomplished with a single word as in "youth flies" or in "the mind burns." A metaphor is a means of changing the meaning of the nominative by either a verb or a complementary object. He reviews, with examples, the theory of the fourfold interpretation, but he deplores its incorrect use. He accepts the old reading of the Song of Songs as the marriage of Christ and the Church, but he finds a recent explanation of it as foreshadowing the Immaculate Conception totally absurd. Noah's Ark as the Church is a sound allegory, but Noah's Ark as the Virgin is not. Allegory, to his mind, is useful for stirring up the languid, consoling the dejected, confirming the wavering, and delighting the fastidious. Its use does not imply that the Bible is uncertain but is to the contrary a sign of its riches. The Holy Spirit wishes the several meanings to be discovered, and those who find them should be thought inspired. Nevertheless, it must be carefully recalled that in Adage 2878 Erasmus takes a position strongly opposed to those who convert the fables of poets into Christian allegories.

English reformers such as Myles Coverdale agree with Erasmus that the interpreter "must have respect to the Spirit and his fruits and not to the flesh and his fruits." There is mystery in both the Bible and the Book of Creatures; "the spirit whereof, and not the bare letter, must specially be searched out, and the allegories handled, not dreamingly or unfruitfully, neither with subtle disputations . . . but well favoredly after the ensample of the old doctors."[140] William Tyndale, Coverdale's presumed associate, shared some of the wariness of Luther and Calvin, but he also saw a value in the study. At the conclusion of his prologue to Leviticus, Tyndale temperately warns the Bible searchers.

---

[137] Melanchthon, *Elementa Rhetorices, Opera* (Halle, 1846), XIII, 466–74.
[138] Calvin, *Opera,* ed. W. Baum, E. Cunlitz, E. Reuss (Brunswick, 1887), XXXV, 466.
[139] Erasmus, *Opera,* ed. Le Clerc (Leyden, 1704), V, 1028–46.
[140] Coverdale, *Writings and Translations* (Cambridge, 1844), p. 511.

Finally, beware of allegories; for there is not a more handsome or apt thing to beguile withal than an allegory; nor a more subtle and pestilent thing in the world to persuade a false matter than an allegory. And, contrariwise, there is not a better, vehementer, or mightier thing to make a man quick witted and print wisdom in him, and make it to abide, where bare words go but in at the one ear and out the other.[141]

Tyndale blames Origen and his followers for distracting men's attention from the literal to the degree that they thought it "served but to feign allegories upon." These specialists were followed by "sophisters" able to draw out of "an antitheme of a half inch" a "thread of nine days long." He knows all about the four methods of "strange speaking," but he fears for the man who leaves the literal way unless he follows Paul's allegorical expounding of the story of Hagar or of Peter's cutting off of Malchus' ear. Even then the allegory does no more than fix the lesson "in the hearer's heart." Now that the Pope has destroyed the whole literal sense, "thou shalt find enough that will preach Christ and prove whatsoever point of the faith that thou wilt, as well out of a fable of Ovid or any other poetry, as out of St. John's gospel or Paul's epistles."[142] An attitude of a similar nature appears toward the end of the sixteenth century when the dissenter William Whitaker complained in his *Disputatio de Sacra Scriptura* of 1588 about those who maintained that there were as many senses as words in the Bible. While admitting allegory, anagogy and tropology, Whitaker insisted that they were but "collections" from the literal, "the true, proper, and genuine sense of Scripture."[143]

As the sixteenth century passed into the seventeenth, Protestants, while preserving a respect for analogy, looked more and more askance at the nonliteral readings of Scripture. This objection led, of course, to problems in the explanation of difficult sections of the inspired texts, problems that the Romans could gloss over with allegory. G. S. Menochio, who flourished in this age and furnished a commentary for all of Scripture, represents the Roman opinion that God made Scripture difficult so that men should labor over it and thus it would be fixed in their memories. Like his great Catholic predecessors, he insists that the literal be understood in accordance with other texts, the tradition, the actions of councils, the glosses of the Fathers and the Scholastics, and the findings of philosophy and science. After the literal is known the mystical

---

[141] Tyndale, *Doctrinal Treatises* (Cambridge, 1848), p. 428.
[142] *Ibid.*, pp. 303–12.
[143] Whitaker, *A Disputation in Holy Scripture* (Cambridge, 1849), pp. 404–5.

senses, if they are present, may be sought, but "they will not be accepted by all." The Church can, however, establish a further "sensus accommodatius," just as the Council of Trent did in the fourth session when it adjusted Ecclesiasticus 44:17 to the work of confessors.[144] What Menochio says is in keeping with Alphonso Salmeron's observations in the ninth, tenth, and eleventh chapters of his prolegomenon to his *Commentarii in evangelicum historiam et in Acta Apostolorum,* published in Cologne in 1602–4. In these sections Salmeron, one of St. Ignatius' original followers, also attacks the Christian allegorizers, who see the creation of Adam in the myth of Prometheus, the story of the Virgin Birth in the tales of Bacchus, Minerva, the Danae, and Perseus, and the Crucifixion in Actaeon's fate. Salmeron points his long finger at Thomas Walleys and cites II Peter 1:16–19 against him and his allegories.

The Protestant theory on the interpretation of Scripture is evident in the *Philologia sacra* of Salomon Glass, published in 1623 and a learned clergyman's *vademecum* until the end of the eighteenth century. The last five hundred columns of Glass' treatise are devoted to the various rhetorical figures to be found in the Bible, which are, consequently, legitimate for ecclesiastical use. His major emphasis is on analogy, but he includes all allegories, both "simple and allusive," which can be found in Holy Writ.[145] For him allegory is basically a continued metaphor, but it may be found infrequently in the Bible as a continued metonymy, irony, or synedoche. He approves of the use of legitimate allegory, but he has no tolerance for the rabbinical cabala or the allegorizations of the *Gesta Romanorum,* the *Legenda aurea,* and the *Metamorphoses* of monks like Berchorius.[146] Glass' *Philologia* stands behind the later lexicons of analogy like Benjamin Keach's *Tropologia: A Key to Scripture Metaphor* of 1682; in fact, the whole first book of the *Tropologia* is little more than a summarized translation of Glass' latter pages; hence, the German theologian is mentioned by Keach in his preface to the reader as a "Precedent," which, indeed, he was.

An occasional Protestant, such as the mystical Henry More, might object to attacks, especially Quaker attacks, on allegory, holding it was a common practice of rhetoricians and poets and praising the ease with which moral lessons can be found in story as opposed to the difficulty of inventing story to illuminate an ethical idea.[147] More recognizes the

---

[144] Menochio, *Commentarius totius Scripturae* (Paris, 1719), I, e3v–e4.
[145] Glass, *Philologia sacra* (Leipzig, 1705), cols. 1425–2076.
[146] *Ibid.,* cols. 408–42.
[147] More, *A Collection of Several Philosophical Writings* (London, 1662), pp. 17–18.

objections to the allegorical method of biblical interpretation, but he defends it in a manner which Glass would have found offensive.

That Natural Things, Persons, Motions and Actions, declared or spoken of in Scripture, admit also many times a Mystical, Moral or Allegorical sense. This is worth proving, it concerning our Souls more nearly then the other. I know this *Spiritual Sense* is as great a fear to some faint and unbelieving hearts as a Spectre or *Night-spirit*. But it is a thing acknowledged by the most wise, most pious, and most rational of the *Jewish* Doctors.[148]

Continental Protestants from Sixtus Amama, who thought allegory "the unskillful study of the insane,"[149] to Francisco Turretini, who argued that because the mind of God is infinite, the Bible is not necessarily so in meaning,[150] would have agreed only with immense difficulty with their British colleague. It can be assumed that when the mystical interpretations of the Bible were increasingly held in doubt, similar readings of Homer, Virgil, Ovid, and the Greco-Roman mythologies were in the same state.

VIII

Some evidence of the steadily altering approval of the interpretive reading of Greco-Roman fable can be observed in the writings of Francis Bacon, the best English allegorizer of mythology. In *The Advancement of Learning* he attacks Paracelsus and his followers for seeking in the Bible "all Natural Philosophy," an effort that not only scandalizes "all other philosophy as heathenish and profane" but also debases Scripture. He advises readers not to be overwise but to fear enigmatical or physical interpretations of the Bible which imitate the manner "of the rabbins or cabalists." Regardless of these admonitions he doubts that the Scripture should be studied "according to the latitude of the proper sense of the place." For him the literal sense is "the main stream," but the church has actually the most use of "the moral sense chiefly, and sometimes of the allegorical or typical."[151] Bacon's sensitive views on biblical exegesis became much bolder when he read ancient poetry and fable.

Parabolical poetry, one of his several classifications, contains "secrets and mysteries of religion, policy, or philosophy." The explication of these secrets and mysteries in Divine Poetry is "authorized" and the

[148] *Ibid.*, p. 54.
[149] Pearson, *Critici sacri* (London, 1660), *ad loc.*
[150] Turretini, *Institutio theologiae elencticae* (Geneva, 1688), I, 165–70.
[151] Bacon, *Works*, ed. J. Spedding, R. L. Ellis, D. D. Heath (London, 1862–76), III, 486–87.

same method used in the reading of fable often results in great felicity. To show how happily the method works, Bacon writes a short explanation of Jupiter's war with the Giants and Achilles' education by Chiron, thereby planting the seed for the fuller treatment of fable in the *De augmentis* and in his allegorized mythology, the *De sapientia veterum*. In the *De augmentis* he admits that there is some doubt about the mystic meanings concealed in myth, but he is ready to confess as indeed he should, that "a mystery is involved in no small number of them."[152] But his earlier opinion in *The Advancement of Learning* is definitely worth knowing.

Nevertheless in many the like encounters, I do rather think that the fable was first, and the exposition devised, than that the moral was first, and thereupon the fable framed. For I find it was an ancient vanity in Chrysippus that troubled himself with great contention to fasten the assertions of the Stoics upon the fictions of the ancient poets. But yet that all the fables and fictions of the poets were but pleasure and not figure, I interpose no opinion. Surely of those poets which are now extant, even Homer himself, (notwithstanding he was made a kind of Scripture by the later schools of the Grecians), yet I should without any difficulty pronounce that his fables had no such inwardness in his own meaning; but what they might have upon a more original tradition, is not easy to affirm; for he was not the inventor of many of them.[153]

The *De sapientia veterum* (1609) appeared midway between *The Advancement of Learning* (1605) and the *Opera* of 1623, in which the Latin version of the *Advancement* became, by the augmentation of the second book into eight, the great *De augmentis*. In this ultimate version, the myths of Pan, Perseus, and Dionysus were rewritten from the texts of the *De sapientia* to make Bacon's theory of hidden mystery more concrete. In spite of the ease with which the material is apparently set forth, the *De sapientia* absorbed an enormous amount of learning, and there are few ancient or recent mythographers unknown to Bacon.[154] Thirty-one myths are expounded, many of them according to Bacon's prime doctrine of utility. Cassandra's troubles can be read as an essay on plainness of speech; Endymion's fate illustrates in practical terms the careers of royal favorites; Homer's Diomedes demonstrates the psychological nature of religious zeal. Other myths such as those of Pan, Coelum, Proteus, Cupid, and the Sphinx help and are helped by the physical philosopher; those of Atalanta and Daedalus, however, put all

---

[152] *Ibid.,* I, 520–21.
[153] *Ibid.,* III, 344–45.
[154] C. W. Lemmi, *The Classical Deities in Bacon* (Baltimore, 1933).

men in touch with the more material aspects of useful learning. But Bacon is also aware of his century's search for Christian doctrine in mythology; hence, his recognition of this movement intrudes quietly into his explications.

Two of the accounts of the generation of Pan can be, in Bacon's view, connected with the Divine Word, "which was entertained by all the more divine philosophers." The "god's horns," or the "universal forms," "reach up to God"; his staff is a symbol of Providence; his office as a messenger suggests that next to the Bible the world is the best witness of divine wisdom and goodness.[155] Proteus stands for the matter of creation,[156] and Cupid, as atom, not only symbolizes the divine creative impulsion in things but makes providential foresight clear in its contrast to his blindness.[157] The preface to the *De sapientia veterum* recapitulates and augments the notions set down in *The Advancement of Learning*. Some will think, Bacon supposes, that he is amusing himself with the discovery of inner meanings; but while he fully realizes the "versatile nature of fable," this is not his intent. He knows that others —Chrysippus and the alchemists—twist the fables to more than was meant. "All this has been explored by us, and we have seen and made not of them all the levity and looseness of wit expended on allegories; however in spite of this, we cannot give up our opinion." Bacon claims that he was fixed in his conclusions by the strange nature of myth and the significance of names, which imply unavoidable meanings. Sometimes the myths contain real history; sometimes matter added for adornment becomes, in due course, important; sometimes there is a confluence of fable resulting in new allegory; and finally, some myths are so absurd that they must have deeper interpretations. He reiterates his old belief that fables came before interpretations, just as hieroglyphics preceded letters; but no matter how the complaints fall, all men must admit that they are the most pleasant means of presenting a lesson.[158]

The vogue of the *De sapientia veterum* was not small, and it is not surprising to find Bacon's name mentioned with those of Heraclitus, Fulgentius, Lavinius, and Conti as one of the principal interpreters of myth as late as 1684 by Andreas Eschenbach in his *Ethica mythologica*. By this time very learned, almost scientific, studies of pagan religion and of individual deities clearly were beginning to elbow out mythologies

[155] Bacon, *Works*, VI, 636–39.
[156] *Ibid.*, VI, 651.
[157] *Ibid.*, VI, 655–56.
[158] *Ibid.*, VI, 625–28.

that emphasized deeper meanings. In 1659, Johannes Stiegler wrote a book about the Dei Selecti in his *De theologia gentili;* but by the end of the seventeenth century and the beginning of the eighteenth, works like J. G. Milich's *De diis, deabusque veterum gentilium Milichiis* (Leipzig, 1699), Joachim Hasenmuller's *De fabulis et mythologia* (Lund, 1705), and Johannes Gnospius' *De Teletis, sive Graecorum theologia physica* (Wittenberg, 1706) were mapping out the positivistic program of classical investigation which would become modern mythological study.[159] Besides this new direction, there had long been—J. V. Andreae's *Mythologia Christiana* of 1619 is an early example—a serious discussion of the old patristic problem of whether or not a Christian poet should use pagan myth. In 1709 George Neumann summarized the whole range of contention in his Leipzig dissertation, *De mythologiae deorum gentilium abusu in poesi Christiana*. He found that none of the common excuses—poetic license, ornamentation, liberty of conscience in matters indifferent to Christianity, the designation of God in the names of the gods, or right of custom—had any validity for a Christian. The mythographers were turning to myth as history or folklore, to the euhemerism of an Abbé Banier, who supplied curious minds, like those of Herman van der Hardt, with historical rope enough for an allegorical hanging.

There is no question that the allegorical technique which enabled the proper interpreters to find so much Christian, moral, or physical wisdom in classical literature, in Homer, Virgil, and Ovid, in the mythographers, or even in the unreadable Egyptian hieroglyphics, was very seriously in trouble by the end of the seventeenth century; nonetheless, it had dominated hermeneutics for two hundred years or more. The demise of the method was hastened to some degree by antiquarianism, which began in the sixteenth century and reached a rather splendid apex with the massive publications of Abbé Montfaucon in the 1720s. But the objects discovered in the soil of antiquity were as hungry for allegorical exposition as the texts of the Greeks and the Romans, and there were antiquarians who could extract as much wisdom from the reverse of a coin, a bas-relief, or an elaborate cameo as the best literary interpreters; in fact both groups of expounders depended on each other, and membership in both professions was often shared by the same man.

[159] Historical accounts of Roman religion and of the Latin pantheon without allegories are found in G. Rosini and Thomas Dempster, *Antiquitatum Romanorum corpus absolutissimum* (Paris, 1632), pp. 107–266; William King, *Heathen Gods and Heroes* (London, 1710); and H. Kipping, *Antiquitates Romae* (Leyden, 1713), pp. 1–156.

IX

❧ THE SYMBOLIC INTERPRETATIONS OF RENAISSANCE ANTIQUARIANS ❧

BEFORE THE NINETEENTH-CENTURY perfection of classical archaeology it is difficult to distinguish the traveler, filled with nostalgia for historical places, from the antiquarian, whose kindred emotion urges him to examine the remains of antiquity as carefully as he reads a classical text. The prehistory of these passions is unknown. In antiquity itself the ruins of Troy were visited by Alexander, who poured libations on the graves of heroes and anointed the tombstone of Achilles.[1] His Trojan expedition was repeated by Julius Caesar, who, since "even the ruins are gone," walked through the "name" of burned Troy to find the bower of Anchises, the seat of Paris, and other famous places.[2] Other Latin admirers of the earlier culture found their way to Greece. Cicero discovered the Athenian ruins made more poignant what he had read in Sophocles, Plato, and Epicurus.[3] Propertius fled to what Horace called "empty Athens"[4] to seek comfort for Cynthia's obdurateness by wandering among its ivories, bronzes, and wall paintings.[5] At a much later time Dio Chrysostom[6] laments the desolation of the country and of the city that Ovid[7] thought proof against

---

[1] Arrian I. 11. 55; VI. 9. 3; Diodorus Siculus XVII. 17–18; XVIII. 5; Justinus XI. 5; Plutarch *Alexander* XV.

[2] Strabo XIII. 1–70; Lucan *De bello civili* IX. 950–95.

[3] Cicero, *De Finibus* I. 1–6.

[4] Horace, *Epistulae* II. 2. 81.

[5] Propertius III. 21. 25–30.

[6] Dio Chrysostom, VII. 38–89; XXXI. 160.

[7] Ovid, *Metamorphoses* II. 797–801.

envy. Cattle graze in the Agora; the images of gods lie smothered in the cornfields. Shortly afterward an unknown poet set a new theme for his successors by describing Rome itself as "the great tomb of greatness."[8]

Not too long after Rome became both the poetical and theological symbol of the transitoriness of mortal worth and imperial splendor, Christian visitors in search of indulgences could purchase handbooks to the holy places and to the instructive wreckage of paganism.[9] Yet even when these pilgrims, led by the crude maps of the city, counted corners

[8] *Anthologia Latina,* ed. A. Riese (Leipzig, 1868), I, 267. The medieval continuation of this motif has been well considered in A. Graf, *Roma nella memoria e nelle immaginazioni de Medio Evo* (Turin, 1882) and in F. Schneider, *Rom und Romgedanke im Mittelalter* (Munich, 1926). The continuing literary tone set, of course, by Alcuin's poem on the vicissitudes of human affairs, *Carmina,* ed. E. Dümmler (Berlin, 1891) I, 230 was augmented by the famous ruin poems of Hildebert of Lavardin. For additional emphases unnoticed by Graf and Schneider, see Sedulius Scottus, *Carmina,* ed. C. Traube (Berlin, 1896), 170–71; F. Novati, *L'influsso del pensiero Latino sopra la civilta Italiana del medio evo* (Milan, 1899), pp. 172–74. The topic comes forward again in a thirteenth-century poem edited by Charles Fierville, "Notices et Extraits des Manuscrits de la Bibliothèque de Saint-Omer," *Notices et Extraits,* XXXI (1883), 100–108.

[9] These guides begin with the ninth-century "Anonymous of Einsiedeln": see *La pianta di Roma dell'Anonimo Einsidlense* (Rome, 1907). The most widely employed handbooks were the so-called "Indulgentiae" and the "Mirabilia" or "Graphia," which derive from the earlier "Notitia," "Curiosa," and "Itineria." On these matters, consult R. Ehwald, *Die Mirabilia Roma* (Gotha, 1847); F. A. Gregorovius, *History of the City of Rome in the Middle Ages,* trans. A. Hamilton (London, 1903), III, 523–28; and A. Nordh, "Libellus de regionibus urbis Romae," *Acta Instituti Romani Regni Sueciae,* III (1949), 58–65. A more readily found example is the anonymous "Itinerarium per urbem et circa urbem," *PL* CXXVIII, 347–66.

The "Indulgentiae," first published in 1475, mention antiquities, but mainly direct the visitor to the right church on the right day (often that of the patron saint) and give the schedule of indulgences. When a pagan monument was nearby it is sometimes mentioned. The earliest guides, published in Latin, are rather small, but about 1491 the "Indulgentiae" thickened and began to be published in two parts. The first part listed 301 churches and the second part glanced at the antiquities. Translated into Italian, French, Spanish, German, and Flemish, the guidebook was augmented and regularly revised by experts at various dates: Antonio Ponto (1524), Andrea Palladio (1554), Fra Santi (1588), Primo da Colle Flaminio (1595), Prospero Parisio (1600), Pompée de Launay (1608), G. B. Cherubini (1609), P. M. Felini (1610), G. Facciotto (1616), Palmerio da Scandriglia (1616), Giovanni Lupardi (1618), Pompilio Totti (1637), D. Franzini (1643), Fioravente Martinelli (1644), Filippo de' Rossi (1645), and M. Rossi (1688).

The "Mirabilia," stemming from the work of Magister Gregorius, who may possibly have been conversant with a manuscript of the *De regionibus urbis Romae* of Publius Victor (published first at Venice in 1505) and/or the similarly titled work of Sextus Rufus (included by Onofrio Panvinio in his book on the Roman Republic of 1558), contains a brief descriptive account of antiquities. It begins with the walls and names the gates, arches, hills, baths, palaces, theaters, places of martyrdoms, cemeteries, the places of the fulfillment of the Tiburtine Sibyl's prophecy to Octavian, of the marble horse, of the columns of Antoninus and Trajan, of the horses of Constantine, of the Pantheon, of the Vatican, of the Castle of Hadrian, of the Capitol, of Trajan's Palace, and of the Temples of Juno, Minerva, the Scipios, Marius, Mercury, and Faunus. Sometimes, but not often, it supplies historical or legendary comments on a monument. See H. Jordan, *Topographie der Stadt Rom im Alterthum* (Berlin, 1871), II, 357–536, 607–41 and particularly Ludwig Schudt, *Le Guide di Roma* (Vienna and Augsburg, 1930).

and houses in order to stand before some noble ruin, they were only sight-seers and not antiquaries. A few men of the twelfth century—Theodulf of Orleans, who wrote a verse description of an ancient vase and of a picture of Tellus,[10] and Magister Gregorius, who wrote a guide to the city and measured the Pantheon[11]—are different only in appearance. Actually, they are like Dante, who can describe himself as "an outlandish visitor gaping at the ruins of Rome,"[12] "ruins worthy of reverence."[13] Francesco Petrarch, born in the next generation, collected imperial coins, read inscriptions, and searched excitedly through the city for places mentioned by Virgil and Ovid.[14] He voiced his feelings in the first modern poem on the ruins of Rome.[15] But Petrarch can hardly be called an antiquarian in the full Renaissance sense; his interest in antiquities was as basically political as his naive faith in Rienzo.

The birthday of true antiquarianism is on the calendar of the fifteenth century, but it is impossible to name the date. It may have been the day when Poggio Bracciolini and Antonio Lusco sat on the Tarpeian Hill and attempted to identify with exactness specific places in "the greatness of the fallen buildings and the widespread ancient ruins."[16] Antiquarianism may have been born when Ciriaco d'Ancona returned from Athens with a packet of transcribed inscriptions,[17] or when aided by an unknown artist, he copied inscriptions and monuments of Rome itself.[18] The profession of antiquary may have come into being when Pomponio Leto founded the Academy of Antiquaries, an establishment abolished by the religious nervousness of the antiquary Pope Paul II.[19] Throughout the fifteenth century men undoubtedly gathered and attempted to date and explain the antiquities of Greece and Rome, but it is truly in the sixteenth century and probably more exactly in the seven-

---

[10] Theodulf, "Versus contra Iudices," *Carmina*, pp. 498–99, also pp. 547–48.

[11] G. McN. Rushfort, "Magister Gregorius, de mirabilibus urbis Romae: A New Description of Rome in the Twelfth Century," *Journal of Roman Studies*, IX (1919), 14–58.

[12] Dante, Paradiso XXXI. 31–40.

[13] Dante, *Convito* IV. 5.

[14] In his letter to Giovanni Colonna di San Vito, *Familiari* II, 112–119, Petrarch walks about Rome identifying the Palace of Evander, the cave of Cacus, and other places known to Aeneas.

[15] Petrarch, *Canzo* 53. 29–42.

[16] Poggio, *De fortunae varietate urbis Romae et de ruina eiusdem* in A. H. de Sallengre, ed., *Novus thesaurus antiquitatum Romanarum* (Hague, 1716), I, 497–507.

[17] E. W. Bonar, *Cyriacus of Ancona and Athens* (Brussels, 1960), pp. 121–85.

[18] *La Roma antica di Ciriaco D'Ancona*, ed. C. Huelsen (Rome, 1907).

[19] G. Tiraboschi, *Storia della Letteratura Italiana* (Venice, 1823), VI, 143, 282–83. I have been unable to find a history of Renaissance antiquarianism better than the short essay in C. B. Stark, *Systematik und Geschichte der Archäologie der Kunst* (Leipzig, 1880), I, 80–161, which would require enormous revision and augmentation before it could be reprinted.

teenth that antiquarianism becomes a systematised discipline. By 1715 Athens and Rome may have been in ruins, but their portable detritus was so safely retained in so many collections and cabinets that Pope, among other men of letters, could have his sport with the avaricious oddness of several thinly veiled English numismatists and think of a Roman imperial as a microscopic emblem of Roman triumphs.[20]

A full century before Pope's epistle to Addison, British classical antiquarianism could be diagnosed as a special aristocratic disease. The Earl of Arundel and the Duke of Buckingham competed for fragments of Greece and Rome with the same eagerness that inspired their search for political favor. By the time thirty-nine of the inscriptions "raked together" by William Petty in Greece were published with a commentary by John Selden as the *Marmora Arundelliana,* the infection had spread to lower social ranks. The endemic nature of the complaint is indicated by Henry Peacham's addition of a chapter on how to collect antiquities to the revised version of his *Compleat Gentleman.* Englishmen also are found wandering fervently through the hallowed spots of antiquity. When George Sandys crossed the Hellespont he was enough of a scholar to know that the ruins he saw there were Roman and not Trojan.[21] However, when Thomas Coryat went to the same site he paused in reverence before Priam's tomb and was knighted "a true Trojane" by Master Robert Rugge. As a certificate of honor he imitated Thomas Dallam's Trojan visit of 1600,[22] and "brake off certaine stones to carrie with mee into my Countrey, and to reserve them in my safe custodie for memorable Antiquities while I live."[23]

A hundred years after Coryat's return from the Levant, Ralph Thoresby, antiquary of Leeds, visited a museum in St. Martins-in-the-Fields recently purchased from the heirs of Lord Carteret by John Kempe. Kempe added so much to this collection, originally begun by Jean Galliard, that when Robert Ainsworth published it as *Monumenta vetustatis Kempiana,* he was unable to cope with its richness and had to

---

[20] Published posthumously, Addison's *Dialogues* are clearly based on his instruction at Rome by a professional numismatist. He had, of course, learned about interpreting the symbolic devices and his readings so impressed Jean Le Clerc, who saw the dialogues in manuscript, that he urged Addison to print his study of "the mystical meanings" of reverses separately. See Peter Smithers, *The Life of Joseph Addison* (Oxford, 1954), pp. 83, 321–22. They eventually appeared, as Le Clerc advised, in a collection of allegorical extracts from various sources edited by H. J. Jansen and published in Paris in 1799 as *De l'Allégorie.*

[21] Purchas, *Purchas his Pilgrims* (Glasgow, 1905), VIII, 102–5.

[22] *Voyages and Travels in the Levant,* ed. J. T. Brent (London, 1893), pp. 49–50.

[23] *Purchas,* X, 399–412.

seek the expert advice of several other antiquaries. Thoresby recorded his visit in his diary under January, 1709.

> I visited Mr. Kempe, who showed me his noble collection of Greek and Roman medals, several of the large medallions in silver, and others larger in copper, valued at vast sums of monies; he had also two entire mummies (in their wooden chests, shaped with human heads), one of which has the Egyptian hieroglyphics painted upon the swathing-bands; he had fragments of another and gave me a piece, which seems converted into a dark coloured rosin or gum by the embalming, which has penetrated the very bones, which are not only outwardly but quite through of a black colour, as is evident per a piece he gave me; but what I was most surprised with was his closet of the ancient deities, lares, lamps, and other Roman vases, some of which were Monsieur Spon's, and are described in print, others not yet; being the noblest collection I ever beheld of this kind.[24]

There is a difference in degrees of sophistication between Dallam and Coryat picking up sherds in Greece and the carefully organized, catalogued, and systematic collections of a Kempe, a Woodward, or a Hans Sloane. John Evelyn, a gentleman antiquary of the later seventeenth century, can be informative on these matters.

From the autumn of 1644 onward Evelyn makes memoranda of his visits to Continental and English museums and collections and mentions various collectors or "curiosi of Antiquities and Medails." In 1675, now an established virtuoso, he was delighted to find himself at the same dinner party as the celebrated numismatist, Ezechiel Spanheim. Within another decade he can stare down his nose at Ralph Sheldon's Greek and Roman coins, "hardly ancient" or, for that matter, worth their appraised value. He is so certain of his antiquarian knowledge five years later that he tells Samuel Pepys how to form a collection of coins and medals, although he admits that good collections are "very few in England."[25] Impelled, perhaps, by Obadiah Walker's *The Greek and Roman History Illustrated by Coins and Medals* (London, 1692), he published in 1697 his own pleasantly illustrated *Numismata: A Discourse of Medals, Antient and Modern*.

Evelyn knew some forty books in French, Italian, and "the most

---

[24] Thoresby, *Diary*, ed. Joseph Hunter (London, 1830), II, 31–32.

[25] Evelyn, *Diary and Correspondence*, ed. W. Bray (London, 1875), III, 297–300. Evelyn refers to Ashmole's collection of British coins and to the private museums of Robert Cotton, Selden, D'Ewes, Hanmer, Paston, and Harvey. He laments the dispersal of Arundel's collection and that of Sir Simon Fanshaw. When in 1697 he again lists antiquarians he adds the names of the Duke of Buckingham, the Marquis of Hamilton, Sir James Long, Sir John Cotton, William Camden, Sir John Marsham, Thomas Henshaw, Abraham Hill, "cum multis aliis" to his list of British virtuosi.

learned Languages" and consequently hesitated to write another book for numismatists; but he trusts that his remarks on modern coins are different enough to be novel. His *Numismata* relies on its continental predecessors to a large extent; but unlike most of them, it puts their findings and methods in a fashion easily comprehended by English amateurs. The third and largest chapter, "Of Reverses Antient and Modern, as they Relate to History, Chronology, and other parts of Erudition," presents the modes of symbolic interpretation to which European numismatists were long accustomed.

For Heads and *Effigies* may be easily distinguished by their *Inscriptions,* not so *Reverses,* which having relation to Symbol only, require particular Explication, as do other *Emblems, Devises* and *Hieroglyphicks,* inclosing Morals, recondite Mysteries and Actions; recommending and representing the most conspicuous Virtues of the Persons and things they relate to.[26]

With this text to guide him, Evelyn lists the traditional symbols of gods and goddesses found on the reverses of classical coins. Among the abstract deities Piety is a veiled matron holding a temple in her hand while a stork stands beside her; Providence touches a globe with her staff; and Security leans negligently on a chair. The four seasons are represented by three naked children—one with a hare for spring, one with a flower basket for summer, and one with a sickle for autumn—and a clothed child of winter. The elephant found on reverses symbolizes eternity; a grazing horse is the sign of prosperity. The serpent symbol of Aesculapius represents genius; but shown under a foot, it should be read as victory. Evelyn was probably not telling men who knew heraldry and the nature of such devices from numerous common practices very much; in fact, he is at the end of the interpretive antiquarian tradition, consonant with that of literary exegetes, which began in the sixteenth century.

II

The year before Ainsworth edited the catalogue of Kempe's collection, Abbé Bernard de Montfaucon began to publish the first of the

---

[26] Evelyn, *Numismata* (London, 1697), p. 64; the essay occupies pp. 48–156. There is no question that Evelyn knew the works of all the great numismatists of the sixteenth and seventeenth centuries. Antiquarian collectors are, however, difficult to count. I have examined the publications of two hundred fifteen Continental antiquarians who published one or more titles during the sixteenth and seventeenth centuries; from their acknowledgments it appears there were at least one hundred sixty-five collectors who published nothing; but this count is, of course, very short of the true number.

fifteen folios of his *L'Antiquité expliquée et représentée en figures.* Within the compass of this great encyclopedia, completed in 1724, were chapters in both French and Latin on the myths, legends, and religious customs of Greece and Rome. Montfaucon drew on many of the great collections of Europe as well as on earlier publications of objects to illustrate his text. Every known ancient representation, whether statue, figurine, painting, or cameo, and whether of Venus, Cupid, Hercules, Theseus, or any other deity or hero, was reproduced to expound their legends and histories. Toward the end of the seventeenth century the Greek and Roman thesauruses of Graefe and Gronov, later supplemented by Sallengre and Poleni, put the best secondary works (some of them unpublished) on all phases of Greek and Roman culture in the hands of classical scholars and antiquarians. Many of the original volumes reprinted in these more than thirty folios were either on antiquarian subjects or used antiquities with the same confidence and authority given to historical and literary documents. With these volumes on his shelves a man who had been only an antiquary could become an archaeologist; but it is hardly necessary to say this because shortly before Montfaucon's first volume was in print, the Brandenburg shoemaker's son Johann Winckelmann was born.

The antiquarian's art was well enough established by the last quarter of the seventeenth century to be sorted out into specialties. In 1685 the Lyons antiquary, historian of Geneva, an expert on Moses' rod,[27] the famous Jacob Spon put together a collection of his papers with the title, *Miscellanea eruditae antiquitatis: in quibus marmora, statuae,*

[27] Spon had published in 1683 at Lyons *Recherches curieuses d'antiquite, contenues en plusieurs dissertations, sur des medailles, bas-reliefs, statues, mosaiques et inscriptions antiques,* a series of learned papers about items in his collection. His account of Moses' rod is found on pp. 397–406. In 1673 came *De l'origine des estrenes;* and in 1674, *Discours sur une piece rare et antique du cabinet de J. S.* The rare item is a vase of bronze which some think an ink-stand; others, the model for a fountain; but which Spon considers to be a cinerary urn. He identifies the standing figure on the cover as Destiny and proceeds to explain the allegory of his vase. He also published in Lyons in 1676 his *Ignotorum atque obscurorum quorundam deorum arae notis illustratae* discovering the gods Dulovio, Trittia, Nehalennia, Togotis, etc. worshiped in Rome and her provinces.

Spon, though by no means the first, probably established the fashion for antiquarian voyages with subsequent reports to the public about what was to be seen and acquired. In 1678–80 his illustrated *Voyage d'Italie, de Dalmatie, de Grece et du Levant fait és années 1675 et 1676* appeared and was quickly translated into Italian by Casimiro Freschot. Charles Cesar Baudelot de Dairval, another distinguished French antiquary, brought out his *De l'utilité des voyages, et de l'avantage que le recherche des antiquitez procure aux savans* (Paris, 1686) in which he published new inscriptions and archaeological finds. The Abbé Bernard de Montfaucon' *Diarium Italicum* (Paris, 1702), which covered the period from 1698–1700, was translated into English in 1712 as *The Travels of the learned Father Montfaucon from Paris thro' Italy.*

musiva, toreumata, gemma, numismata Grutero, Ursino, Boissardo, Reinesio aliisque antiquorum monumentorum collectoribus ignota et hucusque inedita referuntur ac illustrantur. The book, somewhat of a takedown for some earlier experts, contained commentaries and etchings of objects and inscriptions uniquely known to Spon. In his preface Spon defines the study of antiquities as archaeologia or archaeographia. He prefers the second term and delineates its eight important divisions: numismatographia, epigrammatographia, bibliographia, architectonographia, iconographia, glyptographia, toreumatographia, and angeiographia. Although each of these sections is important in itself, it has ancillary worth to all the others. This may or may not be true of some of the lesser branches of archaeographia such as dipnographia, imantographia, doulographia, and taphographia.[28] A knowledge of symbolic and mysterious interpretation is essential to all these antiquarians, but it is of particular value to the numismatographs, or students of coins and medals; the iconographs, or experts on statues, paintings, and figurines; the glyptographs, who collect and explain intaglios and cameos, the toreumatographs, or specialists in bas-reliefs; and the angeiographs, who examine vases and other household and temple implements. The methods of explanation followed by these archaeographs were similar to those followed by their contemporary explainers of classical texts; in fact, the classical hermeneutist and archaeograph were sometimes the same person.

III

The first Renaissance numismatograph to publish the faces and reverses of classical coins was Aeneas Vico, a pupil of Raphael and the first engraver of the *Bembine Tables*. Between 1548 and 1557 he designed three books in which he occasionally attempts to translate a symbolic reverse. But the real problem of the collector, as Vico saw it, was to identify the faces and attempt a chronological exposition of his

---

[28] Spon, *Miscellanea,* pp. a3–a4. Spon's title refers to Jean Jacques Boissard's collection of antiquities with etchings by T., J. T., and J. I. de Bry and extracts from the antiquarian writings of Panvinio, Marliani, Giraldi, Publius Victor, and M. V. Probus. It was published in Frankfort in three folios in 1597–1602 as *Topographia Romae.* His book prepared the way for Fulvio Orsini, *Familiae Romanae in antiquis numismatibus* (Paris, 1663) and for Jan Gruytere, *Inscriptiones antiquae totius orbis Romani* (Heidelberg, 1602-3), supplemented by Thomas Reines, *Syntagma inscriptionum antiquarum* (Leipzig and Frankfort, 1682). The first collection of inscriptions, which also contains an epigraphic vocabulary, is Petrus Apian and Bartholomaeus Amantius, *Inscriptiones sacrosanctae vetustatis* (Ingolstadt, 1534); after this almost every antiquary who writes has a few newly found inscriptions to publish.

collection.[29] Vico's great contemporary Guillaume Du Choul, author of the justly admired *Discours de la religion des anciens Romains* of 1556, was apparently the first student of ancient cult to use the reverses of coins as illustrative documents. Du Choul does not avoid inscriptions, implements, intaglios, statues, and bas-reliefs, but he looks to the religious meaning of more than five hundred symbolic reverses to help illustrate what he had read in ancient texts.

Du Choul naturally finds his descriptions of temples, of forms of worship, and of the priestly orders helped by what he could read on coins; but since his book is about Roman religion he pays close attention to the signs identifying gods, goddesses, demigods, heroes, and abstract divinities. He undertakes to decipher the more complicated symbolism by which Romans signified imperial actions and virtues. Jupiter, he notices, is always shown nude to the waist because the Greeks and Romans "in

---

[29] The first actual publication of drawings of ancient coins was Andrea Fulvio, *Illustrium imagines. Imperatorum et illustrium virorum ac mulierum vultus ex antiquis numismatibus expressi* (Rome, 1517). The same antiquary's *Antiquaria urbis* (Rome, 1513) was the first archaeological account of Rome after Flavio Biondo's 1481 *Romae instauratae liber*; but, unlike Biondo, Andrea Fulvio published various monuments. Fulvio was simply interested in printing portraits of famous people of antiquity. His book, which contains no reverses, could hardly be said to systematize in any fashion the art of Roman numismatics. It was rather slavishly used by Joannes Huttich for his *Imperatorum Romanorum libellus una cum imaginibus ad vivam effigiem expressis* (Strassburg, 1526). If these publications can be ruled out as highly amateurish picture books, then Vico's sixty-eight plates of emperors from Julius Caesar to Verus with Antonio Zantani's brief biographies issued under the title *Le imagini con tutti riversi trovati et le vite de gli imperatori tratte dalle medaglie e dalle historie de gli antichi* (Venice, 1548) is the first attempt at a systematic numismatic publication.

In 1553 Jacob de Strada, a speculator in antiquities, published in Zurich his *Epitome thesauri antiquitatum, hoc est imperatorum Romanorum orientalium et occidentalium iconum ex antiquis numismatibus*, which he dedicated to the wealthy collector J. J. Fugger. Strada claims that all the coins are in his collection, but he publishes only badly done obverses with biographies. Vico's other publications are *Discorsi sopra medaglie degli Antichi* (Venice, 1555) and *Le imagini delle donne auguste* (Venice, 1557). This last work, translated into Latin by N. Conti in 1558, is a series of portraits taken from coins with a biography on the facing page. The *Discorsi* is, however, an important phase in the development of numismatology. It was dedicated to Cosimo de'Medici, contains a dedicatory poem by Dolce, and is Vico's own account of how he worked. He always compared, he states, the inscriptions on coins with those found on stone. He did not accept a face on an obverse at face value but checked it against other portraits on cameos and intaglios. On p. 14 he lists the Italian coin collectors, writes a history of money, an account of the goddess Moneta, and describes the materials used for coinage, the nature of reverses, the famous mints, the value of ancient coins, and the rarest and the largest ancient coins. At the end he gets to the methods of counterfeiting ancient coins (pp. 61–67). Sometimes a new reverse is struck on a corroded side or simply soldered on. Faces and reverses are made by using intaglios as patterns for moulds or by engraving on the coin itself a new face or reverse. He tells how to fake a patina and lists the names of the best counterfeiters of the day; they are V. Gambello, Giovanni dal Cavino, Benevenuto Cellini, Alessandro Greco, Leone Aretino, Jacopo da Tresso, and Federico Bonzagno. He devotes the remainder of the book to the dating of coins and to the importance of comparing the faces on coins with those on other objets d'art.

their occult and mystic theology" believed that higher things should be concealed to earthlings but revealed to the gods.[30] Janus, sometimes represented with the ship which brought Saturn to Italy, has a double face to signify man's progress from savagery to civility; on other coins his double head may be read as peace or as prudence. On coins of the Emperor Hadrian, Janus is also shown with four faces to represent "the four climates of the world."[31] By reproducing some Roman statues, a bas-relief at Narbonne, and twenty-two coins and by consulting Giraldi's life of Hercules and Lucian's account of Hercules Gallus, Du Choul is able to write an essay on the demigod and his symbolism. Statues show him naked to set forth his open virtues and his scorn of wealth. In some of them he holds three apples to signify "no corruption, no avarice, and no voluptuousness." In one coin his face is on the obverse and a falling Phaeton on the reverse in order to contrast reasonable with unreasonable action. Always shown with his vice-quelling club, he is sometimes given a bow to teach that virtue also has the force to strike from afar. Du Choul, like the euhemeristic explicators of myth, does not shun historical fact; hence, he writes in this case as he does in that of other deities about a gentlemanly "Captain Hercules," who really conquered tyrants, punished brigands, diverted dangerous rivers, founded cities, and benefited men in many other ways.[32]

About the time when Du Choul was finishing his book, Gabriel Symeoni, a young Florentine, called on him in Lyons. Symeoni had an Italian reputation as a poet, but when Du Choul, whose book he would turn into Italian, showed him an ancient iron ring from a local Roman vault, he became an instantaneous antiquarian. He had already published an epitaph found in a house in Clermont in his *Le Presage du Triumphe des Gaulois* of 1555,[33] but now he set off through Provence toward Italy to collect inscriptions, view monuments, and gather coins and gems. The account of his journey and his discoveries was published in Lyons in 1558. *Les illustres observations antiques,* though containing much of the same material, is a thinner and more cautious book than *Illustratione degli epitaffi et medaglie antiche* because, fearing French antiquaries more than those of his own land, Symeoni omitted anything at all dubious from the French version. In due time he gathered all the

---

[30] Du Choul, *Discours de la Religion* (Wesel, 1672), p. 54.

[31] *Ibid.,* pp. 18–20.

[32] *Ibid.,* pp. 173–86.

[33] Symeoni, *Le Presage du Triumphe,* p. 14; it is reprinted in *Illustratione,* p. 130. See Toussaint Renucci, *Un aventurier des lettres au XVIe siècle, Gabriel Symeoni* (Paris, 1943), pp. 279–98.

Roman inscriptions in and about Lyons and published them in 1560 in his *Dialogo pio et speculativo con diverse sentenze latine et volgari.*

There is nothing very systematic about Symeoni's book on Roman antiquities except that with associative digressions it pretends to follow the map of his travels. He publishes some twenty coins and medals, beginning with a lead medal in commemoration of Laura found with a non-Petrarchan sonnet about her in her assumed sepulcher at Avignon[34] and concluding with a reverse of "Nobilitas" designed by Symeoni himself and furnished with the "sensi morali dell'autore."[35] Between these two relics, both doubtful, Symeoni publishes and explains genuine Roman coins. His method is perfectly conventional. On a reverse of a coin of Caius Egnatius are two men, one dressed in a toga, the other in a pallium. Some experts, Symeoni notes, think that the former symbolizes war, the latter peace. He hardly agrees with them because the two figures really stand for "arms and letters," a republican requirement. Arms significantly holds Letters by the hand, suggesting the traditional distinction between words and deeds and the necessity in the state for wise counsel.[36] For other coins Symeoni is happy enough to grasp the historical reason for the reverse; but wherever he can he looks for symbol and seeks out allegory. Minerva, for instance, has blue eyes for quiet, a helmet for genius, a rooster for vigilance, and a night-flying owl to signify that "naught is concealed from the wise man."

Symeoni's rather engaging record of what he saw or acquired as he wandered from Rome to Lyons via Ancona, Ravenna, Venice, Verona, and the cities of Provence is the work of an enthusiastic amateur who was essentially a poet and artist. Sebastian Erizzo, whose *Discorso sopra le medaglie de gli antichi* appeared in Venice in 1559, Costanza Landi, compiler of *In veterum numismatum Romanorum miscellanea explicationes,* published in 1560 in Lyons, and Hubert Goltz,[37] designer and commentator of *C. Julius Caesar, sive historiae imperatorum Caesarumque Romanorum,* issued in Bruges in 1563, are all professional numismatists and really the first of the breed. When Antoine Le Pois wrote a history of numismatics as the opening section of his *Discours sur les medalles et graveures antiques principalement Romaines* (Paris,

---

[34] Symeoni, *Illustratione,* pp. 14–15.

[35] *Ibid.,* pp. 165–72.

[36] *Ibid.,* pp. 112–45.

[37] Goltz, artist son of an artist, was regarded in his day as the prince of collectors. His *Opera omnia,* annotated by later men, was printed in five folios in 1645, but the great seventeenth-century numismatists also knew that he had published coins which no one ever could expect to see.

1579),[38] he recognized all of them as his precursors and complimented them on their skill. The interpretive methods used by both Du Choul and Symeoni are known to these numismatographs—less perhaps to Goltz who was an artist rather than a scholar—in their efforts to extract history or meaning from Greek and Roman money. But as symbolic explicators none of the three is in the same class with Antonio Agustin, Bishop of Tarragon, whose *Dialogos de las medallas* was published in 1587, translated into Italian in 1592, and translated into Latin in 1617.

Agustin calls his book "dialogues," although he presents three speakers, A, B, and C, who are the first collectors to specialize in the Roman coins of Spain. Actually they are general experts on all ancient coinage. They illustrate their colloquies with hundreds of woodcuts, and they are almost witty at times. After an inaugural conference on the nature of numismatics they proceed to tell each other how the Romans represented piety, virtue, equality, eternity, religion, faith, concord, peace, hope, justice, clemency, constancy, providence, fortune, and other qualities on reverses. Although some of Agustin's predecessors had also attempted it, his speakers compose the first full and exact symbolic lexicon for provinces, cities, islands, rivers. In the fifth discussion—C is rather a quiet participant—A and B define the heraldic value of various birds and animals on Roman reverses. The eleventh dialogue is an interesting discussion of forgeries: how to do them and how to detect them. Agustin stopped with this section; but when Andreas Schott did the Latin version, he added, after a reported conference with Ortels and the Archbishop of Melines, a monologue of his own on the various numismatic symbols of the twelve gods and goddesses.

[38] There were rather limited catalogues like Wolfgang Lazius, *Commentariorum vetustorum numismatum . . . multarum rerumpublicarum per Asiam, Aphricam et Europam antiquitatis historiam explicans* (Vienna, 1558), which is really a publication of ten coins of Julius Caesar and thirty-eight of Augustus and Tiberius, all illustrated in one plate. Lazius describes the coin, explains the inscription or the significant historical event, and then develops the symbolical meanings. There are also rather desultory publications like the coins reproduced in the appendix to Joannes Sambucus, *Emblemata* (Antwerp, 1564). The custom of doing Roman families according to their coins is popular, and Levinus Hulsius gives the biography of the Caesars from Julius to Domitian and of their wives, children, and parents in *XII primorum Caesarum et LXIIII ipsorum uxorum et parentum ex antiquis numismatibus in aere incisae effigies* (Frankfort, 1597). Alessandro Sardi published an account of the history and nature of money in his *Liber de nummis* (Milan, 1579), a work later attributed to Selden when it was published in London in 1675. Some general catalogues like Adolphus Occo's *Imperatorum Romanorum numismata a Pompeio Magno ad Heraclium quibus insuper additae sunt inscriptiones quaedam veteres, arcus triumphales, et alia ad hanc rem necessaria* (Antwerp, 1579) and M. T. Hostus, *Historiae rei nummiariae veteris libri quinque* (Frankfort on the Oder, 1580) point towards the more professional studies of the late seventeenth century.

The numismatist, both as writer and collector, came into his own in the seventeenth century. When Charles Patin, son of the famous physician Gui Patin, published in 1683 his *Introductio ad historiam numismatum,* he required twenty pages for bibliography and thirty pages for a list of collectors and collections. Besides Patin the second half of the century produced some truly fine numismatists like Pierre Seguin, Jean Foy-Vaillant, Enrico, Cardinal Noris, and Father Jean Hardouin. Reading the reverses of coins, these specialists find the symbols as fixed and certain as the letters of the alphabet. For them the interpretation is no longer, as once it was, a matter of imaginative intuition, but it is, even in its established exactness, still symbolism.[39] One of the great seventeenth-century numismatists, Abraham de Goorle, who sold his collection to James I, omits a discussion of reverses in his *Thesaurus numismatum Romanorum,* which publishes the faces according to gens; however, Jacob de Bie, whose *Imperatorum Romanorum numismata aurea* (Antwerp, 1615) is contemporary with de Goorle's *Thesaurus,* explains the coins published in sixty-four plates and supplies a symbolic index, which is almost as helpful as Valeriano's *Hieroglyphica.* Evelyn's authority, Ezechiel Spanheim, can speak for most of his clan.

Spanheim's *Dissertationes de praestantia et usu numismatum antiquorum* (Rome, 1664) was revised for the Amsterdam reprint of 1671 and further revised for the posthumous edition of 1717. Evelyn read the second version, which has nine dissertations. Baron Spanheim does not,

---

[39] Sections on symbols will be found in the following selected works: Jean Tristan de Saint-Amant, *Commentaires historiques contenants en abregé les vies, eloges, et censures des empereurs . . . iusques à Pertinax* (Paris, 1635); Jean Baptiste Le Menestrier, *Medales illustrées des anciens empereurs et imperatrices de Rome* (Dijon, 1642); Christian Cnorr, *De antiquis Romanorum numismatibus consecrationem illustrantibus* (Leipzig, 1660) (entirely symbolic); Jacob Oisel, *Thesaurus selectorum numismatum antiquorum* (Amsterdam, 1677). This latter book is devoted to classifications of coins according to subjects; the second, third, and fourth classifications are on symbolic meanings. Charles Patin published many antiquarian books but the following deal in part or entirely with symbolical meanings: *Imperatorum Romanorum numismata* (1671); *Theon krisis: judicium Paridis . . . in numismate . . . Antonini Pii* (1679); *Dios genethlia, natalia Jovis in numismate . . . Caracallae* (1681); *De Phoenice in numismate . . . Caracallae,* (1683); and with J. H. Eggeling, *De numismatibus quibusdam abstrusis . . . Neronis* (1681). The *Nummi antiqui populorum et urbium illustrati* (Paris, 1684) of Father Hardouin shows this very rigid and highly literal scholar could also try his hand at symbolic readings. Giuseppe Monterchi attempted explanations of all the reverses when he published *Scelta de medaglioni piu rari nella bibliotheca dell' . . . Cardinale Gasparo Carpegna* (Rome, 1689). The famous numismatist J. Foy-Vaillant works out all the symbolic reverses from Augustus to Magnentius in his *Selectiora numismata e museo Francisci de Camps* (Paris, 1694). One of the most impressive efforts was Francisco Angeloni's *L'historia Augusta . . . illustrata con la verita dell' antiche medaglie,* (Rome, 1641), a work so harshly criticized that Angeloni was attempting to correct it at his death. His nephew, the famous G. P. Bellori, published the Roman edition of 1685, which is illustrated with a thousand faces and reverses explained historically or symbolically.

as his predecessors and contemporaries did, publish plate upon plate of obverses and reverses. Although he draws on the resources of at least two score "cimeliarchiums" besides his own, he reproduces only those coins necessary for documentation. His work, as that of many other numismatists, is no mere catalogue because his purpose is to demonstrate how coins may be used for evidence by historians, chronologists, geographers, grammarians, and epigraphers. He stresses the value of ancient money to students of ethics, who need not search "fables, laws, and precepts alone because this most noble art of life is concealed in symbols." The Egyptians and Greeks, he adds, used ethical symbols "like texts" on the assumption that as coins passed from hand to hand, moral principles would be fixed firmly in the minds of men.[40]

As a consequence of this notion, Spanheim concentrates on the philosophical ideas expressed on coins and devotes his third and fourth dissertations to the entries in the book of creatures found on symbolic reverses. His eye is caught by the hippopotamus, the dromedary, the crocodile, and the strange reptiles of Egypt, Greece, and Macedonia, all of which have rare significances. He calls on Valeriano, Ulisse Aldrovandi, and Bochart for explanatory comfort. Previous explicators— some are to be corrected—aid Spanheim in his researches to ascertain the moral equivalents of the bull, the eagle, the lotus, the "balustio," the palm, and similar natural phenomena.[41] A hardened symbolist of the seventeenth century would hardly consult Spanheim for easy analogues, but he might admire his ingenuity as a searcher. Cosimo III, to whom the volume was dedicated and who is described as a patron interested in "the arcane things of nature and occult mysteries," was probably pleased.

IV

The symbolic interpretations of the numismatists also pleased the iconographs, who published statues, figurines, mosaics, and wall paintings and sought in Greek and Roman texts the material required for commentaries. The earliest guides to Rome are illustrated not only with woodcuts of buildings, theaters, arches, and columns but also with the statues a traveler might see in the city. Beginning with Andrea Fulvio's *De urbis antiquitatibus libri quinque* (*circa* 1527, translated by Paolo del Rosso in 1543 as *L'Antichita di Roma*), it became the custom to publish and

[40] Spanheim, *Dissertationes* (Amsterdam, 1671), pp. 93–94.
[41] *Ibid.,* pp. 122–339.

sometimes to explain statues at Rome. Often the explanation is purely historical, as in the case of the newly discovered Laocoon, the nursing wolf on the Capitoline, and the Dioscuri, at that time assigned to Praxiteles and Phidias. In the case of the Farnese Bull, the visitor is told the legend of Antiope with fitting classical quotations and then is informed that the group is an allegory of the eventual civilization of rude and barbaric people. For the various statues then identified as representations of Hercules (particularly the famous bronze of the infant snake strangler), the guidebook adds a symbolic account of the labors. The custom of explaining and publishing monuments inaugurated by Fulvio was continued by successive compilers of guides to Rome, like Pietro Martire Felini, Federico Franzini, and Famiano Nardini.

Of course many of the iconographs are contented with simply publishing statues which they identify and locate. The *Antiquarum statuarum urbis Romae liber* (Rome, 1569) of J. B. Cavalieri, the *Le statue antiche che in Roma . . . descritta* (Venice, 1542) of Ulisse Aldrovandi (later incorporated in Lucio Mauro's *Le Antichitá de la citta di Roma* published in Venice in 1556), and the third and fourth books of Louis de Montjosieu's *Gallus Romae hospes* (Rome, 1585) do no more than this. The identifications are sometimes curiously wrong, and one can sense the antiquarian frustration of Cavalieri, who labels any baffling female figure as "a Sabine woman." The same sort of picture publication is practiced by Jean Jacques Boissard in the statuary sections of his *Topographia Romae* and by the artist François Perrier, who provided the mid-seventeenth century with a series of pictorial reproductions of statues, but not all the iconographers were so unimaginatively straightforward.

The company of iconographs is large because, in a sense, every Renaissance antiquary had to be one; hence, Symeoni, erstwhile numismatograph, can open the story. When this antiquarian was in Rome, he saw in the loggia of the great collector, Cardinal Cesis, a statue of a woman crowned with towers and drawn in a cart by lions. He quickly identified her as Cybele because her headcovering of turrets represented the cities of the world. Her garment decorated with flowers signified the fruitful earth. In one hand she held a scepter for kingdoms and, in the other, keys with which she unlocked the springtime. The lions harnessed to her chariot were a way of saying that earth is not so savage that it cannot be domesticated. The four wheels of her carriage are the seasons, whereas not only do her cymbals symbolize the earth's rotundity, but also their seven tones indicate the seven planets and their astrological influences. The presence of a pine tree recalls the myth of the transformed Attis and clearly identifies the goddess.[42] Symeoni's interpretation of Cardinal Cesis' statue is paralleled by the interpretations which Lorenzo Pignoria offered for other iconographic remains.

In 1628 Pignoria, famous in Padua as its historian, published a series of fifty letters to other antiquaries as the *Symbolarum epistolicarum liber primus*. By this time he had expounded the *Bembine Tables* and written his book on hieroglyphics and on the Magna Mater. He had also furnished exegetical notes to Alciati's emblems. His symbolic letters, illustrated by cuts of necessary antiquities, are consequently guides to a world of forty-two addressed collectors and scholars. The letters are sometimes no more than corrections of previous interpretations or furnish historical explanations for puzzling inscriptions; but Pignoria also regularly attempts to inform his correspondents about classical symbolic understanding. In the second letter, dated 1596, he explains why a ship's prow is associated with Janus and the significance of Mercury's caduceus and falchion. "There is," he writes, "nothing trite, common, or empty of mystery among our ancestors." In his eighth letter he proposes reasons for the Medusa faces on the reverses of Roman coins. In the thirteenth letter he lists the symbolic attributes enabling the antiquary to identify the effigy of Aesculapius. The crowned basilisk, symbol of "that mysterious people," the Egyptians, is the subject of the twenty-third letter; the bee, which Pignoria contends stands for the Muses in many antiquities from the eastern Roman provinces, furnishes the material for a letter of 1628 to Aleandro. Thanks to his symbolic findings, he informs the expounder of the *Table of Helios*, "we need not envy those ancient Greek and Latin scrutinizers of the mysteries of nature." Pignoria wrote many other books exemplifying the emblematic theories which he had expounded in these letters.[43] In 1625 he used numismatic reverses, inscriptions, and texts to argue, rather foolishly,

[42] *Ibid.*, pp. 18–19. Antoine Le Pois published similar symbolical accounts of four other statues in his *Discours* (pp. 145r–47r).

[43] Behind Pignoria's work stood Pomponio Gaurico, *De sculptura sive staturia* (Florence, 1504); Louis de Montjosieu, *De veterum sculptura, caelatura, gemmarum scalptura et pictura* (Antwerp, 1609), and Jules Cesar Boulenger, *De pictura, plastice, staturaria* (Lyons, 1627). None of these works, which were based mainly on classical sources like the elder Pliny's sections on art or Philostratus' *Imagines,* published antiquities or made any attempts at identification or explanation. They were excellent companion volumes, however, to books of antiquarian drawings published by artists. Pignoria's fascination with symbolic interpretation is apparent in two posthumously published works. The *Magnae deum matris idaea Attidis initia* (Amsterdam, 1669), in which he refers to Symeoni's discussion of the Cesis Cybele, seeks the meaning of the cithara, turtle, pine tree, and other symbols regularly associated with the goddess, and publishes the famous bronze hands which intrigued his generation, some figurines, and reverses. In his *De servis, et eorum apud veteres ministeriis* (Padua, 1656) Pignoria uses various antiquarian objects as scholarly evidence.

that Antenor had established the city of Padua. He published in 1630
the Esquiline fresco commonly known as the "Nozze Aldobrandine" as
Antiquissimae picturae quae Romae visitur . . . explicatus; deftly ex-
ploiting what he knew about ancient wreaths, implements, colors, and
ceremonial postures, he explained the person and functions of each of
the ten figures in this presumed allegorical representation of marriage.

The efforts of Pignoria, of his predecessors, and of many men
living even in the second half of the seventeenth century fade into pure
amateurishness before the *De pictura veterum libri tres* of François de
Jon. De Jon had come to England in about 1620 as the librarian of the
Earl of Arundel, and this book, published in Amsterdam in 1630, was
written at the request of Charles I to whom it was dedicated. The latter
part of the volume contains a catalogue of works of art known through
ancient writers and an alphabetical list of artists commencing with
Aaron, who made the golden calf, and concluding with a certain Zosi-
mus, who is mentioned in one of Gruytere's inscriptions as a maker of
bas-reliefs. Daedalus, Tubal-Cain, Vulcan, and other mythical artists are
not overlooked by de Jon in his directory of masters and their works.

The first part of the *De pictura,* seemingly unknown in the history
of aesthetics, is a learned essay on the purposes and principles of art and
eventuates in a canon of evaluation. God, de Jon writes, created man to
contemplate and imitate creation, but He granted him both memory and
imagination, permitting him to rearrange what he sees and hence to
create surpassingly perfect creatures. The mere variety of things, consequently, allows the artist to work with a great alphabet of art. De Jon
discusses matters of light and shade, proportion, the plastic expression
of emotions, and perspective both in stasis and in motion. His book is an
instructive theoretical masterpiece. There is no section on symbolism, but
as he proceeds with his discursive analysis of art and illustrates his
doctrine with references to pictorial works, he describes and interprets
various symbols. The reader is told why Liber is horned, why Eros has
wings, why the caduceus is made of twined serpents, why some gods are
shown in boats, how gluttons are to be represented, why emperors hold
orbs in the right hand, and what ethical ideas the cypress, pine, and other
trees represent.[44] Like the professional numismatists, de Jon does not
invent interpretations; but since he is confirmed in his belief that poetry
and painting are sister arts, he finds in classical men of letters his
symbolic sources.

De Jon published no statues or pictures to illustrate his history of

[44] Since de Jon supplied his book with three detailed indices, page references are not
given.

ancient art; nevertheless, the work was so authoritative that the great scholar and encyclopaedist J. G. Graefe reprinted it in a splendid format in Rotterdam in 1694. It was the standard book on ancient art until the publication of Winckelmann's *Geschichte.* During the last half of the seventeenth century a few specialized studies of classical art, like François Lemée's *Traité des statues* (Rome, 1688), appeared without symbolic explanations. Other short works—Lucas Holst's *Commentariolus in veterem picturam nymphaeum referentem* (Rome, 1676) or Jacob Gronov *Disquisitio de icuncula Smetiana* (Leyden, 1693)—applied symbolic readings to individual objects. In 1680 Joachim von Sandrart, a not too original antiquary, provided each of his seventy plates of statues in his *Sculpturae veteris admiranda* with brief symbolic commentaries. A more diligent interpreter than he is Gisbert Cuper,[45] whose career flowered in the early eighteenth century; but one of the most impressive seventeenth-century antiquarian efforts is the *Le pitture antiche del'sepolchro de Nasonii* with the text of the by then elderly Giovanni Pietro Bellori and the splendid engravings of Santi Bartoli's drawings. Translated into Latin and provided with additional commentary by Michel Ange de la Chausse, the account of the tomb of the Nasos was printed in Graefe's *Thesaurus* and was regarded in the eighteenth century as a touchstone of Roman taste.

Uncovered in the Via Flaminia in 1674 and easily identified as the mausoleum of Q. Naso Ambrosius and his wife Urbica, supposed lineal descendants of the poet Ovid, the walls, ceiling, and floor of the tomb were copied by Bartoli in a series of fifty-nine plates. In the Latin translation there are thirty-five additional plates by F. Bartoli and Antonio Pazzi of frescoes and mosaics from other Roman sites. The commentaries of Bellori and de la Chausse are mainly concerned with the

---

[45] Cuper was a student of Gronov and a professor of history. When he was twenty-six, he published *Observationum libri tres . . . varii ritus eruuntur et nummi elegantissimi illustrantur* (Utrecht, 1670). In 1683 came his frequently reprinted publication and interpretation of Archelaos of Priene's bas-relief, *Apotheosis vel consecratio Homeri sive lapis antiquissimus in quo poetarum principiis Homeri consecratio sculpta est* (a book attacked in 1714 by Schott in his *Explication nouvelle de l'apothéose d'Homère*) published at Amsterdam. In 1676 he had published a series of figurines and engraved gems with the title *Harpocrates sive explicatio imagunculae argenteae perantiquae quae in figuram Harpocratis formata representat solem,* which was supplemented by a special study of the local appearance of the little god of secrets in *De Mercurii Harpocratis aliisque Romanorum sigillis ad Neomagum erutis et inscriptionibus antiquis* (Noyon, 1704). His masterpiece based on the publication and explanation of every elephant on reverses, figurines, lamps, and bas-reliefs he could find, was the *De elephantis in nummis obviis exercitationes duae* (Hague, 1719). A great series of other monographs, some of which involve symbolic explanation, were published posthumously in Poleni's *Thesaurus,* II and IV. Cuper augmented and emended Pierre Jurieu's *Histoire critique des dogmes et des cultes,* 1704, with his *Suplément* of 1705.

identification of subjects—Apollo, Adonis, Flora, Pluto, Neptune, Ceres, the Seasons, and other figures—by their significant symbols. Since the colors of the garments were discernible, the meaning of the colors is also explained. The commentaries of the antiquarians on Hercules and his exploits as represented in three of the plates suggest that there was a continued interest in ancient symbolism and allegory as late as 1791, when this book was published for the last time.

The mosaic floor of the sepulcher had an elaborate border around a central oblong representing Hercules subduing one of the centaurs. It is surprising that Bellori at this late date looks to Lactantius Placidus and Albericus of London for some of his mythological remarks. He notices, however, that the owl, dove, cock, and eagle in the border are tokens of the four virtues which enabled the demigod to overcome men-beasts. These virtues and their ancillary qualities, wisdom, prudence, honest custom, simplicity, love, clarity of soul, vigilance, providential forebodings, and strength of both body and soul, are all signified by some characteristic of one of the four birds. "All of them combine in the virtue of the hero."[46] Hercules' rescue of Alcestis from the underworld, the subject of a fresco, represents for Bellori the traditional allegory of the salvation of the soul of man; hence, it portrays the fixed symbol of immortality "which is ours under the leadership of virtue, which the figure of Hercules represents." He discloses a quite conventional moral allegory in a third painting of Hercules wrestling with Antaeus while Pallas, or wisdom, stands by and blesses the demigod and Terra, or matter, looks on sadly at her child's defeat.[47] Bellori's allegorical comments are all time-honored; he may have restated them because they were expected.

V

The toreumatographs had the same problems as the iconographs; in fact, the two arts also often claimed the same practitioners. Tombstone reliefs had to be identified historically and explained. The bas-reliefs on sarcophaguses had to be interpreted. More important objects of research than these were the triumphal arches in Rome and the great columns which seemed like stone scrolls half-unrolled. The earliest antiquarian to attempt a historical reading of a column was Alphonse

---

[46] Bellori, *Picturae antiquiae cryptarum Romanarum et sepulchri Nasonis,* ed. and trans. M. A. La Chausse (Rome, 1738), p. 31.
[47] *Ibid.,* pp. 52–53.

Chacon, whose *Historia utriusque belli Dacici a Traiano Caesare gesti ex simulachris quae in columna ejusdem Romae visuntur collecta* was published in Rome in 1576. This work was succeeded by Bellori's and Bartoli's *Colonna Traiana* and Raffaello Fabretti's *De columna Traiani syntagma*. In this volume of 1683 Fabretti printed his *Ad tabellam Iliadis*, the first full-scale treatise on the famous *Tabula Iliaca*. The same bas-relief was republished in 1699 with a more correct commentary by Lorenz Beger as *Bellum et excidium Trojanus*. Bellori, who joined with Bartoli to provide the expositions for his drawings, was the most practised of seventeenth-century toreumatographs as his *Columna Antoniniana Marci Aurelii Antonini Augusti,* and his *Admiranda Romanorum antiquitatum ac veteris sculpturae vestigia*[48] prove. Bellori liked to specialize in commentaries on large antiquarian pieces, of which reproductions were printed in elaborate volumes, but the art of explaining bas-reliefs began much earlier.

Andrea Palladio was the first to sketch the ruins of Rome. His drawings appeared in 1554 as *Dell' antichita di Roma*. When Girolamo Ferrucci edited the 1588 edition of Andrea Fulvio's guidebook of 1513, he included poor reproductions of Palladio's pictures and commented on them. Among the illustrations was a typical Mithraic group also published without interpretation by A. Lafreri in his *Speculum Romanae magnificentiae* (1564) and by J. Camerarius in his *De re rustica opuscula nonnulla* (1577). Ferrucci's allegorical analysis of this fairly traditional group (Fig. 2), which he had seen in the house of Ottaviano Zeno and likened to similar groups in the Palazzo di S. Marco and the Palazzo of Cardinal Cesis, pleased him so much that he also included it in the twelfth edition of Bartolommeo Marliani's *Urbis Romae topographia,*[49] which he edited in the same year.

Marking each figure in the group with a letter, Ferrucci, who either ignored or failed to read the inscriptions on other Mithraic groups, saw this bas-relief of the god Mithra stabbing the bull as an allegory of the perfect farmer, who, having observed the phases of the moon and the

---

[48] Bellori's book may have inspired Claude Menestrier's *Description de la belle et grande colonne historiée dressée à l'honneur de l'Empéreur Théodore* (Paris, 1702) for which G. Bellini furnished the illustrations. A reading of another column was made by Giovanni Vignoli in his *De columna imperatoris Antonini Pii dissertatio* (Rome, 1705), which contains a limited amount of symbolic interpretation. Appended to this volume is the same author's *Veteres inscriptiones,* where a Mithraic bas-relief is published (pp. 174–75) and several altar panels (pp. 194–98) are identified by their symbolic designs.

[49] Marliani, *Urbis Romae topographia* (Venice, 1588), p. 152. In M. J. Vermasren, *Corpus inscriptionum et monumentorum religionis Mithriacae* (Hague, 1956), I, this illustration of the now lost monument is published as fig. 93.

Figure 2

stations of the sun, worked day and night on the land and was aided in his labors by the virtues of strength, providence, faith, and diligence. An adjacent table, alphabetically arranged, furnished the key to each figure in the marble and translated each symbol in the allegorical arrangement. The bull is "the earth stabbed by the knife of labor and shedding the blood of fruitfulness." The identifications of the symbolic Mithraic creatures are easily spelled out: the dog is love and faith; the serpent is providence; the lion is strength and force; and the scorpion is genera-tion. Mithra is Agriculture.[50] Ferrucci was by no means an outlandish allegorist; and though he supports his analogues on no texts or objects, he probably could have offered them to a more learned group of readers

[50] Fulvio, *L'antichità di Roma* (Rome, 1588), pp. 308v-9v.

269

than the purchasers of guides to Rome. In the same book,[51] for instance, he demonstrates by specific documents that a sarcophagus of porphyry previously published as "Sepulcrum Bacci" was the tomb of the Blessed Costanza. Ferrucci's allegorical explanation of the Mithraic bas-relief was sharply criticized by Pignoria, who first pointed to similar inscribed bas-reliefs in his appendix to the 1615 edition of Cartari.[52] In spite of Pignoria's exact criticism, Ferrucci's allegorization was accepted and reprinted in book after book on Roman antiquities; it appears as late as 1672 in Franzini's *Roma antica e moderna*.[53]

Ferrucci had a fellow in antiquarian allegorization in Girolamo Aleandro, whose symbolic commentary on the *Tabula Heliaci* was published in Paris in 1617 as *Antiquae tabulae marmoreae solis effigie symbolisque exculptae, accurata explicatio*. Aleandro, secretary to Cardinal Barberini, saw this square yard of marble bas-relief (Fig. 3) in the Palazzo di Mattei and was teased into its interpretation by what he had read in the Fathers about pagan mysteries.

It is known, as Tertullian points out, that the Ethnics when they were embarrassed by their fables about the gods, took refuge in reading into them a physical interpretation and covered disgrace with cleverness. This was, as Lactantius writes, a feint of the Devil to blind men with an appearance of light. When a wise man was not satisfied with poetic authority proving the false opinions about the gods, he used his wit to excogitate moral or physical interpretations. Athenagoras observes that Empedocles related the gods to the elements; hence, no one can doubt that the designer of this tabula was led by some superstition to suppose that these effigies, which contained allegories of natural things, could be considered as amulets.[54]

With this conviction to guide him, Aleandro separated the whole design into symbols so that he could rearrange them into a proper theological-physical allegory.

When Aleandro saw the clubs wrapped in lionskins he knew that Hercules was symbolically intended. Beneath the youthful head of Helios—the youth with bow and arrows—are the lyre of Apollo, the cup of

---

[51] *Ibid.*, pp. 303v–304v.

[52] Cartari, *op. cit.*, pp. 293–94.

[53] Franzini, *Roma antica e moderna* (Rome, 1672), pp. 596–98. The same group and that on the Capitoline are published and properly explained by Lorenz Beger, *Spicilegium antiquitatis* (Cologne, 1692), pp. 97–100. Four other groups are published by Filippo del Torre, *Monumenta veteris Antii* (Rome, 1700), pp. 157–253 with a full descriptive account of the cult. A much more learned study of Mithraism with publications of monuments, "De origine ac ritibus sacri taurobolii" is in Anthony van Dale, *Dissertationes IX antiquitatibus quin et marmoribus . . . illustrandis inservientes* (Amsterdam, 1702), pp. 1–174.

[54] Aleandro, *Antiquae tabulae* (Paris, 1617), p. 53.

Figure 3

Bacchus, and the caduceuses of Mercury. The pine cones in the garland denote Cybele; the other fruits and flowers represent Ceres, Flora, and Pomona. The garland reminds Aleandro of the one hung before the Temple of Apollo during the Feast of Pyanopsion, a feast sacred to the sun and the seasons. With a little learned juggling, the three gods and the demigod are shown to be solar aspects; but because all of them have some connections with the Muses, they stand for the supremacy in harmony obtained when the sun presides over the other planets. The piles of stone in which the Herculean clubs are thrust represent the

271

presiding validity of all four deities at crossroads. But these four divine powers are also to be identified with the elements: Bacchus is water; Apollo, fire; Hercules, earth; and Mercury, air. Since Apollo is famed for skill with the bow, for prophetic powers, and for the benefits of music and medicine, he can be united with Bacchus, or prophecy, with Hercules, or medicine, and with Mercury, or music. The tones of music help Aleandro symbolize the gods as seasonal figures. Summer is the acute tone; winter, the grave tone; and spring, the middle tone. The ancients made spring and autumn synonymous; and, Aleandro writes, the seasonal analogy fits if the tetrachord is intended. Consequently the Mattei bas-relief is in honor of the sun and the seasons of the sun. Apollo is summer; Bacchus, autumn; Hercules, winter; and Mercury, spring. Aleandro bases his interpretations not only on the texts of Greek and Latin authors and of the medieval mythographers such as Fulgentius, Martianus, and Albericus but also on antiquities. For whatever interpretation he suggests, he finds a text, a reverse, a cameo, or some other antiquarian object which supports his allegorical conclusion.[55]

Although the toreumatograph was mainly interested in verifying or establishing history memorialized in the columns or in the friezes of triumphal arches where symbolism almost never appears, the publication of the deeper meanings of more abstruse bas-reliefs occurs from time to time during the seventeenth century. The so-called epigrammatographs Jan Gruytere,[56] Thomas Reines,[57] Raffaello Fabretti,[58] and Antonio Bosio[59] were regularly faced by the necessity of scholarly pride to explain the symbolism of a funeral monument. Athanasius Kircher, who translated the ancient Egyptian bas-reliefs, wrote a symbolic explanation of the "lithostrotus" in the Temple of Fortune at Palestrina, and some years before Cuper published his exposition of Archelaos of Priene's *Apotheosis of Homer,* gave the world his interpretations of the untitled and hence enigmatic figures in that bas-relief.[60] Spon, not to be outdone by careless predecessors, published the "Marriage of Cupid and

---

[55] In the latter half of this publication Aleandro explains by the cincture on a recently exhumed marble torso that the original complete figure probably represented "solar power, earthly fertility, and hope of harvest." In his *Navis ecclesiam referentis symbolum in veteri gemma annulari insculptum . . . explicatione illustratum* (1626) he finds Christ and Peter on a cornelian engraved with three men, two birds, and a ship.

[56] See note 28 for title of his collection.

[57] See note 28 for title of his additions to Gruytere.

[58] Fabretti, *Inscriptionum antiquarum explicatio* (Rome, 1699).

[59] Bosio, *Roma sotterranea* (Rome, 1632). This account of the catacombs and Christian monuments published posthumously was enlarged and handsomely annotated by Paolo Aringhio for the royal folio edition of 1651.

[60] Kircher, *Latium* (Amsterdam, 1671), pp. 81–87, 97–111.

Psyche''[61] and in the toreumatic section of his *Miscellanea* glanced at the significance of seventeen funeral tablets as well as bas-reliefs of a "suo-vetaurilia" and a "Meleager's hunting."[62]

VI

Both Symeoni and Du Choul can be classified as glyptographs because they were fascinated by intaglios. The earliest angeiograph is probably Stephan Wynants Pighe, who disclosed the myth of Themis and its philosophical understanding painted on a vase in the collection of Cardinal Granvelle. In the same year he published an allegory of the seasons which he read on a covered silver cup of Greek provenience. His *Themis dea seu de lege divina* and his *Mythologia eis tas oras vel in anni partes,* both published in Antwerp in 1568, were reprinted and regarded as models by seventeenth-century antiquarians. Following in the footsteps of both Pighe and his pupil Pignoria, Marquard Freher worked at the symbolism of Constantine as a boar hunter, in which guise the emperor is represented on an intaglio.[63] This study is focused on one object; on the other hand, in his *Dactyliothecae* of 1601, Abraham de Goorle, although he publishes no etchings of stones, attempts to survey glyptography. His book, often reprinted during the seventeenth century with glyptographic studies by Georg Long,[64] Johannes Kirchmann,[65] and Heinrich Kornmann,[66] also had an independent existence of its own and was edited by later antiquarians. In 1695 it appeared in two volumes under the editorial aegis of Jacob Gronov, who supplied each of the 896 intaglios published with a commentary explaining the history, symbolism, or allegory which the engravers intended.

Toward the middle of the seventeenth century, the numismatist Lionardo Agostini also published 214 engraved gems with historical, mythical, and mysterious expositions as *Le gemme antiche figurate* (Rome, 1657). The second volume of this work with illustrations of fifty more intaglios appeared ten years later, and both parts were issued in 1681 with Bellori's additional explanatory remarks. Detailed symboli-

---

[61] Spon, *Recherches curieuses d'antiquité* (Lyons, 1683), pp. 87–97.

[62] Spon, *Miscellanea* (Lyons, 1685), pp. 305–13.

[63] Freher, *Sapphirus Constantii* (Heidelberg, 1602). His *Cecropistomachia* of 1607 describes a sardonyx portraying a gladiatorial combat. Freher discourses on the subject of gladiatorial games and even notices the names of the fighters on the intaglio: Kekrou has overcome Danuvius.

[64] Long, *De annulis signatoriis antiquorum* (Milan, 1615).

[65] Kirchmann, *De annulis* (Leyden, 1623).

[66] Kornmann, *De annulo* (Hague, 1654).

cal interpretations of individual intaglios were written by Jean Chiflet,[67] but the object of enormous seventeenth-century antiquarian interest and speculation was the so-called Great Cameo of France. First published with a historical and symbolic reading by Jean Tristan de Saint-Amant in his *Commentaires historiques,* it was studied further by Jean Le Roy, Jean Hardouin,[68] and Albert Rubens. With each new study—most of them were brought together in the 1683 *Achates Tiberianus sive gemma Caesarea antiquitate, argumento, arte, historia, prorsus incomparabilis, et cui parem in orbe terrarum, non est reperire, D. Augusti apotheosin . . . representans*—symbolism faded and history took its place. However, for a fine view of the symbolic glytograph at work, the great folio of the versatile Fortunio Liceti stands in the front rank.

Liceti composed his autobiography in 1634 and published his correspondence with other scholars in 1640; hence, a great deal more is known about him than about many other men of his generation. When Liceti was nineteen, he wrote the first of his conventional books on the nature of the soul and within a year was elected to the professorship of logic at Pisa. In the accomplished manner of the seventeenth-century intellectual, he transferred to Padua to be Cremonini's successor in the chair of philosophy; then he migrated to the University of Bologna and returned to Padua near the end of his life as Professor of Medicine. Liceti wrote books on many humanistic and scientific subjects, but his antiquarian studies begin with *De lucernis antiquorum reconditis libri quatuor* (Venice, 1621),[69] a work handsomely illustrated with etchings of Greek and Roman lamps in the Udine edition of 1652. This work was succeeded by *Encyclopaedia ad aram mysticam nonarii terrigenae anonymi vetustissimi* (Padua, 1630), in which Liceti, following his commentary in the *De Lucernis,* continued to look for hidden meaning. Like Kircher he was captured by the idea of a mysterious ancient world, and this obsession is clearly responsible for his *De mundi et hominis analogia liber unus* (Udine, 1635), in which he makes an extended comparison of the macrocosm and the microcosm. Liceti's concern with classical occultism is further illustrated by his semiliterary treatment of the Odysseus

---

[67] His two symbolic discussions are *Fons aqua virgo* and *Socrates sive de gemmis eius imagine coelatis iudicium;* both are in the sixth volume of Joannes Wetstein, *Miscellanea Chifletiana* (Amsterdam, 1688).

[68] Hardouin, *Opera selecta* (Amsterdam, 1709), pp. 708–11.

[69] The greatest seventeenth-century publication of Greek and Roman lamps was Bellori and Bartoli's *Le antiche lucerne sepolcrali figurate* (Rome, 1691), which was translated into Latin and supplied with additional explanations of the symbolism by Lorenz Beger in 1704. In its first publication it vied successfully with Giuseppe Malatesta Garuffi's *Lucerna lapidaria . . . via Flaminia et Arimini scrutatur* (Rimini, 1691).

and Circe legend in *Ulysses apud Circen* (Udine, 1636). All of his symbolic analogues and interpretations in these carefully annotated books are based on enormous learning. The same fantastic erudition dominates his antiquarian masterpiece, *Hieroglyphica sive antiqua schemata gemmarum anularium quaesita moralia, politica, historica, medica, philosophica et sublimiora explicata,* published shortly before his death.

The *Hieroglyphica,* dedicated to that famous *virgo* Christine of Sweden, who is informed in the preface that the ancients improvised the devices on gems to save philosophical truths from vulgarization, contains sixty etchings of figured stones with an attached essay on each. Since he was too elderly to be tempted by the passion, Liceti wrote eight essays—a quarter of the volume—on the myths of Eros and ancient theories of love as known to and expressed by lapidaries. He explains, for instance, a gem displaying three Cupids, another showing Eros as a warrior, and others in which Cupid weeps, quenches his torch, or is deprived of his dart by Aphrodite. In his second essay he looks at a gem of Cupid as a boy bird-catcher (Fig. 4), a theme that with modifications enchanted literary men for two thousand years.[70] The motif is found in charming simplicity in Bion, but its didactic variant is an episode in St. John Damascene's *Barlaam and Josaph.* The carver of Liceti's gem converted Bion's Greek bird-catcher, who unwittingly tried to snare winged Eros, into Eros himself as a bird-catcher. Liceti, in his exegesis is unconsciously closer to the *Barlaam and Josaph* "churl and the bird" notion, but he misses the obvious reading. In fact, he misses it eruditely.

When he examines this gem Liceti agrees with Plato and Aristotle that love is a desire to possess the beautiful, the proper desire of the wise man; he notices that the nudity of Eros symbolizes the necessary simplicity of mind required for such intellectual pursuits. The aspiring nature of rational love is signified by the wings and uplifted arms and hands—symbols of prudence—of this Cupid, whose posture also suggests that of the contemplative angels. The limed reeds extended by the Cupid toward the bird are mis-seen by Liceti as ropes by means of which the winged child, or the "avid intellect," seeks through seeing and hearing to elevate himself to the bough on which the bird perches.

The bird, tree, and suspended cage are of course more than they seem. After a learned excursion into the hidden meaning of the Homeric moly and the biblical Tree of the Knowledge of Good and Evil, Liceti decides that this is the Tree of Human Wisdom. It is, consequently, a

---

[70] D. C. Allen, *Image and Meaning* (Baltimore, 1968), pp. 1–19.

Figure 4

laurel tree emblematic of knowledge not imbued by God in man but
secured by hard human labor. The bitter taste of the laurel leaf is an
attribute of this intense labor. The tree of the gem properly has no
flowers "because the end of human wisdom is bare truth, unpleasant, and
sometimes unflattering; only poetry, which has verisimilitude for its end,

mixes the useful with the charming." Although flowerless, the Tree of Human Wisdom "bears fruit, the unreal fruit of symbol, allegory, and metaphor," the fruit "of doctrine or signified wisdom."

The laurel tree and its imaginative fruit are further enriched by the bird and the cage. "The little Cupid, who stands for love of learning, a desire placed in man by Nature, attempts to pull himself towards the summit of the ancient Tree of Knowledge . . . so that he may be closer to the bird and the cage." Essentially the bird is "the word," a metaphoric relationship established by the poetic fact that Homer called words "winged" and "birdlike." Liceti wonders whether or not the bird in this tree is the poetic swan of long symbolic fame, but he rejects this idea and decides it is a nightingale, also an ancient symbol for men "conspicuous in learning and eminent in the world of letters." Through the singing of these significant birds, youthful Cupids are instructed. The cage, a prison for birds, stands for the book in which the accumulated wisdom of mankind is preserved. "Our little gem shows, under the type of a young Cupid, youth desirous of instruction and eager to rise to the tall top of the ancient tree of knowledge in order to capture the melodious nightingale of learning . . . and to take the cage containing the writings of wise men."[71] To support this allegorical explanation Liceti quotes scores of ancient and modern nightingales of learning; hence, while the scheme of his explanation is his own, he finds literary or philosophical authority for what he says.

Though both Kircher and Liceti overdo the symbolizing methods of the seventeenth-century archaeographs, the technique they handle with so much abandon continued to be followed, though becoming less intuitive and more and more historically exact, until well into the eighteenth century. It is regularly used as a tool to explain baffling designs on individual objects,[72] on whole classes of antiquarian items,[73] and on arti-

---

[71] Liceti, *Hieroglyphica* (Padua, 1653), pp. 38–76.

[72] For symbolic explanations of individual items see Domenico Aulisio's *De colo Mayerano* (Naples, 1694). Controversy over symbolic interpretation was not uncommon, and Johannes Eggeling's *Mysteria Cereris et Bacchi in vasculo ex uno onyche* (Brema, 1682) attempted to correct the interpretation of Joachim Feller in the *Acta eruditorum* of the same year. Feller naturally responded in *Vindiciae* (Leipzig, 1685).

[73] Among the many discussions of whole collections, the work of Lorenz Beger, keeper of the Elector of Brandenburg's museum, is of extraordinary interest. In his *Spicilegium antiquitatis fasculi* (Cologne, 1692) he explains reverses, intaglios, bas-reliefs, and statues. In subsequent volumes he collected symbolical serpents, looked at representations of the damned in Avernus, and sought out the legend of Alcestis on various antiquities. Between 1696 and 1701 he published in three folios, with fine plates and explanations, the principal items in the Elector's collection.

facts clustering about one principal symbol.[74] There is, however, a special difference between the method of the antiquaries and their opposites, the literary interpreters and mythographers. The antiquarians, most of whom wrote in the seventeenth century, almost always attempted to support their conclusions by the hard, cold facts of classical history or by Greek and Roman literary material. The allegorical interpreters of Homer, Virgil, and Ovid and of Greek and Roman mythology, with a long tradition behind them, were not nearly so cautiously exact. What the antiquarians often brought to their expositions of objects, certain as they might be, were, however, as symbolic or allegoric in intent and result as the efforts of the others. All of these interpreters added their symbolic emphasis to the Renaissance's conviction of a deep theological and philosophical mystery enshrouding the artistic heritage of Greece and Rome. What theologians from the time of Ambrose onward had seen in the Scripture was also evident in the artistic and monumental remains of pagans who lived under the guidance of the Natural Light or shared in some limited way in the inspiration imparted first to the chosen people and then to true believers. In a world dominated by this connotative climate, European men of letters could hardly help but be warmed by the sun of symbolism and refreshed by the soft winds of allegory.

[74] In addition to Beger's antiquarian studies of special subjects, *Les Sirenes ou discours sur leur forme et figure* (Paris, 1691), by Claude Nicaise, Ignatio Bracci's *Phoenicis effigies in numismatis et gemma* (Rome, 1637), and Charles Gros de Boze's antiquarian essays on Janus and Santé, which appeared in the early years of the eighteenth century, are further examples of this other method of archaeological endeavour.

X

❧ THE RATIONALIZATION OF MYTH AND THE END OF ALLEGORY

ORAL EXPLICATORS OF HOMER, Virgil, and Ovid, symbolical expounders of antiquities, and compilers of mythologies and lexicons of symbolism were haunted in Renaissance times by the same sense of divine mystery that
impelled their associated syncretists to search for evidences of Christian
doctrine or sacred history, fallaciously remembered or diabolically corrupted, in the remains of paganism. Few men living during these centuries were sceptical enough to ask whether the interpretation was in the
text or object explained or only in the imagination of the explainer. As a
matter of fact, the search for a meaning deeper than the superficial one
was a movement that smacked of orthodoxy; each group in the learned
sect depended on the discoveries of the others, and all owed an immense
debt to the long tradition of Christian exegesis. The connection between
the two methods can be found in the late fifteenth century in a clear statement by Pico della Mirandola in which the three worlds of Greek Platonism are accommodated to the three modes of nonliteral biblical elucidation.

Indeed, tied by the chains of concord, all these worlds exchange both their
natures and names. From this fact (if there is anyone unaware of it) is derived
every principle of allegorical interpretation. Nor could those ancient fathers fittingly
represent one thing by another image if they had not known the hidden friendships
and affinities of all nature. Otherwise it would have made no sense to represent one
thing by its seeming opposite. But knowing all things and moved by that **Spirit**

279

which not only knows but creates the Universe, they most aptly represented the nature of one world by what they knew corresponded to it in others. Hence, those who wish adequately to interpret their symbols and their figures, if they are not aided by the same Spirit, have need of the same knowledge.[1]

Pico's opinion is by no means unique. He had been anticipated by Landino, whose *Disputationes* were shelved in his library,[2] and by other members of the Florentine circle. To the syncretists in this group "patres antiqui" might be translated in two ways, but "Spiritus" had only one meaning.

The Hellenists of the fifteenth and early sixteenth centuries found isolated examples of classical symbolism and allegory before they were fully aware of the allegorical procedures of the Homeric apologists. Ficino points to the parabolic myths of Socrates and Plato, but even before his time the famous allegory of Prodicus about Hercules' choice of ways was known to Coluccio Salutati.[3] Until recently Salutati's book was known only in manuscript; but the source of Prodicus' declamation, Xenophon's *Memorabilia,* was published in 1517 in Greek and shortly afterward in Bessarion's Latin translation. The Christian moralizations of the Herculean labors so popular in the Middle Ages were now clearly authorized by this pagan description of the almost Christian conversion of the classical Samson.[4] Lesser Greek allegories might have come to the attention of ardent scholars,[5] and the ancient passion for the exposition of omens and dreams or for enigmatic statement requiring skillful elucidation was probably known to almost every literate man.[6] But the Age of the Renaissance had hardly begun before the *Tabula vitae* of Cebes, published from an incomplete manuscript, furnished everyone with an impressive example of the deeper meaning to be discovered in a mural in

---

[1] G. Pico della Mirandola, *op. cit.,* pp. 188–92.

[2] Pearl Kibre, *The Library of Pico della Mirandola* (New York, 1936), p. 188.

[3] Salutati, *De laboribus,* pp. 182–83.

[4] To Panofsky's study can be added Eugene M. Waith, *The Herculean Hero in Marlowe, Chapman, Shakespeare, and Dryden* (New York, 1962) and Marc-René Jung, *Hercule dans la littérature française du XVIᵉ siècle* (Geneva, 1966).

[5] Pherecydes of Syros, author of a creation allegory, was known to Cudworth and is one of the four secret historians analysed by von der Hardt in his *Aenigmata prisci orbis.* Parmenides' allegorical poem on his meeting with Dame Philosophy and his decision to join her troupe, which had been preserved by Sextus Empiricus (VII, 111), was not in print until the early seventeenth century, but Pico and other scholars had manuscripts of Sextus.

[6] The *Oneirokritika* of Artemidorus and the *Aurea carmina* and *Symbola* of Pythagoras were widely known to Renaissance men; in fact, the fantastic *Hypnerotomachia* of Francesco Colonna, written in 1467, makes clear its author's knowledge of Artemidorus and Hor Apollo. Herodotus' account (IV, 131–32) of the Scythian symbols contrarily interpreted by Darius and Gobryas and Calchas' explanation of the omen in *Iliad* II. 308–35, were, of course, generally mentioned in books on prophecy, symbolism, etc.

the Greek Temple of Cronus. The meaning is not this time only in the imagination of the interpreter, because he simply discloses, with symbolic flourishes, what the artist-allegorist intended.

The *Tabula vitae,* mentioned by Diogenes Laertius[7] and parodied by Lucian,[8] was assumed to be the work of the Theban philosopher who questions Socrates in the *Phaedo*; hence, it was thought to be as old as Platonism and was praised for its foreshadowing of Christian morality. Published in the fifteenth century, it was quickly turned into Latin and then into French, Italian, and English. To make the allegory still plainer some editions were furnished with an imaginary reconstruction, carefully keyed, of the Greek mural depicting the life of man. Since the *Tabula* offered a double dosage of Greek and morality, it was endorsed as a school text by the pedagogical theorist Juan Luis Vives[9] and widely used in Elizabethan grammar schools.[10] When the young teacher John Milton was looking about for "easie and delightful" readings for beginners, he settled on "Cebes, Plutarch, and other Socratic discourses"; but Milton was simply following a pedagogical custom that would continue well into the next century.[11]

Pulling out the folding plate designed by Visscher, the schoolboy of the sixteenth or seventeenth century would attempt to follow in the text the discourse of the elderly disciple of Parmenides and Pythagoras, who simultaneously describes and explains the great mural to an attentive band of presumably youthful Greek tourists. The aged cicerone was allegorist enough to have written a morality play or helped Edmund Spenser with one of his didactic processions. His description actually begins with a version of the Garden of Adonis, for the viewers look first at the lower right corner of the painting to see Genius admit a throng of

---

[7] Diogenes Laertius, *Lives* II, 16.

[8] Lucianus, "Teacher of Rhetoric," *Works*, 6–26. A useful account of editions of Cebes in the Renaissance and of the sixteenth- and seventeenth-century commentaries on the *Tabula vitae* may be found in J. A. Fabricius, *Bibliotheca Graeca* (Hamburg, 1781), II, 703–15. John Davies of Kidwelly, who translated Cebes from the French rendering of G. Boileau, praises the commentaries of Welsen and of Mascardi. It is now supposed that the probable first-century author of the *Tabula* was an initiate in one of the mystery religions; see Robert Joly, *Le Tableau de Cébès et la philosophie religieuse* (Brussels, 1963), pp. 43–51.

[9] F. Watson, *Vives and the Renaissance Education of Women* (New York, 1912), p. 249.

[10] T. W. Baldwin, *William Shakespere's Small Latine and Lesse Greeke* (Urbana, Ill., 1944), I, 347, 417, 535–36, 540; II, 649.

[11] Milton, *Of Education, Works,* ed. F. A. Patterson (New York, 1931), IV, 281. I do not know whether Lessing knew this or not when he saw in Satan's encounter with Uriel evidence of Milton's reading of Cebes; see *Werke,* eds. J. Petersen and W. von Olshausen (Leipzig and Berlin, n.d.), IV, 482. It is interesting to notice that Spenser's eighteenth-century editors, Warton, Upton, and Jortin, were so familiar with the *Tabula* that they looked for traces of it in the *Faerie Queene.*

people into the enclosure of Life, where Deceit offers them a drink from the cup of Error. Embraced by Opinion, Desire, and Pleasure and led away, the newcomers are brought before blind and deaf Fortune, who stands on her sphere and is attended by Thoughtlessness. Those whom the goddess blesses are first flattered by either Avarice or Thriftlessness, then stripped of their goods and handed over to Retribution, Sorrow, Anguish, Despair, and Woe. If Repentance fails to save them they are enthralled to Misery. Those protected by Repentance are presented to Good Opinion and True Education. Should they meet False Education on the way, they are likely to become poets, orators, rhetoricians, musicians, astronomers, or philosophers. True Education, attended by Continence, Endurance, Happiness, and Virtue, dwells on a cliff. Those pilgrims of life who reach her haven are safe and happy; however, many who almost arrive at her palace slip on the road and fall into Grief, Pain, Shame, and Ignorance. The allegory continues in this unexciting fashion until in the eventually discovered Arabic conclusion Senex and Hospes discuss man's personal responsibility for good and evil and the pursuit of the wisest *curriculum vitae*.[12]

The explained picture of Cebes' *Tabula* was the prototype of that major Renaissance literary-artistic invention, the emblem. The first collection, the *Emblemata* of Alciati, appeared in 1531, exactly one generation after the *editio princeps* of the *Tabula*. In this publication, the lemma, or enigma, is followed by a picture which is a congregation of symbols expounded by a suite of verses. Claude Mignault, who annotated the 1571 edition of Alciati and supplied it with a "Syntagma de symbolis," explains the task of the creator and of the explicator. A knowledge of symbolism enables the latter to seek "in myths or in the nature of things moral instruction." The creator, on the other hand, eschews obvious symbols, which are without value, and employs those darker conceits which circle and wind the meaning into obscurity.[13] As the years passed, Mignault's conception of the relation between creation and interpretation was expanded but also refined by other experts who gathered and classified those arcane signs "presenting one thing to the eye but meaning something other to the mind."[14] But critical theory is

[12] Cebes, *Pinax,* ed. R. Parsons (Boston, 1887).

[13] A. Alciati, *Emblemata* (Leyden, 1593), pp. 17–25.

[14] C. Ripa, *La novissima iconologia* (Padua, 1625), sigs. B-B2. He praises symbolic representations as providing the learned with occult wisdom and the ignorant with sweet enjoyment. Filippo Picinelli makes a series of fine distinctions between moral and heroic emblems, aenigmas, moral symbols, hieroglyphs, etc., in the prefatory pages to his *Mondo Simbolico* (Milan, 1669). An enormously learned and careful series of advices on the composition, use, and interpretation of aenigma, allegory, emblem, hieroglyph, symbol, and

never as interesting as practice, and the connection between creator and interpreter can be more fully observed by watching Ariosto and Tasso, epic poets admittedly imitating the poems of Homer and Virgil.

II

When Marino's *L'Adone* was published in 1623, each canto was clarified by a prose interpretation of its myth by Lorenzo Scoto. A modern reader of Marino welcomes any possible expository aid; but Scoto hardly had comfort of this sort in mind because he was simply following an Italian custom, which had begun with the expounders of Ariosto, of probing for a more recondite meaning than a first reading might yield. In the case of Ariosto, who was no more an adversary of allegory than his disciple Spenser, there was a certain justification in expecting more than the lines offered. Ariosto used allegory as he used classical myths, dirty stories, true history, medieval romances, tales of wonder, and anything else that would give his poem variety and keep the reader's interest. The surface of the *Orlando Furioso* is dotted with islands of allegory. The captivity of Astolfo and Ruggiero by Alcina and their escape into the kingdom of Logostilla is patent allegory. The same may be said of Astolfo's voyages to the Earthly Paradise, the moon, and Purgatory. The poem is crowded with symbolic personages like Avarice, Silence, Jealousy, Fraud, and Discord. The rather elaborate treatment in Cantos XXXIV and XXXV of the realms of Life and Death are superb allegory. Given hints of this sort, Renaissance seekers of other meanings were able to see more in the *Orlando* than Ariosto probably intended. By 1600 a great procession of expositors had threaded its way through the poem and deposited many allegorical and moral footnotes. The Italians were naturally better at this work than were the French and the Spanish; Dolce, Valvassori, Ruscelli, Fornari, Toscanella, Porcacchi, Horologgio, and Bonome saw to it that the *Cinque Canti* as well as the

---

other occult devices was provided by Emmanuele Tesauro in his *Il Cannocchiale Aristotelico sia Idea Argutezze Heroiche* (Turin, 1554) (I have used *Idea argutae,* trans. C. Carber [Frankfort and Leipzig, 1698]) where the process is defined as "unity in diversity, clarity in obscurity, deception in expectation" (pp. 455–56). His allegory of "queen" as "rose" (pp. 478–82), which he arranges according to the logical principles of *substantia, quantitas, qualitas, relatio, actio, passio, situs, ubi, quando,* and *habitus* may be schematically presented. Rose: supreme plant/ red of petal/ sweet of odor/ among flowers/ caressed by Zephyr/ feeds bees/ fades/ sits on stem/ in a garden/ at dawn/ bedewed/ with a yellow corolla. Queen: greatest dignity/ purple tunic/ perfumed/ among women/ praised by courtiers/ rewards the good/ dies/ sits on throne/ in a palace/ in youth/ wears pearls/ and a gold diadem.

Orlando Furioso were fully understood on levels higher than that of the literal.[15]

Fornari, Pigna, and Garofalo wrote biographies of Ariosto before the sixteenth century ended; but Fornari followed his life with a full dress account of the poet's work. The *Spositione sopra l'Orlando Furioso di M. Ludovico Ariosto* (Florence, 1549) includes an "Apologia brieva" in which Ariosto is defended against the Neo-aristotelians, who had stated that his poem lacked unity, had an inexact title, and depended too much on the previous poem of Boiardo. The *Spositione,* which follows the biography and the apology and which confessedly utilizes the lifework of Fornari's brother, presents grammatical, historical, geographical, and astronomical material necessary for the reader's understanding of the poem. About one-third of the way along,[16] it occurs to Fornari that he should moralize the song, and he supports this decision by presenting as his own Pico's theory of the three worlds and the three modes of interpretation. An allegory to the poem had already been supplied in the Lodovico Dolce-Gabriel Giolito edition of 1542, but Fornari makes his allegory more extensive to demonstrate how poets hide their wisdom from "the careless" and to encourage those who might be bound down by the "inventiveness of the fable" or the "sweet harmony of the words" to rise to the heights on "intellectual wings."

Fornari's allegorical commentary on Ariosto was followed by that of Clemente Valvassori in 1554, that of Ieronimo Ruscelli in 1558, and that of Tommaso Porcacchi in 1566. In 1574 Orazio Toscanella published at Venice *Bellezze del Furioso di M. Lo. A., scielte da O. T. con gli argomenti, et allegorie dei canti: con l'allegorie de i nomi proprii principali dell'opera.* Toscanella, whose moralizations are sometimes original,[17] is the only interpreter in this group to attach significances to the proper names in the poem. He puts together an alphabetical list in which he notices that Agramante stands for the imperfections and vices of the young, Brandimarte for true friendship, Oberto for the alterations of fortune, and Ruggiero for matrimonial fidelity. In 1584 Francesco de Franceschi, a Venetian publisher, brought out a splendid edition of the *Orlando Furioso* with forty-six plates by Girolamo Porro, who

---

[15] G. Fatini, *Bibliographia della Critica Ariostea (1510–1956)* (Florence, 1958) is the source of my information. Most of the major essays and allegorical expositions were gathered in *Orlando Furioso di M. Lodovico Ariosto delle annotazioni de'piu' celebri autori che sopra esso hanno scritto* (Venice, 1730).

[16] Fornari, *Spositione,* pp. 69–95.

[17] Susannah J. McMurphy, *Spenser's Use of Ariosto for Allegory,* University of Washington Publications: Language and Literature, II (1924), 14–15.

also did the allegorical title page and the illustrations for each of the *Cinque Canti*. The edition contained the lives by Pigna and Garofalo, the commentary of Ruscelli and Alberto Lavezola, the historical expositions of Nicolo Eugenico, the *index verborum* of G. B. Rota, and the "Allegoria" of Gioseffo Bonome. It is from this edition that Thomas Coxon took most of the plates for the Harington translation, and Sir John's "A Briefe and Summarie Allegorie of Orlando Furioso," which comes at the end of his translation, is largely an English rephrasing of Bonome's "Allegoria."[18]

The allegorical readings in Harington's notes are drawn mainly from Fornari and occasionally from Toscanella, but there are times when he rejects the second meanings of his Italian predecessors. Valvassori, Ruscelli, Porcacchi, and Toscanella find moral meaning in Ariosto's fifth canto, but Harington does not. "Allegorie there is none in this book at all." In Canto Four he "touches" on what is notable, leaving the remainder "to each man's private conceipt." Always distinguishing between moral significance and allegory, Harington differs in this respect from the Italians, who were seldom so careful; in fact, no one of them would be so cautious as to write, as Sir John does at the end of Book Two, "For the Allegorie in this Canto I find not much to be said, except one should be so curious to search for an allegorie where none is intended by the Author him selfe." Yet, having delivered himself of this cautionary statement, Harington sees an allegory in the riderless Baiardo's furious pursuit of Angelica, in Angelica's flight from Rinaldo, in Baiardo's striking at Sacripante and yielding to Angelica, and in Rinaldo's following of Angelica on foot, which "some have noted thereby to be meant sensualitie, that is ever in base and earthly, or rather beastly affections, never looking upward." Harington's tendency to blow hot and cold in his commentary on each canto and in his ultimate essay on the "allegorie" is balanced by the prefatory "An Apologie for Poetrie." In this essay he separates the "rine" of the literal or historical sense from "a second rine and somewhat more fine" of the "morall sence." In this sense is kept an understanding of natural philosophy, of "politike government," and of divinity. "These same sences . . . we call the allegorie." After he has illustrated his point with Leo Hebraeus' moral interpretation of the myth of Perseus, Harington takes a leaf from Fornari's book and admits that weaker readers will be enchanted by the fable and the sweetness of the verse, whereas those somewhat stronger will taste the

---

[18] Townsend Rich, *Harington & Ariosto: A Study in Elizabethan Verse Translation,* Yale Studies in English, XCII (1940), 51–66.

moral sense, and "a third sort more high conceited than they, will digest the allegorie."[19]

Ariosto and his heroes appear in Sidney's *An Apology for Poetry* and are recommended for their moral values; but it is Spenser, who desired "to emulate" and hoped "to overgo" Ariosto,[20] who learned so much from the Italian's allegorical procedures and undoubtedly was benefited by the observations of the interpreters. Spenser had many debts to his predecessors, and he gladly admitted them.

> I have followed all the antique Poets historicall, first Homere, who in the Persons of Agamemnon and Ulysses hath ensampled a good governour and a vertuous man, the one in his Ilias, the other in his Odysseis; then Virgil, whose like intention was to doe in the person of Aeneas; after him Ariosto comprised them both in his Orlando: and lately Tasso dissevered them againe, and formed both parts in two persons, namely that part which they in Philosophy call Ethice, or vertues of a private man coloured in his Rinaldo: The other named Politice in his Godfredo.[21]

The distinction that Spenser makes between the epic technique of Ariosto and Tasso is interesting but not original. The annotators of Ariosto had pointed to the double nature of Orlando; Tasso, who was his own best interpreter had announced the true allegorical meaning of his major characters.

Tasso's "Allegoria del Poema" appeared as a preface to the Venice, Parma, Casalmaggiore, and Ferrara editions of the *Gerusalemme Liberata* in 1581 and was the distraught poet's attempt to mollify the objections of critics to whom he had sent his manuscripts. Tasso's letters written to Luca Scalabrino in 1575 state his dislike of the jejeune nature of allegory,[22] but the complaints of his self-sought critics about the supernatural moments in the poem and his own inability to free his romantic inclinations from the classical formalism of his generation drove him into this inescapable corner. In June of 1576 he wrote to Scipione Gonzaga that he had no allegorical intents when he began his poem because Aristotle had said naught on the subject and he himself regarded allegory a vain effort in that every interpreter read allegory according to his own caprice. Halfway through his poem, however, he began to think of allegory as a solution for literary difficulties. It is, he writes, a way of reconciling Plato and Aristotle, a task previously at-

---

[19] Ariosto, *Orlando Furioso in English Heroical Verse* (London, 1591), sig. iv-iv verso.
[20] Spenser, *Prose Works,* ed. R. Gottfried (Baltimore, 1949), p. 471.
[21] Spenser, *The Faerie Queene,* ed. E. Greenlaw, C. G. Osgood, F. M. Padelford (Baltimore, 1932), I, 167.
[22] Tasso, *Le Lettere,* ed. C. Guasti (Florence, 1854), I, 81–89.

tempted by Pico della Mirandola. He reminds Gonzaga that allegory in no sense need fit every particular of the literal; neither Homer nor Virgil was this exact. He then remembers Ficino's remark in the fourth discourse of the *Symposium*: "Not everything presented in a figure should be thought to signify something; many things without significance are there for the sake of order and transition."[23] The passion for allegory, first disclosed here, increased with Tasso's mental disorder; it prevails in the *Apologia* and the *Discorsi del Poema Eroico* and is maintained in the "Giudizio" on *La Gerusalemme Conquistata*, that last infirmity of a noble mind.

The soul of the heroic poem, according to Tasso's "Allegoria," is composed of imitation and allegory. Imitation concerns those human actions obvious to the senses; allegory, to the contrary, not only reveals passions, opinions, and morals, but seeks also to represent them by mysterious signs understood only by those who know the nature of things.

Now the life of the contemplative man is figuratively expressed in every part of Dante's *Divine Comedy* and in the *Odyssey,* whereas the civil life is adumbrated in the *Iliad* and even in the *Aeneid,* although in this poem there is a mixture of action and contemplation. Because the contemplative man is solitary and the active man lives in society, it happens that Dante and Ulysses, after he parts from Calypso, are not represented as accompanied by an army or a multitude of followers but are alone; on the other hand, where Agamemnon and Achilles are described, one is the general of the Greek army and the other is the leader of the great host of Myrmidons. Aeneas is companioned when he fights and when he attends to civil affairs; but when he descends into Hell and to the Elysian Fields, he leaves his comrades except for the faithful Achates, who never leaves his side. In this instance, the poet shows him going alone because the journey allegorizes his contemplation of the rewards and punishments reserved in the next life for the good and the evil; moreover, the operation of the speculative intellect, a single power, is fittingly represented by the action of one . . . but political action cannot be represented unless many together work toward the same end. To these reasons and these examples I have looked when I formed the allegory of my poem.

After formulating this rationale Tasso carefully identifies the symbolic personifications which have historical names in his poem. The Christian Army is really man in his virile age. Jerusalem, described as a strong city situated on a mountainous cliff, is actually the sort of civil felicity a Christian finds agreeable; hence, it is placed on "the peak of an Alpine summit of virtue." Goffredo is the intelligence; Rinaldo, Tan-

[23] *Ibid.,* I, 192–96.

credi, and other princes are qualities of the mind. The common soldiers represent the human body. The amorousness which diverts Tancredi and other knights from Goffredo and the anger which turns Rinaldo aside demonstrate the opposition of the irascible and concupiscible passions to the rational function. Ismeno and Armida, creatures of Satan, are temptations confronting the Christian warrior; the former deceives faith with false opinion; the latter uses the appetites to trick virtue. But characters with proper names are not the only symbolic figures in the poem. Tasso writes:

> The fire, the storms, the shadows, the monsters, and the apparitions are deceiving arguments which make us consider honest pain and honorable dangers as evils. The flowers, fountains, brooks, musical instruments, and nymphs are false syllogisms which present sensual pleasures as something desirable.[24]

Throughout his allegorical preface Tasso pauses to demonstrate how his symbolic persons act out some aspect of Christian ethical theory. When Rinaldo is reconciled with Goffredo, the reader should notice the obedience of the irascible power to the force of reason; at this moment too, Goffredo's civil moderation teaches the observer that reason checks anger not as a king controls a subject but rather as one fellow-citizen reproves another. Reason, in fact, should not suppress anger nor assume the role of anger but make it a companion and servant. When Goffredo, in a manner contrary to his relation with Rinaldo, imperiously imprisons Argillano, the fact that the reason is the complete master of the body is fully shown. When the army with Rinaldo and the other knights returns and obeys the commander, the reader learns that men reenter a state of natural justice when rulers order things rightly and inferiors obey them. "Then in this state of subjection to the divine order, the wood is easily disenchanted, the town is taken, and the enemy defeated; and having overcome without pain all external hindrances, man achieves political happiness." But political happiness is inferior to Christian happiness; hence, Goffredo does not want to hold the city for temporal domination but in order that Christian rites may be celebrated in it. The poem ends with Goffredo's adoration at the Holy Sepulcher, according to the poet's admission, in order to reveal that a "mind weary with civil action ought to repose in prayer and in the contemplation of the beatitudes of a life both blessed and immortal."

[24] All this material is from Tasso, Preface to *La Gerusalemme Liberata* (Pisa, 1830), pp. v-xiv.

III

The expositors of Ariosto of Ferrara as "equall in fame" to Dante and Petrarch, the allegorical procedures of "sage and serious Spenser," and the second reading invented by "magnus Tassus" for his great Christian epic were certainly known to John Milton as he sat in the lonely tower of "Il Penseroso" and turned over in his memory the pages of admired poets.

> And if ought els, great Bards beside
> In sage and solemn tunes have sung,
> Of Turneys and of Trophies hung;
> Of Forests and inchantments drear
> Where more is meant than meets the ear.

It is not improbable that by the time he had written these lines Milton had read Harington's translation for the first time or had summarized in his commonplace book, under the heading "De Mendacio," Sophronia's "glorious" falsehood, for which Tasso's critics had roundly abused him. Later in Naples he visited Giovanni Manso, patron of both Tasso and Marino, and promised him that as their fame brightened, his name would also come to the lips of men. When he memorialized Leonora Baroni, Milton, who may have been told the story by Manso, thought of the "altera Leonora" who drove the poet Tasso out of his mind. His treatise *Of Education* recommends Tasso, Castelvetro, and Mazzoni as the best teachers of the art of poetry, teachers who will inform young Englishmen "what despicable creatures our common Rimers and Play-writers be and show them what religious, what glorious, and what magnificent use might be made of Poetry both in divine and humane things."[25] In *Of Reformation* he quotes twice from the thirty-fourth canto of the *Orlando*; the first quotation is in Harington's translation; the second is clearly Milton's own improvement of Sir John's version.[26] In the autobiographical section of *The Reason of Church Government*, Ariosto advises Milton to fix all the industry and art he has "to the adorning of my native tongue"; in the same vein Tasso, having offered Alfonso his choice of an epic about Godfrey, Belisarius, or Charlemagne, suggests to the hesitating English epic poet that "it haply would

[25] Milton, *Works* IV, 286.
[26] *Ibid.*, III, 27.

be no rashnesse from an equal diligence and inclination to present the like offer in our own ancient stories."[27]

It is impossible to know whether or not Milton always read the epics of Ariosto and Tasso with the recommended moral and allegorical fervor, but it is clear from his marginal annotations in his copy of Harington's Ariosto that he did not fail to read the "morall" and the "allegorie" at the end of cantos. Edward Phillips, who probably read Cebes' *Tabula* in his uncle's classroom, may be recalling the youthful Milton's remarks on the heroic epic when he wrote out his own definition in 1674.

And therefore it is not a meer historical relation, spic't over with a little slight fiction, now and then a personated vice or virtue rising out of the ground and uttering a speech which makes a heroic poem. But it must be rather a brief obscure or remote tradition, but of some remarkable piece of story, in which the poet hath an ample field to enlarge by feigning of probable circumstances: in which, and in proper allegory, invention, the well management whereof is indeed no other than decorum, principally consisteth; and wherein there is a kind of truth even in the midst of fiction. For whatsoever is pertinently said by way of allegory, is morally, though not historically true.[28]

No better description of the tenor of *Paradise Lost* and *Paradise Regained* can be found than Phillips' last sentence, which is actually a prose redaction of Raphael's cautionary preface to his epic of the War in Heaven. But Milton's own symbolical and allegorical readings of Scripture[29] and of classical myth[30] are so well known that conjecture is unnecessary. He read the Old Testament fully aware of St. Paul's rules, and, like his contemporaries, he saw the same sort of faded biblical story or demonically perverted history in classical myth.

In his early use of pagan myth Milton is no different from the European poets who had preceded him. Dante and Petrarch had used classical legend and Christian knowledge as if there were almost no difference between Parnassus and Paradise. Marot, who put both David and Ovid into French verse, can compose a ballad on "The Passion" and expound his Christian symbolism in an expository envoy. Ronsard, who

---

[27] *Ibid.*, III, 236–37.

[28] Phillips, *Theatrum poetarum anglicanorum* (Canterbury, 1800), pp. xxix–xxx.

[29] William G. Madsen, *From Shadowy Types to Truth* (New Haven, 1968) is an excellent analysis and has a fine bibliography.

[30] Since Douglas Bush's account in *Mythology and the Renaissance Tradition in English Poetry* (New York, 1963). pp. 251–305 and *Pagan Myth and Christian Tradition in English Poetry* (Philadelphia, 1968), pp. 1–31, there can be no doubt about the attitude of the Renaissance English poets toward myth.

would gladly adore Ceres, Bacchus, Neptune, Pan, fauns, and nymphs were he not a French Catholic,[31] mixes paganism and Christianity for the glory of French verse. In "Hercule Chrestien," for which Theodore Agrippa d'Aubigné supplied a learned prose,[32] Ronsard is able to ask questions like "Who is this Hercules who left his old wife for a new conquest if not Jesus who refused the Jewish Church as wife in order to wed that of the Gentiles?"[33] English Spenser is not at all disturbed when the Red Cross Knight, having watched in the house of Pluto and Proserpine's daughter a symbolic procession of Christian Vices, fights with Faithlessness, nephew of Night, who goes to Virgil's Hell for Aesculapian medical aid. Subsequently the same hero, who becomes Christlike in the end, loses to Christian Pride, child of Tellus and Aeolus. In the second book Spenser develops a hero who enters Hades like Aeneas and, changing to Odysseus accompanied by a Christian Hermes, destroys un-Homerically the bower of Acrasia after releasing Circe's victims from enchantment. In the fifth book Hercules puts on the medieval armour of Artegall, and although he manages some of his pre-Christian labors successfully, he requires a Shakespearean sort of vigorous heroine to take the spindle of Omphale out of his calloused hands.[34]

Whenever Milton supports a Christian theme or event with a classical myth, he usually invokes "the meaning" rather than "the name." The myths in the Latin poems are likely to be pure adornment, but those in the *Prolusions* and in early poems like the "Fair Infant"[35] often emphasize a Christian position. In *A Mask*, that amazing contamination of pagan and Christian material, the Spirit, who guides and

---

[31] Ronsard, *Oeuvres*, ed. C. Marty-Laveau (Paris, 1891), V, 368–69.

[32] D'Aubigné, *Oeuvres complètes*, ed. E. Réaume (Paris, 1877), II, 226–31.

[33] Ronsard, *Oeuvres* IV, 274.

[34] T. K. Dunseath, *Spenser's Allegory of Justice in Book Five of the Faerie Queene* (Princeton, 1968), pp. 47–59, 84–88, *et passim*.

[35] In Hermias' commentary on the myth of Orithyia in the *Phaedrus*, euhemeristic, physical, and ethical interpretations are suggested. The last reading is etymological and is interesting for Milton's central theme. The name Orithyia is derived from "orouo" + "theio" and "may be said to be a soul aspiring after celestial things"; see Plato, *Phaedrus*, ed. F. Astius (Leipzig, 1810), pp. 13–14. Unfortunately, this commentary was known only in manuscript in the seventeenth century. Of the manuscripts listed by P. Couvreur in *Hermiae Alexandrini in Platonis Phaedrum Scholia* (Paris, 1901), pp. x–xvi, two have interesting proveniences. Hamburg VII. 29, a fifteenth-century manuscript, once belonged to Lucas Holst, and Vienna IV, 327(n) was copied by Holst in 1622 from an Oxford codex which has since disappeared. Milton, of course, did not meet Holst until 1638, when he visited him at the Vatican Library and was shown his fine collection of Greek manuscripts and given two manuscripts from the scholar's pen. In his letter of March 30, 1639, to Holst Milton attributes his three years of study at Oxford as the probable reason for his friendliness to Englishmen. It would be agreeable to find some connection between Holst's Oxford years and some London teachers or acquaintances of the boy Milton, but my whole supposition is probably as absurd as Hermias' interpretation.

advises the elder brother (or memory) and the younger brother (or imagination) as they futilely seek to rescue their sister (or right reason) from the luxuries of pagan temptation, takes an ambiguous view of fable typical of the Renaissance and cautions his charges against too sophisticated an attitude toward the seemingly superstitious.

> Ile tell ye, 'tis not vain nor fabulous
> (Though so esteem'd by shallow ignorance)
> What the sage Poets taught by th' heavenly Muse
> Storied of old in high immortal vers
> Of dire Chimeras and enchanted Isles,
> And rifted Rocks whose entrance leads to hell,
> For such there be, but unbelief is blind (513–19).

In the course of the masque, Comus, whose myth is a Miltonic invention, recalls with suggestive malignancy the myths "of *Saturn's* crew" (805) and of Apollo's passion for Daphne (659–62). As befits his character, Comus looks at their dark readings; the elder brother, however, turns optimistically to the "old Schools of Greece" for symbolic Dianas and Minervas to illuminate the Christian virtue of "Saintly Chastity." The Spirit from the threshold of Jove's court, who has also been in Spenser's Garden of Adonis, finally reminds the audience that (thanks to Fulgentius), the myth of Cupid and Psyche is a Platonized version of a pious soul's union with Christ.

In *Paradise Lost,* contrary to his earlier practice, Milton is agnostic about classical myths and describes them as either "feigned" or "fabled." The classical and oriental myths that he uses to brighten a paragraph in biblical history seem to cluster either before the Fall or after the Repentance. In the fourth book as Satan, now burning with desire but sexually impotent, jealously watches Adam and Eve, Milton finds a metaphor in the Homeric moment when spring blossomed about the fecund couch of Zeus and Hera (497–501); but this fruitful symbol of the primeval hierogamy is made sterile not only by Satan's lustful leer but also by the earlier allusion to "Hesperian Fables true" (250) with its dire implication of a watchful serpent and of a diabolically perverted version of Genesis 2:9. The "silvan lodge" of the first pair may smile like "Pomona's Arbour" (V, 377–78), but the smile is sardonic, because in Book Nine (385–96) Eve is compared in a long simile to Pomona lusted after by protean Vertumnus and to Ceres seduced by Jove, who, like Satan, is able to assume for his salacious purposes a series of animal shapes. Other dark myths of a menacing nature are associated with Eve in Book Four. According to almost sixteen hundred years of tradition, she is placed side by side with Pandora (714–19), who brought evil but also hope into the world of men.[36] The garden in which she named the flowers is compared to the fields of Enna, the grove of Daphne, and the Nyseian Isle (268–79), lovely spots but filled with foreboding and reminding the seeker of the mysterious meanings of the rape of Proserpine, the transformation of Daphne, and the unhappy mother of Ham's eternally cursed son. The comparison in Book Five to Pomona's garden is further qualified by the almost immediate reference to the judgment of Paris in Mount Ida, an event that brought death into the Homeric world and all its woe. The amassing of these fragments of pagan myth undercuts any hopes about the success of Raphael's mission when, like the usually prosperous "Maia's Son," he descends (he is compared to the Phoenix-Christ symbol and is probably for Milton a foreshadowing of the Incarnation) to relate true Heavenly history in terms of Homeric story.

Once Adam and Eve have failed God but discovered the lustral possibility of prayer, Milton finds the mythical reflection in the appeal made by Deucalion and Pyrrha to Themis, or justice. This original analogue brushes aside the traditional comparisons of the Christian interpreters. In 1730 Nicolas Zobel summarized all the pagan theories of the Fall and found Adam represented in Prometheus and Eve in Pandora, Ate, and a bacchante shouting "Evoe." Any Renaissance comparativist knew that Deucalion was the pagan imitation of Noah, and Sandys relates that he built his ark on the advice of his father Prometheus, "which is divine providence."[37] In this instance, as in the earlier cases of the parentage of Euphrosyne or Comus, Milton is skeptical enough of the ordinary mythical equivalents to construct his own.

The mature Milton, who did not hold back from improvising Christian story, would hardly hesitate to invent pagan myth or twist its established meaning to suit his artistic pleasure. In *Paradise Regained* (IV,212–364), Milton, as Christ, places Greek culture second to that of the Jews and accepts the long preserved conclusion of the early apologists "That rather Greece from us these Arts deriv'd;/ Ill imitated." No seventeenth-century reader would have been perplexed by this decision because he would have noticed in *Paradise Lost* that Heaven was as

[36] Dora Panofsky and Erwin Panofsky, *Pandora's Box* (New York, 1965), pp. 11, 64–65, 150–53.
[37] Ovid, *Metamorphosis Englished* (Oxford, 1632), pp. 18–19; see Alexander Ross, *Mystagogus Poeticus*, pp. 368–69.

Hebrew as Hell was Greek or Latin. It is no slip of the tongue when Jehovah consigns the rebellious angels to Tartarus and not to Sheol (VI,52–54), or when Vulcan, assisted by a corps of metallurgists and smiths, constructs a parliament building with a Greek name. The kingdom ruled from this capitol would be better understood by Aeneas or Ulysses than by Dante. The hellions are Hellenes. The demonic heroes, for whom counterparts can be found in the *Iliad* or the *Aeneid,* have read the Greek rhetoricians and make the same sort of speeches that their literary ancestors made in the sea-swamps before Troy; they are all for Greek music and, if *Paradise Regained* is bundled in, for Greek cooking. They have just been through a long and painful conflict. Though they can be likened to Titans and Giants, they are also Achaeans, whose secret weapon, more dangerous than a wooden horse, has failed. Their leader, a sublime demagogue who would have amused Aristophanes, is able even as a serpent-tongued tempter to speak like an orator "renown'd/ In Athens or free Rome" (IX,670–71). Moreover, as a serpent he is the serpent of serpents, the primitive Greek divinity Ophion (X,580–82).[38] But he is somewhat more.

Unlike Spenser, Drayton, or Jonson, whose mythical figures move like men and women through allegorical episodes, Milton, writing variations on a mythical literal, can only use his non-Christian allusions as rephrasings. The gods who retreat in the "Nativity Ode" or who march "in perfect Phalanx to the Dorian mood" in the first book of *Paradise Lost* can do little more than stand outside what is literal and real. Orpheus[39] and Hercules,[40] famous as pagan types of Christ, are openly welcomed by their proper names in Milton's circle of metaphors. But there is even in Spenser an invisible choir; Hercules, Odysseus, Aeneas, and Circe move under more recent aliases in the pageants of the *Faerie Queene.* Ulysses, though somewhat dimmed to view, can also be seen in *Paradise Lost,* where his incognito is "Satan."[41]

Henry Reynolds, whose good friend Michael Drayton had turned the Ovidian myth of Endymion and Phoebe into a scientific lecture on celestial numbers and astrology, was also an ardent seeker of hidden meanings and praised in his *Mythomystes* "our best Mythologians" who

---

[38] M. Y. Hughes, *Ten Perspectives on Milton* (New Haven, 1965), pp. 196–219.

[39] D. C. Allen, "Milton and the Descent to Light," *JEGP,* LX (1961), 618–21.

[40] In addition to Jung and Waith's books see F. M. Krouse, *Milton's Samson and the Christian Tradition* (Princeton, 1949), pp. 44–45 *et passim.*

[41] John Steadman first noticed this possibility in "The Classical Hero: Satan and Ulysses," *MLR,* LII (1957), 81–85. It has been enormously expanded in M. Aryanpur, *"Paradise Lost* and the *Odyssey," Texas Studies in Literature and Language,* IX (1967), 15–66.

had brought out the moral virtues in Ulysses and other classical heroes.[42] By the time that Reynolds wrote this, Ulysses, cleansed of his ancient bad repute, had become a Renaissance model for moral yet sagacious young men. Probably without reading Homer, Shakespeare manages to frame his Ulysses in *Troilus and Cressida* in the approved manner. The wanderer's knowledge of men and manners, his political wisdom, and his celebrated patience are emphasized in the comedy; even his knowledge of astronomy, Calypso's gift, comes forward in the cynical speech on order delivered to a disorderly world. Milton is more cognizant of Ulysses' classical reputation than Shakespeare; his Ulysses is ambivalent, a dignified hero and the polytropic villain.

Not long before Comus, son of Circe by Bacchus, took up residence in a dark wood on the border of Wales and eluded the power of the Christian moly brought by Jehovah's Hermes to an English Ulysses and Eurylochus, Milton, who would have preferred to praise Ovid, admitted in the *Sixth Prolusion* that Homer was the "rising sun and morning star of more refined literature, with whom all learning like a twin was born."[43] In an earlier prolusion he had seen the golden chain of Homer's Zeus as a symbol of harmony;[44] in *Paradise Lost* he would use it to join earth to Heaven and liken it to Jacob's ladder, each stair of which was "mysteriously meant" (III,510–16). In the first elegy Ionian Homer and Virgil are equally ranked, and in the sixth elegy the praises are sung of a temperate Homer, who brought Ulysses safely through the blandishments of Circe and the sirens to control the shades of Hell with a libation. Homer sometimes illustrates or clarifies one of Milton's political or theological opinions. In the *First Defense*[45] Homer supports Solomon's theory of kingship; in the *Christian Doctrine*[46] he annotates a verse from Proverbs. When he is needed Homer takes Milton's part in a debate. On one occasion he talks about "leading each like person to his like, particularly to God Himself,"[47] a not surprising Christian attitude when one remembers that he demonstrates in his epic how "man's own free-will, self-corrupted, is the adequate and sufficient cause of his disobedience besides Fate."[48] Milton's imitations of Homer are familiar enough, and it is known that he owned de Sponde's edition and read the

[42] Reynolds, *Mythomystes*, in *Critical Essays of the Seventeenth Century*, ed. J. E. Spingarn (Bloomington, Indiana, 1957), I, 169.
[43] Milton, *Works* XII, 219.
[44] *Ibid.*, XII, 151.
[45] *Ibid.*, IV, 111.
[46] *Ibid.*, XIV, 175.
[47] *Ibid.*, III, 418.
[48] *Ibid.*, III, 441.

commentary of Eustathius and the continuation of Quintus Calaber. He also knew the writings of Proclus and Porphyry and owned a copy of the *Homeric Allegories* of Heraclitus of Pontus.

It is not improbable that Milton had just reread the *Odyssey* before he wrote *A Mask*. In the earlier "At a Vacation Exercise," Ulysses appears gravely as he listens to Demodocus at Alcinous' feast. In poetry after *Comus* the literal Ulysses appears only infrequently, although he is sometimes mentioned in the prose works as an example of virtue. In *Paradise Lost* allusions to the *Odyssey* or to its hero follow the manner of the other mythological allusions and usually have sinister connotations. When Sin first is shown she is more to be abhorred than "vexed Scylla bathing in the Sea" (II,661); when her father-lover soars into Chaos Milton recalls the occasion when "Ulysses on the Larbord shunned/ Charybdis, and by the other whirlpool steard" (II,1018–19). As the satanic serpent glides into Eden, the garden of Alcinous, "host of old Laertes Son" (IX,441) makes half the metaphor. Eve pays no heed when the same serpent rustles the leaves because she is used to beasts being "more duteous at her call/ Than at *Circean* call the Herd disguis'd" (IX,521–22). The attributes of the comparison are closely applied. The serpent is "disguis'd" and Eve is about to become a Hebraic Circe.

The unattractive Ulysses of Virgil, Philostratus, and Dictys of Crete is not found in the hero presented by Boccaccio,[49] Conti,[50] and Sandys;[51] however, no Renaissance man of letters would be unaware of the dark side of Ulysses. The curious *Moral Interpretations* were based on what Ulysses learned from his mistakes, and when Gesner translated it his Latin title, *Moralis interpretatio errorum Ulyssis*, has a possible ambiguity. When Alexander Ross, praised by Milton,[52] took Homer's hero in hand he was forced to admit, after listing eleven Christian actions of Ulysses, that no life is perfect; hence, Ulysses erred when he bore false witness against Palamedes, robbed the temple of Athena,

[49] Boccaccio, who stands back of Milton's remark in Elegy Six, describes Ulysses as a pattern of providentially enlightened virtues (*op. cit.*, p. 575).

[50] Carlo Dati refers Milton to Conti as if his work was well known to both of them. Milton *Works* XII, 309; see Conti, *Mythologiae*, pp. 492–93.

[51] Ovid, *Metamorphosis Englished* (Oxford, 1632), pp. 264–65. Sandys sees Circe's wand as a poor imitation of the rod of Moses and says: "Yet Ulysses could not lose his shape with the rest, who being fortifyed by immortall power was not subject to mutation." He enlarges this statement by equating Ulysses with the soul and his companions with the elements in a manner similar to that of Calderon.

[52] Milton's epigram on Ross, whose *Mystagogus Poeticus* was printed shortly after the lines were composed, describes Ross as a typical Renaissance bee making sweets out of sours (Milton, *Works* XVIII, 357).

dallied too long in Circe's bed, and failed to control his companions on several notable occasions. Nonetheless, he sees God's Providence effecting Ulysses' return to his kingdom and reminds the reader that "after we have fought the good fight, we shall at last obtain the crown of righteousnesse." It is this other Ulysses who seems to appear in *Paradise Lost*.

Satan, like Odysseus "a stranger," but in another sense, comes, in the course of his odyssey, to the edge of Cimmerian Hades and "swims or sinks or wades or creeps or flyes" until he arrives at the tent of King Chaos and his consort Night, who are as opposite to Alcinous and Arete as the "dark Pavilion" is to their eternal, golden house. The barbaric ruler of the rebelling elements is a mirror image of the great Homeric figure. His subjects are not contented Phaeacians, and the old Anarch of "falt'ring speech and visage incompos'd" is totally different from the king whose name meant "strength of mind"; moreover, he has no ear eager for Satan's earlier adventures. He has personally watched the greatest of Katabases. Unlike Ulysses, Satan is no war hero returning home but a defeated and discredited leader. Both heroes have only their wiles in common. The reversal of events suggests that Satan is the protagonist of an upside-down *Odyssey* and that the direct reference to Ulysses steering between Scylla and Charybdis, with which Satan's venture is compared, is Milton's way of telling the reader to read more closely. But the possibility of an inverted *Odyssey* is made even more plain when, at the beginning of the great tour through space, Satan meets Sin, whose Homeric disguise is that of "th'other whirlpool." To set the stage for this impressive recognition scene the Spanish theater of Calderón is useful.

In 1635 the *El mayor encanto amor* brought Ulysses into the land of Ariosto's Alcina, Spenser's Acrasia, and Tasso's Armida. The Circe of Calderón is both Aphrodite and Athena, and Ulysses becomes an infatuate like Aeneas or Rinaldo and is saved by the urgings of his comrades Antistes, Timates, Polydorus, and the ghost of Achilles. The "afeminado Griego," brought to his senses, imitates Aeneas and leaves Aeaea in secret as the dying Circe-Dido curses him and her luxurious palace collapses. This conflation of the Homeric and Virgilian stories was made into *Los encantos de la culpa* after Calderón had left secular life.

The Ulysses, or rather El Hombre, of the morality has the five Senses and the Understanding as his companions as they journey "through many storms confused and lost" on the Sea of Tribulations.

Sighting land, each Sense hopes for a congenial harbor, but Understanding, which has saved Ulysses from "the burning Troy of the world," prays for a desert. They come to harbor, and while Ulysses sleeps the Senses explore the island and encounter "la Culpa fiera" and her six handmaidens, who entertain them handsomely before turning them into animals. Urged by Understanding to pray and repent, Ulysses, "Christiano Ulises," is visited by Hermes, or Penance, who gives him a saving flower, similar to Milton's "Haemony," which has been dipped "in the Blood of the Lamb." Circe, or Sin, is forced to release the Senses; but while Understanding leads them back to the ship, Ulysses is brought into Circe's garden, where, like Eve and later like Christ, he is offered intellectual temptations, "ciencias prohibidas." Delighted with these intellectual advantages, he is feasting with Sin-Circe when Understanding and Penance enter, reveal the ephemerality of the cates of Circe compared to the Bread of Life, and urge the hero to remember his coming death. Ulysses, or El Hombre, departs as Sin curses him and her manor falls into ruin.[53]

Although Milton describes Sin like Scylla and makes her origin that of Athena *in malo,* she is also similar in some respects to Circe except that the dark Ulysses deceives her rather than she him. The meeting between the daughter-concubine and the father-lover is almost disastrous when Death threatens and the two massive heroes, who will be apocalyptically annihilated, almost engage in a fatal duel. This episode, as any Renaissance man who read about Ulysses in Conti would know, is similar to the extra-Homeric account of Ulysses' death.

In antiquity the contention between father and son begins with Cronus' assault on Uranus and Zeus' overthrow of Cronus. The mortal reflection of these divine contests occurs when Oedipus kills Laius on the road to Phocis. Ulysses was to meet a similar end in one branch of his legend. Parthenius, whose *Eroticon* was reprinted several times during the Renaissance, preserved the plot of the lost *Euryalus* of Sophocles in which Ulysses, prompted by a jealous Penelope, unwittingly killed his son by Evippe. "So Ulysses, as a punishment for his incontinence and lack of moderation, became the murderer of his own son; and not so long after died being wounded by his own offspring."[54] This blind allusion is illuminated by Hyginus, who records that Ulysses had two chil-

---

[53] Calderón, *El mayor encanto, Las comedias,* ed. J. J. Keil (Leipzig, 1830), I, 282–306; *Los encantos, Obras completas,* ed. A. V. Prat (Madrid, 1952), III, 406–21.

[54] Parthenius, *Eroticon,* ed. S. Gaselee (London, 1935), III; in the Renaissance this work was sometimes printed with Achilles Tatius, *Leucippe and Clitophon.*

dren by Circe, Nausithous and Telegonus, and that the latter, born after the hero left "Aenaria," was his murderer.[55] Conti gathered together various accounts of Ulysses' end and recites the Telegonus legend from Dictys of Crete, although he nods and calls the murderer Telemachus.[56]

Whether or not Milton read Parthenius, or Hyginus, or even Conti, cannot be established; but when he translated the fifth ode of Horace he plainly used James Bond's edition. In the commentary on III. 29.8 Bond tells the story of Ulysses' death to explain Horace's "Telegonus the parricide." It is related that Circe sent Telegonus to seek his father in Ithaca. Unaware that he had this son, but warned by a soothsayer of his death at his son's hand, Ulysses sent Telemachus into exile. He and Telegonus meet, fight, and Ulysses is fatally wounded. The heroic meeting may not have influenced Milton's fiction, but once again the facts are reversed. No bloody encounter occurs because Circe-Sin is there to prevent it. There are, however, interesting coincidences. In the Greek myth Telegonus, "driven by hunger," was "beginning to lay the fields waste," and news of this sent Ulysses in search of the stranger. In *Paradise Lost* hungry Death, who stood ready to devour his father, becomes his ally stuffed with promise: "Here ye shall be fed and fill'd/ Immeasurably, all things shall be your prey." Hearing these words, Death puts aside his dart because "his famine should be fill'd." In due course both Sin and Death, who are realities in Hell, ascend to the new world as clear allegorical personifications, and Death begins his universal banquet. Satan, after leaving the realm of Chaos, continues his odyssey through distant stars that seem "happy Isles." Within a few days the polytropic tempter would deceive an angel standing in the sun and, thanks to his knowledge of men and of women, rejoin his daughter-wife and son-grandson in a new Ithaca.

Milton had good reason for rejecting the seventeenth century's high estimate of Ulysses' moral character and the lessons to be learned from his allegorical adventures. The Hebrews had more impressive heroes: Joshua, "whom the Gentiles Jesus call," and *"Gideon and Jeptha and the Shepherd lad."* These heroes were historical; their virtues needed no interpreters; and they prepared the way for the real God. The great figures of Athens and Rome were poor seconds, and the lessons to be drawn from their myths were as worthless as all second-rate things. Milton's mature undervaluing of pagan myth as something virtuously positive is paralleled by his use of allegory. Unlike Ariosto,

[55] *Ibid.,* CVIII, CXI.
[56] Conti, *Mythologiae,* p. 492.

Tasso, or his beloved Spenser, he is most frugal in its use. There is allegory in *A Mask* and in some of the other youthful poems, but then it practically vanishes. One word moral equivalents can, of course, be attached to angels and demons, but they are essentially literal. Mammon is mildly symbolical and so is Belial, but their counterparts unquestionably sat in Charles' Parliament. Figures like Raphael and Michael walked the halls of Christ's but were probably not seen as symbolic persons. Actually the interest in myth and in allegory was waning during Milton's lifetime.

The Elizabethan fondness for mythological decoration or for the literary expansion of ancient myth was beginning to wear out as John Donne was writing his youthful poems. George Herbert may once have been a victim of the contagion, but he was shortly cured. After 1651 Henry Vaughan hardly knows a classical divinity. Other poets of the seventeenth century are still touched by the shadow rather than the substance of the obsession. The spirit of Lucian came from its tomb sometime before Fontenelle overheard the illustrious dead talking together, for in 1650 *L'Odyssée de Homère ou les avantures d'Ulysse en vers burlesques* could be bought in Paris, and in very few years Loredano's *L'Iliade giocosa* was printed in Venice. By 1648 Paul Scarron had begun to publish *Le Virgile Travesty en Vers Burlesque,* and in 1664 *Homer a la Mode* was in the London bookstalls. Bishop Sprat was not particularly daring when he urged English poets to find "in the *Works of Nature* an inexhaustible Treasure of *Fancy,* and *Invention,*" reminding them that:

> The *Wit* of the *Fables* and *Religions* of the *Ancient World* is well nigh consum'd: They have already serv'd the *Poets* long enough; and it is now high time to dismiss them; especially seing they have this perculiar *imperfection,* that they were only *Fictions* at first: whereas *Truth* is never so well express'd or amplify'd, as by those Ornaments which are *Tru* and Real in themselves.[57]

The new century had hardly opened before Swift wrote his burlesque of the almost holy myth of Baucis and Philemon, and John Gay, punning on one of the familiar epithets for the chaste Diana, described a not too classical town consecrated to the filthy goddess Cloacina. A great deal had been said and written between the death of Milton and Gay's *Trivia* which had helped divest the myths and the poets of antiquity of their Adamic wisdom or divine inspiration. A new school of rationalists was looking at the documents of the ancient religions with unblurred

[57] Sprat, *History of the Royal Society of London* (London, 1667), pp. 413–14.

vision and sensing in the diffusion of myth an aspect of man's intellectual and cultural progress. The allegoristic and symbolic modes of interpretation, which had become almost paradigmatic, were increasingly unhelpful as men of letters began to assume idiosyncratic formulas which were almost modern.

IV

About four years before Milton died Benedict Spinoza looked with a cold eye on the myths of the Hebrews but accepted them as "extremely necessary . . . for the masses whose wits are not potent enough to perceive things clearly and distinctly."[58] The apologists for the mythology of Greece and Rome had been saying virtually the same thing, but with a different emphasis, for centuries. Without speaking too loudly, Spinoza was implying that mythologies belonged to the primitive stage of any religion and that anyone in his generation who clung to mythology was as primitive as those peoples with whom it originated. Bossuet, who subscribed to a kind of naive seventeenth-century euhemerism which enabled him to intercalate, as others had before him, the heroes of the mythology with those of the Old Testament, informs the Dauphin that the allegorization of myth into natural processes indicated the collapse of paganism;[59] nonetheless, Bossuet is disturbed by Huet's researches for fear that others will agree with those who have already suggested that "all religion is in pagan books and Christianity has naught to teach men."[60] Bossuet in his way, just as Milton in his, was attempting to fend off what must have been the distressing possibility that religion, just like the Augustinian history of a people, had an infancy, a virile age, and a death. Two French rationalists, the Protestant atheist Bayle and the Catholic atheist Fontenelle, were pushing the minds of men in this new direction.

In impressively written popular pieces, the *De l'origine des fables* and the *Digression sur les anciens et les modernes,* Corneille's clever nephew and biographer Fontenelle revealed that all primitive peoples, be they Lapps, Iroquois, or Greeks, had a similar psychology of religious experience. Confronted and baffled by the phenomena of nature, they

[58] Spinoza, *Tractatus theologico-politicus,* ed. C. H. Bruder (Leipzig, 1846), III, 83.

[59] Bossuet, *Oeuvres* (Paris, 1847), I, 245; later (pp. 278–79) he argues that the Greeks praised Homer because he taught men to live well and celebrated them as superior to the Asiatic barbarians; hence, the divinities supporting the Greeks are the equivalents of virtue, whereas those backing the Trojans are vicious.

[60] Bossuet, *Correspondance* (Paris, 1912), IV, 335–37.

only knew that they could not understand it and that it did not depend on them. Since primitive minds were too undeveloped to grasp even the more modest laws of causality, they assumed the existence of superior and invisible beings responsible for all natural phenomena and all human experience. In the early stages of a religion these beings, like Homer's, are likely to be crude and brutish; however, as a primitive people became more civilized, their gods improved.[61] Fontenelle found it curious that myths continued to be popular long after they lost their pious significance. When he thought of his own country as fourth-century Greece or imperial Rome, he was helped to an explanation. Myths were pleasant to hear and to tell; moreover, priests, mindful of their professional interests, succeeded in explaining myths with the same sort of irrationality that had kept the myth alive. The doubts cast upon ancient religion and its mythology found a place, of course, in the contemporary discussion of the virtues of the ancients and the moderns; but Fontenelle's witty and popular style brought all of this new cynicism to the attention of the average reader, who had no stomach for the scholarship of a Van Dale or the philosophical subtlety of a Spinoza. But Bayle helped too.

In the first edition of Pierre Bayle's *Dictionaire historique et critique,* John Milton received a short notice which, thanks to the publication of Toland's biography, was doubled in the second edition. Bayle's text can wear a fairly somber face (though this is not always the case), but his footnotes, which flood the margins, are filled with scandal and backstage mirth. Had Milton lived to consult this learned and hilarious encyclopedia, he might have been amused by Bayle's account of the nepenthes, which "Jove-born Helena" got in Egypt, and by Bayle's salacious remarks about the queen's virginal exploits with Theseus. Milton would not have been so pleased, perhaps, when a few folios farther along he came on Bayle's account of Hercules, the pagan Samson, "who passed for the son of Jove and Alcmena." The euhemeristic emphasis present in the verb "passed" became louder as Bayle related the demigod's prodigious appetite for food, drink, and women and reported that, considering Hercules' feats at table and in bed, "some have doubted

---

[61] Fontenelle, *Oeuvres* III, 270–96. It is rather interesting that the germ of Hume's notion of primitive religious psychology as expressed in the *Natural History of Religion* is here. As late as 1758, Hume argued that "allegory really has a place in the heathen mythology" because anyone can see the myths themselves stand on allegory; but one should not expect perfect allegory from ignorant superstition, "there being no work of genius that requires a nicer hand, or has been more rarely executed with success": *Essays* (London, 1788), II, 381–83. Voltaire (*Oeuvres* XXXIII, 167) agrees that the classical allegorists were men of genius, far superior to those of his day and were the instructors of the Fathers; he could, and probably does, have his tongue in his cheek.

his heroic achievements." With insinuations of this sort Bayle converts one of the most famous of pagan types of Christ into a Greek Falstaff. To destroy the myth more thoroughly he remembers that the hero wiggled his ears as he ate, and, to the tacit demolition of the disciples of Stillingfleet or Gale, adds, "It is said that he was three days in the belly of a whale and that he came out safe and sound having lost nothing but his hair."

In spite of this Rabelaisian treatment of myth not all men ceased to sort through the pagan pantheon for Old Testament faces. Samuel Shuckford found unfallen Adam in Plato's account of the Golden Age and disobedient Adam when Porus wanders drunkenly in the garden of Zeus. In *The Sacred and Prophane History of the World Connected* (1728), he considered how well his views were supported by the early apologists and concluded that the fragments of the ancients properly interpreted supported, rather than contradicted, the Bible and were "an additional Argument of its uncorrupted Truth and Antiquity."[62] Shuckford's book did not want popularity, and it was joined shortly by Guillaume Lavaur's *Conférence de la fable avec l'histoire sainte,* a great annex to Huet which was reprinted as late as 1835. Lavaur finds the forty years in the Wilderness in the myth of the Argonauts; Abraham and Sara, in Baucis and Philemon; Job, in Niobe. But his theories had already been questioned by Euhemerus' great French disciple Abbé Antoine Banier in a brief monograph of 1711 completed in the definitive version of 1738–40 as *Explication historique des fables, où l'on découvre leur origine et leur conformité avec l'histoire ancienne.*

Banier, by finding sixteen reasons for the origin of fable, cogently refined the suppositions of Fontenelle, even though he then proceeded, to the joy of Herman von der Hardt, to find fairly commonplace historical events beneath the cover of some of the most lurid ancient myths. His interpretations, though often very shaky, were so overwhelming that centuries of theological, physical, and Christian readings were simply submerged. In his opening theoretical chapters Banier considered the problems of the early Christian apologists and their pagan opponents, who had to invent "allegorical explanations" to defend their theology. Truth has now come into its own, but Banier, noticing that mythology is still the subject of poets, dramatists, and artists, urges its understanding and preservation, provided it is detached from "moralizing and trivial allegories." He warns mythologists against the interpretive methods of

[62] Shuckford, *Sacred and Profane History* (London, 1743), pp. xxv–vi.

the Neo-platonists and the "atheist Stoics," with whom he associates Spinoza; nevertheless, he is ready to grant that "sometimes" there is allegory. He treats the opinions of Kircher and Bochart with a certain delicacy and praises the latter scholar for the premises he had given to other euhemerists like the fabulous Jean le Clerc. He is less cautious with Thomassin, Huet, Clasen, Fourmont, and "the author of Homer Hebraizing," ingenious men who find Christian doctrine or Old Testament history in every primitive legend. They are interpreters who begin with a theory which they attempt to establish by forced comparisons. Fables are unquestionably "beautiful veils," but they are hardly concerned with the fermentation of wine, the growth of grain, the marriage of earth and sky, or the inner combats of the human passions. To some of these veils poets may have added ornaments, but Banier proposes to strip them away to expose a more simple and lovely truth.[63]

Banier's exhaustively documented theory was welcomed in England, where the deistic disciples of Herbert of Cherbury had already altered the conventional view of mythological religion.[64] By mid-century, when Warburton's *The Divine Legation of Moses Demonstrated* was completed, seventeenth-century radical theological opinion was practically episcopal. The traditional notion that speculative wisdom was mythologized and could be demythologized to unhull a pristine truth was hardly doubted. Warburton assumes that the early pagan thinkers were sparing in the use of types and allegory and that their successors "allegorized all the traditional stories of their gods into natural, moral, and divine entities."[65] He deplores the demythologizers who search for "mysterious wisdom" or biblical history; "those who esteem the fables a corruption of pagan history appear in general to be right."[66] In spite of his objection the bishop likes and reprints the conventional Christian interpretation, "which fits the fable," of Apuleius' myth of Cupid and Psyche; however, he is clever enough to inquire "did the author write the tale for the moral or did the critic find the moral for the tale?"

Nay, when a rage of allegorizing happens to prevail, as it did a century or two ago, the author himself will be either tempted or obliged, without the commentator, to encourage this delusion. *Ariosto* and *Tasso*, writers of the highest reputation, one of whom wrote after the *Gothic* romances, as the other after the *classic* fables,

[63] Banier, *La mythologie et les fables expliquées par l'histoire* (Paris, 1764), I, 14–15, 22–35.
[64] See F. Manuel, *The Eighteenth Century Confronts the Gods* (Cambridge, 1959), pp. 57–84.
[65] Warburton, *Divine Legation,* ed. R. Hurd (London, 1837), II, 527; I, 574–81.
[66] *Ibid.,* I, 463–65.

without ever concerning themselves about any other moral than what the natural circumstances of the story conveyed; yet to secure the success of their poems, they submitted, in compliance to fashion and false taste to the ridiculous drudgery of inventing a kind of posthumous allegory, and sometimes more than one; that the reader himself might season their fables to his own taste.[67]

Warburton's temporal estimate is incorrect by a century, but his remark about "fashion and false taste" points backward to an essay that Pope called "Bossu's admirable treatise of the Epic Poem."

In the *Traité du poème epique* (1675), epic poets are said to be as important for morality as divines were for theology. In primitive times the divine clarified the nature of the Absolute by distributing its attributes among numerous deities; the poet, to the contrary, gathered all possible human virtues and perfection and presented them in the person of his protagonist.[68] The honest epic provides instruction for the readers in its allegorical actions, which are "a tissue or suite of metaphors" collected into one body. Le Bossu piles up examples of ethical allegory in Homer and Virgil[69] and finds little that is comparable in other classical epics lacking "deguisements et allegories."[70] Virgil's allegories are more sophisticated than those of Homer because he wrote for an advanced culture; even Homer's literal would not have been tolerated in the age of Augustus. In seventeenth-century France taste was changing and in supporting this method—in fact. in assuming that the epic was written around a preconceived moral center—Le Bossu realized that he was not without opposition.

The taste of antiquity both sacred and profane, both Greek and Barbarian, for fables, parables, and allegories (all the same) gave a great liberty to ancient poets that moderns do not have and make beauties in Homer that would not be considered so were they found in modern works. These also expose this poet to criticisms, resulting more from our own ignorance than his fault. It was a practice in this age to hide mysteries from people and not explain allegories. The wisemen made an especial study of discovering the hidden sense, and this penetration was a very considerable part of their doctrine. Our age, so enlightened and so curious, has neglected this knowledge.[71]

Le Bossu's notion of the ethical allegories in the epic is a far softer principle than that of the ancient allegorizers of Homer or of the sixteenth-century disciples of the medieval interpreters of Ovid and

---

[67] *Ibid.*, I, 326–27.
[68] Le Bossu, *Traité du poème epique* (Paris, 1708), p. 7.
[69] *Ibid.*, pp. 470–532.
[70] *Ibid.*, p. 29.
[71] *Ibid.*, pp. 124–27.

Virgil; but his critical views were impressive and, like Boileau, Rapin, André Dacier, and Segraïs, he helped instruct the English.

One of Le Bossu's most fervent English converts was, of course, John Dryden, who salutes him in the preface to *Troilus and Cressida*;[72] a score of years later Dryden regrets that Spenser, otherwise a good poet, had no chance to read Le Bossu's epic laws.[73] Dryden's devotion is not difficult to understand because he agreed with Le Bossu before he knew him, asserting in the "Defense of the Essay of Dramatic Poesy" that "moral truth is the mistress of the poets as much as of the philosopher."[74] Dryden's "moral truth" is similar to Le Bossu's "deguisements et allegories," but both principles are less exacting and more generally applied than Landino's close and unrelenting moralization of the *Aeneid*. Although Dryden was endorsing as late as "A Parallel of Poetry and Painting" Le Bossu's mischief-making theory that the better epic poets adjusted their fable to a preestablished moral pattern,[75] he was very temperate when he wrote about the moralization of epic in his preface to his translation of the *Aeneid*. A hero's piety, magnanimity, constancy, and patience arouse, Dryden assumes, admiration and emulation; his opposite characteristics turn a reader the other way.

> The courage of Achilles is proposed to imitation, not his pride and disobedience to his general, nor his brutal cruelty to his dead enemy, nor the selling of his body to his father. We abhor these actions while we read them; and what we abhor we never imitate. The poet only shows them like rocks or quicksands, to be shunned.[76]

Although he would mock Le Bossu's epic prescriptions in "Of the Art of Sinking in Poetry" and cynically define the moral allegory as something "you may extract out of the Fable afterwards at your leisure: be sure you strain them sufficiently," Pope introduced his translation of the *Odyssey* with the *Traité* epitomized. Both of his Homeric translations are supplied with interesting critical apparatus, and the *Iliad* is furnished with an important preface. In this essay Pope, having sepa-

[72] Dryden, *Essays*, ed. W. P. Ker (Oxford, 1900), I, 211.
[73] "Dedication of the *Aeneis*," ibid., II, 220.
[74] *Ibid.*, I, 121.
[75] *Ibid.*, II, 127–28. Although Le Bossu's views were accepted in France by Anne Dacier in her preface to her translation of Homer and by critics like Antoine Houdar de La Motte and Henri Richer, they were stoutly opposed in 1753 by Charles Batteux in *Cours de Belles-Lettres* (Paris, 1773), who, though admitting that the ancients were infatuated by allegory, observed that all historical figures have some moral emphases. Le Bossu's popular notion is, he thought, simply based on names. Alexander and Octavius Caesar would be as useful to moralists as Achilles and Agamemnon. "Can anyone describe them without mentioning their actions or characteristics?" (II, 62–80).
[76] Dryden, *op. cit.* II, 159.

rated the epic fable, to the consequent horror of John Dennis,[77] into the probable, the allegorical, and the marvellous, extends his remarks on allegories.

If we reflect upon those innumerable Knowledges, those Secrets of Nature and Physical Philosophy which *Homer* is generally suppos'd to have wrapt up in his *Allegories,* what a new and ample Scene of Wonder may this Consideration afford us? How fertile will that Imagination appear, which was able to cloath all the Properties of Elements, the Qualifications of the Mind, the Virtues and Vices, in Forms and Persons; and to introduce them into Actions agreeable to the Nature of the Things they shadow'd? This is a Field in which no succeeding Poets could dispute with *Homer;* and whatever Commendations have been allow'd them on this Head, are by no means for their Invention in having enlarg'd his Circle, but for their Judgment in having contracted it. For when the Mode of Learning chang'd in following Ages, and Science was deliver'd in a plainer manner, it then became as reasonable in the more modern Poets to lay it aside, as it was in Homer to make use of it. And perhaps it was no unhappy Circumstance for *Virgil;* that there was not in his Time that Demand upon him of so great an Invention, as might be capable of furnishing all those Allegorical Parts of a Poem.[78]

Pope's readiness to agree to the existence of allegory in a primitive Homer resulted in the moral index to his *Odyssey* and the fuller moral and physical analysis of the *Iliad.*[79] It is a learned attitude hardly in keeping with the more advanced views of the early eighteenth century.

Sometime before 1711 Joseph Trapp, who became the first Professor of Poetry at Oxford in 1708, presented his judgment of allegory in what might have been his inaugural lecture. He confessed to his lack of interest in fables or in their allegorical meaning. Let "the mythologists" seek out the meaning of the two peaks of Parnassus, the symbolical number nine of the nine muses, the wings and hoofprints of Pegasus. These are the "stains of poetry" and the products of a paganism which infected true religion and should now be abandoned. He urged his

[77] John Dennis, who had sustained Le Bossu's doctrine of the preconceived moral in a letter of December 5, 1716, to Richard Blackmore, attacks Pope for, among other things, distinguishing these three aspects of the *Iliad.* See *The Critical Works,* ed. E. N. Hooker (Baltimore, 1943), II, 115–61.

[78] Pope, *Poems,* ed. M. Mack (London and New Haven, 1967), VII, 6.

[79] In his first observation on the *Iliad* Pope complains that commentators on Homer had been more interested in setting down philosophical, historical, geographical, and allegorical remarks "rather any thing than Critical or Poetical." He castigates those pedants who are always looking for new or uncommon meanings and "are apt to fancy Two Meanings for want of knowing One." He speaks of Eustathius as not free of "some of the foregoing Censures," although he asked William Broome to translate any of the Bishop's comments concerned with Homer's art or beauties. "What are allegorical, if obvious and ingenious, abstract; if far-fetched, omit." See *Works,* eds. W. Elwin and W. J. Courthope (London, 1871–89), VIII, 33.

audience to despise these legends and remove the alloy of falsehood from both poetry and religion.[80] Later, in the preface to his translation of Virgil, Trapp stated that the moral found by Le Bossu in the *Iliad* was "too narrow and particular to be the *Grand Moral* of an Heroic Poem," but there is for him a difference between allegory and moralization.[81]

Writing about the same time that Trapp was speaking, Joseph Addison, who admitted to reading Le Bossu, hoped for pardon if he failed to pick out "the particular MORAL which is inculcated in *Paradise Lost*" though he is sure that there never was a heroic poem "from whence one great Moral may not be deduced."[82] Within less than six months he praises Tickell's "On the Prospect of Peace" because he has not "amused himself with Fables out of the Pagan Theology" or compared beautiful women to Venus or Helen. What the burlesquing of the mythology had indicated about its loss of reverence is openly announced by Addison.

> When we are at School it is necessary for us to be acquainted with the System of Pagan Theology, and may be allowed to enliven a Theme, or point an Epigram with an Heathen God; but when we would write a manly Panegyric, that should carry in it all the Colours of Truth, nothing can be more ridiculous than to have recourse to our *Jupiters* and *Junos*.

Myths are usable, Addison concedes, in mock heroics, but "for a Christian Author to write in the Pagan Creed . . . would be downright Puerility, and unpardonable in a Poet that is past Sixteen."[83]

Addison's 1712 statement seems to be a turnabout in light of some of his earlier literary performances. In 1709, for instance, he had rewritten Prodicus' Herculean parable[84] and composed an allegorical[85] disquisition on some lines in the *Iliad*. In the same year Richard Steele had followed suit with an essay on the famous cestus of Venus.[86] There is a certain amount of wit in all these pieces, but the symbolic equivalents are carefully repeated. About the same time John Hughes defines allegory as the "Fairy Land of Poetry," which is both visionary and "typical" to an almost shocking degree "if the Mind did not attend to the mysticke

---

[80] Trapp, *Praelectiones poeticae* (Oxford, 1711), p. 43.

[81] Virgil, *The Works Translated into English Blank Verse*, trans. J. Trapp (London, 1735), pp. xliii–iv.

[82] *The Spectator*, ed. D. Bond (Oxford, 1965), III, 390–91.

[83] *Ibid.*, IV, 361–64; Steele imitates both Cebes and Boccalini, *ibid.*, IV, 324–30.

[84] *The Tatler* (London, 1759), II, 366–72.

[85] *Ibid.*, III, 203–8.

[86] *Ibid.*, III, 209–13.

Sense." He assembles the enchanting women of Homer, Virgil, Ariosto, Tasso, and Spenser into one symbolic tableau before he brings in as their male counterpart the Comus of Milton. Addison had praised the Sin and Death of *Paradise Lost* as superb allegories, and Hughes finds them to be examples that do not strain the imagination. He wishes that the critics had published rules for allegory, but in lieu of such a canon the reader can observe Mr. Addison at work.[87] The indefatigable Richard Blackmore, while admitting that all myth is primitive and allegorical,[88] and while agreeing with Hughes that Milton's Sin and Death are "elegant instances," feels that Ariosto and Spenser "have run too far into allegory."[89] By 1725 the allegorization of myth and the symbolized universe were breathing hard, but they were not yet ready for the knacker; nevertheless, it would not be too long before myth would become folklore, and allegory and symbol, once a kind of lingua franca, would become completely idiosyncratic. But myth and allegory found an English Don Quixote in Thomas Blackwell, who fought a last-ditch defense before the critical generation of Samuel Johnson ousted the gods and goddesses from the land of literature.

In his *An Enquiry into the Life and Writings of Homer,* Blackwell defined myth as a "delicate" and "majestic" means of expressing the effects "of those natural powers" on man's body and mind[90] and also as a way of inculcating morality.[91] His *Letters upon Mythology* (1747) are actually a series of attempts to argue for a mysterious but generalized philosophical understanding of myth. "The wise and learned" among the

---

[87] E. Spenser, *The Works,* ed. J. Hughes (London, 1750), I, xix–xli.

[88] "An Essay upon Epic Poetry," *Essays upon Several Subjects* (London, 1716), I, 22, 27–78. "Some important moral should arise from the Whole Fable" (p. 76).

[89] *Ibid.,* I, 41–42. In "A Discourse upon Epick Poetry," in F. Fenelon, *The Adventures of Telemachus the Son of Ulysses* (London, 1720), Alexander Ramsay observed that although his religion was "a Heap of Fables," we owe to Homer the personalizing of divine attributes, human passions, and physical causes (p. xxxvi). In his subsequent "Of the Theology of the Antients" appended to his *The Travels of Cyrus* (London, 1727) the key to Egyptian myths is said to be metaphysical, whereas science is the basis of Greek myth (II, 15). Ramsay finds Christian doctrine everywhere but attributes it to a general diffusion and not to Hebraic influence (II, 143–44). His views (II, 22–23) on poetry and allegory can be repeated. "Poetry deifies all the various Parts of Nature, and gives Spirit to Bodies, as well as Body to Spirits. It expresses the Operations and Properties of Matter by the Actions and Passions of such invisible Powers as the Pagans supposed to be the Directors of all the Motions and Events that we see in the Universe. The Poets pass in a Moment from Allegory to the literal Sense and from the literal Sense to Allegory; from real Gods to fabulous Deities and this occasions that jumble of their Images, that Absurdity in their Fictions, and that Indecorum in their Expressions, which are so justly condemned by the Philosophers." For an enlightening essay on this subject, one can turn to Albert J. Kuhn, "English Deism and the Development of Romantic Mythological Syncretism," *PMLA,* LXXI (1956), 1094–1116.

[90] Blackwell, *Enquiry* (London, 1735), p. 142.

[91] *Ibid.,* p. 213.

ancients did not believe in gods who were like men and who had adventures;[92] hence, for them mythology was "instruction conveyed in a Tale," or, on occasion, in signs and symbols.[93] Fables have latent truths but not necessarily the truths discovered by Banier,[94] Pluché, Voss, Bochart, Huet, Fourmont, and Prideaux.[95] Some modern poets like Ariosto, Marino, and Tasso "sit gravely down and compose a moral to each book which they call the Allegory" and some readers find in this a "double Pleasure,"[96] but Blackwell has doubts. His skepticism about modern allegorical poets does not extend to the interpreters of ancient texts, although there are some who say that they "find out Meanings and Mysteries which the Authors or their Cotemporaries never thought of." But few men, even Francis Bacon, can read these fables without sensing a hidden meaning.[97] Every myth has a gown of triple tissue, "a Tale, monstrous, yet moving, of feigned allegorical Personages," who act and talk as to "represent *Causes,* narrate *Transactions,* and irresistibly convey *Instruction* to the Mind, by striking the Fancy, and winning the heart."[98] But this is generalized, in "Out-Lines," and details must not be demanded. "The minute Application must be therefore left, as Religion was of old, to every one's own particular Turn and Extent of Capacity."[99]

Blackwell's modest propositions are shared by his contemporaries. Mark Aikenside prefaced his "Hymn to the Naiades" with a description of these powers of nature, who give motion to the air, nourish plants, maintain commerce and maritime strength, furnish healing waters, and provide "the true inspiration which temperance only can receive in opposition to the enthusiasm of more licentious poets."[100] But the question of whether pagan myth had *this* meaning or *that* meaning or *no* meaning at all was dissolving in the greater question of the place of classical mythology in English literature.

Blackwell had not yet published his letters on mythology when the seventeenth-century opinion of Bishop Sprat was restated with eighteenth-century elegance by William Melmoth. In a letter to Clytander dated February 8, 1739, but not printed until 1742, Melmoth complains

[92] Blackwell, *Letters* (London, 1748), pp. 63–64.
[93] *Ibid.,* p. 70.
[94] *Ibid.,* pp. 119–31, 216.
[95] *Ibid.,* pp. 232–45.
[96] *Ibid.,* p. 184.
[97] *Ibid.,* p. 186.
[98] *Ibid.,* p. 82.
[99] *Ibid.,* pp. 409–10.
[100] *A Collection of Poems by Several Hands,* ed. R. Dodsley (London, 1766), VI, 2.

that the gods of Greece and Rome continue to be worshipped in modern verse, a confession that "fancy is enlivened by superstition."

> I will own, however, that I think there is something ridiculous in this unnatural adoption, and that a modern poet makes but an awkward figure with his antiquated gods. When the pagan system was sanctified by popular belief, a piece of machinery of that kind, as it had the air of probability, afforded a very striking manner of celebrating any remarkable circumstance, or raising any common one. But now that this superstition is no longer supported by vulgar opinion, it has lost its principal grace and efficacy, and seems to be, in general, the most cold and uninteresting method in which a poet can work up his sentiments. . . . To speak my sentiments in one word, I would leave the gods in full possession of allegorical and burlesque poems: in all others I would never suffer them to make their appearance in person and as agents but to enter only in simile or allusion.[101]

Melmoth defines the new direction of taste already exemplified in literary performance. Samuel Johnson, who will eventually blame Milton, Dryden, Waller, Prior, Granville, Pope, Thomson, and even Gay for their poetic penchant for classical myth, was in this decade already on the edge of Melmoth's conclusion. It is implied in the prologue to *Irene* which asks pardon of "intriguing wits" and "beauties":

> Nor Gods his Heroes, nor his Lovers Fools.
> If no wild Draught depart from Reason's Rules,

After almost two thousand years the Christian apologists had lost and had won.

[101] Melmoth, *The Letters of Sir Thomas Fitzosborne on Several Subjects* (London, 1795), pp. 298–99, 302.

❦ BIBLIOGRAPHY ❧

The titles and dates of first publications are given in the text; the items listed here are those consulted and cited in the notes. There is, consequently, a difference in title and date. Usually full titles are given in the text; short titles are frequently used in the notes and in this listing. When the native name of an author could be found, it is given and followed by his Latinized name in brackets.

I. SOURCES BEFORE 1800

The following abbreviations are used for J. P. Migne, *Patrologiae cursus completus*: *PG* = *Series graeca*, Paris, 1857–1903; *PL* = *Series latina*, Paris, 1844–1903.

Abelard, P. *Introductio ad theologiam, PL* CLXXVIII. 982–114. *Sermones, PL* CLXXVIII. 379–610. *Theologia Christiana, PL* CLXXVIII. 1123–330.

Addison, J. *Miscellaneous Works in Verse and Prose.* London, 1726. ——, and R. Steele. *The Spectator,* ed. D. Bond, Oxford, 1965.

Aelianus *Varia historia,* ed. R. Hercher. Leipzig, 1870.

Agostini (Augustinus), L. *Le gemme antiche figurate.* Rome, 1657.

Agrippa, H. C. *De incertitudine et vanitate omnium scientiarum et artium liber.* Leyden, 1643. *Opera omnia.* Lyons, n.d.

Agustin, A. *Antiquitatum Romanarum Hispanarumque in nummis dialogi XI,* trans. A. Schott. Antwerp, 1617. *Dialoghi sopra le medaglie,* trans. D. Sada. Rome, 1698. *Dialogos de las medallas.* Tarragona, 1587.

Ainsworth, R. and J. Ward *Monumenta vetustatis Kempiana ex vetustis scriptoribus illustrata.* London, 1700.

Alberti, L. B. *Opera inedita,* ed. G. Mancini. Florence, 1890. *Opusculi morali.* Venice, 1568.

Alciati, A. *Emblemata.* Leyden, 1593.

Alcuin *Carmina,* ed. E. Dümmler. Berlin, 1891.

312

Aldrovandi, U. *Le statue antiche che in Roma . . . descritta.* Venice, 1542.

Aleandro (Aleander), G. *Antiquae tabulae marmoreae, solis effigie symbolisque exculptae, accurata explicatio.* Paris, 1617. *Navis ecclesiam referentis symbolum in veteri gemma annulari insculptum . . . explicatione illustratum.* Rome, 1626.

Alexander ab Alexandro *Genialium dierum libri sex.* Rome, 1522.

Alexandre, Nöel. *Conformité des Cérémonies Chinoises avec l'Idolatrie Grecque et Romaine.* Paris, 1700.

Allacci (Allatius), L. *De patria Homeri.* Lyons, 1640.

Ammianus Marcellinus *Rerum gestarum libri,* ed. V. Gardthausen. Stuttgart, 1967.

Amyraut, M. *Brief traité de predestination.* Samur, 1634.

Ancona, C. d' *La Roma antica,* ed. C. Huelsen. Rome, 1907.

Andreae, J. V. *Mythologiae Christianae sive virtutum et vitiorum vitae humanae imaginum libri tres.* Strassburg, 1619.

Anecdota Graeca, ed. F. Matranga. Rome, 1850.

Angelocrator, D. *Chronologiae.* Hamburg, 1597.

Angeloni, F. *L'historia Augusta . . . illustrata con la verita dell' antiche medaglie.* Rome, 1641.

Annio (Annius) of Viterbo, G. *Antiquitatum variarum volumina XVII.* Paris, 1515.

Anthologia Latina, ed. A. Riese. Leipzig, 1868.

Apianus, P. and A. Bartholomaeus *Inscriptiones sacrosanctae vetustatis.* Ingolstadt, 1534.

Apin, J. P. *De religione Senecae.* Wittenberg, 1692.

Apollodorus *Bibliotheca,* ed. and trans., J. Frazer. London, 1921.

Apuleius, L. *Metamorphoseon libri XI,* ed. J. van der Vliet. Leipzig, 1897.

Aquinas, T. *Summa theologica.* Turin, 1901.

Ariosto, L. *Orlando Furioso in English Heroical Verse,* trans. J. Harington. London, 1591. *Orlando Furioso . . . dell annotazioni de' piu' celebri autori che sopra esso hanno scritto.* Venice, 1730.

Arminius, J. *Opera.* Leyden, 1629.

Arnobius *Adversus gentes, PL* V. 714–1290.

Arrianus, F. *Anabasis,* ed. C. Abicht. Leipzig, 1871.

Ascham, R. *The Scholemaster,* ed. E. Arber. London, 1927.

Athenaeus *Deipnosophistae,* ed. A. Meinke. Leipzig, 1858–59.

Athenagoras *Legatio pro Christianis, PG* VI. 889–971.

Auctores mythographi Latini, ed. A. van Staveren. Leyden and Amsterdam, 1742.

Augustine *Contra Academicos, PL* XXXII. 905–58. *Contra Faustus Manichaeum, PL* XLII. 207–518. *De civitate Dei,* ed. J. E. C. Welldon. London, 1924. *De consensu evangelistarum, PL* XXXIV. 1041–230. *De doctrina Christiana, PL* XXXIV. 15–122. *De utilitate credendi, PL* XLII. 63–91. *De vera religione, PL* XXXIV. 121–71. *Epistolae, PL* XXXIII. *Liber de divinatione daemonum, PL* XL. 581–91.

Aulisio (Aulisius), D. *De colo Mayerano.* Naples, 1694.

Bacon, F. *The Works,* eds. J. Spedding, R. L. Ellis, D. D. Heath, London, 1862–76.

Bacon, R. *Opus maius,* ed. J. H. Bridges. London, 1900.

Balbi (Balbus), G. *De civili et bellica fortitudine liber ex mysteriis poetae Vergili nunc depromptus.* Rome, 1526.

Banier, A. *La mythologie et les fables expliquées par l'histoire.* Paris, 1764.

Bardi, F. *Favole d'Ovidio istorico, politico, morale con le allegorie.* Venice, 1684.

Barga (Bargaeus), P. A. *Commentarius de obelisco.* Rome, 1586.

Barthelémy, J. J. "Sur la langue Cophte," *Memoires de l'Academie des Inscriptions,* LVII (1773), 387–401.

Bateman, S. *The Golden Boke of the Leaden Gods.* London, 1577.

Batteux, C. *Cours de Belles-Lettres.* Paris, 1773.

Baudelot de Dairval, C. C. *De l'utilité des voyages, et de l'avantage que le recherche des antiquitez procure aux savans.* Paris, 1686.

Bax, M. *De Busiride.* Leyden, 1700.

Bayle, P. *Pensées diverse sur la comète,* ed. A. Prat. Paris, 1939.

Beger (Begerus), L. *Bellum et excidium Trojanum.* Leipzig, 1699. *Spicilegium antiquitatis fasculi.* Cologne, 1692.

Bellori, G. and P. Bartoli *Admiranda Romanarum antiquitatum ac veteris sculpturae vestigia.* Rome, 1685. *Columna Antoniniana Marci Aureli Antonini Augusti.* Rome, 1672. *Colonna Traiana.* Rome, 1673. *Le antiche lucerne sepolcrali figurate.* Rome, 1691. *Picturae antiquiae cryptarum Romanarum et sepulchri Nasonis,* ed. and trans. M. A. La Chausse. Rome, 1738.

Benedict, T. *Interpretationem allegoriae Homericae de errore et precibus incipit.* Leipzig, 1784.

Bergmann, N. *De theologia Homeri.* Leipzig, 1689.

Bernard of Silvester *Commentum super sex libros Eneidos Virgilii,* ed. W. Riedel. Greifswald, 1924.

Beroaldo (Beroaldus), F. *Symbola Pythagorae moraliter explicata.* Paris, 1505.

Bersuire (Berchorius), F. *Cy commence Ovide . . . son livre entitule Metamorphoses contenant XV livres particuliers, moralise par Maister Thomas Waleys . . . translate et compile par Colard Mansion.* Bruges, 1484. *Bible des poetes methamorphoses.* Paris, 1493. *L'Ovidius moralizatus,* ed. F. Ghisalberti, *Studi Romanzi,* XXIII (1933), 5–136. *La bible des poetes.* Paris, 1531. *Metamorphosis Ovidiana moraliter.* Paris, 1515. *Reductorium morale, liber XV, Cap. 1., De formis figurisque deorum,* ed. J. Engels. Utrecht, 1962. *Six Books of Metamorphoseos,* trans. W. Caxton, ed. G. Hibbert. London, 1819. *Ovyde hys Booke of Methamorphose,* trans. W. Caxton, ed. S. Gaselee. London, 1924.

Bertels (Bertelius), J. *Deorum sacrificiorum gentilium.* Cologne, 1606.

Bessarion *Opera.* Venice, 1516.

Bianchini, F. *Le istoria universale provata con monumenti e figurata con simboli de gli antichi.* Rome, 1687.

Bie, J. de *Imperatorum Romanorum numismata aurea.* Antwerp, 1615.

Biondo (Blondus), F. *Romae instauratae liber.* Rome, 1481.

Blackmore, R. *Essays upon Several Subjects.* London, 1716.

Blackwell, T. *An Enquiry into the Life and Writings of Homer.* London, 1735. *Letters upon Mythology.* London, 1748.

Blumberg, C. G. *Fundamenta linguae Copticae.* Leipzig, 1716.

Boccaccio, G. *Genealogie deorum gentilium libri,* ed. V. Romano. Bari, 1951.

Boccardo (Buccardus Pylades), G. *Deorum genealogiae,* s. i., 1498.

Bocchi (Bocchius), A. *Symbolicarum quaestionum de universo genere libri quinque.* Bologna, 1574.

Bochart (Bochartus), S. *Opera omnia.* Leyden, 1712.

Böck (Bockius), J. *De bello Troiano praecipue Jacobo Hugoni . . . opposita.* Jena, 1672.

Boecler (Boeclerus), J. H. *De scriptoribus Graecis et Latinis ab Homero ad initium saec. post. Chr. nat. decimi sexti commentatio.* Strassburg, 1674.

Bogan, Z. *Ebraizon: sive comparatio Homeri cum Scriptoribus Sacris quoad norman loquendi.* Oxford, 1658.

Boissard (Boissardus), J. J. *Typographia Romae.* Frankfort, 1597–1602.

Bompart (Bompartius), J. *Parallela sacra et profana sive notae in Genesim.* Amsterdam, 1689.

Bosio, A. *Roma sotterranea.* Rome, 1632.

Bossuet, J. B. *Correspondance.* Paris, 1912. *Oeuvres.* Paris, 1847.

Boulenger, J. C. *De pictura, plastice, staturaria.* Lyons, 1627.

Bourgueil, B. de *Les oeuvres poétiques,* ed. P. Abrahams. Paris, 1826.

Boxhorn (Boxhornius), M. *Orationes tres.* Leyden, 1686.

Bracci (Braccius), I. *Phoenicis effigies in numismatis et gemma.* Rome, 1637.

Brammer (Brammerus), B. *Veritas creationis mundi prout a Mose descripta est ostensa in traditionibus gentium ac vetustissimus antiquitatis profanae monumentis ad convincendos atheos.* Kilon, 1668.

Breganio (Breganius), R. *Theologiae gentium de cognitione divina enarrationes.* Venice, 1621.

Briga, M. à *Fascia Isiaca statuae Capitolinae nunc primum in lucem edita.* Rome, 1716.

Brucker (Bruckerus), J. J. *Historia critica philosophiae.* Leipzig, 1766.

Buchner (Buchnerus), A. *Orationes academicae.* Dresden, 1682.

Buenting, H. *Chronica Catholica.* Magdeburg, 1608.

Burnet, T. *Archaeologiae philosophicae . . . libri duo.* London, 1733.

Calderón, P. *Las comedias,* ed. J. J. Keil. Leipzig, 1830. *Obras completas,* ed. A. V. Prat. Madrid, 1952.

Calvin, J. *Opera,* ed. W. Baum, E. Cunlitz, and E. Reuss. Brunswick, 1863–82.

Camerarius, J. (the younger) *De re rustica opuscula nonulla.* Nuremberg, 1577.

Campanella, T. *Atheismus triumphatus seu reductio ad religionem per scientiarum veritates.* Rome, 1631.

Carmina a variis auctoribus in obeliscum conscripta. Rome, 1586.

Carmina Burana, ed. A. Hilka and O. Schumann. Heidelberg, 1941.

Carpozov (Carpozovius), F. B. *De P. Virgili Maronis ecloga quarta.* Leipzig, 1669.

Cartari, V. *Delle Imagini de gli Dei de gli antichi* (1647). Graz, 1963.

Casalio (Casalius), J. B. *De veteribus Aegyptiorum ritibus.* Rome, 1644. *De profanis Aegyptiorum, Romanarum, et sacris Christianorum ritibus libri tres.* Rome, 1681.

Casaubon, M. *The vindication or defense of Isaac Casaubon against those impostors that lately published an impious and unlearned pamphlet intituled The Original of Idolatrie etc., under his name.* London, 1624.

Cassianus, J. *Collationes, PL* XLIX. 479–1327.

Cassiodorus, F. *Variae,* ed. T. Mommsen and L. Traube. Berlin, 1894.

Castalio, G. *De frigido et calido potu apologeticus . . . Vergili . . . adversus Pierum Cassianum.* Rome, 1607.

Caussin, N. *Electorum symbolorum et parabolum historicarum syntagma.* Paris, 1618.

Cavalieri (Cavallerius), G. B. *Antiquarum statuarum urbis Romae liber.* Rome, 1569.

Cebes *Pinax,* ed. R. Parsons. Boston, 1887.

Chacon (Ciaconnius), A. *Historia utriusque belli Dacici a Traiano Caesare gesti ex simulachris quae in columna ejusdem Romae visuntur collecta.* Rome, 1576.

Chiflet (Chifletius), J. *Miscellanea Chifletiana,* ed. J. Wetstein. Amsterdam, 1688.

Cicero, M. T. *Opera omnia,* ed. J. G. Baiter and C. L. Kayser. Leipzig, 1860–69. *Rhetorica ad Herennium,* ed. H. Caplan. New York, 1968.

Ciofani (Ciofanus), E. *In omnia P. Ovidii Nasonis opera observationes.* Antwerp, 1575.

Clasen (Clasenius), D. *Theologia gentilis.* Frankfort, 1684.

Classicorum auctorum e Vaticanis codicibus editorum tomus I (-x), ed. A. Mai. Rome, 1828–38.

Claudianus, C. *Carmina,* ed. J. Koch. Leipzig, 1893. *Il ratto di Proserpine,* trans. G. Bevilacqua. Palermo, 1586.

Clement of Alexandria *Opera,* ed. W. Dindorf. Oxford, 1869.

Clement of Rome *Epistola I ad Corinthios, PG* I. 199–328.

Cnobloch (Cnoblochius), J. *De Apide bove atque idolo Aegyptiorum.* Wittenberg, 1694.

Cnorr, C. *De antiquis Romanorum numismatibus consecrationem illustrantibus.* Leipzig, 1660.

Colberg, E. D. *Unicum, proprium, adaequatum remedium therapeuticum aetheologiae.* Rostock, 1680.

Collection of Poems by Several Hands, ed. R. Dodsley. London, 1766.

Collius, F. *De animabus paganorum libri quinque.* Milan, 1622.

Columella, L. *Opera,* ed. W. Lundstrom. Upsala, 1897–1940.

Commodianus *Adversus gentium deos, PL* V. 202–82.

Conti (Comes), N. *Mythologiae sive explicationis fabularum libri decem.* Padua, 1616.

Convenzio (Conventius), S. *De ascensu mentis in Deum ex Platonica et Peripatetica doctrina.* Venice, 1563.

Cornutus *De natura deorum,* ed. F. Osann. Gottingen, 1844. *Theologiae Graecae compendium,* ed. C. Lenz. Leipzig, 1881.

Coverdale, M. *Writings and Translations,* ed. G. Pearson. Cambridge, 1844.

Crenius (Crusius), T. *Animadversionum philologicarum et historiarum liber.* Leyden, 1702.

Crinito (Crinitus), P. *De honesta disciplina.* Lyons, 1554.

Crispo (Crispus), G. *De ethnicis philosophis caute legendis disputationum.* Rome, 1594.

Croese (Croesius), G. *Omeros Ebraios: sive historia Hebraeorum ab Homero conscripta.* Dordrecht, 1704.

Cudworth, R. *The True Intellectual System of the Universe.* London, 1743.

Cuper (Cuperus), G. *Apotheosis vel consecratio Homeri sive lapis antiquissimus in quo poetarum principiis Homeri consecratio sculpta est.* Amsterdam, 1683. *De elephantis in nummis obviis exercitationes duae.* Hague, 1719. *De Mercurii Harpocratis aliisque Romanorum sigillis ad Neomagum erutis et inscriptionibus antiquis.* Noyon, 1704. *Harpocrates sive explicatio imagunculae argenteae perantiquae quae in figuram Harpocratis formata representat solem.* Amsterdam, 1676. *Observationum libri tres . . . varii ritus eruuntur et et nummi elegantissimi illustrantur.* Utrecht, 1670.

Cuper (Cuperus), L. *Paratitla tes chronologias et historiae sacrae a mundo condita usque ad ten Exodon Jisraelitarum ex Aegypto; profanam quae explicat prout desumpta ex libris Metamorphoseon Publii Ovidii Nasonis ad haec tempora spectat.* Amsterdam, 1721.

Cyrillus of Alexandria *Contra Julianum, PG* LXXVI. 503–1058.

D., D. W. J. *Hippocrates atheisimi falso accusatus.* Rudolstadt, 1719.

Dante, *Comento di Christophoro Landino Fiorentino sopra la Comedia di Danthe Alighieri Poeta Fiorentino* Florence, 1481. *Epistolae,* ed. P. Toynbee. Oxford, 1966. *Il Convito,* ed. G. Giuliani. Florence, 1874. *La Divina Commedia,* ed. G. A. Scartazzini. Milan, 1922.

Darcie, A. *The Original of Idolatries, or the Birth of Heresies.* London, 1624.

D'Aubigné, T. A. *Oeuvres complètes,* ed. E. Réaume. Paris, 1877.

Demetrius of Phaleron *De elocutione,* ed. L. Rademacher. Leipzig, 1901.

Dennis, J. *The Critical Works,* ed. E. N. Hooker. Baltimore, 1943.

Dickinson, E. "Diatribe de Noah in Italiam adventu," *Opuscula quae ad historiam ac philologiam sacram spectant.* I (Rotterdam, 1693).

Dilherr (Dilherrus), J., "Farrago rituum sacrorum et secularium," *Opuscula quae ad historiam, ac philologiam sacram spectant,* VIII (Rotterdam, 1693).

Dio Chrysostom *Orationes,* ed. J. W. Cohoon. London and New York, 1932–51.

Diodorus Siculus *Bibliotheca historica,* ed. L. Dindorf. Leipzig, 1866–68. *The Historical Library,* trans. G. Booth. London, 1700. *The History,* trans. H. Cogan, London, 1653.

Diogenes Laertius *Lives of the Eminent Philosophers,* ed. R. D. Hicks. London and New York, 1925.

Discours en forme de comparaison sur les vies de Moyse et d'Homère. Paris, 1604.

Donatus, A. *Interpretationes Virgilianae,* ed. H. Georg. Leipzig, 1905.

Drelincourt, C. *De divinis apud Hippocratem dogmatis sermo,* trans. C. Drelincourt [the younger]. Leyden, 1689.

Dryden, J. *Essays,* ed. W. P. Ker. Oxford, 1900.

Du Choul, G. *Discours de la Religion des anciens Romains.* Wesel, 1672.

Du Halde, J. B. *Description géographique, historique, chronologique et physique de la Chine et de la Tartarie Chinoise.* Paris, 1735.

Duport, J. *Homeri gnomologia.* Cambridge, 1660.

Eggeling (Eggelingus), J. H. *Mysteria Cereris et Bacchi in vasculo ex uno onyche.* Brema, 1682.

Elizabethan Critical Essays, ed. G. G. Smith. Oxford, 1904.

Emmerling, J. T. *Schediasma de Schilo in Silenum atque Mose in Bacchum a profanis converso.* Jena, 1667.

Ennius *Carmina reliquiae,* ed. L. Müller. St. Petersburg, 1884.

Epiphanius *Adversus haereses, PG* XLII. 9–832.

Erasmus, D. *The Colloquies,* trans. C. Thompson. Chicago, 1965. *Opera,* ed. J. Le Clerc. Leyden, 1703–6.

Erizzo, S. *Discorso sopra le medaglie de gli antichi.* Venice, 1559.

Eschenbach, A. *Ethica mythologica, sive dissertatio de fabularum poeticarum sensu morali.* Altdorf, 1684.

Eucherius *Liber formularum spiritualis, PL* L. 727–71.

Euhemerus *Reliquiae,* ed. G. Némethy. Budapest, 1889.

Eusebius *Evangelicae praeparationis libri XV,* ed. E. H. Gifford. Oxford, 1903. *Historia ecclesiastica, PG* XX. 47–906.

Eustathius *Commentarii ad Homeri Iliadem.* Leipzig, 1827–29. *Commentarii ad Homeri Odysseam.* Leipzig, 1825–26.

Evelyn, J. *Diary and Correspondence,* ed. W. Bray. London, 1875. *Numismata: A Discourse of Medals, Antient and Modern.* London, 1697.

Eysson, R. *Silvae Virgilianae prodromus.* Groningen, 1695.

Fabretti (Fabrettus), R. *De columna Traiani syntagma.* Rome, 1683. *Inscriptionum antiquarum explicatio.* Rome, 1699.

Fabricius, J. A. *Bibliotheca Graeca.* Hamburg, 1781.

Faust, J. *Examen theologiae gentilis quam docuit Aristotle.* Strassburg, 1667.

Feith, E. *Antiquitatum Homericarum libri IV.* Leyden, 1677.

Fenestella, L. *De Romanorum magistratibus.* Venice, 1490.

Ficino (Ficinus), M. *Opera omnia.* Basel, 1576.

Filelfo, F. *Epistolarum libri sedecim.* Paris, 1613.

Firmicus Maternus, J. *De errore profanarum religionum,* ed. K. Ziegler. Leipzig, 1907.

Fletcher, Giles and Phineas. *The Poetical Works,* ed. F. Boas. Cambridge, 1908.

Fontenelle, Bernard de. *Oeuvres.* Paris, 1761–67.

Fornari, S. *Spositione sopra l'Orlando Furioso di M. Ludovico Ariosto.* Florence, 1549.

Fourmont, E. *Reflexions critiques sur les histoires des anciens peuples.* Paris, 1735.

Fournival, R. de *La vielle ou les derniers amours d'Ovide,* trans. J. Lefevre, ed. H. Cocheris. Paris, 1861.

Foy-Vaillant, J. *Selectiora numismata e museo Francisci de Camps.* Paris, 1694.

Fragmenta historicorum Graecorum, ed. C. Muller and T. Muller. Paris, 1841.

Franzini, F. *Roma antica e moderna.* Rome, 1672.

Fraunce, A. *The Third Part of the Countesse of Pembrokes Yuychurch.* London, 1592.

Freher (Freherus), M. *Cecropistomachia.* Heidelberg, 1607. *Sapphirus Constantii.* Heidelberg, 1602.

Fréret, N. *Oeuvres completes.* Paris, 1796.

Fulgentius, F. P. *Opera,* ed. R. Helm. Leipzig, 1898.

Fulvio (Fulvius), A. *Antiquaria urbis.* Rome, 1513. *De urbis antiquitatibus libri quinque.* Rome, 1527. *Illustrium imagines.* Rome, 1517. *L'antichità di Roma,* trans. P. de Rosso. Rome, 1543. *L'antichità di Roma,* ed. G. Ferrucci. Rome, 1588.

Galanti, L. *Christianae theologiae cum Platonica comparatio quin imo cum tota veteri sapientia ethnicorum, Chaldaeorum nempe, Aegyptiorum et Graecorum.* Bologna, 1627.

Gale, T. *The Court of the Gentiles or Discourse Touching the Original of Human Literature Both Philologie and Philosophie from the Scriptures and Jewish Church.* Oxford, 1669–78.

Galesino, P. *Ordo dedicationis obelisci quem S.D.N. Sixtus V. Pont. Max. in foro Vaticano ad limina Apostolorum erexit.* Rome, 1587.

Garuffi, G. M. *Lucerna lapidaria . . . via Flaminia et Arimini scrutatur.* Rimini, 1691.

Garzoni, T. *La piazza universale di tutte le professioni del mondo.* Venice, 1600.

Gassendi, R. *De vita Peireskii.* Hague, 1655.

Gataker, T. *Opera critica.* Strassburg, 1698.

Gaurico, P. *De sculptura sive staturia.* Florence, 1504.

Gautruche (Galtruchius), P. *L'Histoire poétique pour l'intelligence des poètes et autheurs anciens.* Caen, 1673. *The Poetical Histories,* trans. M. d'Assigny. London, 1672.

Gelli, G. B. *La Circe.* Milan, 1804.

Génébrard (Genebrardus), G. *Chronographia.* Paris, 1567.

Gentilis, A. *Lectionis Virgilianae variae liber.* Hanover, 1603.

Gesta Romanorum, ed. H. Oesterley. Berlin, 1872.

Giraldi (Giraldus), G. G. *Opera omnia.* Leyden, 1696.

Glass (Glassius), S. *Philologia sacra.* Leipzig, 1705.

Gnospius, J. *De Teletis, sive Graecorum theologia physica.* Wittenberg, 1706.

Goltz (Goltzius), H. C. *Julius Caesar, sive historiae imperatorum Caesarumque Romanorum.* Bruges, 1563.

Goorle (Gorlaeus), A. de *Dactyliothecae liber.* Leyden, 1601. *Thesaurus numismatum Romanorum,* ed. D. de Goorle. Amsterdam, 1608.

Gordon, A. *An Essay towards Explaining Hieroglyphical Figures on the Coffin of the Ancient Mummy belonging to Capt. William Lethieullier. An Essay towards Explaining the Ancient Hieroglyphical Figures on the Egyptian Mummy in the Museum of Dr. Mead.* London, 1737.

Gorp (Goropius Becanus), J. van *Hieroglyphica.* Antwerp, 1580.

Goulart, S. *A Learned Summary upon the Famous Poeme of William of Saluste, Lord of Bartas. Wherein are Discovered all the Excellent Secretts in Metaphysicall, Physicall, Morall, and Historicall Knowledge,* trans. T. Lodge. London, 1621.

Graefe (Graevius), J. G. *Thesaurus antiquitatum Romanorum.* Leyden, 1694–99.

Gregorii, F. *De miraculis Providentiae apud gentes antiquas.* Leipzig, 1714.

Gregory of Tours *Liber miraculorum, Monumenta Germaniae Historica.* Berlin, 1885. *Libri historiarum X,* ed. B. Krush and W. Levison. Hanover, 1951.

Gronov (Gronovius), J. *Disquistio de icuncula Smetiana.* Leyden, 1693.

Groot (Grotius), H. de *De veritate religionis Christianae.* Leipzig, 1709. *Opera.* London, 1679.

Gros de Boze, C. *Dissertation sur le culte que les anciens ont rendu à la Déese de la Santé.* Paris, 1705. *Dissertation sur la Janus des anciens et sur quelques médailles qui y ont rapport.* Paris, 1705.

Gruytere (Gruterus), J. *Inscriptiones antiquae totius orbis Romani.* Heidelberg, 1602–3.

Gundling (Gundlingius), N. H. *Historia philosophiae moralis*. Halle, 1706.

Gurtler (Gurtlerus), N. H. *Origines mundi*. Amsterdam, 1708.

H., T. *The Fable of Ovid treting of Narcissus*. London, 1560.

Halloix (Halloisius), P. *Illustrium ecclesiae orientalis scriptorum qui sanctitate iuxta et eruditione . . . vitae et documenta*. Douai, 1633.

Hardouin (Harduinus), J. *Nummi antiqui populorum et urbium illustrati*. Paris, 1684. *Opera selecta*. Amsterdam, 1709.

Hardschmidt, N. *De Seneca notitia Dei naturali*. Jena, 1668.

Hartzheim, C. *Explicatio gentilium fabularum et superstitionum quarum in sacris scripturis fit mentio; vario hinc inde sensu, praeter literalium, ut allegorico, morali anagogico exornata*. Padua, 1731.

Hasenmuller, J. *De fabulis et mythologia*. Lund, 1705.

Haurech (Julianus Aurelius), J. *De cognominibus deorum*. Basel, 1543.

Heinz (Heinsius), D. *Aristarchus sacer, sive ad Nonni in Johannem metaphrasin exercitationes*. Leyden, 1627.

Henning, J. *De polytheismo gentilium*. Marburg, 1677.

Heraclitus of Pontus *Allégories d'Homere*, ed. E. Buffière. Paris, 1962.

Herbert, E. *De religione gentilium errorumque apud eos causis*. Amsterdam, 1663. *The antient religion of the Gentiles, and the causes of their errors*, trans. W. Lewis. London, 1705.

Hermias *In Platonis Phaedrum scholia*, ed. P. Couvreur. Paris, 1901.

Herodotus *The History*, ed. A. D. Godley. New York and London, 1921.

Herwart ab Hohenburg, J. G. *Admiranda ethnicae theologiae mysteria propalata*. Munich, 1623. *Thesaurus hieroglyphicorum ex museo J.G. H. ab H*. Munich, 1610.

Herzog, C. *Essay de mummio-graphie*. Leipzig, 1718.

Hildebert of Lavardin *Carmina miscellanea*, PL CLXXI. 1441–48.

Hildebrand (Hildebrandus), F. *Centuria gemina epistolarum: prior epistolas varii argumenti, altera fabulas ad moralia applicata complectitur juventis*. Nordhausen, 1671.

Holst (Holstenius), L. *Commentariolus in veterem picturam nymphaeum referentem*. Rome, 1676.

Homer *Quae extant omnia*, ed. J. de Sponde. Basel, 1583. *Works*, trans. G. Chapman, ed. A. Nicoll. New York, 1956. *Les oeuvres*, trans. A. Dacier. Amsterdam, 1731. *L'Omero Toscana*, trans. B. Bugliazzini. Lucca, 1703. *Ilias*, ed. T. W. Allen. Oxford, 1931. *Ilias*, ed. O. Gifanio. Basel, 1572. *Odyssea*, trans. F. Porta. Geneva, 1609. *Odysseae libri XXIIII*, trans. S. Lemnius. Basel, 1549. *L'Ulisse*, trans. L. Dolce. Venice, 1573.

Hor Apollo *Hieroglyphica*, ed. F. Sbordone. Naples, 1940. *The Hieroglyphics*, trans. G. Boas. New York, 1950.

Horace *Opera omnia*, ed. E. C. Wickham. Oxford, 1891–96.

Hostus, M. T. *Historiae rei nummariae veteris libri quinque*. Frankfort on the Oder, 1580.

Huet (Huetus), P. *Alnetanae quaestiones de concordia rationis et fidei*. Paris, 1690. *Demonstratio evangelica*. Venice, 1732. *The History and Commerce of the Ancients*. London, 1717.

Hugo of St. Victor *Didascalion*, PL CLXXVI. 74–838.

Hugues (Hugo), J. *Vera historia Romana, seu origo Latii vel Italiae ac Romanae urbis.* Rome, 1655.

Hulsius, L. *XII primorum Caesarum et LXIIII ipsorum uxorum et parentum ex antiquis numismatibus in aere incisae effigies.* Frankfort, 1597.

Hume, D. *Essays.* London, 1788.

Hutten, U. von and Crotus Rubianus *Epistolae obscurorum virorum,* ed. and trans. F. G. Stokes. New Haven, 1925.

Huttich (Huttichius), J. *Imperatorum Romanorum libellus una cum imaginibus ad vivam effigiem expressis.* Strassburg, 1526.

Huygens, C. *Oeuvres complètes.* The Hague, 1888–1950.

Hyginus *Astronomica,* ed. E. Chatelain and P. Legendre. Paris, 1909. *Fabulae,* ed. H. J. Rose. Leyden, 1934.

Incerti scriptoris graeci fabulae aliquot Homericae de Ulixis erroribus ethice explicatae, ed. J. Columbus. Leyden, 1745.

Irenaeus *Adversus haereses, PG* VII. 433–1224.

Isidorus of Seville *Etymologiarum, sive originum libri XX,* ed. W. M. Lindsay. Oxford, 1911.

Itinerarium per urbem et circa urbem, PL CXXVII. 347–66.

Jablonski, P. E. *Pantheon Aegyptiorum.* Frankfort, 1750.

Jameson, W. *Spicilegia antiquitatum Aegypti atque ei vicinarum gentium.* Glasgow, 1720.

Jansen, H. J. *De l'allégorie.* Paris, 1799.

Jerome *Adversus Jovinianum, PL* XXIII, 222–352. *Commentarius in evangelium Matthaei, PL* XXVI. 15–228. *Epistolae, PL* XXII. 325–1191. *Liber de viris illustribus, PL* XXIII. 631–759.

John of Garland *Integumenta super Ovidium Metamorphoseos,* ed. F. Ghisalberti. Milan, 1933.

John of Salisbury *Polycraticus,* ed. C. C. I. Webb. Oxford, 1907.

Jon (Junius), F. de *De pictura veterum libri tres.* Amsterdam, 1630.

Jones, S. *De origine idolatriae apud gentes et Christianos.* Lyons, 1708.

Jordan, C. E. *Histoire de la vie et ouvrages de M. la Croze.* Amsterdam, 1741.

Josephus, Flavius. *Contra Apion,* ed. T. Reinach, trans. L. Blum. Paris, 1930.

Jouvency, J. de *Appendix de diis et heroibus poeticis,* in Ovid, *Metamorphoseos.* Paris, 1705.

Julianus *The Works,* ed. W. C. Wright. London and New York, 1913–23.

Justin Martyr *Apologia pro Christianis, PG* VI. 327–470. *Dialogus cum Tryphone Judaeo, PG* VI. 471–800.

Justinus, *Historiarum . . . libri XLIV,* ed. N. E. Lemaire. Paris, 1823.

Kaewitz, G. *De Christianismo Senecae.* Wittenberg, 1668.

Kapp, J. E. *Clarissimorum virorum orationes selectae.* Leipzig, 1722.

Keach, B. *Tropologia: A Key to Scripture Metaphor.* London, 1682.

King, W. *Heathen Gods and Heroes.* London, 1710.

Kipping, H. *Antiquitates Romae.* Leyden, 1713.

Kircher (Kircherus), A. *China illustrata.* Amsterdam, 1667. *Latium.* Amsterdam, 1671. *Lingua Aegyptiaca restituta.* Rome, 1664. *Obelisci Aegyptiaci nuper inter Isaei Romani rudera effossi interpretatio hieroglyphica.* Rome, 1661. *Obeliscus Aegyptiacus, hoc est universalis hieroglyphicae veterum doctrinae temporum iniuria abolitae instauratio.* Rome, 1650. *Obeliscus Pamphilius.* Rome, 1650. *Prodromus Coptus, sive Aegyptiacus.* Rome, 1636. *Sphinx mystagogus.* Amsterdam, 1676.

Kirchmann (Kirchmannus), J. *De annulis.* Leyden, 1623.

Kornmann (Kornmannus), H. *De annulo.* Hague, 1654.

Kortholt, C. *De calumniis paganorum in veteres Christianos sparsa.* Rostock, 1663. *De tribus impostoribus.* Kilon, 1680. *Tractatus de origine, progressu, et antiquitate philosophiae barbaricae.* Jena, 1660.

Krentzheim, L. *Observationum chronologicarum . . . libri IIII.* Ligne, 1605.

Lactantius, L. *Divinae institutiones, PL* VI. 111–322.

Lactantius Placidus *Commentarios in Statii Thebaida et commentarium in Achilleida,* ed. R. Jahnke. Leipzig, 1898.

Lafreri, A. *Speculum romanae magnificentiae (1554),* ed. C. C. F. Huelsen. Munich, 1921.

La Mothe le Vayer, F. de. *Oeuvres.* Paris, 1662.

Landi, C. *In veterum numismatum Romanorum miscellanea explicationes.* Lyons, 1560.

L'Anglois, P. *Discours des hiéroglyphes Aegyptiens.* Paris, 1584.

La pianta di Roma dell' Anonimo Einsidlense. Rome, 1907.

La Seine (Lasena), P. *Homeri nepenthes.* Lyons, 1624.

Lazius, W. *Commentariorum vetustorum numismatum . . . multarum rerumpublicarum per Asiam, Aphricam et Europam antiquitatis historiam explicans.* Vienna, 1558.

Le Bossu, R. *Traité du poème epique.* Paris, 1708.

Leibnitz, G. W. *Opera.* Geneva, 1768.

Lemaire de Belges, J. *Oeuvres,* ed. J. Stecher. Louvain, 1882–91.

Lemée, F. *Traité des statues.* Rome, 1688.

Le Menestrier, J. B. "De colo antiquo ad Mayerum," in A.de Sallengre, *Novus thesaurus antiquitatum Romanorum* (The Hague, 1716–19), III, 937–43. *Medales illustrées des anciens empereurs et imperatrices de Rome.* Dijon, 1642.

Leonberger (Leonbergerus), G. *Ad Vergili opera omnia loci aliquot.* Ingolstadt, 1542.

Le Pois, A. *Discours sur les medalles et graveures antiques principalement Romaines.* Paris, 1579.

Le Roy, J. *Achates Tiberianus, sive gemma Caesarea . . . D. Augusti apotheosin . . . representans.* Amsterdam, 1683.

Lessing, G. *Werke,* ed. J. Petersen and W. von Olshausen. Berlin and Leipzig, n.d.

Liceti (Licetus), F. *De lucernis antiquorum reconditis libri quatuor.* Venice, 1621. *De mundi et hominis analogia liber unus.* Udine, 1635. *Encyclopaedia ad aram mysticam nonarii terrigenae anonymi vetustissimi.* Padua, 1630. *Hieroglyphica, sive antiqua schemata gemmarum anularium quaesita moralia, politica, historica, medica, philosophica et sublimiora explicata.* Padua, 1653. *Ulysses apud Circen.* Udine, 1636.

Linck, M. *De bello Troiano in qua contra omnes fere historicos ostenditur, Trojam in illo bello quod decennale putatur, minime a Graecis flammis ruinisve fuisse deletam.* s.l., 1674.

Lipse (Lipsius), J. *Opera omnia.* Antwerp, 1637.

Lloyd, N. *Dictionarium historicum, geographicum, poeticum.* Oxford, 1670.

Lodge, T. *Works.* Glasgow, 1883.

Long (Longus), G. *De annulis signatoriis antiquorum.* Milan, 1615.

Lucanus, M. *De bello civili,* ed. G. Steinhardt. Leipzig, 1892.

Lucianus *Works,* ed. A. M. Harmon, K. Kilburn, and M. D. Macleod. New York and London, 1913–67.

Luther, M. *Works,* ed. J. Pelikan. St. Louis, 1955–64.

Lycophron *Cassandra,* ed. N. Gerbel. Basel, 1546.

Lynche, R. *An Historical Treatise of the Travels of Noah into Europe.* London, 1601.

Macrobius, A. *Saturnalia,* ed. J. Willis. Leipzig, 1953.

Maffei (Maffejus), R. *Commentariorum urbanorum libri triginta.* Paris, 1511.

Maichin, A. *La theologie payenne.* St. Jean d'Angely, 1657.

Maier, M. *Arcana arcanissima: hoc est hieroglyphica Aegyptio-Graeca . . . sex libris exposita.* Oppenheim, 1614.

Maioli, S. *Dies caniculares.* Mayence, 1607.

Maranta, B. *Lucullianarum quaestionum libri quinque.* Basel, 1564.

Marliani (Marlianus), B. *Urbis Romae topographia.* Venice, 1588.

Marolles, M. de *Tableaux du temple des muses.* Amsterdam, 1676.

Marot, C. *Oeuvres,* ed. C. Marty-Laveaux. Paris, 1891.

Marsham, J. *Chronicus canon Aegypticus Ebraicus et disquisitiones.* London, 1676.

Martianus Capella *De nuptiis philologiae et Mercurii et de septem artibus liberalibus libri novem,* ed. U. F. Kopp. Frankfort, 1836.

Martin, D. *Traité de la religion naturelle.* Amsterdam, 1713.

Marulic (Marulus), M. *Dialogo di M. M. delle eccelenti virtu et maravigliosi fatti di Hercole,* trans. B. Christolpho. Venice, 1549.

Masen (Masenius), J. *Speculum imaginum veritatis occultae.* Cologne, 1664.

Matthaeus, J. *Quod bene vortat Nisum Samsonis symbolum.* Wittenberg, 1724.

Mauro, L. *De antichitá de la citta di Roma.* Venice, 1556.

Maximus *Homiliae, PL* LVII. 222–530.

Mehl, M. *Pterelaum Samsonis symbolum.* Wittenberg, 1724.

Meier, G. *De papatu per ethnicisum impraegnato.* Frankfort, 1634.

Melanchthon, P. *Opera,* eds. G. Bretschneider and H. E. Bindseil. Halle, 1834–60.

Melmoth, W. *The Letters of Sir Thomas Fitzosborne on Several Subjects.* London, 1795.

Mencken, J. B. *De charlataneria eruditorum.* Leipzig, 1725.

Menestrier, C. F. and G. Bellini. *Description de la belle et grande colonne historiée dressée à l'honneur de l'Empéreur Théodore.* Paris, 1702.

Menochio (Menochius), G. S. *Commentarius totius Scripturae.* Paris, 1719.

Mercati (Mercatus), M. *De gli obelischi di Roma.* Rome, 1589.

Micraelius, J. *Ethnophronii liber contra gentiles de principiis religionis Christianiae dubitationes.* Stettin, 1647.

Milich (Milichius), J. G. *De diis deabusque veterum gentilium Milichiis.* Leipzig, 1699.

Milton, J. *Works,* ed. F. A. Patterson. New York, 1931–40.

Minucius Felix, M. *Octavius,* ed. H. Boenig. Leipzig, 1903.

Modio (Modius), F. *Novantiquae lectiones*. Frankfort, 1584.

Moebius, G. *Tractatus de oraculum ethnicorum origine, propagatione, ac duratione*. Leipzig, 1660.

Moneta, J. *Problema mythologicum utrum immolatio Phrixi eadem sit ac Isaaci necne*. Wittenberg, 1721.

Montefalcio (Montefalcius), P. *De cognominibus deorum*. Perugia, 1525.

Monterchi, G. *Scelta de medaglioni piu rari nella bibliotheca dell'* . . . *Cardinale Gasparo Carpegna*. Rome, 1689.

Montfaucon, B. de *Diarium Italicum*. Paris, 1702. *L'antiquité expliquée*. Paris, 1719–24. *The Travels of the learned Father Montfaucon from Paris thro'Italy*. London, 1712.

Montjosieu (Demontiosius), L. de *De veterum sculptura, caelatura, gemmarum scalptura et pictura*. Antwerp, 1609. *Gallus Romae hospes*. Rome, 1585.

More, H. *A Collection of Several Philosophical Writings*. London, 1662. *Conjectura cabbalistica*. London, 1662. *The Theological Works*. London, 1708.

Morlot, M. *De idolatria gentili*. Strassburg, 1688.

Mornay, P. de *De la verité de la religion Chrestienne*. Paris, 1585.

Mythographi Graeci, ed. N. Festa. Leipzig, 1902.

Mythographi Latini, ed. T. Muncker. Amsterdam, 1681.

Mythologici Latini, ed. J. Commeline. Heidelberg, 1599.

Muller, J. H. *De miraculis Vespasiani*. Jena, 1707.

Musaeus, J. *Examen Cherburianismi sive de luminis naturae insufficientia ad salutem*. Jena, 1675.

Nashe, T. *Works*, ed. R. B. McKerrow. London, 1904.

Neckham, A. *De naturis rerum*, ed. T. Wright. London, 1863.

Neuman, G. *De mythologiae deorum gentilium abusu in poesi Christiana*. Leipzig, 1709.

Newton, I. *The Chronology of Ancient Kingdoms Amended*. London, 1728.

Nicaise, C. *Les Sirenes ou discours sur leur forme et figure*. Paris, 1691.

Nonnos *Dionysiaca*, ed. W. H. D. Rouse. London and New York, 1940.

Novarini, L. *Schedismata sacro-prophana, hoc est observationem antiquis Christianorum, Hebraeorum, aliarumque gentium ritibus in lucem eruendis*. Lyons, 1635.

Occo, A. *Imperatorum Romanorum numismata a Pompeio Magno ad Heraclium*. Antwerp, 1579.

Oisel (Oiselius), J. *Thesaurus selectorum numismatum antiquorum*. Amsterdam, 1677.

Oncieu, G. de *Colloquia mixta*. Geneva, 1620.

Origen *Contra Celsum, PG* XI. 641–1632. *De principatibus, PG* XI. 115–414.

Orosius, P. *Historiarum libri VII, PL* XXXI. 663–1174.

Orsini (Ursinus), F. *Familiae Romanae in antiquis numismatibus*. Paris, 1663.

Ortell (Ortelius), A. *Deorum dearumque capita e veteribus numismatibus*. Anvers, 1573.

Ovid *Amatoria cum doctorum virorum commentariis*. Basel, 1549. *Erotica et amatoria opuscula*, ed. M. Goldast. Frankfort, 1610. *Heroides*, ed. A. Sabinus and G. Morillionius. Venice, 1583. *Metamorphoseos*, ed. Bonus Accursius and B. de Novaria. Venice, 1486. *Metamorphoseos libri XV. In eosdem libris Raphaelis Regii . . . et Petri Lavinii commentarii non ante impressi.* Milan, 1540. *Metamorphoseos,* ed. R. Regius and J. Moltzer (Micyllus). Basel, 1543. *Metamorphoseos . . . enarrationibus autem et allegoriis . . . versu expositae,* ed. J. Spreng. Frankfort, 1563. *Metamorphoseon,* ed. J. Spanmueller. Antwerp, 1610. *Metamorphoseon, plerarumque historica naturalis moralis ekphrasis,* ed. J. L. Gottfried. Frankfort, 1619. *Metamorphoseon,* ed. H. Magnus. Berlin, 1914. *Les Metamorphoses d'Ovide traduittes en prose Francoise . . . Avec XV discours contenans l'explication morale des fables,* trans. N. Renouard. Paris, 1614. *Les Metamorphoses d'Ovide en Latin et François,* ed. and trans. P. du Ryer. Paris, 1660. *Les Metamorphoses,* ed. and trans. A. Bannier. Amsterdam, 1732. *Trois premiers livres de la Metamorphose,* trans. C. Marot and B. Aneau. Lyons, 1556. *Le Sommaire en Prose des Metamorphoses d'Ovide dans le Manuscript Burney 311,* ed. U. D. Hunt. Paris, 1925. *Le grand Olympe des histoires poétiques du prince de poesie Ovide Naso en sa Metamorphose.* Lyons, 1532. *Metamorphoseos vulgare,* trans. G. Bonsignori. Milan, 1519. *Di Ovidio le Metamorphosi . . . con sue allegorie significatione e dichiaratione della Fabole in prosa,* trans. N. di Agostini. Venice, 1533. *Le Metamorfosi,* eds. G. Horloggi, F. Turchi, and G. dell' Anguillara. Venice, 1584. *Metamorphosis Englished, Mythologized and Represented in Figures,* ed. and trans. G. Sandys. Oxford, 1632. *Metamorphosis,* trans. J. Brinsley. London, 1618. *Opera,* ed. R. Ehwald. Leipzig, 1912. *Ovide Moralisé,* ed. C. de Boer, M. G. de Boer, J. T. M. Van't Sant, *Verhandelingen der Koninklijke Akademie van Wetenschappen: Afdeeling Letterkunde, N.R.,* XV (1915), XXI (1920), XXX (1931), XXXVII (1936), XLIII (1938). *Le Commentaire de Copenhague de l'Ovide Moralisé,* ed. J. T. M. Van't Sant. Leyden, 1929.

Ovid (Pseudo) *De vetula,* ed. P. Klopsch. Leyden, 1967.

Owen, J. *Theologoumena pantodapa, sive de natura, ortu, progressu, et studio verae theologiae libri sex.* Oxford, 1661.

Pacard, George. *Théologie naturelle.* Paris, 1606.

Palaephatus *De incredibilibus,* ed. N. Festa. Leipzig, 1901.

Palladio, A. *Dell'antichitá di Roma.* Rome, 1554.

Pansa, M. *De oscula ethnicae et Christianae philosophiae.* Chieti, 1601.

Panvinio (Panvinius), O. *Republicae Romanae commentariorum libri tres.* Venice, 1558.

Paquelin, G. *Apologeme pour le grand Homère contre la reprehension du divin Platon sur aucunes passages d'icelvy.* Lyons. 1577.

Parthenius *Eroticon,* ed. S. Gaselee. London, 1935.

Patin, C. *Dios genethlia, natalia Jovis in numismate . . . Caracallae.* Padua, 1681. *Imperatorum Romanorum numismata.* Strassburg, 1671. *Introductio ad historian numismatum.* Arusterdan, 1683. *Theon krisis: judicium Paridis . . . in numismate . . . Antonini Pii.* Padua, 1679. and J. H. Eggeling. *De numismatibus quibusdam abstrusis . . . Neronis.* Brema, 1681.

Peacham, H. *Compleat Gentleman.* London, 1634.

Pearson, J. *Critici sacri.* London, 1660.

Perkins, W. *Armilla aurea.* London, 1590.

Persona, J. B. *Noctes solitariae sive de iis quae scientifice scripta sunt ab Homero in Odyssea*. Venice, 1613.

Petau, D. *Rationarium temporum . . . libros decim tributum*. Paris, 1633.

Peter of Cluny *Tractatus contra Petro Brusiango, PL* CLXXXIX. 719–850.

Petit (Petitus), R. *Homeri nepenthes*. Utrecht, 1689.

Petrarch, F. *Lettere delle cose familiari*, ed. G. Fracassetti. Florence, 1892. *Lettere senili*, ed. G. Fracassetti. Florence, 1892. *Opere*, ed. E. Bigi. Milan, 1966. *Rerum memorandarum libri*, ed. G. Billanovich. Florence, 1943. *Scritti inediti*, ed. A. Hortis. Trieste, 1874. *Francisci Petrarcae Vergilianus Codex*, ed. G. Galbiati and A. Ratti. Milan, 1930.

Pfanner (Pfannerus), T. *Systema theologiae gentilis purioris*. Basel, 1679.

Phillips, E. *Theatrum poetarum anglicanorum*. Canterbury, 1800.

Philo Judaeus *Works*, trans. and ed. F. H. Colson and G. H. Whitaker. London and New York, 1929–62.

Picinelli, F. *Lumi reflessi o dir vogliamo Concetti della Sacra Bibbia osservati ne i volumi non sacri*. Milan, 1667. *Mondo simbolico*. Milan, 1669.

Pico della Mirandola, G. *De hominis dignitate, Heptaplus, de ente et uno, e scritti vari*, ed. E. Garin. Florence, 1942.

Pico della Mirandola, G. F. *Examen vanitatis gentium et veritatis Christianae disciplina*. Mirandola, 1520.

Pictor (Pictorius), G. *Apotheseos tam exterarum gentium quam Romanorum deorum libri tres*. Basel, 1558. *Theologia mythologica*. Antwerp, 1532.

Pignoria (Pignorius), L. *Antiquissimae picturae quae Romae visitur . . . explicatus*, Padua, 1630. *De servis, et eorum apud veteres ministeriis*. Padua, 1656. *L'Antenor*. Padua, 1625. *Magnae deum matris idaea Attidis initia*. Amsterdam, 1669. *Symbolarum epistolicarum liber primus*. Padua, 1628. *Vetustissimae tabulae aenae sacris Aegyptiorum simulachris coelatae accurata explicatio, in qua antiquissimarum superstitionum origines . . . enarrantur*. Venice, 1605.

Pladek (Pladecius), P. H. *De tribus hypostasibus Plotini*. Wittenberg, 1694.

Plato *Opera*, ed. G. Serrano. Paris, 1578. *Phaedrus*, ed. F. Astius. Leipzig, 1810.

Plautus *Comoediae*, ed. W. M. Lindsay. Oxford, 1924.

Pletho, G. B. *De Platonicae et Aristotelicae philosophiae differentia, PG* CLX. 890–932.

Plinius, C. *Naturalis historiae libri XXXVII*, ed. C. Mayhoff. Leipzig, 1882–97.

Plotinus *Opera*, ed. and trans. M. Ficino. Basel, 1580. *Enneades*, trans. E. Bréhier. Paris, 1924–31.

Plutarch *Moralia*, ed. D. Wittenbach. Leipzig, 1832.

Poetae Latini minores, ed. E. Baehrens. Leipzig, 1881.

Poggio Bracciolini (Poggius), G. F. *De fortunae varietate urbis Romae et de ruina eiusdem*. In *Novus thesaurus antiquitatum Romanarum*, ed. A. H. de Sallengre, I, 497–507. Hague, 1716.

Poleni, G. *Utriusque thesauri antiquitatum Romanarum Graecarumque nova supplementum*. Venice, 1737.

Polenton, S. *Scriptorum illustrium latinae linguae libri XVIII*, ed. B. L. Ullman. Rome, 1928.

Poliziano (Politianus), A. *Opera omnia*. Paris, 1519.

Pomey, F. *Pantheum mythicum, seu fabulosa deorum historia*. Amsterdam, 1730.

Pontano (Pontanus), G. G. *Opera*. Venice, 1515.

Pope, A. *Works,* ed. W. Elwin and W. J. Courthope. London, 1871–89. *Poems,* ed. M. Mack. London and New Haven, 1967.

Porphyry *Opuscula,* ed. A. Nauck. Leipzig, 1886. *Quaestiones Homericarum,* ed. H. Schrader. Leipzig, 1880.

Proclus *In Platonis Rem Publicam commentarii,* ed. W. Kroll. Leipzig, 1901.

Propertius, S. *Carmina,* ed. J. S. Phillimore. Oxford, 1901.

Publius Victor *De regionibus urbis Romae.* Venice, 1505.

Purchas, S. *Purchas his Pilgrims.* Glasgow, 1905.

Quintilian, M. *Institutionis oratoriae libri XII,* ed. L. Rademacher. Leipzig, 1907–35.

Rabelais, F. *Gargantua and Pantagruel,* trans. T. Urquhart and P. Motteux. London, 1863.

Raleigh, W. *History of the World.* Edinburgh, 1820.

Ram, D. *Hercules et Samson seu dissertatio mythologico-critica.* Copenhagen, 1707.

Ram, J. *Ulysses et Otinus unus et idem, sive disquisitio historica et geographica, qua, ex collatis inter se Odyssea Homeri, et Edda Island.* Copenhagen, 1702.

Ramsay, A. *The Travels of Cyrus.* London, 1727.

Regoli (Regulus), S. *In primum Aeneidos Virgili librum ex Aristotelis de arte poetica et rhetorica praeceptis explicationes.* Bologna, 1563.

Reineck (Reineccius), R. *Historia Julia, sive syntagma heroicus,* Helmstadt, 1593.

Reines (Reinesius), T. *Syntagma inscriptionum antiquarum.* Leipzig and Frankfort, 1682.

Remigius of Auxerre *Commentum in Martianum Capellam,* ed. C. E. Lutz. Leyden, 1962.

Reusner, N. *Emblemata . . . partim ethica, et physica; partim vera historica, et hieroglyphica . . . in quatuor libros digesta.* Frankfort, 1581. *Symbolorum imperatoriorum classis prima-tertia.* Frankfort, 1588.

Reverend, D. *Lettres à Monsieur H*** sur les premiers Dieux ou Rois d' Egypte.* Paris, 1733.

Reynolds, H. *Mythomystes.* In *Critical Essays of the Seventeenth Century,* ed. J. E. Spingarn, I, 141–78. Bloomington, Ind., 1957.

Ribondeault (Ribondeauldus), P. de *Sacrum Dei oraculum Urim et Thummin.* In *Thesaurus antiquitatum sacrum complectens selectissima,* ed. B. Ugolino (Ugolinus), XII. Venice, 1751.

Riccheri (Richerius), L. C. *Lectiones antiquae.* Lyons, 1560.

Richard of Bury. *Philobiblon,* ed. E. C. Thomas. Oxford, 1960.

Ridewall, J. *Fulgentius metaforalis,* ed. H. Liebeschütz. Berlin and Leipzig, 1926.

Rigord, J. P. "Lettre de Monsieur Rigord Commissaire de la Marine aux journalistes de Trévoux sur une ceinture de toile trouvée en Egypte autour d'une mumie. In *Mémoire pour l'Histoire des Sciences et des Beaux Arts,* pp. 978–1000. Trévoux, 1704.

Ripa, C. *La novissima iconologia.* Padua, 1625.

Roetel, A. *Deorum gentilium praecipuorum origines ex sacra scriptura derivatas.* Jena, 1674.

Ronsard, P. *Oeuvres,* ed. C. Marty-Laveau, Paris, 1891.

Rosini, G. and T. Dempster *Antiquitatum Romanorum corpus absolutissimum.* Paris, 1632.

Ross, A. *Mystagogus Poeticus.* London, 1647.

327

Roth, E. *De ludicra Jacobi Hugonis deliratione bello Trojano.* Jena, 1672.

Roth, J. *De philosophia Homeri.* Wittenberg, 1704.

Rotth, A. *Trinitas Platonica.* Leipzig, 1693.

Rufinus *Historia ecclesiastica, PL* XXI. 463–540.

Sabinus Floridus, F. *Lectiones subsicivae.* In J. Gruter, *Lampas sive fax artium liberalium,* I, 996–1223. Frankfort, 1602.

Saint-Amant, J. T. de *Commentaires historiques contenants en abregé les vies, eloges, et censures des empereurs . . . iusques à Pertinax.* Paris, 1635.

Sallustius *Concerning the Gods and the Universe,* ed. and trans. A. D. Nock. Cambridge, 1926.

Salmeron, A. *Commentarii in Evangelicum Historiam et in Acta Apostolorum,* Cologne, 1602–4.

Salutati, C. *Epistolario,* ed. F. Novati. Rome, 1891. *De laboribus Herculis,* ed. B. L. Ullman. Zurich, 1951.

Sambucus, J. *Emblemata.* Antwerp, 1564.

Sandrart, J. von *Sculpturae veteris admiranda.* Nuremberg, 1680.

Sanford, H. *De descensu domini nostri Iesu Christi ad inferos.* London, 1611.

Sardi, A. *Liber de nummis.* Milan, 1579.

Saumaise (Salmasius), C. *Epistolae.* Leyden, 1656.

Scaliger, J. J. *Opus novum de emendatione temporum.* Paris, 1583.

Schaevius, H. *Mythologia deorum et heroum.* Stargard, 1660.

Scheffer, G. *Coelum poeticum seu sphaera astronomica.* Prague, 1686.

Schelhorn, J. G. *Amoenitates literariae.* Frankfort and Leipzig, 1728–30.

Schmidt, J. A. *De Seneca ejusque theologia.* Jena, 1686.

Schott, J. C. *Explication nouvelle de l'apothéose d'Homère.* Amsterdam, 1714.

Schroer, P. *De Serapide Aegyptiorum deo maxime.* Bratislava, 1666.

Schubart (Schubartus), G. *De diluvio Deucalionis.* Jena, 1642.

Schuler (Sabinus), G. *Fabularum Ovidii ethica, physica et historica interpretatio tradita in Academia Regiomontana.* Cambridge, 1584.

Scriptores rerum mythicarum Latini tres Romae nuper reperti, ed. G. H. Bode. Celle, 1834.

Sedulius Scottus *Carmina,* ed. C. Traube. Berlin, 1896.

Seelen, J. von *Miscellanea.* Lubeck, 1734–39.

Seerup, G. N. *De legis Mosaicae divina origine et auctoritate diatribe adversus Edoardum Herbertum.* Copenhagen, 1678.

Selden, J. *Marmora Arundelliana.* London, 1628.

Seneca (pseudo), *Epistolae divi Pauli Apostoli . . . epistolae ad Senecam sex,* ed. Lefèvre d'Etaples. Paris, 1517. *Epistolae Senecae ad Paulum et Pauli ad Senecam,* ed. C. W. Barlow, Papers and Monographs of the American Academy in Rome, X, 1938.

Sennert (Sennertus), A. *Exercitationum theologicarum trias.* Wittenberg, 1667.

Servius Honoratus, M. *Commentarii in Virgilium,* ed. H. A. Leon. Gottingen, 1826.

Sextus Empiricus *Opera,* trans. R. G. Bury. London and New York, 1933–49.

Seyssel (Seyssellus), C. *De divina providentia tractatus.* Paris, 1520.

Shuckford, S. *The Sacred and Profane History of the World Connected.* London, 1743.

Sidney, P. *Apology for Poetry.* In *Elizabethan Critical Essays,* ed. G. G. Smith, I, 150–207. Oxford, 1964.

Sidonius, C. M. A. *Opera,* ed. W. B. Anderson. London and New York, 1936–65.

Sieber, J. *De salute Christiana et philosophica, id est, de Christianorum vera et philosophorum gentilium ut Hermetis Tresmegisti, Platonis, Aristotelis, Ciceronis et Senecae praeprimis falsa beatitudines considerationes.* Dresden, 1657. *Seneca divinis oraculis quodammodo consonans.* Dresden, 1675.

Souverain, M. *Le Platonisme dévoilé.* Cologne, 1700.

Spanheim, E. *Dissertationes de praestantia et usu numismatum antiquorum.* Amsterdam, 1671.

Spanmueller (Pontanus), J. J. *Symbolarum libri XVIII quibus P. V. M. Bucolica, Georgica, Aeneis declarantur, comparantur, illustrantur.* Lyons, 1604.

Spencer, J. *De legibus Hebraeorum ritualibus.* Cambridge, 1727.

Spenser, E. *The Faerie Queene,* ed. E. Greenlaw, C. G. Osgood, F. M. Padelford. Baltimore, 1932–38. *Prose Works,* ed. R. Gottfried. Baltimore, 1949. *The Works,* ed. J. Hughes. London, 1750.

Spinoza, B. *Tractatus theologico-politicus,* ed. C. H. Bruder. Leipzig, 1846.

Spon, J. *De l'origine des estrenes.* Lyons, 1673. *Discours sur une piece rare et antique du cabinet de J. S.* Lyons, 1674. *Ignotorum atque obscurorum quorundam deorum arae notis illustratae.* Lyons, 1676. *Miscellanea eruditae antiquitatis.* Lyons, 1685. *Recherches curieuses d'antiquité.* Lyons, 1683. *Voyage d'Italie, de Dalmatie, de Grece et du Levant.* Lyons, 1678–80.

Spontone, C. *Hercole defensore d'Homere.* Verona, 1595.

Sprat, T. *History of the Royal Society of London.* London, 1667.

Stephanus, J. *Theologia Hippocratis.* In J. A. Fabricius, *Bibliotheca Graecae,* XIII, 192–246. Hamburg, 1746.

Steuco (Steuchus), A. *Opera omnia.* Venice, 1591.

Stiegler, J. *De theologia gentili ex antiquis nummis eruta et antiquitate illustrata.* Wittenberg, 1659.

Stillingfleet, E. *Origines sacrae, or a Rational Account of the Christian Faith.* London, 1662.

Stockmann, P. *Elucidarius deorum dearumque gentilium, variaeque idolatatriae in usum antiquitatis studiosorum, necnon ad loca tam Scripturae S. quam profanorum scriptorum, huius argumenti, facilius intelligenda et explicanda, e probatis autoribus congestus et in ordinem alphabeticum redactus.* Leipzig, 1697.

Strabo *The Geography,* ed. J. R. S. Sterrit. London and New York, 1917–32.

Strada, J. de *Epitome thesauri antiquitatum, hoc est imperatorum Romanorum orientalium et occidentalium iconum ex antiquis numismatibus.* Zurich, 1553.

Suetonius *Reliquiae,* ed. A. Reiffersheid. Leipzig, 1860.

Sulpitius Severus, *Epistolae, PL XX.* 175–85.

Symeoni, G. *Dialogo pio et speculativo con diverse sentenze latine et volgari.* Lyons, 1560. *Illustratione degli epitaffi et medaglie antiche di M. G. S.* Lyons, 1558. *Le presage du triumphe des Gaulois.* Lyons, 1555. *Les illustres observations antiques.* Lyons, 1558.

Symmachus, Q. A. *Opera,* ed. O. Seeck. Berlin, 1883.

Tacitus, C. *Annales,* ed. C. Stegmann. Leipzig, 1909–10.

329

Tasso, T. *Dialoghi,* ed. E. Raimondi. Florence, 1958. *La Gerusalemme Liberata.* Pisa, 1830. *Le Lettere,* ed. C. Guasti. Florence, 1854.

Tatian *Oratio adversus Graecos, PG* VI. 803–88.

Tertullian *Ad nationes, PL* I. 559–608. *Apologeticus, PL* I. 256–556. *Contra Marcion, PL* II. 239–526. *De anima, PL* II. 642–752. *De coronis, PL* II. 75–102. *De idolatria, PL* I. 662–96. *De praescriptione haereticorum, PL* II. 10–74. *De resurrectione carnis, PL* II. 791–886. *De spectaculis, PL* I. 627–62. *De testimonio animae, PL* I. 607–18.

Tesauro, E. *Idea argutae,* trans. C. Carber. Frankfort and Leipzig, 1698.

Theodoretus *Curatio Graecorum affectionum,* trans. P. Canivet. Paris, 1958.

Theodulf of Orleans *Carmina,* ed. E. Dümmler. Berlin, 1881.

Theophilus *Ad Autolycum, PG* VI. 1023–168.

Thomassin, L. *La méthode d'étudier et d'enseigner Chrétiennement et solidement les lettres humaines par rapport aux Lettres et aux Ecritures.* Paris, 1681–95.

Thoresby, R. *Diary,* ed. J. Hunter. London, 1830.

Tibullus, A. *Carmina,* ed. J. P. Postgate. Oxford, 1905.

Tilenus, D. *Consideratio sententiae J. Armini de praedestinatione, gratia Dei, et libero arbitrio hominis.* Frankfort, 1612.

Tixier de Ravisi (Ravisius Textor), J. *Epitheta.* Paris, 1523. *Officina.* Paris, 1520.

Tooke, A. *Pantheon of Heathen Gods and Illustrious Heroes.* London, 1698.

Torre, F. del *Monumenta veteris Antii.* Rome, 1700.

Toscanella, O. *Observationi . . . sopra l'opere di Virgilio.* Venice, 1566.

Trapp, J. *Praelectiones poeticae.* Oxford, 1711.

Trigland (Triglandus), J. *De Josepho patriarcha in sacris bovis hieroglyphico.* Leyden, 1700.

Tritonio (Tritonius), M. A. *Mythologia.* Bologna, 1560.

Trömler, C. H. *Bibliothecae Copto-Jacobiticae specimen.* Leipzig, 1767.

Turretini (Turretinus), F. *Institutio theologiae elencticae.* Geneva, 1688.

Tyndale, W. *Doctrinal Treatises.* Cambridge, 1848.

Typoest (Typotius), J. *Symbola divina et humana.* Prague, 1601–1603.

Ugolini (Ugolinus), B. *Thesaurus antiquitatum sacrarum complectens selectissima.* Venice, 1744–69.

Ursinus, J. H. *Analectorum sacrorum libri sex.* Frankfort, 1658.

Usher, J. *Annales Veteris Testamenti.* London, 1650.

Valeriano, P. *Hieroglyphica, sive de sacris Aegyptiorum literis commentarii.* Basel, 1556.

Valio, D. C. *Teatro morale e poetico overo commentarii.* Bari, 1630.

Valkenier, J. *Roma paganizans.* Franecker, 1656.

van Bashuysen, H. *De Iside magna dearum matre.* Zerbst, 1719.

van Dale, A. *De oraculis veterum ethnicorum dissertationes duae.* Armsterdam, 1683. *De origine et progressu idolalatriae et superstitionum.* Amsterdam, 1696. *Dissertationes IX antiquitatibus quin et marmoribus . . . illustrandis inservientes.* Amsterdam, 1702.

Vegio (Vegius), M. *De educatione liberorum et eorum claris moribus libri sex,* ed. M. W. Fanning and A. S. Sullivan. Washington, D. C., 1933, 1936. *Mapheus Vegius and his Thirteenth Book of the Aeneid,* ed. A. C. Brinton. Palo Alto, 1930.

Vico, E. *Discorsi sopra medaglie degli antichi.* Venice, 1555. *Le imagini delle donne auguste.* Venice, 1557. *Le imagini con tutti riversi trovati et le vite de gli imperatori tratte dalle medaglie e dalle historie de gli antichi.* Venice, 1548.

Vieri, F. de *Compendio della dottrina di Platone in quello che elle è conforme con la fede nostra.* Florence, 1577.

Vignoli (Vignolus), G. *De columna imperatoris Antonini Pii dissertatio.* Rome, 1705.

Virgil *Opera . . . C. Landini prohemium.* Florence, 1487. *Opera . . . C. Landini interpretationes.* Venice, 1491. *Opera omnia,* ed. Mancinelli, Beroaldo, Datho, Calderini. Paris, 1507. *Opera Virgiliana,* ed. Leto, Valeriano, Mancinelli, Badius Ascensius. Lyons, 1539. *Opera,* ed. P. Melanchthon. Cologne, 1545. *Opera,* ed. F. Campani. Venice, 1566. *Opera,* Basel, 1577. *Opera,* ed. F. Orsini. Heidelberg, 1589. *Opera omnia,* ed. F. Taubmann. Wittenberg, 1618. *Opera,* ed. F. A. Hirtzel. Oxford, 1900. *L'opere di Virgilio Mantoano,* ed. C. Malatesta, F. Venuti, G. Fabrini. Venice, 1615. *Bucolicorum Vergilii expositio potissimum allegorica,* ed. J. L. Vives. Antwerp, 1544. *Bucolica,* ed. R. Gorraeus. Lyons, 1554. *Bucolica,* ed. M. Barth. Leipzig, 1570. *The Works translated into English Blank Verse,* trans. J. Trapp, London, 1735.

Vitae Vergilianae, ed. J. Brummer. Leipzig, 1912.

Vitry, P. de. *Les Oeuvres,* ed. P. Tarbe. Rheims, 1850.

Voltaire, F. M. A. *Oeuvres.* Paris, 1819–25.

von der Hardt, H. *Aenigmata prisci orbis: Jonas in luce in historia Manassis et Josiae, ex eleganti veterum Hebraeorum stilo solutum aenigma. Aenigmata Graecorum et Latinorum ex caligine Homeri, Hesiodi, Orphei . . . enodata.* Helmstadt, 1723. *Arion . . . a delphine in marii servatus . . . pro rebus Jonas . . . illustrandus.* Helmstadt, 1719. *Aureum vellus Argonautarum ex Orphei thesauro . . . detectum.* Helmstadt, 1715. *De Rhea Cybele magna Deum matre.* Helmstadt, 1720. *Hercules ex Carcharia.* Helmstadt, 1719. *Musa Virgilii Augusta patula fagus duodecim frondium.* Helmstadt, 1740. *Mythologiae Graecorum detecta.* Leipzig, 1716. *Prooemium in Botanica et Bucolica Virgilii, hortulans Tityro, Alexi, et Sileni.* Helmstadt, 1739. *Proteus cum Phocis illustrata.* Helmstadt, 1719. *P. V. M. Deus Pan sylvarum et pastorem numen . . . O. Caesar pro paronomasiae divinitate.* Helmstadt, 1740. *P. V. M. dulcia arva Q. Varus literatissimus bellorum dux in Octavi Caesaris Augusti Romana curia excellens.* Helmstadt, 1740. *P. V. M. famosa Amaryllis marmorae Roma, Maecenate, Vero et Pollione in Caesarea Romana curia.* Helmstadt, 1740. *P. V. M. fatidici poetae Alexis.* Helmstadt, 1740. *P. Virgilii Silicernum.* Helmstadt, 1740.

Voorbroek (Perizonius), J. *Aegyptiarum originum et temporum antiquissimorum investigatio.* Leyden, 1711. *Origines Babylonicae et Aegyptiacae.* Leyden, 1711.

Vos (Vossius), G. *De theologia gentili et physiologia Christiana, sive de origine et progressu idolatriae.* Amsterdam, 1668 *Opera omnia.* Amsterdam, 1686.

Voyages and Travels in the Levant, ed. J. T. Brent. London, 1893.

Walker, O. *The Greek and Roman History Illustrated by Coins and Medals.* London, 1692.

Walsingham, T. *De archana deorum,* ed. R. A. van Kluyve. Durham, N.C., 1968.

331

Warburton, W. *The Divine Legation of Moses Demonstrated,* ed. R. Hurd. London, 1837.

Webb, J. *An Historical Essay Endeavouring a Probability that the Language of the Empire of China is the Primitive Language.* London, 1669.

Webbe, W. *Of English Poetry. In Elizabethan Critical Essays,* ed. G. G. Smith, I, 236–302. Oxford, 1964.

Wedel, G. W. *De nepenthe Homeri.* Jena, 1692.

Wendelin, M. *Admiranda Nili, commentatione philologica, geographica, historica, physica, et hieroglyphica ex 318 autoribus.* Frankfort, 1623.

Whitaker, W. *A Disputation in Holy Scripture,* trans. W. Fitzgerald. Cambridge, 1849.

Wicel, G. *Parallela affinia, sive correspondentia ex nostris hoc est sacris et gentilium libris.* Mayence, 1544.

Wilkins, J. *Essay towards a Real Character.* London, 1668.

Willich, J. *De consilio et scopo Aeneidos Virgilianae.* Frankfort, 1551.

Wits (Witsius), H. *Aegyptiaca et Dekaphulon, sive de Aegyptiacorum sacrorum cum Hebraicis collatione libri tres.* Amsterdam, 1696.

Wolff, C. *Quod Hercules idem sit ac Josua.* Leipzig, 1706.

Worm, C. *De corruptis antiquitatum Hebraearum.* Copenhagen, 1693.

Wynants Pighe (Pighius), S. *Mythologia eis tas oras vel in anni partes.* Antwerp, 1568. *Themis dea seu de lege divina.* Antwerp, 1568.

Xenophon *Symposium,* ed. O. J. Todd. London and New York, 1932.

Young, A. *An Historical Dissertation on Idolatrous Corruptions in Religion.* London, 1734.

Zesen, P. von *Coelum astronomico-poeticum, sive mythologia stellarum fixarum.* Amsterdam, 1682.

Zimmerman, J. *De praestantia religionis Christianae collata cum philosophia Socratis,* in J. G. Schelhorn, XI, 369–510. *Exercitatio de atheismo Platonis,* in Schelhorn, IX, 827–968. *Vindiciae dissertationis de atheismo Platonis.* In Schelhorn, XI, 93–212.

Zobel, N. *De lapsu primorum humani generis parentum a paganis adumbratio.* Altdorf, 1730.

Zwingli, U. *Werke,* ed. M. Schuler and J. Schulthess. Zurich, 1828–42.

II. SOURCES AFTER 1800

Agahd, R. M. "Terenti Varronis, Antiquitates rerum divinarum." *Jahrbücher für classische Philologie, Supplementband,* XXIV (1898), 5–220.

Allen, D. C. *Image and Meaning.* Baltimore, 1968. *The Legend of Noah.* Urbana, Ill., 1949. "Milton and the Descent to Light," *JEGP,* LX (1961), 614–30. "The Predecessors of Champollion," *Proceedings of the American Philosophical Society,* CIV (1960), 527–47. "Some Theories of the Growth and Origin of Languages in Milton's Age," *PQ,* XXVIII (1949), 5–16.

Alphandery, P. "L'Euhémerisme et les debuts de l'histoire des religions au Moyen Age," *Revue de l'Histoire des Religions,* CIX (1934), 5–27.

Arnou, R. "Platonisme des Pères," *Dictionaire de Théologie Catholique,* XII (Paris, 1935), 2258–393.

Aryanpur, M. *"Paradise Lost* and the *Odyssey," Texas Studies in Literature and Language,* IX (1967), 15–66.

Atti del Convegno Internazionale Ovidiano. Rome, 1959.

Baldwin, T. W. *William Shakespere's Small Latine and Lesse Greeke.* Urbana, Ill., 1944.

Bartsch, K. *Albrecht von Halberstadt und Ovid im Mittelalter.* Quedlingburg and Leipzig, 1861.

Battaglia, S. "La tradizione di Ovidio nel medioeva," *Filologia Romanza,* VI (1959), 185–224.

Baylis, H. J. *Minucius Felix.* London, 1928.

Benoit, P. "Sénèque et St. Paul," *Revue Biblique,* LIII (1946), 7–33.

Bezold, F. von *Das Fortleben der antiken Götter im Mittelalterlichen Humanismus.* Bonn and Leipzig, 1922.

Boissier, G. *La fin du paganisme.* Paris, 1891.

Bonar, E. W. *Cyriacus of Ancona and Athens.* Brussels, 1960.

Born, L. K. "Ovid and Allegory," *Speculum,* IX (1934), 362–79.

Boyer, C. *Christianisme et Néo-Platonisme dans la formation de S. Augustin.* Paris, 1920.

Bréhier, E. *La philosophie du Moyen Age.* Paris, 1949.

Buffière, F. *Les mythes d'Homère et la pensée Grecque.* Paris, 1956.

Bush, D. *Mythology and the Renaissance Tradition in English Poetry.* New York, 1963. *Pagan Myth and Christian Tradition in English Poetry.* Philadelphia, 1968.

Capéran, L. *Le problème du salut des infidèles.* Paris, 1912.

Carré, J. R. *La Philosophie de Fontenelle.* Paris, 1932.

Cassirer, E. *Die Platonische Renaissance in England und die Schule von Cambridge.* Leipzig and Berlin, 1932.

Chadwick, H. *Early Christian Thought and the Classical Tradition.* Oxford, 1966.

Chenu, M. D. *"Involucrum:* Le mythe selon les theologiens mediévaux," *Archives d'histoire doctrinale et littéraire du Moyen Age,* XX (1956), 74–79. *La Théologie au Douzième Siècle.* Paris, 1957.

Comparetti, D. *Vergil in the Middle Ages,* trans. E. F. M. Benecke. London, 1895.

Cooke, J. D. "Euhemerism: A Mediaeval Interpretation of Classical Paganism," *Speculum,* II (1927), 396–410.

Coulter, C. "The Genealogy of the Gods," *Vassar Mediaeval Studies* (New Haven, 1923), pp. 317–41.

Courcelle, P. *Les lettres grecques en occident.* Paris, 1943.

Danielou, J. *Origen,* trans. W. Mitchell. New York, 1955.

Dannenfeldt, K. "Egypt and Egyptian Antiquities in the Renaissance," *Studies in the Renaissance,* VI (1959), 7–27.

Davis, R. B. "Early Editions of George Sandys' 'Ovid': The Circumstances of Production," *The Papers of the Bibliographical Society of Virginia,* XXXV (1941), 225–76. *George Sandys, Poet-Adventurer.* London, 1955. *"In re* George Sandys' 'Ovid,'" *Studies in Bibliography,* VIII (1956), 226–30.

Decharme, P. *La critique des traditions religieuses chez les grecs.* Paris, 1904.

Dictionnaire d'Archéologie Chrétienne et Liturgie, eds. F. Cabrol and H. Leclercq. Paris, 1963.

Dill, S. *Roman Society from Nero to Marcus Aurelius*. New York, 1904. *Roman Society in the Last Century of the Western Empire*. New York, 1905.

Drews, P. "Die Anschauungen reformatorischer Theologen über die Heidenmission," *Zeitschrift für praktische Theologie*, XIX (1897), 202–3.

Dunseath, T. K. *Spenser's Allegory of Justice in Book Five of the Faerie Queene*. Princeton, 1968.

Ehwald, R. *Die Mirabilia Roma*. Gotha, 1847.

Elliott, K. and J. P. Elder. "A Critical Edition of the *Vatican Mythographers*," *Transactions of the American Philological Association*, LXXVIII (1947), 189–207.

Ellspermann, G. L. *The Attitude of Early Christian Latin Writers toward Pagan Literature and Learning*. Washington, D. C., 1949.

Engels, J. "Berchoriana," *Vivarium*, II (1964), 62–124. *Etudes sur l'Ovide Moralisé*. Groningen, 1945.

Fassbinden, F. *Das Leben und die Werke des benedikter Pierre Bersuire*. Bonn, 1917.

Fatini, G. *Bibliographia delle critica Ariostea* (1510–1956). Florence, 1958.

Fierville, C. "Notices et extraits des manuscrits de la Bibliotheque de Saint-Omer," *Notices et Extraits*, XXXI (1883), 110–108.

Finsler, G. *Homer in der Neuzeit.* Leipzig and Berlin, 1912.

Fleury, A. *Saint Paul et Sénèque*. Paris, 1853.

Fontaine, J. *Isidore de Seville et la culture clássique dans l'Espagne Wisigothique*. Paris, 1959.

Freundenberger, T. *Augustinus Steuchus*. Münster, 1935.

Frey-Sallman, A. *Aus dem Nachleben antiker Göttergestalten*. Leipzig, 1931.

Garin, E. *Studi sul Platonismo médiévale*. Florence, 1938.

Gasquy, A. *De Fabio Planciade Fulgentio Virgilii Interprete*. Berlin, 1887.

Gaul, P. L. *Albert des Grossen Verhältnis zu Plato*. Munich, 1913.

Geffcken, J. *Sokrates und das alte Christentum*. Heidelberg, 1908.

Ghisalberti, F. "Arnolfo d'Orleans, un cultore di Ovidio nel sec, XII," *Memorie del Reale Instituto Lombardo di Scienze e Lettere*, XXIV, 4 (1932), 157–234. "Fulgenzio, Alberico, Giovanni di Virgilio, Folchino de Borfoni," *Archivum Romanicum*, VII (1923), 95–154. "Giovanni del Virgilo espositore delle *Metamorfosi*," *Giornale Dantesca*, XXXIV, n.s. IV (1933), 3–110. "Mitografi latini e retori medievali in un Codice Cremonese del sec. XIV: Fulgenzio, Alberico, Giovanni di Virgilio, Folchino de Borfoni," *Archivum Romanicum*, VII (1923), 95–154.

Giehlow, K. "Die Hieroglyphenkunde des Humanismus in der Allegorie der Renaissance," *Jahrbuch der Kunsthistorischen Sammlungen der allerhochsten Kaiserhauses*, XXXII (1915), 1–218.

Graf, A. *Roma nella memoria e nelle immaginazioni de Medio Evo*. Turin, 1882.

Gregorovius, F. A. *History of the City of Rome in the Middle Ages*, trans. A. Hamilton. London, 1903.

Grindle, G. E. A. *The Destruction of Paganism in the Roman Empire*. Oxford, 1892.

Gruppe, O. *Geschichte der Klassischen Mythologie*. Leipzig, 1921.

Guyer, F. E. "The Influence of Ovid on Crestien de Troyes," *Romanic Review*, XII (1921), 97–134, 216–47.

Harent, S. "Infidèles," *Dictionnaire de Théologie Catholique,* VII (Paris, 1935), 2, 1726–1930.

Harnack, A. *The Expansion of Christianity in the first three Centuries,* trans. J. Moffatt. London and New York, 1904–1905.

Hauréau, B. "Mémoire sur un commentaire de Métamorphoses d'Ovide," *Mémoires National de France, Académie des Inscriptions et Belles-Lettres,* XXX (1883), 45–55.

Hauvette, H. *Boccacce.* Paris, 1914.

Helm, R. "Der Bischof Fulgentius und der Mythograph," *Rheinisches Museum,* LIV (1899), 111–34.

Henle, R. J. *St. Thomas and Platonism.* Hague, 1956.

Hennebert, F., *Histoire des traductions françaises d'auteurs grecs et latins pendant le XVI° et le XVIII° siècles.* Brussels, 1861.

Hortis, A. *Studi sulle opere latine de Boccaccio.* Trieste, 1879.

Hughes, M. Y. *Ten Perspectives on Milton.* New Haven, 1965.

Hunt, U. D. *Le Sommaire en Prose des Métamorphoses d'Ovide dans le Manuscript Burney 311.* Paris, 1925.

Hyde, W. W. *Paganism to Christianity in the Roman Empire.* Philadelphia, 1946.

Janssen, J. *Geschichte des deutschen Volkes.* Freiburg, 1891.

Joly, R. *Le tableau de Cébès et la philosophie religieuse.* Brussels, 1963.

Jones, J. W. "Allegorical Interpretation in Servius," *CJ,* LVI (1961), 217–26.

Jordan, H. *Topographie der Stadt Rom im Alterthum.* Berlin, 1871.

Jung, M. R. *Hercule dans la littérature française du XVI° siècle.* Geneva, 1966.

Keim, C. T. *Rom und das Christenthum.* Berlin, 1881.

Keseling, F. *De mythographi Vaticani secundi fontibus.* Halle, 1908.

Kibre, P. *The Library of Pico della Mirandola.* New York, 1936.

Klibansky, R. *The Continuity of the Platonic Tradition during the Middle Ages.* London, 1939.

Klibansky, R., E. Panofsky, and F. Saxl. *Saturn and Melancholy.* Cambridge, 1964.

Kocher, P. H. *Christopher Marlowe.* Chapel Hill, 1946.

Koerting, G. *Petrarca's Leben und Werke.* Leipzig, 1878.

Kristeller, P. O. *The Philosophy of Marsilio Ficino.* New York, 1943.

Krouse, F. M. *Milton's Samson and the Christian Tradition.* Princeton, 1949.

Kuhn, A. J. "English Deism and the Development of Romantic Mythological Syncretism," *PMLA,* LXXI (1956), 1094–1116.

Kuntze, P., *Le Grand Olympe, eine Alchimistische Deutung von Ovids Metamorphosen.* Halle, 1912.

Kurfess, A. "Zum dem Apokryphen Briefwechsel zwischen dem Philosopher Seneca und dem Apostel Paul," *Aevum,* XXVI (1952), 42–48.

Labriolle, R. de. *La réaction paienne.* Paris, 1934.

Landi, C. *Demogorgone, con saggio di nuova edizione delle Genealogie Deorum Gentilium del Boccaccio e silloge dei frammenti di Teodonzio.* Palermo, 1930.

Langlois, E. "Une rédaction en prose de *l'Ovide Moralisé,*" *Bibliothèque de l'École des Chartes,* LXII (1901), 251–55.

Lemmi, C. W. *The Classical Deities in Bacon.* Baltimore, 1933.

Lenz, F. W. "Einführende Bemerkungen zu den mittelalterlichen Pseudo-Ovidiana," *Das Altertum,* V (1959), 171–82.

Leutsch, E. von. "Homeros im mittelalter," *Philologus,* XII (1857), 366–68.

Lidonnici, G. "La correspondenza poetica di Giovanni del Virgilio con Dante e il Mussato, e le postille di Giovanni Boccaccio," *Giornale Dantesco,* XXI (1913), 205–43.

Lord, G. de F. *Homeric Renaissance.* New Haven, 1956.

Lubac, H. de. *Exégèse médiévale.* Paris, 1959.

Lungo, I. de. *Fiorentia.* Florence, 1897.

McManaway, J. G. "The First Five Bookes of Ovids Metamorphosis, 1621, Englished by Master George Sandys," *Papers of the Bibliographical Society of Virginia,* I (1948–49), 71–82.

McMurphy, S. J. *Spenser's Use of Ariosto for Allegory.* University of Washington Publications: Language and Literature, II. Seattle, 1924.

Madden, M. D. *The Pagan Divinities and Their Worship As Depicted in the Works of St. Augustine Exclusive of The City of God.* Washington, D. C., 1930.

Madsen, W. G. *From Shadowy Types to Truth.* New Haven, 1968.

Mahly, J. *Angelus Politanus.* Leipzig, 1864.

Manitius, M. "Beitrage zur Geschichte des Ovidius und anderer romischen Schriftsteller im Mittelalter," *Philologus,* Supplement, VII (1899), 723–67.

Manuel, F. *The Eighteenth Century Confronts the Gods.* Cambridge, 1959.

Marcel, R. *Marsile Ficin.* Paris, 1958.

Marchesi, C. "L'allegorie ovidiane di Giovanni del Virgilio," *Studi Romanzi,* VI (1909), 85–135.

Marrou, H. I. *Saint Augustin et la fin de la culture antique.* Paris, 1938.

Masai, F. *Pléthon et le platonisme de Mistra.* Paris, 1956.

Micheli, P. *La vita e le opere di Angelo Poliziano.* Livorno, 1917.

Momigliano, A. *Paganism and Christianity in the Fourth Century.* London, 1963.
———. "La leggenda del Cristianesimo di Seneca," *Rivista Storica Italiana,* LXII (1950), 325–44.

Muller, L. *Q. Enni reliquiae.* St. Petersburg, 1884.

Munari, F. *Ovid im Mittelalter.* Zurich, 1960.

Nolhac, P. de. "Les scholies inédites de Pétrarque sur Homère," *Revue de Philologie de Littérature et d'Histoires Anciennes,* XI (1887), 97–118. *Pétrarque et l'Humanisme.* Paris, 1892.

Nordh, A. "Libellus de regionibus urbis Romae," *Acta Instituti Romani Regni Sueciae,* III (1949), 58–65.

Novati, F. *L'influsso del pensiero Latino sopra la civiltà Italiana del medio evo.* Milan, 1899.

Otis, B. "The *Argumenta* of the So-called Lactantius," *Harvard Studies in Classical Philology,* XLVII (1936), 131–63.

Pannier, L. "Notice biografique sur le bénédictin Pierre Bersuire, premier traducteur français de Tite Live," *Bibliothèque de l'École des Chartes,* XXXIII (1872), 325–64.

Panofsky, E. *Hercules am Scheidenwege.* Leipzig and Berlin, 1930.

Panofsky, E. and D. Panofsky. *Pandora's Box.* New York, 1965.

Paris, G. "Chrétien Legouais et autres Traducteurs ou Imitateurs d'Ovide," *Histoire Litteraire de la France,* XXIX (Paris, 1885), 455–525.

336

Pépin, J. *Mythe et allégorie.* Paris, 1958.

Pichon, R. *Lactance.* Paris, 1901.

Praz, M. *Studies in Seventeenth-Century Imagery.* Rome, 1964.

Rahner, H. *Greek Myths and Christian Mystery.* London, 1963.

Rand, E. K. "Is Donatus' Commentary on Virgil Lost?" *CQ,* X (1916), 158–64.
   Ovid and his Influence. New York, 1928.

Raschke, R. *De Alberico mythologo.* Bratislava, 1912.

Rathbone, E. "Master Alberic of London, Mythographus Tertius Vaticanus,"
   Mediaeval and Renaissance Studies, I (1941–43), 35–38.

Renucci, T. *Un aventurier des lettres au XVIe siècle, Gabriel Symeoni.* Paris,
   1943.

Rex, W. *Essays on Pierre Bayle and Religious Controversy.* The Hague, 1959.

Rich, T. *Harington & Ariosto: A Study in Elizabethan Verse Translation.* Yale
   Studies in English, XCII. New Haven, 1940.

Rothe, C. "Dante Dresdensia," *Deutsches Dante-Jahrbuch,* XII (1930), 136–38.

Rushfort, G. McN. "Magister Gregorius, De mirabilius urbis Romae: A New
   Description of Rome in the Twelfth Century," *JRS,* IX (1919), 14–58.

Sade, J. F. P. A. de. *Memoires pour la vie de F. Petrarque.* Amsterdam and
   Avignon, 1764–67.

Saitta, G. *Il pensiero Italiano nell' umanesimo e nel Rinascimento.* Bologna, 1950.
   Marsilio Ficino. Bologna, 1954.

Samaran, C. "Pierre Bersuire, Prieur de Saint-Eloi de Paris," *Histoire Littéraire de
   la France,* XXXIX (Paris, 1900), 259–451.

Schanz, M. *Geschichte der romischen Litteratur.* Munich, 1914–20.

Scharz, E. "De Varronis apud sanctos patres vestigiis," *Jahrbücher für Classische
   Philologie, Supplementband,* XVI (1888), 407–99.

Schiavone, M. *Problemi filosofici in Marsilio Ficino.* Milan, 1957.

Schmidt, B. *De Cornuti theologiae Graecae compendio.* Halle, 1912.

Schneider, F. *Rom und Romgedanke im Mittelalter.* Munich, 1926.

Schoell, F. L. *Etudes sur l'humanisme continental en Angleterre à la fin de la
   Renaissance.* Paris, 1926.

Schudt, L. *Le guide di Roma.* Vienna and Augsburg, 1930.

Schulz, R. *De mythographi Vaticani primi fontibus.* Halle, 1905.

Sedlmayr, H. "Beitrag zur Geschichte der Ovidstudien in Mittelalter," *Wiener
   Studien,* VI (1884), 142–58.

Sevenster, J. N. *Paul and Seneca.* Leyden, 1961.

Seznec, J. *The Survival of the Pagan Gods,* trans. B. F. Sessions, New York,
   1953.

Slater, D. A. *Towards a Text of the Metamorphosis of Ovid.* Oxford, 1927.

Smithers, P. *The Life of Joseph Addison.* Oxford, 1954.

Spargo, J. W. *Virgil the Necromancer.* Cambridge, Mass., 1934.

Stanford, W. B. *The Ulysses Theme.* Oxford, 1954.

Stark, C. B. *Systematik und Geschichte der Archäologie der Kunst.* Leipzig, 1880.

Steadman, J. "The Classical Hero: Satan and Ulysses," *MLR,* LII (1957), 81–85.
   Milton's Epic Characters. Chapel Hill, 1968.

Stein, R. von. *Verhältniss des Platonismus zur Philosophie der Christliche Zeit.*
   Göttingen, 1875.

Strathman, E. *Sir Walter Raleigh.* New York, 1951.

Sudre, L. *Ovidii Metamorphoseon libros quomodo nostrates medii aevi poetae imitati interpretati sint.* Paris, 1893.

Taylor, J. W. "Bessarion the Mediator," *APA Transactions,* LV (1924), 120–27. *Georgius Gemistus Pletho's Criticism of Plato and Aristotle.* Chicago, 1921.

Thomas, A. "Chrétien de Troyes et l'auteur de *l'Ovide Moralisé,*" *Romania,* XXII (1893), 271–74. "Extraits des archives du Vatican pour servir à l'histoire littéraire, *Romania,* XI (1882), 181–87.

Tiraboschi, G. *Storia della Letteratura Italiana.* Venice, 1823.

Torre, A. delle. *Storia dell'Accademia Platonica di Firenze.* Florence, 1902.

Ussani, V. "In margine al Comparetti," *Studi Medievali, n.s.* V (1932), 1–42.

Vermasren, M. J. *Corpus inscriptionum et monumentorum religionis Mithriacae.* Hague, 1956.

Viarre, S. *Le survie d'Ovide dans la litterature scientifique des XII⁰ et XIII⁰ siècles.* Poitiers, 1966.

Volkmann, L. *Bilderschriften der Renaissance.* Leipzig, 1923.

Wace, A. J. B. and F. H. Stebbing. *A Companion to Homer.* London, 1926.

Waith, E. *The Herculean Hero, in Marlowe, Chapman, Shakespeare, and Dryden.* New York, 1962.

Warburg, A. *Gesammelte Schriften.* Leipzig, 1932.

Watson, F. *Vives and the Renaissance Education of Women.* New York, 1912.

Wehrlie, F. *Zur Geschichte der allegorischen Deutung Homers in Altertum.* Leipzig, 1928.

Wickstead, P. H. and E. C. Gardner. *Dante and Giovanni del Virgilio.* Westminster, 1902.

Wilkins, E. H. "Description of Pagan Divinities from Petrarch to Chaucer," *Speculum,* XXXII (1957), 511–22. *The University of Chicago Manuscript of the Genealogia deorum gentilium.* Chicago, 1927.

Wipprecht, F. *Quaestiones Palaephatae.* Bonn, 1892.

Wolf, E. "Die Allegorische Vergilerklärung des Cristoforo Landino," *Neue Jahrbücher für das Klassische Altertum Geschichte,* XXII (1919), 453–79.

Wolfson, H. A. *The Philosophy of the Church Fathers.* Cambridge, Mass., 1956.

Zabughin, V. *Vergilio nel Rinascimento Italiano da Dante a Torquato Tasso.* Bologna, 1921.

Zaman, F. *L'attribution de Philomena à Chrétien de Troyes.* Amsterdam, 1928.

❧ INDEX ❧